*Set the Stage!*

# Contributors

*Salvatore Bancheri,* University of Toronto–Missisauga
*Frances Boyd,* Columbia University
*Laura Colangelo,* University of Notre Dame
*Gian Giacomo Colli,* Franklin and Marshall College
*Antonella Del Fattore-Olson,* University of Texas–Austin
*Dario Fo,* Italy (Italian playwright, Nobel laureate, artist)
*Pietro Frassica,* Princeton University
*Giuseppe Gazzola,* Yale University
*Dacia Maraini,* Italy (Italian poet, playwright, novelist)
*Nicoletta Marini-Maio,* Dickinson College
*Daniela Noè-Le Sassier,* Barnard College
*Elena Past,* Wayne State University
*Franca Rame,* Italy (Italian playwright, artist)
*Colleen Ryan-Scheutz,* Indiana University–Bloomington
*Francesca Savoia,* University of Pittsburgh
*Walter Valeri,* Harvard University
*William Van Watson,* University of Arizona–Tucson

# Set the Stage!
## Teaching Italian through Theater

*Edited by*

NICOLETTA MARINI-MAIO and

COLLEEN RYAN-SCHEUTZ

*Yale University Press*  New Haven and London

Publisher: Mary Jane Peluso
Editorial Assistant: Elise Panza
Project Editor: Timothy Shea
Manuscript Editor: Jessie Dolch
Production Editor: Ann-Marie Imbornoni
Production Controller: Maureen Noonan

Set in New Aster and Helvetica type by Duke & Company, Devon, Pennsylvania.
Printed in the United States of America by Hamilton Printing Co.

Library of Congress Cataloging-in-Publication Data
Set the stage : teaching Italian through theater / edited by Nicoletta Marini-Maio and Colleen Ryan-Scheutz.
    p.  cm.
  Includes bibliographical references and index.
  ISBN 978-0-300-10985-6 (pbk. : alk. paper)  1. Italian language—Study and teaching—Foreign speakers.  2. Drama in education.  I. Marini-Maio, Nicoletta, 1961–  II. Ryan-Scheutz, Colleen.
  PC1066.S44 2009
  458.071—dc22
                                                        2008024107

A catalogue record for this book is available from the British Library.

This paper meets the requirements of ANSI/NISO Z39.48-1992 (Permanence of Paper).

10  9  8  7  6  5  4  3  2  1

*A Vittorio e Matthias*

*A Costanza, Riccardo, Clara e Aeneas*

# Contents

*Illustrations follow p. 382*

# *Acknowledgments*

It is often the case that edited volumes take time and perseverance to bring to fruition and depend on the support of many people and organizations throughout the process. This work has certainly been no exception to the rule. Therefore, we express our deepest thanks to all of the authors for their invaluable contributions and for their patience during the different phases of this work. In particular, we thank Dacia Maraini, Dario Fo, and Franca Rame for having graciously accepted to contribute to this volume with their inspiring reflections on Italian theater. We also thank Dario Fo, Franca Rame, and Walter Valeri for providing the original photographs that may be found in the last part of this book.

Our home institutions were also a great source of support during this project, as were the colleagues who edited and translated for us. We wish to extend our gratitude to the Nanovic Institute for European Studies at the University of Notre Dame and to Middlebury College for grants that facilitated work meetings and cooperative research for this book. We are equally indebted to Debra L. Karr for her excellent, punctual editorial work, and to Giuseppe Gazzola and Elena Past for their translations of the Fo and Rame and Maraini interviews.

Our warm thanks also go to the colleagues and friends who sustained our willingness to explore the pedagogical applications of theater even much before the project of this book. Without their help, we could not have developed our expertise in teaching Italian through theater. Nor could we have conceived and produced this collected work. Among these special people are, first and foremost, Millicent Marcus, who promoted the establishment and development of theater production courses and workshops at the University of Pennsylvania with the support of the Center for Italian Studies; and Dayle Seidenspinner-Núñez, Theodore Cachey, John Welle, Christian Moevs, and the Institute for Scholarship in the Liberal Arts, who encouraged and supported the Italian Theater Workshop at the University of Notre Dame. We also thank Silvia Carlorosi, Fabiana Cecchini, Laura Colangelo, Michela Ronzani, and Mike Vanacore, who assisted us over the years with many energy- and time-consuming activities related to our productions at the University of Pennsylvania, the University of Notre Dame, and Middlebury College. On a similar note, we recognize the time and efforts of all those who helped provide technical equipment, personal assistance, and theater space at the three institutions: Frank Pellicone (Harriton College House at the University of Pennsylvania), John MacDermott (SAS Computing at the University of Pennsylvania), Sarah Prince (DeBartolo Performing Arts Center at the University of Notre Dame), Antonio Vitti (director of the Italian Language School at Middlebury College), and Allison Rimmer alongside the staff of the Wright Theatre at Middlebury College.

We were also fortunate to have numerous engaged reviewers whose many constructive suggestions led to important changes in content and organization. We thank Elvira DiFabio (Harvard University), Victoria Kirkham (University of Pennsylvania), Bettina Matthias (Middlebury College), Claudio Mazzola (University of Washington), Cinzia Noble (Brigham Young University), and Laura Salsini (University of Delaware) for their time, contributions, and recommendations, especially those regarding the literary overview and secondary school curriculum. And we thank all the staff at Yale University Press for their support during the process of preparation, revision, and copyediting: Mary Jane Peluso, Elise Panza, Ann-Marie Imbornoni, and Jessie Dolch.

Finally, a wholehearted applause goes to our students and families. The hard-working and passionate learners at Penn, Middlebury, and Notre Dame have made teaching Italian through theater a truly unique and satisfying endeavor. Their enthusiastic responses and wonderful performances onstage prompted us to undertake an intense journey of searching, discussing, testing, and sharing of ideas. And our families' unwavering support, selfless understanding, and great sense of humor have inspired us each step of the way.

# *Introduction*

NICOLETTA MARINI-MAIO
AND COLLEEN RYAN-SCHEUTZ

Ciò che dobbiamo imparare a fare, lo impariamo
facendolo.
—ARISTOTELE

Both the study of theater and the study of foreign languages have long-standing traditions at all levels of education. Yet only in recent decades has an interdisciplinary approach joining the two come to light as a subject of both practical and scholarly interest. *Set the Stage! Teaching Italian through Theater* is founded on the belief that theatrical texts and techniques have the ability to catalyze learning and foster curricular innovation in numerous interesting ways. With this premise, this book intends to "set the stage," if you will, for a meaningful dialogue among scholars and practitioners who wish to move in new pedagogical directions by integrating various aspects of the Italian studies curriculum through theater. In particular, the contributions to this work support a performance-based approach to theater. Whether through brief in-class exercises or full-scale theater productions, the common aim is to engage students' whole being in the learning process and to make Italian language, literature, and culture come alive.

This book contains theoretical and practical discussions of different kinds with the aim of inspiring instructors of all levels and learning environments to undertake new projects and embark on new teaching and learning trajectories within their curriculum; to renew and enrich their current courses or curricula by adding or altering their use of theater materials; to create new courses and types of learning experiences for their students; and to reconceive teaching and learning through this theatrical lens and unique interactive framework. Furthermore, *Set the Stage!* includes a "Director's Handbook"—a collection of concrete, detailed, and practical activities and information for both the novice and veteran instructor who would like to start right now.

## Using Theater to Reach Diverse Learning Goals

Theater has been central to humanistic studies since Aristotle's *Poetics* and comprises one of the primary literary genres across canons, cultures, and continents. Yet this prominent art form and cultural tradition does not necessarily play a leading role in foreign language study programs, neither in individual courses nor across whole curricula. In the case of Italian studies, an informal survey of programs reveals that theater only occasionally appears to be the primary subject of undergraduate and graduate course offerings. Certainly, one finds a smattering of courses on topics such as Renaissance theater, commedia dell'arte, or twentieth-century Italian theater, or monographic courses on Carlo Goldoni or Luigi Pirandello. But more often than not, theatrical works comprise only a small fraction of the primary texts selected for literature courses, treating a given author, time period, or theme. Moreover, courses that include authentic dramatic texts typically represent the upper-division or advanced level of a program, indicating that students of Italian might not be exposed to dramatic works, if at all, until their third or fourth year of study. While the reasons for this reality may range from faculty strengths and student preferences to the prominence of other works, authors, and genres in a foreign language tradition, such factors do not justify the lower or less frequent status of theater vis-à-vis narrative, poetry, music, and cinema in Italian courses and curricula.

At the same time, for several years now, research in foreign language acquisition and pedagogy has highlighted the positive effect of drama—particularly improvisation, scenarios, and role-plays—on language learning, and the interest in this field continues to grow. These types of drama activities have become standard, everyday practices in Italian classes and have, in fact, proved successful in developing and reinforcing students' communication skills and in promoting student interaction. By their very nature, drama-based materials, learning objectives, and pedagogical approaches incorporate the understanding of, participation in, and demonstrable appropriation of social practices across time and space. Even for beginner students of Italian, a brief role-play about meeting one of their professors on the street can integrate oral production of basic vocabulary and structures with cultural knowledge regarding linguistic registers and appropriate behaviors, accompanying gestures, and topics for conversation.

Instructors can use theatrical texts and techniques to help their students reach an array of learning objectives in both college and high school–level Italian curricula. Thanks to its diverse subgenres (for instance, comedy, satire, melodrama, farce), its characteristic quality of featuring relatively short communicative interchanges (alternating with lengthier monologues, of course), and the broad range of historical, social, and cultural topics it may contain, theater can aid the student of Italian in the following ways: acquiring and practicing grammatical forms in context; developing language proficiency; focusing on phonetics, cadence, and intonation; grasping and engaging in socio-pragmatics relative to Italy; augmenting comprehension of cultural facts and discourses; improving overall communicative competence; and understanding and analyzing authentic Italian texts. From day one, in other words, it is easy to see the long-term potential and pedagogical benefits of theater or performance-based activities for the class.

## Uses of Theater for a Multidimensional Pedagogy

### *Communicative Language Teaching*

As several chapters in this book highlight, the study of theater (meaning of literary texts and their sociocultural discourses) and the use of drama techniques (role-play, improvisational interchanges with language and/or body, exercises with nonverbal language) uphold the primary principles of communicative language teaching. Among these principles are the presence of rich, comprehensible input; the expression, understanding, and negotiation of meaning; the emphasis on student-centered tasks and information gap assignments; and opportunities to employ and practice linguistic, social, strategic, and discourse competencies that contribute to greater communicative ability.[1] The study of language through theater can, therefore, place equal emphasis on receptive and productive skills. Indeed, the production of a play (or even smaller-scale skit) can be likened to the production of language. Students/actors listen, watch, think, study, consider, and experiment as they "take in" and process input before putting the information in context and creating their own unique product or performance.

Theater performance is an ideal setting for communicative language teaching to unfold thanks to the interpersonal and contextualized practice it requires. When rehearsals are conducted solely in Italian, students rely on and reinforce many facets of oral communication in the social interactions that lead up to the final performance: from lexicon to morphological and syntactic norms all the way to supra-segmental (accent, stress, intonation, and length) and paralinguistic (kinesthetic and proxemic: gestures and body distance) elements. In other words, students use the language for real "speech acts": to negotiate their roles, physical appearances, and interpretations of the text; to state goals and requirements; to make plans; and to propose changes. Moreover, learners use the second language (L2) both as a means to interact and as a literary artifact to read, interpret, and perform. In this framework, speaking the L2 fluently and accurately turns from a learning objective into a necessary means of communication among the members of a community enacting, as it were, a full-immersion experience.

In this communicative scenario, teachers and students gradually find themselves reshaping their relationships and roles in new and creative ways, accomplishing the goals of a student-centered pedagogy. Teachers provide input and suggestions for the adaptation and the mise-en-scène. Besides being available to consult on technical matters, they also help the student-actors find their own acting pace, intonation, and expression. Often, they leave the center stage that teachers habitually inhabit in the classroom and step into the wings to silently monitor their students' performance. Students, on the other hand, speak most of the time, are dynamically involved in all the practical endeavors of the production, and consult their teacher for linguistic, cultural, or technical matters. Overall, in theater performance courses, teachers naturally become the facilitators of their students' learning process, while students become active protagonists of the production and gain confidence in using the target language.[2]

## A Collaborative Learning Environment

Though the affective barriers to such immersion-style learning can be somewhat daunting at first, drama techniques also constitute a powerful means for breaking down the psychological mechanisms that often inhibit students and, in time, help promote collaborative learning. First, the interactive nature of drama and theater elicits the dialogic mental and sociocultural processes in which language learning is grounded and helps the instructor build positive relationships among students. Second, the collective task of the theatrical performance, be it a full-scale play production or a small in-class recital, encourages the creation of a "team-based, high-performance organizational structure," which helps to raise the achievements of all students and replaces the notion of competition with that of cooperation.[3]

The interactional group activities intrinsic to drama and theater courses prove very conducive to learning. In the many stages that lead to the performance, students show a tendency to either offer to or seek in their fellow students some linguistic, social, and affective support in the understanding, pronunciation, and memorization of the play; in organizational issues; and in all the aspects that the preparation of a public performance requires. Usually, students who feel least secure about their linguistic competence turn to more proficient ones for suggestions and corrections, while they often provide their support for practical endeavors and emotional issues.[4] By participating in such cooperatively oriented tasks, students interact in an independent and democratic fashion, thus replicating the conditions of natural communication. These peer-to-peer relationships are extremely useful not only for establishing a positive affective climate in the group, but also for promoting language learning and helping students develop critical thinking skills.

The social interactions that take place in the target language during the different phases of the production process—group and peer reading and discussion, collective adaptation and mise-en-scène of a play—mirror real-life experiences in that they emphasize the concrete content and outcomes of the communicative exchanges among the members of the group.[5] By discussing the cultural, political, literary, and human questions a play raises, and by planning, rehearsing, negotiating, and re-creating meanings and texts, students become a community of language learners who gradually forget to be such and focus instead on the collective goal of the final performance.[6] It is through this many-sided process of collaboration that theater students undergo an impressive cultural, linguistic, and psychological metamorphosis from a "bare class" to a live, dynamic, and interactive theater troupe.[7]

## Approaching Theater as Both a Product and a Process

No matter what the shape or size of the theatrical task, the final performance is a tangible product encompassing several processes that often overlap.[8] The three main phases of the production process—reading the text, negotiating the modes and style of its adaptation and mise-en-scène, and performing it for a real audience—entail a series of linguistic and cultural exchanges among different interlocutors. And, whether aimed at close textual reading, interpretation and stage direction, rehearsal notes, or set, costume, lighting, or scene design, they require a variety of communicative tasks. Clearly, this threefold process focuses on a specific form of text, one that is written not to be read in solitude, but to be adapted and performed, and pertains, therefore, to the semiotics of theater.[9] For this reason, the reading and interpretive stages expand into the semiosis of textual typology and encompass the specific elements of the theatrical medium, namely, the pragmatic context (physical presence of spectators and theater) and paralinguistic communication (voice, tone, gestures) enacted in the presentational and dialogic forms (staged monologues, scenarios, storytelling, choruses).[10]

The detailed reading and performance of a play can be central to the development of multiple literacies in varied and interconnected ways.[11] In the case of actors, the memorization of lines requires perceiving the text as a sociocultural script through which they will become part of and contribute to a cultural message. The learners' study of rhythm, movements, and vocal intonation and their relationships to other characters, objects, and spaces will contribute to what Janet Swaffar and Karen Arens call "discernment of patterns within more complex cultural performances and texts: their narrative point of view, structure, content, and context (macro-systems within the culture)."[12] Likewise, a designer (of sets, costumes, etc.) must engage with a variety of foreign language texts—resource books, websites, artworks, films, music, etc.—in order to conduct research, run meetings, make presentations, gather input from the director and troupe, and make decisions about the "text" they themselves are creating. Ultimately, students of the theater workshop or performance-oriented course will "read texts in ways that reveal how those functions are variously created and enacted in different times and places" and will practice "decoding and encoding such textual information about behaviors, attitudes, and values."[13]

Generally speaking, the nonpermanent, interactional nature of dramatic texts allows students to establish a dynamic relationship with the language used and the culture that this language reflects. As a result, in their theatrical apprenticeship, learners become progressively more aware that, in order to avoid a mechanical replica of the original play, they must submit the text to an important process of cross-cultural transformation. This process takes students "past the basic literacy of language into various literacies of social practice and texts," signaling a path for maximizing the learning potential of each one, and sets the stage for more advanced and interdisciplinary modes of learning.[14]

Furthermore, the multifaceted activity leading to the performance of a play that has not been created for a foreign audience entails additional interpretation and negotiation from a cross-cultural perspective. From their first approach to the play, students will need to address the questions raised by topics that are embedded in the L2 culture and start planning how to tailor such topics to their audience, typically composed of native English speakers. This two-way process becomes a sort of dialogue between the students, bearers of their own linguistic and cultural system, and the culture of the target language.[15] Through such a dialogue, the intrinsic relationships between language and culture are brought to light alongside their shared systems of values and knowledge.

## Theater as a Tool for Curriculum Design

With respect to the Italian program at large, theater-oriented courses can offer a cohesive framework for achieving more comprehensive curriculum design. That is, the inclusion of theater texts and techniques throughout the curriculum—from beginning language courses through senior or graduate-level seminars—would represent a significant step in establishing continuity and graduation of both content material and skill building, thereby diminishing the formidable gap between lower- and upper-division classes or between language and literature study. Clearly, not all texts, techniques, or performance-based tasks can be appropriate for every level of study. At the same time, some texts, exercises, or activities can be adapted to accommodate different levels and learning objectives. Just as content areas such as history, music, gender relations, cinema, politics, economics, or dialectology are often currently introduced into the Italian curriculum in a gradual and systematic fashion, so can theater. It suffices to start simply with just an excerpt or set of exchanges. One can start with the *Tragedie in due battute* by Achille Campanile and work up to whole scene studies, homemade mini-dramas inspired by literary texts, or the full-scale performance of a three-act play.[16]

Furthermore, a wide range of supplementary cultural topics will surface naturally from the study of an excerpt or play. For example, the lesser-known comedy by Campanile, *Il campionato di calcio ovvero fare l'amore non è peccato*, integrates the subjects of social class, linguistic registers, soccer culture and stadium behavior, and gender relations, all in the first two scenes. This play also encourages the study of early twentieth-century Italian history and theories of comedy, most notably Pirandello's *umorismo*. While the original language of these scenes may be inaccessible for first-year students, novice-to-intermediate students can infer a lot of information from observing the performance of a theater workshop or troupe or by adapting and enacting some scenes themselves in the form of simplified role-plays that summarize the basic plot and main idea.[17]

Some brief selections from Pirandello's work, too, could be included early in the curriculum in theater performance courses. Most of his texts are too complicated for beginners, and the intricacy of their metatheatrical discourse is more suitable to upper divisions, but some extracts from, for example, *Così è (se vi pare)* may offer students a first contact with issues of gender and class relations in early twentieth-century Sicily and southern Italy.[18] If seen from a sociocultural perspective, Pirandello's dramas may become accessible as soon as learners have developed the linguistic skills necessary to formulate hypotheses, express uncertainty, and understand a certain degree of ambiguity. Again, the interactive nature of theater can facilitate the comprehension and use of Pirandello's often sophisticated language and content. Dacia Maraini's and Dario Fo's works are other examples of dramatic texts dealing with stimulating and current topics in the fields of history, politics, and gender.

Among numerous theatrical works, Maraini has authored such dramas as *Veronica Franco, meretrice e scrittora* and *La lunga vita di Marianna Ucrìa*, which emphasize the gendered position of the female protagonists in different epochs (the Renaissance and the nineteenth century) and regional settings (Venice and Sicily).[19] Similarly, Fo's politically engaged theater provides a great deal of information on historical and political themes, such as the sociocultural changes of Italian society during the years of the boom (for example, *Non tutti i ladri vengono per nuocere, Gli arcangeli non giocano a flipper*), the turmoil of the late 1960s and early 1970s (for example, *Morte accidentale di un anarchico, Non si paga! Non si paga!*).[20] Since Fo's earlier plays are brief and entertaining, the use of his texts (or extracts from them) may significantly ease the encounter of learners with content and reduce the work of the instructor. Moreover, his language is rich and idiomatic and may be very fruitful for class exchanges. Even selections from the texts of the *teatro di narrazione* (narrative theater), an original dramatic movement developed in Italy during the 1990s, may stimulate students' interest in cultural topics and enhance their communicative skills. An interesting example of this new genre might be Marco Paolini's *Vajont,* the *orazione civile* (civic oration) that denounces the responsibility of political and economic powers in the collapse of the Vajont dam in 1963, an event that destroyed a town of two thousand in just four minutes.[21] Paolini's text is a combination of several rhetorical forms: it is not only an indictment, but also a conversation with the public, a documentary speech, and a public recollection of shared memories. Accordingly, it presents an assortment of linguistic registers for the analysis of communicative strategies and enhancement of presentational skills. Many other texts lend themselves to skill-building and cultural understanding in different ways. For a complete discussion, see the "Director's Handbook" in this book.

These plays are just a few examples of the rich terrain we might draw from in conceiving a curriculum with dramatic texts and techniques at its core. Establishing theater as a fundamental curricular component fosters creativity and continuity in the overarching pedagogical approach that places the students—their engagement, interaction, and learning—at the center of events. Finally, theater inspires students to invest more of themselves, in terms of their critical capacity and personal commitment, in every class experience.

## Theater as Explored in *Set the Stage!*

*Set the Stage!* joins the theoretical perspectives and practical experiences of teachers of Italian who use theater in high schools and universities in different parts of North America. The essays are written by scholars and teachers with backgrounds in both Italian and theater and years of experimentation and practice in combining the two. The book begins with opening remarks by renowned Italian writer and playwright Dacia Maraini, and it ends with an interview with Franca Rame and Dario Fo, celebrated Italian actors and playwrights. Their plays have a solid tradition of study and performance in the United States and Canada, and both authors are well acquainted with the pedagogy of Italian theater in North American universities and across the world.

In the prologue, Maraini highlights the positive effect of a performance-based approach to Italian theater in enabling students to gain an in-depth understanding of contemporary Italian culture. She illustrates her point by sharing her experiences with several student productions in North America, in which she participated as an author-in-residence.

Part I explores the centrality of theater in Italian culture from literary, cultural, and anthropological perspectives. To begin, Pietro Frassica offers in Chapter 1 an overview of the theatrical genre in the Italian literary canon from the Middle Ages to the present. The panorama of authors and movements over time that he discusses can guide instructors who wish to expand their knowledge of the genre and consider the study of different authors and texts. In Chapter 2, claiming that "Italian theater is a redundancy," William Van Watson explores the cultural dimensions of Italian theater. He emphasizes the intrinsic theatricality of Italian culture in all its manifestations, from social interaction in the piazza up to the use of body and gestures in any act of communication. Grounded in semiotic and ethno-semiotic theories of culture, his analysis offers a theoretical and literary rationale to explain the "self-conscious theatricality of Italian behavior."

Part II discusses the features and goals of courses with a performance-based approach to teaching theater. Notwithstanding the contextual differences among the several models presented, all the authors stress the positive effects these courses can have on students and programs. Chapter 3, by Salvatore Bancheri, outlines many steps involved and many practical issues that arise in performance-oriented courses. Bancheri analyzes the organization, requirements, timing, and constraints of such courses at two institutions—one a large urban university and one a small liberal arts summer program—and maintains that both models provide a "360-degree experience" and unique means to approaching literature and perfecting communication skills.

Francesca Savoia in Chapter 4 presents a teaching model that applies the methods of L2 teaching to the study of literary texts. Her theatrical workshop is designed to introduce third-year students to Italian literature through a performance-oriented approach that regularly integrates theater and performance in class to pursue three objectives: to integrate the study of language and literature; to help students avoid misconceptions about literature in general; and to improve learners' abilities to read, rewrite, and interpret literary productions.

Laura Colangelo's and Colleen Ryan-Scheutz's study in Chapter 5 focuses on the use of theater texts and techniques for teaching high school Italian. Drawing upon Howard Gardner's theory of multiple intelligences, the authors claim that dramatic literature is "inherently accessible to learners who excel in each of the seven intelligence areas." They also argue that theater can be highly instrumental for developing the national standards (the five Cs: communication, comparisons, connections, cultures, and communities); for creating a challenging variety of production- and performance-based assessments that reflect the methods and tasks in their teaching; and for designing an advanced placement (AP) Italian language and culture course that helps prepare students for the AP exam.

In Part III, the authors discuss the different genres of Italian theater they use in their language and literature courses. In Chapter 6, Walter Valeri highlights the artistic and pedagogical value of Fo's and Rame's satires as a means for exploring Italian culture, politics, and language. He emphasizes the central position of Fo's work in the tradition of comic theater (beginning with Aristophanes and developing through Shakespeare and the commedia dell'arte), elucidates the unique features of Fo's comic style as an author and actor, and advocates for the efficacy of this style in understanding comic discourse, which, Valeri maintains, is "a decisive step in the students' mastery of the Italian language."

In Chapter 7, Gian Giacomo Colli establishes an original parallel between the work of the commedia dell'arte actor and that of the L2 learner. Colli's argument derives from his career as an actor, director, and theater instructor and is grounded in the belief that communicative language teaching is based upon role-playing and improvisation techniques that are very similar to the performance process of commedia dell'arte. After providing a brief history and outlining the main features of the genre, he expounds his method for teaching a course on commedia dell'arte that is both informative and performance-oriented, but does not necessarily culminate in a final production.

Daniela Noè-Le Sassier and Frances Boyd in Chapter 8 examine the pedagogical value of opera, a genre that shares many of the comic and melodramatic qualities of theater and holds a distinct place in the Italian canon. By exploring opera as both genre and subject, the authors demonstrate how a thematic approach to the genre helps develop communicative and literacy competences. The authors delineate several opera-related strategies and activities for promoting language learning and critical thinking, encouraging collaborative work, introducing students to different cultural settings, sustaining their motivation, and assessing their progress.

Part IV delineates different versions of Italian theater workshop courses with a focus on methodologies and assessments. Extending Peter Brook's theatrical metaphor of the "empty space" to L2 education, Nicoletta Marini-Maio claims in Chapter 9 that a performance-based approach to teaching theater can fill the gap between lower- and upper-division courses and be a transformative experience for cultural learning and psychological growth. She argues that this twofold goal may be achieved by combining subject matter study, textual analysis, improvisation techniques, and the production of a full-scale play in a three-part course (content study, workshop, performance), and she illustrates her method with three case studies based on Fo's and Pirandello's theater.

In Chapter 10 Antonella Del Fattore-Olson focuses on advanced-level language courses to suggest that performance-based methods can harmonize the perfection of the language skills with the development of cultural and literary competence. She argues for a preliminary phase of study in which reading and research strategies alternate with language review and practice. At the same time, the instructor and students must work to build a strong sense of community in order to prepare for their final performance. Del Fattore-

Olson applies her model to Dacia Maraini's and Eduardo De Filippo's plays, which "provide endless sources" for students to explore controversial topics and study an array of linguistic varieties, including dialects.

In Chapter 11, Colleen Ryan-Scheutz addresses the topic of assessments in the hands-on, full-immersion-style theater workshop course. Here, she affirms that in addition to the personal and community value of play production within a program, it is important to remember that such advanced-level, credit-bearing courses merit a clear set of learning objectives with appropriate forms of assessment for evaluating progress toward these goals. On the basis of her experiences, Ryan-Scheutz prioritizes a set of learning outcomes as well as a hybrid plan for assessment. This plan includes a series of tests and assignments that span the four main skills as well as cultural knowledge and literary analysis. In addition, she describes qualitative assessments designed to gauge students' motivation, self-perceived progress, and satisfaction.

Following the four main parts is a "Director's Handbook," which provides a collection of practical instructions and considerations for Italianists at any level who wish to teach language, literature, and culture through theater. The topics range from preproduction organization and advice on the selection of appropriate texts, to finding an appropriate space, garnering financial resources, and organizing auditions and rehearsals. In addition, the handbook offers many in-class or in-production activities that range in nature and scope from improvisation and acting exercises, monologue projects, translations and surtitle creation to the full development of nonacting (artistic, directorial, and technical) student roles. Our hope is that this information will encourage our colleagues to undertake new theater-based, performance-oriented projects of their own.

Finally, the Afterword features an interview with maestri Dario Fo and Franca Rame. In this conversation with Walter Valeri, Fo traces the evolution of his theater and discusses both the values and dangers of theater as a pedagogical tool. In illuminating the relationship between laughter and the comic, Fo discusses cultural factors that strengthen or weaken theater's effect in our lives. Similarly, Rame revisits her theatrical trajectory, reflecting on the public versus private aspects of her work and the extent to which the condition of women has changed in the past thirty-five years.

## Raising the Curtain

The dramatic genre and performance-based approach constitute a unique gateway for learning about language, literature, and culture. Students not only learn terminology, historical and contextual information, and literary concepts but they also grow in cultural competence (empathy, ability to compare native and target culture, etc.). Through these texts, exercises, and productions, students make a personal investment—intellectual, emotional, and physical—in their study of Italian, which enables them to analyze cultural notions from their roles "inside" and "outside" the text or linguistic task at hand. That is, they learn to comprehend the text from up close, as they are intricately connected to the *pièce* and directly involved in the social problems and cultural debates that arise from the dialogues and exchanges they read and present. At the same time, students gain understanding from a position "outside of" or detached from the text from which they can engage in critical thinking through a more objective lens. The integration of their "inside" and "outside" analyses of the text allows student-actors to fully realize their characters onstage. Moreover, their awareness of the sociocultural elements underlying the spoken or written words helps to transform the production of language as a linguistic act into a multifaceted sociolinguistic endeavor. Using their minds, bodies, and spirits all at once, students find that Italian comes alive for them as never before and learning takes place in its most comprehensive form.

The integration of theater and performance in the Italian curriculum offers endless opportunities for character development and language learning. As instructors continue to incorporate more and more theatrical elements into their classrooms, they will discover both the rewards of this new pedagogy and the challenges of organizing such varied approaches and assignments into a coherent whole. In the future, they will need to "translate" the activities associated with theater performance into a system with clear learning objectives and sound methods for evaluating student progress.

What follows is an attempt to reveal some of the backstage magic involved in learning Italian language, literature, and culture through theater. We hope that it will help you set the stage for a fruitful educational endeavor. *Buono spettacolo!*

## Notes

1. For a discussion of linguistic competencies contributing to communicative abilities, see Canale and Swain, "Theoretical bases," and Savignon, *Communicative Competence.* For a landmark discussion of communicative language teaching in today's foreign language classroom, see Lee and Van Patten, *Making Communicative Language Teaching Happen.* And for a very recent text on communicative teaching methodologies, see Brandl, *Principles.*
2. For a thorough discussion of the role of the teacher as a facilitator in communicative language teaching, see Larsen-Freeman, *Techniques and Principles.*
3. See Johnson, Johnson, and Holubec, *Cooperative Learning in the Classroom,* 2.
4. In sociocultural theory, this process of interactional support in the classroom environment is called *scaffolding.* For a detailed explanation of scaffolding, see Donato, "Collective Scaffolding."
5. With regard to the proximity of drama and theater learning activities to real life, see Via, "The Magic 'If' of Theater," 123.
6. For a discussion about collaborative learning methods in L2 teaching, see Bassano and Christison, *Look Who's Talking,* xvi.
7. Here we are applying Peter Brook's theatrical metaphor of the "bare stage" to the field of L2 teaching. See Brook, *The Empty Space,* 9.
8. For an informed and convincing discussion about the nature of drama activity and theater performance as processes versus products, see Moody, "Undergoing Process."
9. With regard to the semiotics of theater, see De Marinis, *The Semiotics of Performance,* and Essif, *The French Play.*
10. For a definition of textual typologies, see Mortara Garavelli, "Textsorten/ Tipologia dei testi."
11. Swaffar and Arens's concept of multiple literacies maintains that in order to truly achieve advanced competence in a foreign language, one needs to be able to navigate and communicate in the language through a broad variety of text types and cultural contexts or situations. This diversity in navigation and communication abilities necessitates more than the study of foreign language as a tool and as a means to understanding different literary genres. It also implies students' ability to use and understand different rhetorical strategies, different textual formats, and/or different communication/artistic/cultural media. Educators embracing this concept would likely devise individual assignments, whole courses, and, eventually, entire curricula in such a way that "content and discourse remain mutually informing at all levels of

teaching and learning." See Swaffar and Arens, *Remapping the Foreign Language Curriculum*, 40–41.

12. Ibid., 43.
13. Ibid., 43–44.
14. Ibid., 43.
15. For the relationship between language and culture in L2 teaching, see Kramsch, *Context and Culture in Language Teaching*, and Kramsch, "Language and Culture."
16. See Campanile, *Tragedie in due battute*.
17. See Di Pietro, *Strategic Interaction*.
18. See Pirandello, "Così è (se vi pare)."
19. These two dramas by Maraini are included in *Fare teatro*, 343–395.
20. Fo, *Teatro*.
21. See Paolini, *Vajont*.

## Bibliography

Armstrong, Thomas. *Seven Kinds of Smart: Identifying and Developing Your Many Intelligences*. New York: Plume, 1993.
———. *Multiple Intelligences in the Classroom*. Alexandria, VA: Association for Supervision and Curriculum Development, 1994.
Bassano, Sharron, and Mary Ann Christison. *Look Who's Talking*. San Francisco: Alemany Press, 1981.
Brandl, Klaus. *Principles of Communicative Language Teaching in Action*. New York: Prentice Hall, 2007.
Brook, Peter. *The Empty Space: A Book about the Theatre: Deadly, Holy, Rough, Immediate*. New York: Atheneum, 1968.
Campanile, Achille. *Tragedie in due battute*. Milan: Rizzoli, 1987.
Canale, Michael, and Merrill Swain. "Theoretical Bases of Communicative Approaches to Second-Language Teaching and Testing." *Applied Linguistics* 1.1 (1980): 1–47.
De Marinis, Marco. *The Semiotics of Performance*. Translated by Áine O'Healy. Bloomington: Indiana University Press, 1993.
Di Pietro, Robert. *Strategic Interaction: Learning Languages through Scenarios*. Cambridge: Cambridge University Press, 1987.
Donato, Richard. "Collective Scaffolding in Second Language Learning." In *Vygotskian Approaches to Second Language Research*, edited by James P. Lantolf and Gabriela Appel, 33–56. Norwood, NJ: Ablex, 1994.
Essif, Les. *The French Play: Exploring Theatre 'Re-creatively' with Foreign Language Students*. Calgary: University of Calgary, 2006.
Fo, Dario. *Teatro*. Turin: Einaudi, 2000.

Gardner, Howard. *Frames of Mind: The Theory of Multiple Intelligences.* New York: Basic, 1983.

———. *Multiple Intelligences: The Theory in Practice.* New York: Basic, 1993.

———. *Intelligence Reframed: Multiple Intelligences for the 21st Century.* New York: Basic, 2000.

Haggstrom, Margaret A. "A Performative Approach to the Study of Theater: Bridging the Gap between Language and Literary Courses." *French Review* 66.1 (1992): 7–19.

Johnson, David, Roger Johnson, and Edythe Johnson Holubec. *Cooperative Learning in the Classroom.* Alexandria, VA: Association for Supervision and Curriculum Development, 1994.

Kramsch, Claire. *Context and Culture in Language Teaching.* Oxford: Oxford University Press, 1993.

———. "Language and Culture: A Social Semiotic Perspective." *ADFL Bulletin* 33.2 (2002): 8–15.

Larsen-Freeman, Diane. *Techniques and Principles in Language Teaching.* Oxford: Oxford University Press, 1986.

Lee, James, and Bill Van Patten. *Making Communicative Language Teaching Happen.* 2d ed. New York: McGraw-Hill, 2003.

Maraini, Dacia. *Fare teatro.* Vol. 2. Milan: Rizzoli, 2000.

Moody, Douglas J. "Undergoing Process and Achieving a Product: A Contradiction in Educational Drama?" In *Body and Language,* edited by Gerd Bräuer. Westport, CT: Ablex, 2002.

Mortara Garavelli, Bice. "Textsorten/Tipologia dei testi." In *Lexikon der Romanistischen Linguistik,* edited by Günter Holtus, Michael Metzeltin, and Christian Schmitt, 157–168. Tübingen: M. Niemeyer, 1988.

Paolini, Marco. *Vajont.* Turin: Einaudi, 2002.

Phillips, June K., ed. *Foreign Language Standards: Linking Research, Theory, and Practices.* Lincolnwood, IL: National Textbook Co., 1999.

Pirandello, Luigi. "Così è (se vi pare)." In *Maschere nude,* edited by Alessandro D'Amico, 417–509. Vol. 1. Milan: Mondadori, 1993.

———. "Sei personaggi in cerca d'autore." In *Maschere nude,* edited by Alessandro D'Amico. Vol. 2. Milan: Mondadori, 1993.

Pratt, Mary Louise. "Building a New Public Idea about Language." *ADFL Bulletin* 34.3 (2003): 5–9.

Richards, Jack C., and Theodore S. Rodgers. *Approaches and Methods in Language Teaching.* Cambridge: Cambridge University Press, 2001.

Savignon, Sandra. *Communicative Competence: Theory and Classroom Practice.* 2d ed. New York: McGraw-Hill, 1997.

Swaffar, Janet, and Karen Arens. *Remapping the Foreign Language Curriculum: An Approach through Multiple Literacies.* New York: MLA, 2006.

Via, Richard. "The Magic 'If' of Theater: Enhancing Language Learning through Drama." In *Interactive Language Teaching,* edited by Wilga M. Rivers. Cambridge: Cambridge University Press, 1987.

Vygotsky, Lev Semenovich. *Mind in Society: The Development of Higher Psychological Processes.* Cambridge, MA: Harvard University Press, 1978.

———. *Thought and Language.* Cambridge, MA: MIT Press, 1986.

# *Prologue: Theater Performance with American Students*

DACIA MARAINI, TRANSLATED BY
ELENA PAST

Working alongside people who portray one's own characters onstage is always a good thing for a playwright. The theater is the most choral of the arts, one that is elaborated in a group, in the presence of and with an exchange among professionals who act, direct, and handle the lights, music, sets, and costumes. Each of these specialists is a necessary part of the performance, and it would be impossible to do without them. In theater, an author cannot reach the public without good actors, good directors, a good lighting director, good musicians, a good costume designer, and a good scenographer. If any one of these experts does not know how to do his or her job, the entire result is compromised. Thus playwrights must have the humility to listen to each of the technicians who collaborate with them, putting themselves in a dialectical relationship with the entire company without pretending to impose or isolate themselves in a personal paradise closed to those not "sanctified" by the gift of creation.

All of this increases a hundredfold if, in the place of professional actors, aspiring actors or students perform the work, seeking with curiosity and generosity to enter the world of theater perhaps for the first time in their lives.

In my life as a playwright, I have mainly worked with professional companies, sometimes arguing furiously with the director and actors, sometimes cutting, sometimes rewriting parts of the text that, when rendered onstage, were too long or not suitable for the chosen actors.

The question of the credibility of the staging is essential for an author. Everything can be said in a dramatic text: one can choose a symbolic style, a realistic style; one can favor an erudite language or one that is dialectal and popular. Yet the sentences enunciated must be convincing in the mouths of the actors who appear onstage. Theater is not like poetry or narrative, which testify to their credibility on paper, and make the rest unimportant. Dramaturgy that works only on the printed pages of a book is not true dramaturgy. The words of an author must become a voice in the mouth of the actor and must be able to reach the attentive ear of the spectators, with a tone of truth that wins them over, binds them to that text, that representation. This is not, then, a naturalistic truth, but an internal, poetic, sensual truth.

I have also worked with amateur companies and often with university students or theater schools. I have conducted seminars on dramaturgy in Germany, Brazil, Holland, and Italy. Each time, I have learned something new about theater. A relationship with students who want to deepen their knowledge of a subject like dramaturgy compels an author to clarify the creative process, render it legible and accessible. It obliges an author to find the words to rationally explain that which sometimes is born of an unconscious creative instinct.

I have also worked many times in the United States with non-professional actors and each time returned enriched. Those who seek to learn from professionals with long theatrical experience ask them to draw heavily upon their relationship with the theater, asking question after question. What do the words we are using mean? Why the choice of one plot over another? How is a character born? What are the ties with the history of theater? With classic texts? To what degree do authors have to revise their own work through their relationship with the company, the director, and the actors? To what degree do they have to be faithful to the characters chosen? Should the relationship with characters be one of detachment or identification? Where is the *drama*? How important is timing in dramatic narration? Does the demand for unity of time and place still hold? How much influence has cinema had on the dramaturgical creative process?

Students ask authors to clarify their thought process and to make their thoughts explicit, in the moment they witness the students' taking possession of the text. The students' attitude is experimental, and authors must confront this fact, questioning their certainties, ready to start, each time, from the beginning.

The students from California State University, East Bay (actually, the female students), under the guidance of Rhoda Kaufman, first accompanied me down the difficult path of the representation of a concise and symbolically contracted text, *Maria Stuarda,* translated as *Mary Stuart.* The text has been represented in twenty-two countries around the globe, from Tokyo to Lisbon, from Amsterdam to Rio de Janeiro.

Under the direction of Kaufman (who in 1994 edited a book titled *Only Prostitutes Marry in May* for Guernica Editions, containing four of my theatrical texts), and with two young aspiring actresses, I discussed my text, which has a structure that is rigid in its circularity. The two characters, Maria and Elisabetta, are always onstage speaking between themselves, even if they never actually meet. When one of the two women plays the queen, the other acts the part of the lady companion and vice versa. How to distinguish these two roles that become four during the performance? How to make the public enter into the Pirandellian *gioco delle parti* (role play)? How to make clear, without having time to change costumes, that the actress is changing from the body of the queen to that of the lady companion? And from the companion to that of the queen?

I think that this specular construction is at the base of the success of the text (it continues to be performed today without seeming dated). It is a challenge for the two actresses, who must give the best of themselves, must continually face two—or in fact four—very different characters, all the while maintaining an artistic credibility that includes historic veracity and psychological analysis.

In 1996 in Rome, during the spring semester, students from Temple University staged my text titled *Dialogo di una prostituta col suo cliente,* under the direction of Pia Candinas. And in 1999, other students from Temple University organized a dramatic reading, which in French is called a *mise en espace,* of a theatrical text called *I sogni di Clitennestra.* In this case, I met with students only after the production. The text had been translated and staged at the Judith Anderson Theater in New York by a young director, who sadly died of AIDS at the age of twenty-seven. The students were familiar with the translation but then worked on the Italian original.

The necessarily greater linguistic mastery of students who live in Italy for a year or two gave the performance a surprising fluency. The stage, as in all schools, was humble, without costumes or sets. The text, presented in a bare, severe *aula magna,* had the effect of a theatrical body laid bare and dissected for the purposes of study.

The result, while perhaps not particularly spectacular, had the merit of giving great emphasis to the words that, alone, filled the emptiness of a bare stage.

I then worked with students from the Department of French and Italian at the University of Texas at Austin, directed by Antonella Del Fattore-Olson in her course on language and theater, the Italian Drama Workshop.

In three years, the students performed an extremely varied selection of my works. *Una casa fra due palme* (1998), inspired by the writings of Eugenio Montale (one of the greatest poets of the twentieth century in Italy), recounts Montale's imaginary return to the Ligurian village where he was born. Set in 1944, it depicts his encounter with his wet nurse, his father, his mother, and some old friends who had died years before, loveable and tormenting ghosts who come to console him during the painful years of the war.

In the summer of 1999, another group of students from the University of Texas staged a work of mine called *Bianca Garofani*. It is the story of a woman without memory who lives alone, and who each morning must laboriously and painfully reconstruct the itinerary that takes her to her office, forgotten again each time.

Still in 1999, but six months later, there was the representation of *Veronica Franco, meretrice e scrittora*. Veronica was a sixteenth-century courtesan poetess who lived in Venice. She was the daughter of a prostitute who brought her onto the streets when she was only fifteen. But the intelligent Veronica wants to learn and thus begins to study on her own and manages to achieve a level of erudition, an extremely rare accomplishment among street prostitutes. From prostitute, she transforms herself into a courtesan, a more elegant job to define a woman who does not sell herself on the street or in brothels but rather in rich salons with the most important members of the aristocracy and the clergy of her city.

Veronica becomes so famous that even the king of France, Henry III, is curious about her when he visits Italy. The city of Venice gifts him with a night with the famous courtesan, a night of exquisite food, erudite conversation, music, and dance, but not of sex. Veronica was not even particularly beautiful, was already older than thirty years of age (considered in those times close to old age), and had four children.

Her poems, extraordinarily, exceed the limits of the amateur production linked to the customs of her times. They are formally elegant but also have a strong emotional effect; they courageously stage sexual love and the solitude of a condition as difficult as hers. She is the only courtesan who dares to speak in her poems of "bed" and the "battles of love," without hiding behind sentimentality or mannerist sophisms.

Finally, in 2003, still with the University of Texas, and still under the direction of Antonella Del Fattore-Olson, there was the performance of *La lunga vita di Marianna Ucria,* a theatrical text that I drew from one of my most popular novels of the same title. The text was performed in theatrical form by the theater company of Catania two years later. The writing is choral and thus appropriate for a school. It presupposes the presence of many actors. The protagonist, Marianna, deaf and mute, is multiplied by three. One is a child-Marianna who watches a more grown-up self act. A twenty-year-old Marianna observes the sufferings and despondency of the child she was, and a forty-year-old Marianna rereads her past through the memories of the twenty-year-old who is no longer there.

There is a father in love with his daughter, who, however, finds nothing strange in giving her in marriage to the uncle who raped her when she was six years old; there is a mother who does not want to see or understand; there is a grandmother who patiently teaches the child how to write in order to afford her the possibility of expressing her will; there are children, grandchildren. There is the Sicily of the eighteenth century, with its violence, sumptuousness, its hateful feudal habits—habits that begin to be called into question by the insinuations of a new, fresh wind, a wind that speaks of equality and liberty, something absolutely revolutionary in a time of fixed, oppressive social hierarchies.

This may have been the text on which I worked most with students, speaking with them at length, responding to the thousands of questions provoked in the performance of a world so complex and distant, investigating the characters one by one. Days and days of discussions and in-depth study were necessary.

The effort, however, was overmatched by the extraordinary desire of the students Del Fattore-Olson directed to learn and to participate. I was moved by the enthusiasm with which they donned the clothing of characters so distant from them, seeking to identify with women and men who lived four hundred years ago, in a grandiose, impoverished Sicily.

The encounter with the students from the University of Texas was fortuitous, owing to the personal initiative of one teacher. And yet it produced great results, both in local theater and in the form of a book that recounts the experience to a wider, more diverse public. For this reason, I believe that the experiment should be diffused as a means for better understanding the new Italian culture. Theater brings one closer to a country's spoken language, to its ethical and historical problems, to the most humble and profound practices of a changing population. It is certainly a greatly effective educational tool that professors of Italian in the United States can use as a testimony to and as encouragement in the difficult didactic process of getting to know a culture that is often neglected, or else understood in its most conventional, folkloristic aspects.

For a playwright, this type of experience is one of great intellectual enrichment. Certainly, it is one of the best ways to better understand what and why one writes. For the students, I hope, it is the most advantageous introduction to the secrets of a language, to the internal rhythms of a creative process as complex, musical, profound, and actual as the theater.

I thank California State University, East Bay, and in particular the University of Texas at Austin, who generously wanted to repeat the theatrical experiment, thus assigning to teachers and students a trust that affirms the importance of theater as an instrument of both knowledge and education.

# *I* Theater in Italian Literature and Culture

# CHAPTER 1

# Authors, Texts, and Innovative Movements: An Overview of the Italian Theatrical Canon

PIETRO FRASSICA

In every period of Italian literature, many writers and poets have often found a congenial form of expression in the theater. This brief overview of Italian theater highlights those authors and works that more than others may best fit in university curricula of Italian literature, in order to help students better understand the broader historical sweep of drama in Italy and of Italian culture in general. To this end, this overview provides a chronological outline of some of the most significant moments in Italian theatrical expression from the Middle Ages to the present.

## Medieval Theater

Two forms of theatrical expression in early medieval Italy merit discussion as a starting point for this overview: secular mimes of the minstrel tradition and *sacre rappresentazioni,* or religious dramas. The *Contrasto* by Cielo d'Alcamo is an example of a kind of minstrel mime in dialogue form that seems written for performance. Written in a southern dialect between 1231 and 1250, the *Contrasto* presents an impudent young man who speaks in insinuating tones of his love for a girl, who at first is reluctant but little by little gives in to his flattering enticements. The *Contrasto* brings to life a certain freshness and a witty humor that would be hard to attribute to an author unfamiliar with literary tradition, revealing as well a notable artistic experience, psychological finesse, and fine instinct for observing reality.

As for the medieval religious dramas that were also diffused throughout Europe, it is commonly held that they began in the thirteenth century with the spiritual *laude,* a naïve and passionate expression of ardent medieval religiosity. The *laudi* were rather simple compositions that arose in central Italy, in particular the region of Umbria. Linked directly with specific evangelical texts, they offered paraphrased reworkings of these texts—of certain scenes from the Passion, from the life of Mary, or from saints' lives—that encouraged disdain for earthly goods, thoughts of mortality, penitence, and prayers. These are comparable to similar religious dramas in England and France of the same period. Of the three forms that laudi assumed—lyrical, narrative, and dialogue—the latter gradually prevailed. Beginning in the thirteenth century and continuing over the next two centuries, laudi written in dialogue form developed into real dramatic compositions, though they were still quite simple in structure and were performed with very little stage settings. They gave place, in time, to sacred representations that became very popular in the middle of the thirteenth century. In the majority of sacre rappresentazioni, where the characters of the play are drawn from daily life—peasants and thieves, clerics and doctors, judges and assassins—the comic contends with the serious, and the audience's laughter is provoked by many means.

These sacre rappresentazioni had no act or scene divisions and normally began with an angelic announcement explaining the theme and inviting the audience to silence and devout attention. The angel would appear again at the end with an envoi to the performance. Within this structure the action acquires a more realistic and human dimension, and it is also enriched with comic and fictional elements. Normally, this kind of drama took place during important religious holidays in oratories, vestries, or the entryways of churches. The action would occur on a stage where, as far as possible, the different settings would be placed side by side. Often, these were places very far from each other, such as heaven and hell; the latter would be positioned below the stage, in a crude and primitive form, while the former would be above the stage, depicted with veils and angels (often these were children suspended with ingenious devices). With ropes and pulleys, the souls of the righteous would be drawn up into heaven, and angels let down; and through trapdoors devils and the wicked descended into hell. Animals also frequently appeared on the stage.

About one hundred dramatic laudi have been preserved. That they were the work of many authors is indicated by their differing qualities, but few of the authors of the laudi will ever be known by name. The major exception is Jacopone da Todi (1236–1306), author of a significant number of the surviving laudi, some in lyrical, others in dialogue form. With an unmistakable poetry, the author drew on his extraordinary and dramatic and religious experience of a man who had explored the pains of the world, the conflicts between body and soul, of the vanity and misery of earthly things. During the course of the fifteenth century, the *rappresentazioni* spread to Florence and other parts of Italy, and in 1450 Feo Belcari (1410–1484) wrote his very solemn *Abraham and Isaac* and *The Angel Raphael and Tobit,* Lorenzo de' Medici wrote his *St. John and Paul,* and Castellano de' Castellani his *Last Supper and Passion.*

## Renaissance Theater

By this time, the *sacre rappresentazioni* had moved far from the hieratic solemnity of the early representations of the Passion of God and the Lament of the Virgin Mary. The time demanded a new form of theater. In the second half of the fifteenth century, Angelo Poliziano (1454–1494), with his *Orfeo,* and Matteo Maria Boiardo (1441–1494), with his *Timone,* gave the earliest examples of secular plays in the vulgar tongue. Poliziano's *Orfeo* (considered the first secular drama written in vernacular Italian) combined tragedy, the pastoral, and opera in a mixed work in which songs of shepherds anticipated the pastoral drama of Baldassare Castiglione's (1478–1529) *Tirsi,* Torquato Tasso's *Aminta,* and Giovanni Battista Guarini's *Pastor Fido.* If in the form of his *Orfeo* Poliziano employed the structure of religious dramas, its originality consisted in replacing a religious with a classical subject. He wrote it in a mere two days, on the occasion of a courtly celebration in 1480, while he was in Mantua at the court of the Gonzaga family. The myth of Orpheus' recovery of Eurydice from the underworld through the power of song is not presented by Poliziano with dramatic conflicts or tragic accents. The poet treats this material as a lovely fable, one freed from every realistic reference. Orpheus' conquest of the underworld and of beasts symbolizes poetry, which draws humanity out of barbarism into civilization and to a heightened life of the spirit. Matteo Maria Boiardo followed a different direction in his *Timone.* The subject was borrowed from Lucian, who recites the prologue; later, the main character leaves the stage before the end of the fifth act, and the conclusion is narrated by an allegorical figure. Indeed, in the second half of the fifteenth century, there was a rich blossoming of allegorical masquerades. The flowering of this type of spectacle in the Renaissance is often attributed to Jacopo Sannazaro (1457–1530), who early in his career wrote several "farces," dramatic compositions that would present a series of allegorical scenes to accompany the pomp and splendor of courtly audiences.

Slowly the religious aspect was becoming less important, to the point of becoming a pretext. The passage was brief from theatrical representations like these to a more modern secular theater. This development was made possible through the presence of classical Greek and Latin drama, in an atmosphere of imitation rather than intentional secularization. The appearance of distinct genres of tragedy and comedy in the sixteenth century indicates an important stage along this line of development. Moreover, in the attempt to imitate the forms of classical theater on which were modeled the emerging vernacular theater, religious drama faded away, leaving the city and the main courts, but surviving in remote country churches as entertainment for rustic audiences. Thanks to this process, Italian theater moved from the early simplistic structure of religious dramas to complex and sophisticated forms.

The Renaissance in Italy, as in the rest of Europe, was marked by increased attendance to and dependence on classical models. Fundamental rules for this new drama, drawn from interpretations of Aristotle's *Poetics,* were the three unities—of time, of place, and of action. Specific classical plays were also widely emulated. For example, after a codex containing twelve comedies by Plautus was discovered in Germany in 1429 by Niccolò Cusano, Plautus' *Menaechmi* enjoyed wide popularity in the courtly theaters of the fifteenth and sixteenth centuries. The play seems to have been appreciated most of all for its intricate interplay of mistaken identities, a fact that is most evident in the numerous plays inspired by this theme, including Bernardo Bibbiena's *Calandria,* Agnolo Firenzuola's *I Lucidi,* Giovanni Giorgio Trissino's *Simillimi,* Pietro Aretino's *L'Ipocrito,* and Annibale Caro's *Gli Straccioni.* The popularity of *Menaechmi* spread far outside of Italy: Shakespeare's *Comedy of Errors* is the reworking of it that is most well-known to English audiences. Following its popularity in Renaissance comedy, the theme of misunderstood identity due to a similarity of appearances was carried over into the commedia dell'arte beginning in the mid-sixteenth century and was then taken up by Carlo Goldoni in his *Due gemelli veneziani*.

The time was ripe for the birth of the regular Italian comedy of the classic type, and its importance in the history of Italian theater is evident when we consider that it produced authors like Ludovico Ariosto (1474–1533), Niccolò Machiavelli (1469–1527), and Pietro Aretino (1492–1556). In particular, Ariosto's work had a great influence. Among his important comedies are *Cassaria* and *Suppositi*. Although the former is not derived from Plautus or Terence, it reproduces the spirit of the Roman theater with its predilection for intrigues and stratagems. As sources for the *Suppositi*, Ariosto himself indicated the *Eunuchus* of Terence and the *Captivi* of Plautus.

In the same setting one can also recall Machiavelli's first work, a translation and reworking of Terence's *Andria*, written in a highly energetic vernacular style. Later, his *Mandragola*, in 1518, and his *Clizia*, in 1521, would also evoke Plautus' *Casina*, clearly marking Machiavelli's inclusion among Renaissance classical imitators. In the *Clizia* one glimpses the shadow of an autobiographical episode (at the age of fifty Machiavelli fell in love with a young woman), and the humor of an old man in love becomes a sort of satire of himself; whereas in the *Mandragola*, considered his best work, we find the same vision of the world that is represented in his political writings. The *Mandragola* is a microcosm of society as Machiavelli knew it—and as it had to be to justify his own philosophy. It is a world where simple people are easily deceived, although they feel wise and knowing, and of cunning people who deceive the simple with the help of priests, ready to perform any ignominious deed as long as they are well rewarded. The laughter that emerges from the plot and the lively dialogue is full of bitter irony. Machiavelli portrays a corner of the world, in which he does not want to become entangled, as a microcosm of human brutality.

For his originality, liveliness, and native intellect, Aretino occupies a most important place in the history of sixteenth-century Italian theater. Composed between 1525 and 1542, his five comedies (*Marescalco, Cortigiana, Ipocrita, La talanta,* and *Filosofo*) offer only slight traces of classical imitation. He peoples his scenes with pleasing, hastily drawn figures: crafty servants, lost women, braggart soldiers, and dissolute youths.

But if Plautus and Terence offered structures and basic dramatic forms, the playwrights of the Renaissance treated their models with great liberty, not only commingling elements from two or more classical plays, but also translating into their own compositions the large repertoire of type-scenes, situations, intrigues, and jokes that they found in contemporary prose, especially Giovanni Boccaccio's *Decameron,* in addition to many elements and themes deriving from more popular literary forms in regional dialects. This variety of sources is characteristic, for example, of the plays of Ruzante and, more generally, of the theatrical culture of Renaissance Venice. Angelo Beolco (Padua, 1502–1542), better known as Ruzante (the frolicker), was a writer and actor whose significant literary cultivation helped him develop his tastes and refine his artistic talents. The critical positions he assumed on literary matters did not arise from ignorance or from disdain for culture, but rather from a discriminating artistic involvement and a desire to regain for the author a greater freedom for creativity and expression. His best comedies, written in rustic Paduan dialects, are *Il reduce* (or *Parlamento*), *Bilora, Moschetta, Anconitana,* and *Fiorina.* These draw vivid pictures of country life in all its freshness, vivacity, and good humor. From the same area came Andrea Calmo (1510–1571), an eccentric Venetian who used in his comedies not only Venetian but also the dialects of Padua, Bergamo, Dalmatia, and the hybrid speech of the Stradioti (Greek mercenaries who spoke a mixture of Venetian and neo-Greek).

The Neapolitan Giambattista della Porta (1535–1615) was also gifted with a versatile intellect. He devoted much time to researching the history of science, and from his studies of philosophy, alchemy, and magic, he sought retreat in the composition of plays. He wrote some twenty-nine comedies (including *Olimpia, Astrologo, Turca, Sorella, Fantesca, Cintia, Trappolaria, Due fratelli simili,* and *Due fratelli rivali*), three tragedies, and a tragicomedy.

As far as the genre of tragedy in Italy is concerned, in the sixteenth century it remained faithful to traditional forms, and it never really gained a larger public outside of the courts. For the most part, the plots used protagonists from high social levels—historical persons, classical heroes, or biblical figures—cast into dramatic conflicts between personal passions and the ruthless logic of political necessities. Strongly influenced by the climate of the Counter-Reformation, and in particular the theatrical theory and practice developed by the Jesuits, tragedy was understood as having a didactic purpose leading one toward catharsis, achieved through pity and fear provoked by the extreme misfortunes of those onstage. Numerous authors wrote tragedies, both conforming with the traditional aesthetic canons laid down by Aristotle and also pursuing novel experiments. Torquato Tasso (1544–1595) introduced a conformity to the rules of the art (he devoted extensive time and study to the principles of Aristotle) and produced a mixture of the most admired Hellenic tragedies in his *Torrismondo*. This tragedy is an excellent example of the mingling of past and present in the drama, and of the new romantic elements still confined in the old classic structure. Giambattista Giraldi Cinzio's (1504–1573) tragedies, meanwhile, especially his *Orbecche,* determined the direction of numerous Italian tragedies in the second half of the century: characters were more numerous than they had been in other Greek imitations, and he introduced prologues that were delivered by supernatural beings.

The most important tragic playwrights of the seventeenth century were Federico della Valle (1560–1628) and Carlo de' Dottori (1618–1686). In 1595, della Valle staged his tragicomedy *Adelonda di Frigia* for the Savoia family in Turin. Soon thereafter, because of differences of opinion concerning the Savoias' politics, in 1601 he moved to Milan and served Count Fuentes. There, between 1627 and 1628, he published his tragedies *La reina di Scozia* (about Mary, Queen of Scotland), *Judit,* and *Ester.* Della Valle's heroines are of the noblest natures, never forgetting the duties and responsibilities proper to their social roles. In accordance with the model of Greek tragedy, no violence is shown onstage. Thus, for example, the execution of Mary of Scotland is narrated to her nurses by the steward who accompanied her to the gallows. In *Aristodemo,* de' Dottori's best-known tragedy, the plot is based also on the merciless dynamics of political expediency. The protagonist Aristodemus embodies the archetypical tyrant and the judgment of one who possesses absolute power. Although the theatrical genre of tragedy was never as widely popular as comedic genres, it nevertheless had an important place in sixteenth- and seventeenth-century Italian theater, not least because it gave poets and audiences creative space for cultivating links with the heroic figures of ancient and more recent history.


## Commedia dell'Arte and Melodrama

In the seventeenth century courtly theater continued to flourish, but from the middle of the sixteenth century public theaters also began to grow as a parallel institution, addressing larger and more diverse audiences than the elite aristocratic circles of the courts. In addition, Jesuit colleges became an ever more prominent site for theatrical productions of a marked educational nature. Overall, however, literary production for the theater did not, relatively speaking, enjoy great prestige in seventeenth-century Italy. The modest means of most rulers left the cultural life of the courts in a depressed state, while pressures from religious authorities, strongly concerned with Counter-Reformation efforts, greatly limited the freedom of writers, artists, and, above all, playwrights. Moreover, changing tastes were heightening demand for entertaining spectacles, in which different artistic media—from poetry to music to visual arts—were mixed and exploited to construct fantastic and elaborate scenes. This demand for entertainment both in the courts and in public audiences was met by the emerging genres of commedia dell'arte and melodrama.

Commedia dell'arte began around the middle of the sixteenth century but reached its apex of success in the following century, thanks to professional acting troupes that, under the guidance of a director, prepared their own performances and toured from town to town. The performances were largely based on actors' improvisations. The plays were not fully scripted but rather were introduced in the form of a *canovaccio* (outline), a word that indicates a summary script at the actors' disposal that suggests the plot for the play and the characters to appear scene by scene. On this foundation the actors improvised their lines and constructed the dialogue. The actors' inventiveness was buttressed by a repertoire of common scenes, committed to memory, that constituted the regular tools of the profession. This repertoire was filled out by skilled mimicry, required for the so-called *lazzi* (jokes), which were wordless mimes that drew laughter by their exaggerated gestures, by repetition, and by the frequent recourse to obscenities. Here, too, the actor had scope for improvisation and could vary the usual scheme with personal touches. Another element that characterized commedia dell'arte was the use of masks, or stereotyped characters. Inherited from ancient Latin theater, these characters of fixed social and psychological identity were highly elaborated during the Renaissance. Some of the types that are recognizable inheritances from antiquity are the braggart soldier and the bawd or procuress. In addition, there were regional masks, characters typifying "ethnic" or regional stereotypes, such as Arlecchino, Brighella, Pantalone, and Pulcinella. These were often recognized by a specific costume, and they would speak in regional dialects. The success of this form of entertainment contributed to an eclipse of traditional literary theater. In commedia dell'arte the actor had a preeminent role compared with the author and gave life to a theater that was very popular among all social strata for a good part of the eighteenth century.

The rise of melodrama can also be ascribed to the good fortune of theatrical spectacles, which became more and more independent of literary production and dependent on professional theater workers. By the late sixteenth century the innovative energies that arose out of classical humanism had nearly been exhausted. This period is historically defined as *mannerism,* a word that, although coined by art critics, is nevertheless perfectly suited for literature and theater as well. Fewer and fewer new ideas were arising in the courts, which had long played host to the active literati and had been important settings for lively dialogue and the exchange of ideas necessary for artistic activity. As the courts declined as the most important institution for artistic and philosophical patronage, private academies began to take their place. The idea of the academy was not new; already in the mid-fifteenth century Lorenzo the Magnificent had encouraged Marsilio Ficino to found the Platonic Academy in Florence, where students of Plato could discuss and delve into the ideas of the great Greek philosopher.

Later in Florence, beginning toward the end of the sixteenth century, a collection of friends formed the Camerata dei Bardi, which met in the house of Giovanni Bardi (1534–1612), count of Vernio. Among them were musicians and mathematicians like Vincenzo Galilei (1520–1591), an illustrious composer and father of Galileo; Jacopo Peri (1561–1633); and Ottavio Rinuccini (1562–1621), who wrote the first opera librettos. This group developed the theory and first examples of melodrama, in which words and music played equal parts, and the music was meant to be an interpretation of the words. Melodrama was perhaps the genre that best answered the new taste for glamour and grandiosity. Also typical were pastoral themes and settings, which were fashionable among the aristocratic audiences. It was in this context that Rinuccini wrote his four melodramas *Arianna, Dafne, Euridice,* and *Narciso.* He was the first poet who devoted himself fully to this genre. His melodramas repeat and amplify the passionate lyricism that one already finds in Tasso. This is most apparent in the prologue of *Euridice,* where the personification of Tragedy comes onstage to announce that she has entered a new phase. Whereas in the past she has been painted with dark hues and in an atmosphere of gloom, now she would like more delicate tones in order to reawaken "sweeter passions in the heart."

The reference here to Greek tragedy constituted an important theoretical premise for the new genre. The theorists and first practitioners of melodrama referred back to Greek tragedy as an example of theatrical production in which music and poetry blended in harmony. The innovative aspect of melodrama was that it linked the musical score strictly to the dramatic text, according to the formula *recitar cantando* (to act by singing), which attributed primacy to the poetic word. The preeminent composer for the melodrama was Claudio Monteverdi (1567–1643), whose famous works include *Orfeo,* his setting of Rinuccini's libretto *Arianna;* the *Ritorno di Ulisse in patria;* and his last work, *Incoronazione di Poppea.* The operatic aria began its rise to prominence with Monteverdi. Entrusted to a solo performance by the female protagonist, the aria became the emotional nucleus of the melodrama and provided a privileged moment for singers to display their virtuosity.

In fact, the singers' demands for more opportunities to show off their vocal talents onstage led, over the course of the seventeenth century, to a sort of decline of the libretto, as the poetic script became ever more subordinate to the melodic execution. This led, in turn, to a kind of reformation at the beginning of the eighteenth century by Apostolo Zeno (1668–1750) and, above all, Pietro Metastasio (1698–1782). Metastasio was introduced to the musical milieu of Rome by the famous singer Marianna Benti Bulgarelli, and his *Didone abbandonata* was first performed to great success in 1724. From that moment, his career became a crescendo. He had found the perfect balance between poetry and music, inspired by mythology, legend, history, and anything else that could provide him with stimulation for tragic plots, which he then would revive with a wholly Arcadian sensibility that shunned real tragedy and tended instead toward melancholy and idyllic musical works. Between 1724 and 1729 he composed *Catone in Utica, Semiramide riconosciuta,* and other melodramas, all considered inferior to the *Didone abbandonata.* In Vienna from 1730 to 1740 Metastasio wrote his best and most celebrated works: *Adriano in Siria, Demetrio, Olimpiade, Clemenza di Tito,* and *Attilio Regolo.* In later years his poetic inspiration dried up, and he turned to composing more theoretical works, which set out to explain, after the fact, those principles that had inspired his melodramas. The success of his works, praised universally throughout Europe, proved that Metastasio had understood his times and was able to express the tastes of the eighteenth century and to rescue melodrama from its literary decline.

As already mentioned, in the eighteenth century commedia dell'arte reigned triumphant on the Italian stage. But the genre had, over time, reached a point of excess because the fixed character types became fossilized and actors were more and more liberal in their use of vulgar and obscene expressions to please the public, abandoning the clever and vivacious wit that had earlier marked the art form. For this reason Carlo Goldoni (1707–1793) decided to create a new type of play. He wanted to replace the old cast of type figures (the clever servant, the greedy father, the shiftless son, etc.) with characters that reflected real life and depicted their psychologies in all their variety. Moreover, in order to avoid the actors' improvised interventions, which were not always appropriate, he wanted to have a scripted text written entirely by the playwright.

In order not to clash with the tastes of a public long habituated to the standards of commedia dell'arte, Goldoni introduced his reforms gradually. His first fully scripted comedy was *La donna di garbo* (1743). Goldoni's prolific body of work includes *La famiglia dell'antiquario, La bottega del caffé, Il bugiardo, La locandiera,* and *Le smanie per la villeggiatura,* all written in Italian. In the Venetian dialect he wrote *I rusteghi, Sior Todero Brontolon,* and *Le baruffe chiozzotte.* During his long stay in France he also wrote, in lively and clever French, his *Memoirs.*

Despite the fact that he achieved great popularity in Italy, in 1762 he left Venice for Paris to direct the Italian Theater. Goldoni decided to leave his native land because of the great bitterness that resulted from strong polemics against him by two literati, Pietro Chiari and Carlo Gozzi. Chiari was a rival of Goldoni who could not bear the sudden and unexpected success of his plays. Gozzi was an aristocrat who regarded Goldoni's realism as socially subversive and a threat to the dignity of the aristocracy as well as a mystified exaltation of life and the rights of the people.

Carlo Gozzi (1720–1806)—whose writings are a testimony to the social, moral, and political crises of eighteenth-century Venice—was an important figure in Italian theater in his own right. Gifted with a strong polemical spirit, he became an implacable opponent of the culture and myths of the Enlightenment. On the literary plane, his criticisms were directed above all against Goldoni, whom he accused of literary defects, moral decadence, and excessive indulgence in his representations of human vices. Intending to demonstrate to Goldoni that dramatic spectacles for children could also be successful in the theater, without rejecting the ingredients of commedia dell'arte, Gozzi began to write *Fiabe* ("Fables"), such as his *L'amore delle tre melarance, Re cervo, Turandot, L'augellino belverde,* and others. In these, fabulous tales are mixed with dramatic elements as well as literary polemics. Despite some uneven roughness in structure, the *Fiabe* reveal their author's measure of fair-minded artistic talent, his taste for the marvelous, and a lively imagination.

Before the eighteenth century, tragedy in Italy had had only limited success and influence. After the middling results of the sixteenth and seventeenth centuries, at the beginning of the eighteenth century Scipione Maffei (1675–1755), with his *Merope,* prepared the ground, in a sense, for Vittorio Alfieri (1749–1803), who in turn found an open and nearly unexplored artistic field. What drew him toward tragedy was his intuition that this ancient literary form might provide a congenial way to express the fullness of his interior life, which was always preoccupied with a search for balance between the urgency of desires and the will toward reflection. Onstage he set steady and rigid scenes, reducing them to essentials; he limited the actions and number of characters; and he introduced the protagonist either in the second act or when the tragic mood seemed already poised on the edge of catastrophe. By these means, tragic tension itself came to dominate, highlighting the conflict of divergent passions. Moreover, Alfieri's tragedy answered Italian aspirations for freedom. More than he loved liberty, he hated tyranny. In his first tragedy, *Filippo,* the protagonist is the very personification of tyranny, while his *Saul* is torn by contrary passions. He struggles with God and with himself, but in the end he expresses a majesty that inspires compassion and admiration. In *Mirra,* Alfieri's final masterpiece, the drama lies in the horrible struggle of a chaste soul with an incestuous obsession. The importance of Alfieri's theater in the history of Italian literature was enormous, inspiring many other Italian tragedies in the early nineteenth century.

## Nineteenth-Century Theater

In fact in 1797, on the eve of the Italian *Risorgimento,* Ugo Foscolo (1778–1827) dedicated to Alfieri his tragedy *Tieste,* written in Alfierian style and having a broad political purpose. While the character Altreo is the symbol of perfidious tyranny, Tieste is the vindicator of justice and liberty. Foscolo's second tragedy, *Aiace,* is a heroic poem with many exquisite lines and in which the spirit of antiquity has been reproduced. His third tragedy, *Ricciarda,* composed in 1813, was the least successful of the three. Politics were very important in the vicissitudes of nineteenth-century Italian theater. It was in the climate of conspiracy against the Austrian domination that Silvio Pellico (1789–1854) wrote his *Francesca da Rimini,* a tragedy that was performed by the famous actress Carlotta Marchionni and, although the plot was weak and versification poor, enjoyed a tremendous success.

Religious and historical themes informed the two tragedies of Alessandro Manzoni (1785–1873), *Il conte di Carmagnola* (1820), based on the conflict between conscience and expedience, and *Adelchi* (1822), which centers on the inscrutable suffering of the innocent son of an oppressive Lombard king. Manzoni expounded his program for Romantic tragedy in his letter to monsieur Chauvet *sur l'unité de temps et de lieu dans la tragédie* (1820), in which he repudiates as cumbersome the classical rules of the unity of time and place. He also abandoned mythological and classical subjects and substituted national, medieval, and modern historical themes. Moreover, he revived and transformed the function of the chorus that in Greek tragedy had narrated events happening offstage or interpreted collective emotions in response to the action. It had fallen out of use in recent times, and Manzoni restored it with a new function: he reserved it as his own special space for expressing freely his own lyrical feelings without affecting the course of the action.

His first tragedy, *Il conte di Carmagnola,* deals with Carmagnola's seven-year rise and fall in the service of the Venetian commonwealth. Francesco Bussone, better known as Carmagnola, was one of those soldiers of fortune who led mercenary troops for different princes. In times when there were no national armies, the importance of these mercenaries was enormous. The play's action covers historical events from 1426 to 1432, from Carmagnola's entering the service of Venice until his execution. In trying to reveal the soul of the protagonist,

Manzoni obscured history and depicted a spiritualized Christian character very different from the fifteenth-century soldier.

*Adelchi* is like a great fresco of the events that preceded the fall of the Lombard kingdom in Italy between 772 and 774. Manzoni injects into these events an intense Christian compassion for the conquerors and the conquered and a somber pity for the Italian people who suffered from the foreign invaders. In nineteenth-century Italy, which was in turmoil because of conflicts between the French and the Austrians, the story of the Franks' intervention to aid the pope when threatened by the Lombard king Desiderio must have had great resonance. In the play, faith and political machinations intermingle, contaminating Charlemagne himself and compelling the Frankish king to repudiate his wife, Ermengarda, who had been given to him as a pledge of the alliance between Charlemagne and Desiderio. Here, moral and spiritual dilemmas interact with those of history and transcend them, such as the relation between devotion to fatherland and faith in divine principles and the mystery of historical conflicts—or of providence—by which the innocent Adelchi (ever faithful to his duty and maintaining peace as long as possible) and Ermengarda pay for the crimes of their bloodthirsty fathers.

During the second half of the nineteenth century, theater changed along with the changing times, especially after the unification of Italy in 1861. Plays focusing on social issues prevailed; in these, contemporary society was presented and critiqued from a moral point of view. At the same time, throughout the nineteenth century, operatic melodrama became more and more popular. Besides such prominent composers as Gioacchino Rossini, Vincenzo Bellini, and Giuseppe Verdi, important contributions were made by Arrigo Boito (1842–1918), who wrote many successful librettos and was involved with the Milanese *scapigliatura* movement, an artistic rebellion against bourgeois conventions and culture that flourished between 1860 and 1880. Toward the end of the nineteenth century, several playwrights were influenced by the literary movement of *verismo;* these included Marco Praga (1862–1929), whose greatest work was *Moglie ideale* (1890), and the three Sicilian authors Luigi Capuana (1839–1915), who wrote *Malia* and *Lu paraninfu;* Nino Martoglio (1870–1921), with his *L'aria del continente;* and Giovanni Verga (1840–1922), best known for his *Cavalleria rusticana, La lupa,* and *Dal tuo al mio.*

## Twentieth-Century Theater

At the beginning of the twentieth century, Italian theater was dominated by the imposing figure of Gabriele D'Annunzio (1863–1938), who broke with the well-worn naturalistic conventions of drama. He brought onstage a kind of poetic tragedy set amid stunning backdrops and capable of expressing to a larger public ideological themes evocative of Friedrich Nietzsche's Superman. D'Annunzio as a playwright relished his role as the great artist and in the newly unified Italy enjoyed a genuinely national celebrity. His tragedies are simple in their structure, with an atmosphere that favors the most intense emotions. The scenes are set in ancient times or in some period of decadence when the crust of civilization has thinned or has been torn off by violence. The souls of his characters are not tortured by remorse, nor do they struggle against temptation. Such a conception ignores the classic notion that drama is a battle in the soul between good and evil. Since such primitive characters cannot easily be set within the frame of modern life, D'Annunzio presents an abundance of scenic arrangements, with magnificent descriptions colored by his magical vocabulary. Although D'Annunzio wrote numerous plays (*Fedra, La Gioconda, La gloria, Francesca da Rimini, Più che l'amore, La fiaccola sotto il moggio,* and *La nave*), his lasting fame rests on *La figlia di Iorio,* a drama original in conception and style and harmonious in all its parts. It takes place in a legendary land where reality is transposed with a spiritual loftiness, pastoral rites, and mystic worship.

Filippo Tommaso Marinetti (1876–1944) leveled criticisms against both traditional and poetic theater, proclaiming in *Manifesto* (1911) that futurism was the next rightful stage of theater. Drama, he claimed, should be a synthesis of life along its more typical and significant lines, thus anticipating the main thesis he would express in *Manifesto del teatro sintetico* (1915), which delved into the controversial themes of the variety show stage. Futurist synthetic theater attacked the useless and boring prolixity of contemporary theater, which was to be replaced by the barest essentials of words and gestures, artfully chosen to engage and provoke the audience. It was no accident that the model of this new theater was the popular variety show, with its quick and fantastic characters and actions, which the futurists exaggerated in absurd and paradoxical directions. Marinetti and his followers assailed the public in their notorious and unpredictable "futurist evenings." The dramatic works of Marinetti are *Roi Bombance/Re Baldoria* (1905), inspired by Alfred Jarry's *Ubu roi, Elettricità sessuale* (1909), *Il tamburo di fuoco* (1922), *Bianco e rosso* (1923), and many others. In many aspects they anticipated the anguished abstractions of Eugene Ionesco's absurdist theater.

As already mentioned, in the early twentieth century the variety show had an important role in various aspects of Italian theater. Born from the performances in French singing cafés (songs, parodies, skits, jokes, nonsense), these were shows without a plot and tied exclusively to the performers' talents. Variety shows were much appreciated among the avant-garde, thanks especially to their imaginative and quixotic character. The greatest variety show performer of the time was the extraordinary Roman actor Ettore Petrolini (1886–1936), whose famous gags were a great success. He also wrote comedies (such as *Benedetto fra le donne* and *Chicchignola*) that have been performed even in recent years. Petrolini was unsurpassable, especially for his irresistible monologues (*I salamini, Antico romano, Fortunello, Ma l'amore mio non muore, and Nerone*), which were modern satires that grew out of an awareness of the folly and stupidities of a petty society easily duped by myths. With plays on words, puns, and double entendres often pushed to the point of absurdity, Petrolini targeted his satires at the fashions and ridiculous obsessions of the petite-bourgeoisie. Despite his mockery of the grandiose idea of "Romanità" and the many veiled allusions in his *Nerone,* the Fascist regime put up with him, perhaps because in comedies, variety shows, and popular films the state found more conformity and collaboration than any danger of subversion. The paradoxical humor in the plays of Achille Campanile (1900–1976) is also based on everyday language. In all his dramas, from *Centocinquanta la gallina canta* (1924) to *L'eroe* (1976), a taste for wordplay and surrealist nonsense predominates.

An important avant-garde development of a vaguely expressionist nature was the "theater of the grotesque." Flourishing between 1916 and 1920, some of the important works in the movement were *La maschera e il volto* by Luigi Chiarelli (1884–1947), *L'uomo che incontrò se stesso* by Luigi Antonelli (1882–1942), and *Marionette, che passione!* and *La bella addormentata* by Pier Maria Rosso di San Secondo (1887–1956). The grotesque developed out of the same critical impulses toward demystification that drove Luigi Pirandello in his plays. A distrust of the identity of the self, common to all expressionist art, leads these authors to insist on the fictitious quality of the person, who seems more like a mask or a marionette. From this derives the technique of grotesque decomposition of character and of the unity of perspective, and the insertion into the plot of a *raisonneur* or philosopher who acts as the author's mouthpiece and becomes the critical conscience of the play. An example of such a figure is Laudisi in Pirandello's *Così è (se vi pare)*.

Living amid the feverish atmosphere of futurism and the theater of the grotesque, and influenced as well by Henrik Ibsen's symbolism and by Pirandello, Massimo Bontempelli (1878–1960) was another subtle and sophisticated author, although his plays never attained a wide audience. Nevertheless, he still provokes interest among critics and scholars. His best work includes *La guardia della luna* (1920), *Siepe a Nord-ovest* (1923), *Nostra Dea* (1925), and *Minnie la candida* (1928), each of which expresses the author's unique voice and originality.

Far and away the most studied playwright of the twentieth-century Italian stage is Luigi Pirandello (1867–1936). Raised in rural Sicily, he studied in Rome and later in Germany. From writing poetry, essays, and short fiction in his early days, he turned to the theater around 1910 when his first stage productions were performed in Rome. Thereafter, he quickly established himself as an important modern playwright, composing and staging many plays in the teens and early twenties, including, in 1913, *Il dovere del medico;* in 1916, *Pensaci, Giacomino!* and *Liolà;* in 1917, *La giara, Così è (se vi pare),* and *Il piacere dell'onestà;* in 1918, *Il giuoco delle parti;* in 1919, *L'innesto* and *L'uomo, la bestia e la virtù;* in 1920, *Tutto per bene, Come prima meglio di prima, Cecé,* and *La signora Morli, una e due;* and his greatest early success, *Sei personaggi in cerca d'autore* in 1921. With *Sei personaggi* Pirandello rose to prominence both in Italy and in the wider European world, gaining a name as an important figure in contemporary theater. With this play he began to portray onstage the "uneasiness" of representation, dramatizing the tensions between the text, the characters, and their author. These metatheatrical developments were in many ways revolutionary, and they continued to occupy Pirandello for the rest of his career. In 1922 were performed his *Enrico IV* and *Vestire gli ignudi,* in 1923 *L'uomo dal fiore in bocca* and *La vita che ti diedi,* and in 1924 *Ciascuno a suo modo.*

In Pirandellian theater, human identity is the product of perception and circumstance. Like mirrors, people are reflections of the world around them, and his characters often enact struggles between their personal identities and the identities that society imposes on them. Pirandello's plays explore such complex issues as the multiplicity of human personality, the relativity of truth, and the difficulty if not impossibility of establishing a dividing line between reality and its illusions. The focus, however, is usually on the characters' interactions with these concepts, as they struggle to deal with the effects such ideas have on their lives. Pirandello realized that a character's theatricality need not be unexamined or unconscious but that it can be used by its possessor for certain ends. Thus he used the theater self-consciously in the same way, to examine itself and its relationship to life. In the plays that are usually referred to as his theater trilogy—*Sei personaggi in cerca d'autore, Ciascuno a suo modo*, and *Questa sera si recita a soggetto*—Pirandello pushes the theater into modernism by attempting an exploration of the theatrical process and its relationship to the world it mirrors. All three of the theater trilogy plays break through the imaginary "fourth wall" of the realistic theater in an attempt to destroy the barrier between auditorium and stage.

In the author's last creative period, which began around 1928 to 1929, Pirandello entrusted his tortured investigations of truth to "myths," as a last hope for coherence, even if illusory, in the face of the relentless fragmentation of forms. The rejection of the world of contingency, against which Pirandello had first reacted with irony and then with dramatic contempt, developed finally into a nostalgic aspiration to that mythic absolute which generated a new form of fabulous and surrealistic theater. Another decisive element that intervened in his life and work at this time was his encounter with Marta Abba, the actress for whom he wrote, among others, *Diana e la Tuda* (1926), *L'amica delle mogli* (1927), *La nuova colonia* (1928), and *Come tu mi vuoi* (1930). The work from this time is suffused with autobiography, reflecting his love for Abba and displaying a depth of emotional expression not found in his earlier work. *La nuova colonia* is the first stage of his new "mythic theater," followed by *Lazzaro* (1929), and—although unfinished at the time of his death—*I giganti della montagna*, which he considered his dramatic masterpiece.

If Pirandello aimed to criticize any society founded on rules and laws, by negating the legitimacy of the patriarchal family, the primal site of human alienation, Eduardo De Filippo (1900–1984) instead fixed his sights on the moment of mutual recognition between father and son, in which family represents a kind of lost paradise. A dream fated to destruction in the face of the reality of human social life, family provokes isolation and animosity. So in *Natale in casa Cupiello* (1934), De Filippo's first real success, the fundamental theme, as in all his plays, is the Neapolitan family, a knot of affections and latent hostilities often exacerbated by poverty and lack of education. Moving from descriptions of inside the house, its daily objects, and routines (waking, morning coffee, encounters with neighbors, etc.), De Filippo gradually plumbs to the depths of his characters' solitude, the misunderstandings that divide them, and the repressed animosities that explode into drama. It is the same atmosphere found in some of Pirandello's works. Luca Cupiello cannot avoid confronting reality: his puerile preoccupation with building the Christmas nativity allows him to escape the mediocre reality of his family. His son, who despises the nativity, shows no interest in relating with his father, while his daughter is on the verge of destroying her marriage for the sake of a lover. Before their familial myth collapses, just as in other of De Filippo's characters, Luca reacts with malaise, immobility, silence, and thoughts of death. Ultimately, in a humorous upturn that seems to mock the values of marital fidelity, the daughter unites with her lover, mistaking him for her husband. Such are the themes found in his most famous plays, *Napoli milionaria* (1945), *Questi fantasmi* (1946), *Filumena Marturano* (1946), *Le voci dentro* (1948), *De Pretore Vincenzo* (1957), *Il sindaco del rione Sanità* (1960), and *Gli esami non finiscono mai* (1974). In representing the tragicomic vicissitudes of family, always set in Naples, De Filippo normally uses the Neapolitan dialect that from Eduardo Scarpetta (1853–1925) to Raffaele Viviani (1888–1950) had been used to express the range of emotional ordeals of contemporary life.

After the futurist revolution, the great Pirandellian moment, and the plays of De Filippo, the work of Ugo Betti (1892–1953) is the most important in twentieth-century Italian theater. From the end of the 1920s to the mid-1950s, Betti pursued his conception of theater, which was founded on investigation. From his first play (*La padrona*, 1927), Betti tended to present situations of psychological conflict, especially of the individual tormented by the longing for justice. As a judge, his profession for much of his life, he observed life's dramas, great and small, and was forced to sentence people who betrayed and killed in order to steal. As a playwright he was able to bring onstage the very same events and to rail, almost like an accuser, against excessive desire of people to acquire and possess.

Betti deftly explores such themes in his works with a depth of analysis and a stylistic tension uncommon on the Italian stage in the 1930s and 1940s. Among his best works are *Frana allo scalo nord* (1932) and *Corruzione al palazzo di giustizia* (written in 1944 and produced in 1948), based, respectively, on an investigation into the death of workers killed in a landslide and another into a homicide in a courthouse—ironically, the very seat of justice.

Closely linked to Betti's characteristic dramatic structure of legal and moral investigation are the plays of Diego Fabbri (1911–1980), a Catholic author who grafts onto the theme of the investigation of historical, religious, and large social dilemmas (war, Nazism, racism). *Processo a Gesù* (1953), his best work, employs the Pirandellian device of "a play within a play": the life of Christ is debated by actors (playing Jews who have betrayed one of their companions) and spectators, ending in a general prayer for grace from the Son of God, who has died for all.

The latter half of the twentieth century was particularly difficult for Italian playwrights, since theater had been undergoing an evolution toward new conceptions of drama. This time witnessed the rise and institutionalization of the modern system of city theaters (Teatri Stabili), the diffusion of Bertolt Brecht's political theater, and large companies preferring to choose their repertoires from among the classics or from among plays with international success. Faced with the new difficulties of this cultural context, Italian playwrights generally were not able to compete with works that met the new market demands. A marginalization of the author developed with a simultaneous rise in the power of stage directors. A forerunner in this development was Carmelo Bene, who did not limit himself to directing, but more and more invaded the sphere of the author with his liberal arrangements of the texts of plays. In such a difficult situation, few spaces existed for new authors, and only rarely were new works capable of reaching a large audience.

However, among the most significant theatrical episodes of the latter part of the twentieth century was the case of Giuseppe Patroni Griffi, whose plays were produced in close collaboration with one of the largest companies of the 1960s and 1970s, that of Giovani, formed by Rossella Falk, Romolo Valli, and Giorgio De Lullo. Griffi's plays arose from his close attention to current events, without imposing a social or moralistic perspective. His great work *D'amore si muore* (1958) scrutinizes the world of cinema from the perspective of those who try to succeed in it but encounter a world so strange that, not able to give up their bourgeois moralities, they end up burning out. Griffi's most successful play, however, is *Metti una sera a cena* (1967), a bourgeois comedy that trespassed conventional moral limits and presented a picture of—and encouraged—a new freedom of casual sexual relations.

Also significant during this period were the works of Pier Paolo Pasolini (1922–1975), whose verse tragedies (*Orgia, Calderòn, Affabulazione,* and *Pilade*) use myths to explore diversity and social marginalization, themes very familiar to him. Another significant and complex playwright of the time was Giovanni Testori (1923–1993), with his subtle trilogy *Ambleto* (1972), *Macbetto* (1974), and *Edipus* (1977). After his conversion to Catholicism, Testori's plays took on a religious character (*Conversazione con la morte,* 1978; *Interrogatorio a Maria,* 1979). Another figure, known especially for his grotesque and surreal humor, was Ennio Flaiano (1910–1972), who wrote the scripts for several of Federico Fellini's films (for example, *La dolce vita*). His comedy *Un marziano a Roma* (1960) is a brilliantly ironic treatment of the intellectual world of Rome.

Last, an intense experimentalism has marked the work of Dario Fo (1926– ), author and actor of great appeal (often performing with his wife, Franca Rame, herself the author of a number of satirical plays). His whimsical imagination and surreal and minstrel-like humor marked his first theatrical farces: *Comica finale, Non tutti i ladri vengono per nuocere, L'uomo nudo e l'uomo in frac, Gli imbianchini non hanno ricordi, I cadaveri si spediscono e le donne si spogliano, Gli arcangeli non giocano a flipper,* and *Chi ruba un piede è fortunato in amore.* In 1963, with *Isabella, tre caravelle e un cacciaballe,* an evolution began on the wave of political events in Italy that would draw Fo toward a theater ever more in conflict with the political system. Several of his works arose under the influence of ideological concerns of the time: *Settimo: ruba un po' meno, La colpa è sempre del diavolo,* and *La signora è da buttare.* Others grew out of his political activities within the radical left wing, including *Morte accidentale di un anarchico, Pum pum chi è? La polizia!,* and *Fanfani rapito.* His (original) reconstruction of medieval minstrel culture, viewed from the angle of the modern popular culture of protest and unrest, led to his *Mistero buffo* in 1969, a minstrel play that he wrote in the fifteenth-century dialect of the Po Valley on the basis of his free interpretation of contemporary popular sources. This delightful text continues to be staged today with great success. In 1997, for his extraordinary talents and achievements as writer and actor, he was awarded the Nobel Prize in literature.

During the last decades of the twentieth century, Italian theatrical production received new energy and direction thanks to the work of a number of female writers who have become more active in this genre. Natalia Ginzburg (1916–1991) was among these who acquired visibility as a playwright with her first play *Ti ho sposato per allegria* (1964), followed by *L'inserzione* (1968). Her plays, ten in all, are often based on comic humor that cloaks a tragic sense of desperation. Their plots and themes are similar to those of her novels and short stories in which the narrative tends to center on family dynamics.

Also considerable and steady have been the contributions to Italian theater of Dacia Maraini (1933– ), one of Europe's most important contemporary female playwrights. A prolific writer with more than fifty publications of novels, poetry, plays, and screenplays, she has been, ever since the publication of her first two novels *La vacanza* (1962) and *L'età del malessere* (1963), an active participant in the debate concerning the status of women and their struggles in Italy during a period of great social and political change. Of the more than thirty plays Maraini has written, one may recall *Cuore di mamma* (1969), *La donna perfetta* (1975), *Dialogo di una prostituta con un suo cliente* (1978), *Suor Jana* (1980), *I sogni di Clitennestra* (1981), *Veronica, meretrice e scrittora* (1992), *Memorie di una cameriera* (2001), and *Maria Stuarda* (2001). More than a dozen have been translated and performed outside of Italy. Maraini's innovative plays have been influential not least because of their decisive explorations of sexuality, gender, and power. Her theatrical texts do not speak only to women, however. They have also helped to open a dialogue on issues that affect all individuals and the whole of society.

Because of these compelling and fascinating new voices within the Italian theatrical panorama, the beginning of the new millennium appears not only vibrant but also more balanced, where both male and female playwrights explore (often with humor and a keen sense of the absurd) such fundamental issues as social repression, identity, political upheaval, and the struggle for real and lasting social change. The Italian stage thus continues to be, as it has been since its medieval beginnings, a vital artistic forum for critical representation of and intervention into Italian and European society. And indeed, as the landscape of human concerns continues to shift rapidly with the complex revolutions of globalism and technology, Italy's contemporary playwrights, both men and women, able to draw on a rich and unique tradition, seem well poised to apply their varied talents to providing significant dramaturgical responses to these challenges.

# CHAPTER 2

# Acting Italian: From the Piazza to the Stage

WILLIAM VAN WATSON

## Preliminaries

The essence of drama is conflict, and conflict comes from the desires and drives of the characters and forces—social, divine, natural, psychological, or ideological as they may be—in a play that are at cross-purposes with one another or in opposition to one another. Konstantin Stanislavski (1863–1938), the foremost theorist of modern acting, considered the focus or goal of these desires and drives to be the "objective" of the character. The character's objectives provide him or her with motivations for actions. Aristotle (384–322 B.C.), in his *Poetics* (360–322 B.C.), defined drama as "the imitation of a perfect action, but also of actions which are terrible and piteous, and actions principally become such . . . on account of each other" (12). The dramatic actions of characters should not be confused with mere physical activity that can, on occasion, embody a dramatic action but more often does not. The clashing objectives of the characters are set into conflict by the actions they take. These actions become "perfect," "terrible," and "piteous" "on account of each other" as they continually escalate through a series of crisis situations until the climax of the play—an ultimately decisive action—is reached. The accumulation of the objectives of any given character cultivated throughout the course of a play comprises that character's *through-going action, through-line,* or *superobjective,* terms Stanislavski used interchangeably (*Legacy* 192). For Stanislavski, the superobjective forms "[the] innermost center, [the] core of the role" (*Creating* 77), and thoughts of the character related to this superobjective constitute his "inner monologue." Conversely, a character's superobjective could be divided into his or her momentary objectives that, as they

intersect with those of the other characters, form the beats and set
the rhythm of the play and its action. The play text is thus analyzed
or scored for motivations, tactics, and strategies. The character may
or may not know why he or she enters a room, but the actor had
better know why he or she enters the stage. Such calculative scoring
does not preset the performance, however. Instead, the actor must
then adapt, adjust, and react to the actions of the other actors, all
varying somewhat from one evening to the next, hopefully creating
what Stanislavski called "the illusion of the first time." Theater performances are thus replicated, not duplicated, and in fact, Italians
call a theatrical performance *una replica.*

## Metatheatricality and the Piazza

Italian theater is a redundancy. In Greek, *theatron* means the seeing-
place. To take part in the seeing-place means to make things seen,
to express, not only to exist, but to create signs of this existence.
Semiotics is the study of sign systems. Ethnosemiotics and cultural
semiotics examine not only what signs are used and deployed within
varying ethnic groups and cultures, but also how these groups con-
ceive of and perceive such signs. Semiologist Irene Portis Winner
asserts that "the semiotics of culture is concerned with the most
abstract and . . . invariant cultural models" (Winner and Umiker-
Sebeok 182).[1] As Italian and Anglo-American societies presuppose
different "invariant cultural models" with regard to signs, Italian
theater should be viewed within the context of these differences. To
be American is to want to mistake the sign of the thing for the thing
itself. Italians do not make this mistake. In his landmark book *The
Italians* (1964), Luigi Barzini described the Italian sensibility as one
in which "nothing is ever what it looks like, and one can never trust
appearances; everything then takes on a double outline. In fact,
the thing and its representation often coincide exactly. They may
also coincide approximately, or may not coincide at all. There is no
sure way of telling" (85). Theater as an art form is an amalgam of
semiotic systems, and so consequently, two cultures having disparate conceptions of the sign will also have disparate conceptions
of theater. In semiotic terms, then, Italians know that the signs
are duplicitous, that they are constituted of signifier and signified,
and that the relationship between these parts can be arbitrary and

even perverse. The Anglo-American and Italian cultures occupy two distinctly different positions vis-à-vis the sign. The Anglo-American position is comparatively semiotically naïve, believing in an imagined primordial wholeness of an Ur-sign, while the Italian position is semiotically savvy, the result of an ancient and wary culture dating back to the Etruscan.

Theater is an intensified, compacted, scripted representation of life, and as such, life functions as the prototype of theater. As a representation of life, theater is a re-presentation of life. Sociologist Erving Goffman explains that "the common social relationship is in itself organized like a staged scene, with an exchange of theatrically exaggerated actions, counteractions and exiting 'lines'" (*Presentation* 88–89). Shakespeare's poetic insight—that "All the world's a stage. / And all the men and women are merely players. / They have their exits and their entrances. / And one man in his time plays many parts"—has its basis in social reality (*As You Like It,* II, vii, 139–142). Theater functions as a microcosm of the macrocosm of the world. Goffman notes, "A character staged in a theater . . . involves use of *real* techniques—*the same techniques by which everyday persons sustain their real social relations*" (254). The key difference between social and staged reality, other than the pre-scripting of the latter, seems to lie in the presence of an audience, but not even this proves entirely true, as interpersonal interactions and altercations between individuals sometimes occur in the presence of onlookers. Alternatively, the actual addressee may be conceived as an onlooker to what is being communicated. Goffman observes, "Often what the speaker tries to do is to present dramas to an audience rather than to convey information to the addressee. It seems that we devote less time to conveying information than to performing" (*Frame* 508). Cultural semiologists Marcel Danesi and Paul Perron have divided human expression into "*representational* and *communicative* structures," but the former is merely a less abstract form of the latter (14).

Given the Italian propensity to externalize the internal, Italians tend to prefer the more representational over less illustrative forms of the communicative. Their culture truly appears very much as a seeing-place. Pier Paolo Pasolini noted: "The archetype of the theater occurs before our eyes every day in the street, at home, in the public meeting places, etc. In this sense social reality is itself a performance that is *not entirely unaware of itself as being such,* and has, therefore, its own code" (italics mine, 143). Anglo-American social interaction constitutes a performance as well, but most often it remains *entirely unaware of itself as being such.* In contrast, Italians revel in the semiosis of social interaction and put on a display in every piazza, at every fountain, inside every *cortile,* and outside every *trattoria.* Entire conversations transpire on busses and on the sidewalks without a word being spoken. For Anglo-Americans, making a scene may serve as a source of embarrassment, but for Italians, the art of making a scene, or *fare una scenata,* can be a defense strategy, a weapon, or a method of manipulation. Barzini describes an Italy where "the show can be so engrossing that many people spend most of their lives just looking at it. . . . There are balconies along the facades of all streets, as convenient as boxes at the theater. . . . Italians [are] the actors, playwrights, choreographers and *metteurs en scène* of their own national drama" (60, 77). With such a daily display, Italian theater proper becomes virtually redundant. As a result, much formal Italian theater is metatheatrical; that is, it is theater that is aware of itself as such. It is self-reflective theater, theater about theater. Luigi Pirandello's (1867–1936) famous "trilogy of the theater" epitomizes this tendency. *Six Characters in Search of an Author* (1921), *Each in His Own Way* (1924), and *Tonight We Improvise* (1929) all take place in theaters and involve the staging of plays as their basic situation. Even Pirandello's more realistic works, while being less explicitly metatheatrical, nevertheless remain implicitly so. In *Right You Are If You Think You Are* (1917), Signora Frola and Signor Ponza are forced to perform their private family melodrama for their overly inquisitive neighbors. In the play, Laudisi describes their public confrontation in overtly theatrical terms. He exclaims: "It will be a most interesting scene! The curtain rises at eleven, precisely!" (103). Eduardo De Filippo's *Grand Magic* (1948) reveals a similar use of metatheatricality within a realist context, as the guests at the resort serve as spectators for the jealous scenes Calogero and Marta enact. Signora Zampa comments, "Every summer there's always a couple who turn out to be the star attraction . . . it was like a Victorian melodrama" (100–101).

Theater may be divided into the presentational and the representational. Presentational theater is avowedly metatheatrical, acknowledging the presence of the audience. Such acknowledgment usually comes in the form of the actor speaking directly to the audience. In contrast, representational theater maintains "the illusion of the fourth wall." This concept dates to a period in history in which theater was performed almost exclusively on a proscenium stage, rather than in a round or on a thrust stage, so that the audience was configured on only one of four sides of the stage. This was the side of "the fourth wall" that the actors, as their characters, imagined to be there. Much of Italian theater, from the commedia dell'arte–inspired texts of Carlo Goldoni (1707–1793) and Carlo Gozzi (1720–1806) to Dario Fo (1926– ), falls into the more overtly metatheatrical presentational category. For instance, Fo's *We Won't Pay! We Won't Pay!* (1974) calls for the roles of the State Trooper, Police Sergeant, Gravedigger, and Grandfather all to be played by the same actor. Furthermore, just in case the audience does not notice this unrealistic casting convention, the character Giovanni comments to the Gravedigger: "I'm sorry for laughing, but you are the spitting image of the sergeant without the mustache who looks like the state trooper with the mustache. I feel like I'm in a play I saw when I was a kid" (51–52). Already parodying scenes from several Shakespearean plays, Fo's *Elizabeth, Almost by Chance a Woman* escalates metatheatricality and self-referentiality still further. The character Big Mama, a servant originally played in drag by Fo himself, threatens an arrogant Elizabeth: "Dario Fo wrote this play, and he wouldn't like to see your treating me like this. One word from me and he'll cross out 'Queen' next to your lines and write in 'Maid'" (175). Like Pirandello before him, Fo must up the ante of the metatheatricality of his texts because of the already theatrical culture that produced him, and to both came Nobel Prize–winning results. Alberto Moravia's (1907–1990) *Il dio Kurt* (1968) puts a macabre twist on such metatheatricality, as a production of *Oedipus Rex* transpires within a Nazi concentration camp. Also, other Italian plays, such as the carefully wrought *Theater of Moral Trials* of Ugo Betti (1892–1953) and works by Diego Fabbri (1911–1980), may be covertly metatheatrical. Substituting the courtroom for the theater stage, Betti's *Landslide on the North Slope* (1932) and Fabbri's *Trial of Jesus* (1955) both present court cases that involve testimony, related with a certain degree of consciousness of role-play and performance upon the stand, and an audience of onlookers who sometimes become witnesses themselves.

The observations of Pasolini and Barzini regarding the self-conscious theatricality of Italian behavior are not new. German traveler Carl Augusto Mayer noticed the parallel between balconies on the street and boxes in the theater in his travelogue *Neapel und die Neapolitaner oder Briefe aus Neapel in die Heimat*, originally published in 1840. Mayer points out how, through the use of gesture, messages could be communicated across a noisy street or down to vendors below. The *locus classicus* of Italian social interaction is the piazza, a wide open space, requiring amplification of expression; a sunny place where people of various classes intermingle and mix; a public place where communication occurs across distances from balconies to cobblestoned streets. In contrast, the *locus classicus* of English social interaction, England with its miserable climate, is indoors; in the parlor, a private space in keeping with English reserve; a quiet, muted, and sometimes dark place where curtains muffle sound, where interaction remains within one class, where raising one's voice is forbidden, and merely raising one's eyebrow constitutes gestural bravura. Mayer's contemporary Andrea De Jorio studied and recorded the behavior of his fellow Italians. He observed "a woman whose particular movement caused the scene to change, seeing the spectators amused by it, repeats the gesture voluntarily that at first was involuntary or done by chance, just for the sake of further entertaining the bystanders" (civ). Gestures, or for that matter, any form of expression, may be conscious or unconscious. A formerly spontaneous behavior, gesture, expression, or word can become a learned behavior that may be deployed with calculation.

## Knowing about Feeling, and Feeling in the Know

This dynamic between an immediate authentic response and a planned social or interpersonal maneuver echoes the performative dilemma delineated in Denis Diderot's (1713–1784) *Paradox of Acting,* written in the 1770s, first published in 1830, and considered perhaps the first important treatise on the subject of acting. Diderot comments: "But they say an actor is all the better for being excited, for being angry. I deny it. He is best when he imitates anger. Actors impress the public not when they are furious, but when they play fury well. . . . What passion itself fails to do, passion well imitated accomplishes" (71). For Diderot, there is a difference between being furious and playing fury onstage. Actors, paradoxically, must be in control of their characters' lack of control. Actors should remain somewhat removed from their characters. Actors should certainly not be self-conscious, but they should be self-aware in a manner in which their characters should not, with the important caveat that some characters, and some Italian characters in particular—given Italian behavioral patterns—*are* self-aware. Diderot claims that the actor's "talent depends not, as you think, upon feeling, but upon rendering so exactly the outward signs of feeling, so that you fall into the trap" (12). In other words, if the actor feels it, it is therapy; if the audience feels it, it is theater.[2] Diderot distinguishes the emotion of the actor onstage from that of a person in life: "The player's tears come from his brain, the sensitive being's from his heart" (20). Elsewhere he notes, "The great actor watches appearances; the man of sensibility is his model; he thinks over him and discovers by after-reflection what it will be best to add or cut away" (37). For Diderot, great acting was primarily an intellectual process. The actor observed "the man of sensibility," thought "over" him or analyzed him, and then, in accordance with certain aesthetic criteria, selectively duplicated his "appearances." Writing as an eighteenth-century rationalist, Diderot can think only in terms of a brain–heart dichotomy of intellect and emotions. He does not realize that both thought and passion manifest themselves in the brain, the nerve center of the body. Somatized illnesses can provoke real physiological symptoms. For Diderot, the actor can only "imitate" and not "replicate." In the eighteenth century, characters may dissemble, but, at least for Diderot, actors may not have known how to simulate. Lacking Pirandello's distinctly Italian and existentially ironic sensibility, Diderot fails to realize that "there are real appearances and—merely apparent appearances" (Eric Bentley in Pirandello xii).

Stanislavski conceded that "some part of [the actor's] senses must remain free from the grip of the play to control everything that he attempts and achieves as the performer of his part" (Cole 35). For the most part, however, Stanislavski's concepts of acting remain distinct from those of Diderot. While Stanislavski also stressed the importance of observation for the actor in building a character, he nevertheless asserted that "characters cannot be 'shown,' they can only be *lived*" (*Legacy* 82). To create a believable "imitation of a perfect action" for an audience, or better yet to replicate rather than merely imitate feelings, actors must first believe it themselves, through both stimulation and simulation. Stanislavski writes, "When you believe, you feel that your objectives and actions have become something real, living, purposeful" (*Creating* 135). For Stanislavski, as for Diderot, feelings and emotions should not be the goal of actors, but merely a side effect, an affect, of their commitment to an objective. Stanislavski notes: *"It is therefore impossible to act feelings 'in general.' One must perform the task which will evoke the specific feeling"* (*Creating* 67). For Stanislavski, feelings are stimulated by the actions toward the objective and therefore will be simulated by the actor. He states, *"The objective is the lure for our emotion"* (*Creating* 51). However, when Stanislavski claims that *"one cannot play or represent feelings, and one cannot call forth feelings point blank"* (*Legacy* 187), he writes as an actor who obviously has never been to Italy. In fact, he seemingly contradicts himself in a passage when he speaks of the actor's use of *"affective memory,* calling up from its secret depths, beyond the reach of consciousness, elements of already experienced emotions, [to] regroup them" (*Legacy* 187). Elsewhere, and most often, Stanislavski prefers the term *emotional memory.* Actors produce emotional memory by asking themselves how they might have felt in a situation similar to that of their characters. While actors may not "call forth feelings point blank," they can nevertheless, with the self-manipulation of emotional memory, "call forth feelings." Of course, actors may confront characters very unlike themselves, in a situation foreign to their personal experience. In order to build a character, actors must take into consideration what Stanislavski calls "the given circumstances" of the play, and by this he means "the plot of the play, the epoch, the time and the place of the action, the conditions of life . . . the setting" (Moore 33). To further resolve this dilemma, Stanislavski posited the use of what he called "the magic ifs" (*Legacy* 46). Basically, actors must imagine how they might behave *if* they were in that situation. Actors must search for points of connection between themselves and their characters. The Stanislavskian actor asks, "What circumstances of my own inner life—which of my personal, human ideas, desires, efforts, qualities, inborn gifts and shortcomings—can oblige me, as a man and actor, to have an attitude toward people and events such as those of the character I am portraying?" (*Creating* 181). The actor seeks out something in himself or herself in which to ground the character and the character's actions, if only this something is an unrealized alter ego. Given Stanislavski's emphasis on internalization as a means of grounding the character in the actor, when the Actors Studio in the United States became the primary disseminator of his acting method, many actors who trained there—Geraldine Page, Paul Newman, Shelley Winters, and Steve McQueen among them—found their techniques more effective when used before the close proximity of a movie camera, especially in close-up, rather than in the seeing-place of a theater, where internal states must be somewhat externalized to be seen.

Without even an alter ego connection to the character, Stanislavski recognized a final alternative, conceding that "if a part does not of its own accord shape itself inside an actor he has no recourse except to approach it inversely, by proceeding from the externals outward" (*Creating* 149). Here, Stanislavski returns to Diderot. Psychologically, externals may include the actor's observation of and familiarity with the lived experience of others. Physically, externals may include a specific walk, a nervous tic, a particular manner of speech, or a habitual gesture. Such physical elements also constitute a viable part of building a character. Stanislavski notes, "An actor on the stage need only sense the smallest modicum of organic physical truth in his action or general state and instantly his emotions will respond to his inner faith in the genuineness of what his body is doing" (*Creating* 150). This technique, working from the outside in, rather than from the inside out as was generally preferred by Stanislavski, was Sir Laurence Olivier's approach to a character and has also been frequently used by Meryl Streep, despite her Actors Studio training. Nevertheless, for Stanislavski, *"every pose, every gesture will have an inner justification"* (*Legacy* 189), even if the actor comes up with the justification afterwards. Stanislavski, like many Italians, realized that to be most truly effective as an actor, or as an Italian, each expression, gesture, or action must access something of the original motivation that inspired it. In *Six Characters in Search of an Author*, the Manager acknowledges, "I am aware of the fact that everyone has his own interior life which he wants very much to put forward" (Pirandello 258). In other words, whether a person or a character expresses himself or herself spontaneously or with some degree of calculation, the impulse to express, to communicate, or to achieve something motivates both.

Italians are perhaps more self-aware of their social self-presentation, and so are more capable of calculation than Anglo-Americans, who tend to equate naïveté with authenticity. Consciousness and self-awareness do not necessarily preclude sincerity. Whereas Americans tend to be hypocritical in their sincerity, Italians are sincere in their hypocrisy. They know that the sign is a show, and that a show is an illusion, and that in illusion resides the potential for hypocrisy and deception. Niccolò Machiavelli (1469–1527), Baldassare Castiglione

(1478–1529), and Count Alessandro Cagliostro (1743–1795) all wrote treatises—*The Prince* (1532), *The Book of the Courtier* (1528), and *Compendio sulla vita e sulle gesta* (1791), respectively—on the art of show, gesture, illusion, hypocrisy, and deception in negotiating the political societies of their times. For all three writers, important social interaction does not merely happen naturally, but rather, to be effective, must be undertaken in a conscious and calculated manner. Such "calculated" behavior may sound sinister to Anglo-American moralist ears, but for an Italian, it simply means playing *il furbo* (the clever one) rather than the fool. The Italian prioritization of *furbizia,* or cleverness, contrasts sharply with the parallel cultural stereotype of the self-ignorant *pollo americano,* or American chicken, ready and waiting to be plucked by the first clever Italian to come along. From Machiavelli to Fo, many, if not most, of the characters in Italian theatrical texts fall into one of these two categories. For example, in Machiavelli's *The Mandrake* (1519), the quicker-witted Callimaco, Timoteo, and Ligurio actually persuade the pompously naïve Messer Nicia to encourage his own wife to cuckold him. As empathy in *The Mandrake* gravitates toward Callimaco, Timoteo, and Ligurio, rather than to Messer Nicia, the Italian prioritization of *furbizia,* of being in the know, supersedes traditional morality. As Machiavelli's preference for the functionally effective presupposes a pervasive skepticism regarding ideals, popular Anglo-American culture, in its naïve moralism, has converted the term *Machiavellian* into an inaccurate synonym for "evil." Machiavelli's landmark text merely demonstrates what Barzini considers part of the Italian social ideology in general. He claims that in Italy "the poor in spirit, the gullible, the naïve . . . are derided" (172). Just as cleverness determines the value system of *The Mandrake,* it proves an important element in the Italian value system in many other plays as well. In Fo's *The Archangels Do Not Play Pinball* (1959), the deceptively clever Lanky purposefully allows his friends to take advantage of him merely so that he can take advantage of them. Lanky states, "For me playing the fool is something of a profession" (259). He appears as a descendant of Arlecchino and Truffaldino, commedia dell'arte characters who recur throughout the plays of Carlo Goldoni and Carlo Gozzi. Goldoni's *The Servant of Two Masters* (1745) features Truffaldino as its chief protagonist. In the play, Pantalone comments on Truffaldino, "I think the man's a fool," and Dr. Lombardi responds, "I think the man's playing a fool" (Bentley 84). While playing the fool can be *furbo,* Lanky and Truffaldino remain a bit of both.

The stock characters of commedia dell'arte, such as those found in the plays of Goldoni and Gozzi, are traditionally divided into three groups: (1) the older men, or *vecchi,* (2) the lovers, or *innamorati,* and (3) the servants, or *zanni.* These groups can be further subdivided into *furbi* and fools. The primary *vecchi,* namely, Pantalone, il Dottore, and il Capitano, are almost always fools, as they all suffer from that most lethal of Italian social diseases, self-ignorance. A dotard, Pantalone makes a fool of himself by still fancying himself a potent lover. A pedant of limited intelligence, il Dottore deludes himself that his intellect exceeds all those who surround him. A cowardly braggart, il Capitano imagines himself a courageous man of valor. The *innamorati* are often, though not always, fools, but almost never to the extent that their foolishness inhibits audience empathy. Their investment in love itself renders them fools, as a passage from *The Servant of Two Masters* illustrates. Discovering Clarice having what he believes to be a liaison with another man, Silvio, overcome with jealousy, confronts her:

> *Clarice:*   I love you with all my heart.
>
> *Silvio:*   I hate you with all my soul.
>
> *Clarice:*   I will die, if you are not to be appeased.
>
> *Silvio:*   I would sooner see you dead than unfaithful.
>
> *Clarice:*   Then you shall have satisfaction. (Bentley 119)

Only the intervention of the savvy *zanni* servant girl Smeraldina manages to put an end to such impulsive foolishness. As Smeraldina's behavior demonstrates, the *zanni,* also including Colombina, Arlecchino, Brighella, Truffaldino, Scapino, and Pulcinella, can be either clever or foolish, depending on the circumstances and plot of the play. The characters in Goldoni's more realistic plays, such as *La bottega del caffè* (1750) and the *Trilogia della villeggiatura* (1761), while more subtle, nevertheless follow a similar pattern of division into the *furbi* and the foolish.

**Question: "How do you get an Italian to shut up?"**
**Answer: "Hold his hands."**

Italians interpret signs with great wariness and employ signs with even greater calculation. It is their calculation, their self-consciousness in the use of signs that renders the Italian culture so pervasively and seductively theatrical. Stanislavski notes: "In every *physical action*, unless it is purely mechanical, there is concealed some *inner action*, some feelings" (*Creating* 228). Gestures externalize and express internal states of being. Gestures in life communicate to other people; gestures onstage communicate to other characters and to the audience. Danesi and Perron write, "In social contexts, bodily posture and body image are perceived to be part of Self-presentation" (113). Life again serves as a prototype for theater. Life is theatrical, even as theater is lifelike. Barzini has noted: "Italian gestures are justly famous. Indeed, Italians use them more abundantly, efficiently, and imaginatively than other people" (62). What Barzini observed personally, kinesiologists have ratified professionally. Kinesiology is the study of human movement. Danesi and Perron have catalogued some 1,000 different body positions, 5,000 different hand gestures, and approximately 250,000 different facial expressions that, when used in various combinations, form a lexicon of more than 700,000 possible gestures (104). The degree to which various cultures exploit this lexicon varies from culture to culture. Kinesiologist W. LaBarre has ranked Italian culture, along with the Greek, as among the most gesticularly evolved on the planet. Given this prominence of Italian gesture, not surprisingly, De Jorio's *Gesture in Naples and Gesture in Classical Antiquity*, originally published in Naples in 1832, constituted the world's first treatise on gesture, composed before kinesiology even existed as a field of study. De Jorio's division of gestural sources into body position, hands, facial expressions, and the use of combinations of these thus predates Danesi and Perron's categorizations by more than a century and a half.

"It is a fine thing to say that people of the North do not gesture," De Jorio writes. "It is a fact, however, that some gesture more, some less" (lxiv). A century and a half later, Barzini draws a similar distinction: "Italians are often disconcerted, unhappy and lonely in the north of Europe, and seldom know what is going on, surrounded as they are by blank faces on which little can be read and the little seldom exciting. They wrongly conclude that, as the people show no feelings, they have no feelings worth showing. The proverbial impassivity of the English is believed to be proof of definite coldness and insensibility" (61). The English, along with the cultural heritage they bequeathed to the majority of the first white Americans, constitute one such "people of the North." English reserve contrasts with Italian effusiveness. Danesi and Perron observe: "*Kinesic codes* are fashioned from bodily movements, postures, etc., believed to bear meaning during social interaction; *facial codes* are based on the expressive qualities of the face and on eye contact; *proxemic codes* are fashioned from the distances people feel they should maintain between each other and the orientation their bodies should assume during interaction; *tactile codes* are based on the meanings that certain touch patterns are felt to have in certain social situations; and *gestural codes* are made from the properties of the hand" (104). In every category, Italian social interaction demonstratively exceeds that of its Anglo-American counterparts. Kinetically, Italians may appear more animated than Anglo-Americans, and they may knowingly assume a posture, or even strike a pose, when an Anglo-American more often simply falls into a default position determined by his or her place in the surroundings. Facially, Barzini has referred to "the transparency of Italian faces. Conversations can be followed at a distance by merely watching the changing expressions of those taking part in them" (61). Italian faces are certainly not more physiologically expressive than those of other people; anatomically Italians do not have more facial muscles than other humans; but they are culturally more expressive. As opposed to members of other cultures, Italians express "[u]ndisguised emotions" (Barzini 61). These emotions may appear both more intense and more mutable than those of Anglo-Americans who, in their hypocritical sincerity, may become slaves to consistency. Proxemically, Italians stand closer to one another than Anglo-Americans and have a more intimate sense of space, even when they take space by invading that of another person. Tactically, Italians touch one another much more often than Anglo-Americans and those of more "northern" temperaments. Finally, Danesi and Perron note, "Clearly, eye contact and eye configuration patterns may in part be . . . cultur[ally] specific—southern Europeans will tend to look more into each other's eyes during conversation than do North Americans" (118). In other words, Italians catch and maintain eye contact more than Anglo-Americans. When performing a play, however, such eye contact also functions as a way of directing the audience's focus. If all the actors onstage are looking at one particular character, the audience's attention will end up on this character, as any attention given temporarily to the other actors will eventually be rerouted to this character by the other actors' gazes. The Italian tendency to "look more into each other's eyes" thus serves as a prototype for the actor onstage who, like the Italian and his or her addressee, uses the gaze to manipulate the focus of the audience.

Semiologist A. K. Halliday claims that "dialogue . . . is linguistically coded behaviour" (Fawcett et al. 33). As such, it can be thought of almost as a verbal gesture, especially when used by an Italian. De Jorio describes the quintessential Italian speaker:

> The greatest richness is found in our language and in our gesturing, where one deals with hyperbole in discourse. The simple enunciation of a proposition, however magnificent and grandiose one might wish, is not enough. . . . To impress his hearer with something in the same way in which he feels it himself, he employs every technique. He will adopt a lively and efficacious expression which he changes and adorns with various additions, either with words, or with accents, with tones or with lyrical passages, with reticences or with interpositions. He adds one proposition to another, each one as lively and as well adapted as the last. Whether in crescendo or diminuendo, he sustains a long discourse, always expressive and touching, never departing from his object, that of expressing his idea and of getting his listeners to share it. (92–93)

Dialogue is not merely talk, and an Italian does not merely talk. Instead, Italian speech and dramatic speech may embellish, enhance, expand, and exaggerate. Robert Benigni, in the film *Life Is Beautiful* (1998), may describe mushrooms with the hyperbolic "fritti, fritti, fritti," but no nonstuttering English speaker would ever order or serve "fried, fried, fried" mushrooms. There is, after all, no *-issimo* in the English language. The use of repetitive sounds and rhythms exists innately within the Italian language in a manner and to a degree that far exceeds their use in English. With the emphasis on the penultimate syllable in most Italian words, a regular pronunciation of Italian already incorporates its own cadences, cadences that can easily aspire to the musical or lapse into sing-song. Furthermore, Italian speech may be punctuated with interjections, exclamations, and sighs, like so many musical *fermate* that also serve to regulate the verbal pace.

Pierangela Diadori explains: "Every oral pronouncement, in fact, can assume a particular meaning, depending on the gesture that accompanies it" (16). The physical communication of gesture can modify the verbal communication of words. In fact, gesture may trump dialogue or contradict what is said. "Spoken words may be sometimes at variance with the grimaces that accompany them," Barzini notes. "The words should then be overlooked" (61). Italian social interaction transpires primarily in the *theatron,* the seeing-place, rather than the auditorium, the hearing-place. Whereas English gestures tend to be more abstract, Italian gestures sometimes serve as a substitute for untrustworthy verbal communication. Kinesiologist Michael Argyle describes Italian gestures as "pictorial illustrations" (54), while for De Jorio they are "allegorical and metaphorical" (lxxxviii). De Jorio points out that some gestures may have their origins in nature, such as a hanging head and slumped shoulders to indicate tiredness as deriving from the actual physical results of tiredness (lxxxii). Others, such as the *schiopetto,* or snapping of the fingers to indicate joy, scorn, or a confidential summons, seem more arbitrarily conventional (273). Compared with other cultures, Italian abounds in these more arbitrarily conventional gestures. Diadori's *Senza parole: 100 gesti degli italiani* (1990) delineates numerous Italian gestures, some of which are quite complex and composed of multiple parts. As a point of comparison, Diadori also notes the "reserve" and "coldness" of the English (20).

Gesturally speaking, another non-Western culture provides an even sharper point of contrast with the Italian than does the Anglo-American. Argyle points out that "the Japanese have a display rule that one should not show negative emotions. The Japanese smile is used as a mask, and may express reserve or embarrassment" (52). For the Japanese, *saving face* can be tantamount to *hiding the face* behind a mask. For the Japanese, "one should not show negative emotions," but Italians maintain no such prohibitions. Sociologists Monica McGoldrick and Marie Rotunno note that "Italians do not have the problems with disallowed feelings that some cultural groups do" (345). Italian personal interaction overtly expresses what other cultures, such as the Anglo-American, and especially the Japanese, covertly repress. Not surprisingly, given the diametric behavioral oppositions between Italian and Japanese cultures in particular, a "1988 poll in Japan ranked the Italians as the 'most stupid' among major nations because of their perceived lack of seriousness. The poll was received with incredulity and mirth in Italy. . . . The stupid ones are the Japanese because they work too hard and never have a good time" (Hoffman 197). The Italian and the Japanese present keenly divergent "invariant cultural models."

## Self-Awareness and the Problem of Sincerity

This "perceived lack of seriousness" of the Italian, this propensity not only for role-play but also for play itself, distinguishes Italian social interaction. For Italians, it is the importance of not being too earnest. In Goldoni's play *The Servant of Two Masters,* Clarice and Silvio are earnest lovers, and their earnestness risks Clarice's death. As proof of love, Clarice's attempted suicide constitutes not the only such drastic act in the play. Later, Beatrice and Florindo, the ostensibly smarter lovers, mistakenly believe one another dead and hover on the brink of suicide before seeing each other alive at the last minute. The fact that a potential love suicide serves as a source of comedy in Italian theater, rather than as a source of tragedy, as in William Shakespeare's *Romeo and Juliet* (1595), or in the love suicide plays of the Japanese dramatist Chikamatsu Monzaemon (1653–1725), illustrates the radical difference with regard to "earnestness" and "seriousness" that separates Italian from English and Japanese cultures. Given the potential fatality of a passion too keenly felt, in his book *That Fine Italian Hand,* Paul Hoffman describes the Italian relative lack of earnestness in terms of a survival strategy. "By not being too earnest for too long a time," he comments, "the Italians as a nation have gotten away with a lot of things" (193). As Italian opera director Italo Nunziata has stated, "Italians are the first to talk about killing themselves for love, and the last to do it." Not only biological survival, but also the survival of the ego, the self-image, and the reputation—one's image with others—become a major issue. As Goldoni repeatedly demonstrates in *The Servant of Two Masters,* being too earnest or serious in one's feelings can make one appear ridiculous. Two centuries later, in Luigi Chiarelli's *The Mask and the Face* (1916), the character Cirillo discusses "the terror of the ridiculous" risked by the overly passionate (41). In this play, Paolo confronts his unfaithful wife, Savina, knowing full well that he may kill her in a fit of jealousy and, for committing a crime of passion, avoid legal punishment. Unable to kill her, but afraid of appearing as a cuckold, he sends her away and counterfeits her death. Chiarelli thus ironically demonstrates how the Italian terror of the ridiculous can actually make one behave ridiculously. In Pirandello's *Henry IV* (1921), Henry asserts, "We're all fixed in good faith in a certain concept of ourselves" (169). Henry thus appears as an atypical Italian in his commitment to this "fixity" of identity, to his "good faith" in his role as lover, and to his unbridled commitment (fittingly, he falls from his horse) to his passion for Donna Matilda. For her part, Matilda responds in a more characteristically Italian manner, safeguarding her heart. She notes: "One of the many misfortunes which happen to us women, Doctor, is to see before us every now and again a pair of eyes glaring at us with a contained intense promise of eternal devotion. [She bursts out laughing.] There is nothing quite so funny" (156). The perceptive Henry indicts this "perceived lack of seriousness," this "terror of the ridiculous" as emotional resignation. He comments, "When we are not resigned, out come our desires" (169). Characters who desire something are essential to drama, as desires at cross-purposes create the conflict essential to dramatic action. Whereas Henry gives rein to his desire for Donna Matilda, she desires the safety of emotional resignation. They are not even at cross-purposes as regards their feelings for one another, but rather as regards their attitudes toward their feelings for one another. Perhaps the most ridiculous of modern tragic heroes, Henry must confront "that obscure and fatal power which sets limits to our will" (169). That power may be nature, God, society, or in Henry's case, the will of another person, Matilda, whose "terror of the ridiculous" prompts her fear of the intensity of Henry's love. Matilda's "good faith" in the "fixity" of her identity as a dispassionate woman does not fit Henry's desired romantic life scenario. Using Henry's exact same terminology, De Filippo's *Grand Magic* puts this dialectic regarding "good faith" in the absoluteness of passion and desire metaphorically in a box. Following in the tradition of Chiarelli, yet another unfaithful wife, De Filippo's Marta, reduces her husband, Calogero, to suffering the terror of "making [him]self ridiculous" out of love for her (103). The hypnotist Otto convinces the desperate Calogero that Marta has not actually abandoned him but remains trapped in a small box. Despite the blatant physical impossibility of this, Otto claims that if Calogero truly loves his wife and opens the box, she will be there, and, if she is not there, this merely proves that his love was not in "good faith." The conflict between

Pirandello's Henry and Donna Matilda regarding amorous passion becomes the paradox of De Filippo's Calogero. Living this paradox, Calogero can neither discard nor open the box. In the meantime, his life becomes perpetually postponed, even as it passes him by, a metaphor for all who live life as a dress rehearsal rather than an actual performance.

In his book *The Semiotics of Performance*, Marco De Marinis asks, "Who is so stupid as not to know the difference between being and pretending?" (97). This simple question quickly proves more problematic than it seems, as if there were no continuum between a completely serious investment and a superficially playful investment in performing life's roles. The conflict between Henry's passion and Matilda's hysterical (in both senses of the word) aversion to passion, while appropriate to their characters and the action of the play, constitutes a false dichotomy in terms of conceptualizing human behavior in general, and Italian behavior in particular. Barzini answers De Marinis's question with regards to the Italian lover: "He may be an honest lover like any other, perhaps a little more skillful. He may be, at the opposite end of the scale, an accomplished performer, a complete impostor. He may also be anything in between. . . . He himself often does not know where truth ends and invention begins. He may sincerely think he is in love but may only be a lukewarm and temporary *innamorato* carried away by emotions and his own ability" (86). A huge continuum exists between absolute earnestness and purely cynical dissimulation. The central inner conflict of the male protagonist Eugenio in Diego Fabbri's *The Seducer* (1951) demonstrates precisely the dilemma posited by Barzini. Eugenio claims to love three different women, Norma, Wilma, and Alina; his infidelity to each is contingent upon his belief in the genuineness of the sincerity of his feelings for the others, but he protests too much. He himself realizes: "I said 'I love you'—and I was aware that the words, the emotion was much more vast than the feelings for the person I was saying it to . . . I love you!!! But whom—whom—do we really love when we say this? Whom? Ourselves? The other person? Love?" (794). While Fabbri arguably provides no definitive answer to Eugenio's question, Norma expresses a view both cynical and sympathetic. She says: "He was a man who needed to be believed. . . . I can honestly say he lived his own . . . lies. His very dear lies" (814–815). From Goldoni's *Il bugiardo* (1750) to Fabbri's own *La bugiarda* (1954), the seducer who seduces himself, the liar who deceives himself serves as a prototype both in and of Italian theater. Hypocrisy and sincerity prove neither absolute nor mutually exclusive.

Although self-awareness merely opens the possibility of conscious hypocrisy and does not actually preclude sincerity, the question of sincerity obsessively recurs throughout Italian drama. As Italians implicitly recognize the precarious rift in the sign, the potential duplicity in the sometimes arbitrary relationship between signifier and signified, the issue of the divided sign-person of human identity persistently haunts much of Italian theater. If Eugenio wants to believe he is in love, he nevertheless knows his love is predicated on the quagmire of his own identity, an identity that to a certain extent is itself an artifice, a construct, a duplicitous sign. The word *person* comes from ancient Etruscan, arguably the first culture to flourish on the Italian peninsula, but in its original language the word "person" meant "mask." For Italians then, in contrast to the Japanese, the ostensibly natural behavior of the "person" and the socialized role-playing of the "mask" are not necessarily oppositional categories. After all, for an Italian, role-playing, if not outright natural, is at least second nature. The crisis comes when role-playing seems to usurp or even erase identity, giving rise to an Italian dramatic tradition that addresses the dilemma of self-alienation. Chiarelli's aptly titled *The Mask and the Face* focuses on precisely this dilemma. Savina tells Paolo: "Take away this mask of crime, and be sincere with yourself, read your own heart, and don't be the slave of your own words and conventional behavior! . . . Let's play with our own destiny" (23). Man versus himself, as epitomized early in the history of theater in Sophocles' *Oedipus Rex*, has long been a staple of conflict in drama, but in Italian drama, particularly of the twentieth century, this conflict expands to psychological and existential proportions often beyond that found in other dramatic traditions. Mirrors, photographs, and portraits have long served not only as devices, but also as metaphors for self-confrontation. In Betti's *Landslide on the North Slope,* the legal councilor Parsc looks nostalgically at a photograph of his former self and says: "I used to . . . live. That's it: I used to be alive!" (*Frano* 66). In contrast to his seemingly more vital past, Parsc in the present can only self-deprecatingly mimic his own current rote-like behavior as a hollow functionary of the Italian justice system. "Today I watched myself," Parsc notes. "What a face I put on" (*Frano* 67). For Parsc, his mask has permanently replaced his face; his role has ultimately usurped his identity. Masks and masquerades form a recurrent motif in Italian theater from commedia dell'arte to Dario Fo. For feminist playwright Dacia Maraini (1936– ), femininity itself appears as a masquerade in which one may or may not choose to invest. Under the apparently oxymoronic collective title *Naked Masks*, much of Pirandello's theater plays upon the ostensibly oppositional, but actually paradoxical, relationship of the mask to the face. In *Henry IV*, Henry recognizes that an earnest investment in role-play can supersede any ostensible authenticity of identity. He charges Matilda, "You too, Madam, are in a masquerade, though it be in all seriousness" (170). Wearing a mask, deploying strategies and tactics, being effective in a role, all form part of the serious business of social survival. In contrast, attempts to approach an originary identity can prove hysterical, especially in the plays of Pirandello, Fabbri, and Betti. In *Henry IV* such an attempt results in murder; in *The Seducer* it provokes suicide; while in Betti's *Crime on Goat Island* (1950), it prompts the protagonist Agata to get down on her knees and bleat with the goats in her effort to subvert human (self-)consciousness. In *Henry IV*, Henry momentarily erases the dialectic between mask and face when he describes life as "that other continuous, everlasting masquerade, of which we are the involuntary puppets, when, without knowing it, we mask ourselves with that which we appear to be" (205). The portraits of both Henry and Matilda in their youth serve as ostensible mirrors to an originary identity that both precedes and transcends the "everlasting masquerade" of their role-play. When the portraits are taken down, and Matilda's daughter, Frida, and Henry's nephew, Charles Di Nolli, pose as look-alike mannequins in the place of the older couple, Pirandello reinscribes the dichotomy of mask and face that Henry had earlier erased. Henry, in his present "artificial" role, must confront both himself and Matilda in their supposed original identities. In his "conscious madness," Henry is perhaps the most penetratingly lucid of all Italian protagonists, and as he sees through the vertiginous transparency of the sign-person, of both himself and Matilda, trauma and drama erupt.

In *Six Characters in Search of an Author*, the Manager directs the Leading Man: "you, who act your own part, become the puppet of yourself" (Pirandello 214). The question becomes one of whether or not one is a conscious puppet(eer) or an unconscious puppet(eer) of oneself, a division that somewhat replicates the division of Italian characters into *furbi* and fools. However, as the theater of Fabbri, Betti, and Pirandello painfully demonstrates, being a conscious puppet(eer) of oneself does not necessarily prevent one from becoming a fool. In this sense, their dramatic works constitute perhaps a more successful attempt at a truly modern tragedy than those found in other national literatures. Like sincerity and hypocrisy, consciousness and unconsciousness form more of a continuum than a set of oppositional categories, as various characters in plays from Machiavelli to Fo reveal differing degrees of self-awareness and self-consciousness. In contrast to the hyperconsciousness of Pirandello's Henry or Betti's Agata, many characters function as puppets without being aware of—or in existential terms, without taking responsibility for—the fact that they are also their own puppeteer. Instead, they may abdicate this role and allow someone else to play them for a puppet. The division of life into the roles of puppet and puppeteer roughly replicates what the existentialist philosopher Jean-Paul Sartre describes as living *en soi,* inside oneself, or *pour soi,* for oneself. Since the myth of Eden and against all Socratic tradition, a persistent Western Puritanism that has tended to equate self-ignorance with innocence also tends to perceive living inside oneself as the morally preferable, prefallen condition. In *Six Characters in Search of an Author,* the Father concedes, "I know that for many people this self-blinding seems much more 'human'" (Pirandello 267). Characters who live more fully inside themselves often more readily take action, proving themselves more dramatic than those awash in the drift of their own consciousness. While internal conflicts within characters remain a viable source of drama, the sometimes interminable (self-)reflective set speeches by Pirandello's protagonists can risk becoming burdensome. In *Six Characters in Search of an Author,* the Manager advises: "Drama is action, sir, and not confounded philosophy" (270). Great literature and good theater are not the same thing. On the opposite side of the spectrum from Pirandello's philosopher-protagonists are the puppetlike commedia-inspired stock characters of Goldoni and Fo and the melodramatic *vinti,* or victims, of Giovanni Verga. In *The Servant of Two Masters,* Truffaldino lacks all consciousness of foresight despite his plotting to earn a double salary. He readily admits, "I am learning my part as I go along" (Bentley 103). At one point his animal-like, monomaniacal appetite virtually prevents him from serving his two masters, as he eats more food than he serves either one. In contrast, Fo's Queen Elizabeth in *Elizabeth: Almost by Chance a Woman* appears simply monomaniacal, jealous of her own power, stabbing imagined assassins behind arrases, mounting armies against counterinsurgents, and threatening censorship of perceived Shakespearean attacks against her. An unknowing puppet of the puppeteer of her own paranoia, her hysteria is hysterical. Similarly, in Fo's *We Won't Pay! We Won't Pay!*, Giovanni first appears as the puppet of every bureaucratic and authoritarian institution that wields power over him. During the course of the play, as Giovanni gains consciousness, he also gains class consciousness. He can thus become his own puppeteer, not so much psychologically or philosophically—those levels upon which Pirandello operates—but rather politically, in accord with Fo's Marxist agenda. Verga's nineteenth-century peasant characters do not suffer from the mitigating, mostly bourgeois twentieth-century consciousness that afflicts the characters of Pirandello, Betti, and Fabbri. Instead, in Verga's collection of short stories *Don Candeloro e C. i.* (1894), Verga configures himself as a puppeteer, leaving his characters the sole role of puppet to perform their rash and drastic actions. In *Cavalleria rusticana* (1886), Santuzza, as a woman scorned, incites two men, Alfio and Turiddu, to a duel, while in *La lupa* (1894), the title character openly lusts after her own daughter's husband. In such texts, southern Italian overt expression readily overcomes any potential covert repression, be it northern (Italian) or otherwise.

## To the Stage

The Freudian concept of repression predicates an unconscious with drives and desires that must be suppressed in order for an individual to be socialized. The Freudian unconscious serves as both a parallel to and corollary of the Stanislavskian concept of the subtext. "Spectators come to the theater to hear the subtext," Stanislavski claimed. "They can read the text at home" (Moore 35). The text is like the tip of the iceberg; the subtext, the largest, deepest, and potentially most dangerous part of the iceberg, lies beneath the surface. Stanislavski defines "the subtext [as] the underlying current of the play which provokes the superficial waves of action" (*Creating* 175). For Freud, the bulk of the human psyche was unconscious. Accordingly, for Stanislavski, the bulk of the character's psyche was also unconscious. The actor's analysis of the text leads him or her to this unconscious, "to the underlying meaning which shapes the line of

[the] role" (*Creating* 140). The same holds true for the character's actions, as textual analysis, like psychoanalysis, reveals "what underlies them, gave rise to them, is hidden behind them" (*Creating* 18). Stanislavskian-based acting aims not only at understanding the sometimes unsavory impulses and drives that society and the self would repress, but also at provoking and evoking them, stimulating and simulating them in a performance live onstage. Stanislavski sought to access the unconscious consciously. Acting scholar Sonia Moore observes that Stanislavski "became aware that, though an actor has no real reason to suffer or to rejoice onstage, he begins to have true emotions when he is inspired. This fact brought Stanislavski to the idea that the subconscious—the uncontrolled complex of emotions—is not altogether unapproachable, and that there must be some kind of key which would intentionally 'turn on' this mechanism. He began studying the possibility of deliberately arousing emotions" (13). Stanislavski's methodical approach to textual analysis aspires to be this "key." Theater can serve as therapy, but hopefully for the audience even more than for the actor, furnishing the sort of social catharsis of repressed feelings prescribed by Aristotle in his *Poetics*.

The psychology of Freudian repression, so central to Realistic acting, may be very much in keeping with American Puritanism and English reserve, but remains very much anathema to Italian demonstrativeness. Similarly, the Freudian unconscious often finds itself at odds with Italian self-awareness. Not surprisingly then, the so-called Stanislavskian-Realist school of acting never quite took root in Italy. In Italy, Realism as a formal aesthetic arrived in one generation only to be exploded by Pirandello in the next. The plays of Roberto Bracco (1861–1943), who was known in the late nineteenth and early twentieth centuries as "the Italian Ibsen," have since sunk into relative obscurity, and the work of Italy's best Realist playwrights of the period, Giuseppe Giacosa and Verga, was often co-opted by the quintessential Italian metatheater, namely, opera, the performance art that allows for the greatest license in semiotic revelry. Raul Radice, former head of Italy's National Academy of Dramatic Art, dismissed the Stanislavskian system as "a mere vogue," declaring, "A public institution such as ours cannot be a school of any particular tendencies, such as those of Copeau or Stanislavski, which were conceived for private institutions" (Di Giammarco 30). In stark contrast, the Stanislavskian method became the basis of acting training in the United States for most of the twentieth century, to the extent that it was almost considered the only viable form of acting training.

As a formal aesthetic, Realism attempts to minimize the disparity between the signifier and signified, a disparity with which Italians are relatively comfortable, while Anglo-Americans are not. Realism, as practiced by Anglo-American culture, constitutes a supreme attempt to resurrect the Ur-sign, to approximate a unity between signifier and signified, to make the sign integral and whole. Semiologist C. S. Peirce defined the icon as a specific kind of sign where the correspondence between signifier and signified was most immediate, so much so, in fact, that the icon may actually possess some of the qualities attributed to its signified. Keir Elam has rightly discussed the theater as the most iconic of art forms. Theater is the art form wherein a human being most likely represents a human being, a chair a chair, an apple an apple, and a candle a candle. It is more iconic than film, despite the greater potential of film for iconic *visual* representation, because, unlike film, theater exists in the same time and space as its public. Not accidentally then, since the nineteenth century, Realism as an aesthetics of iconicity has heavily influenced and still influences concepts of theater in general, if not Italian theater in particular. The first tenet of Realism is the maintenance of an illusion of reality. Luigi Pirandello repeatedly exposed this illusion as a hollow sham because reality itself is constructed of, or at least communicated and understood through, a precarious network of potentially unreliable signs.

The primary means for creating such illusionism is the iconization of reality, to ground the theatrical moment in the real "emotional memory" of the actor. Such iconization in Stanislavskian method acting produces actors concerned mostly with whether or not their impulses are rooted in natural, observed, or experienced behavior, and yet simultaneously and spontaneously remain fresh to the theatrical moment, the so-called illusion of the first time. In this manner, Stanislavskian actors attempt to fuse the *face* of their own person with the *mask* of their character. Jacques Derrida has claimed that "the actor is born out of the rift between the representer and the represented" (305), but it is precisely this rift that the Stanislavskian-Realist actor in particular and most actors in general endeavor to minimize or erase. Prompting genuine feelings from artificial causes, the actor attempts to recompose the divided sign "actor/character" into a unified being, to transcend its innate division. Tellingly, Stanislavski's use of such amorphous, unplayable, and undefined (by him) terms and phrases as "spiritual content" (*Legacy* 77), "spiritual life of the role" (*Creating* 175), and "human soul" (Moore 25) bespeaks a Romantic residue in his ostensibly methodical approach. Despite such late and latent Romanticism, Stanislavski remains the most important figure in the systematic demystification of the process of acting, delineating a practical technique of scoring a text in accordance with a character's motivation. In this sense, he managed to moderate acting into an accessible series of tasks, prompting an "inspired" performance of "true emotions" in a reliably methodical manner.

The Realist actor attempts to straddle the rift between representer and represented, to fuse himself or herself with the character, at least to a certain degree, for the duration of the performance. As the representer, the actor should not necessarily presume that the represented character is itself an integrated whole. The ultimate Stanislavskian goal of total temporary immersion in or fusion with the character as an integrated whole may actually be at odds with the fissures in the character, those multiple roles demanded not of the actor but of the character itself. Pirandello, Betti, Fabbri, De Filippo, and Maraini have repeatedly invoked such psychic fissures in their works, some of which address not only social alienation, but also self-alienation as their primary theme. As some of these alienated characters are left to address the audience, some of these plays merge the representational theater of Giacosa, Verga, and Bracco with the presentational theater of Goldoni, Gozzi, and Fo. Self-identity, the ego, is a construct susceptible to self-deconstruction. Italians have long extended their skepticism regarding the ostensibly integral, but often divided, nature of the sign to the ostensibly integral, but often divided, sign-person of human identity. Italian theater started questioning the divided nature of identity long before Freudian psychology shattered the notion of the human psyche as an integrated whole. Even a cursory examination of the history of Italian theater reveals its preoccupation with the slippery and sometimes duplicitous relationship between face and mask, between identity and role, and between natural behavior and social performance. As a result, Stanislavskian techniques—emotional memory, building a character, scoring a text for motivations, objectives, and super-objectives—cannot always be taken at *face* value, as they might when dealing with English or American theater. Instead, the *mask* value of Italian theater must be taken into consideration. In other words, Italian theater may present an actor with a character who is quite consciously, or perhaps even semiconsciously, already playing a role. Given the Italian penchant to *fare una scena,* the subtext of a character may percolate up and expose itself directly in the text of an Italian play. The stock characters of commedia dell'arte, and their descendants in the plays of Goldoni, Gozzi, and Fo, and to a lesser extent of De Filippo and Maraini, might have little or no subtext at all, speaking their desires, drives, and objectives outright. While for Stanislavski, as for Freud, a gesture might unconsciously betray a character, for an Italian a gesture might quite consciously relay the character. Stanislavskian tradition relegates emotion to incidental affect, but Italian characters, like Italians themselves, might often employ emotion for intentional effect. In general then, Stanislavski's emphasis on internalization runs counter to Italian culture's emphasis on externalization. "Orson Welles once acutely observed that Italy is full of actors—fifty million of them" (Barzini 61). As theater re-presents Italian life, acting Italian must take into consideration the real phenomenon, demonstrated throughout the daily life of Italy, of Italians acting.

## Practicalities

Given the differences discussed above between Italian and Anglo-American behavior, Stanislavskian principles may need modification when applied to Italian theater. Furthermore, certain principles may not be applicable at all. For instance, does Machiavelli supply a subtext? Does Truffaldino actually have an unconscious, or for that matter, just exactly how conscious is Henry IV of the motivations of his actions from one moment to another? How could Pina in Verga's *La lupa* ever possibly be considered repressed when it is her direct expression of desire that disrupts the repression of others? Nevertheless, inasmuch as Stanislavski provides a methodical way—literally known as "the method"—in which to play a character, certain aspects of this method prove almost universally serviceable.

While not discounting inspiration, Stanislavski believed in an intellectual approach to the role, involving study and analysis of the dramatic text. In developing his or her role, an actor should first determine a character's superobjective, that is, what the character wants, what the motivation is, for the entirety of the play. This superobjective must then be broken down into the character's more specific objectives for each scene of the play, which in turn can be broken down into the character's minor objectives, his or her momentary strategies or tactics for each moment of the play. At this level, the play is considered to be broken down into individual beats. The objectives, strategies, and tactics of the individual beats are traditionally marked with active verbs—"to win," "to seduce," "to intimidate," etc.—to keep the actor thinking in terms of action. This is the scoring of the text to set a basis for performance. As one character's superobjective, objectives, tactics, and strategies encounter those of other characters and forces, either at cross-purposes or in direct opposition to his or her own, conflict results, in accordance with Aristotle's premise that the essence of drama is conflict. Conflict may be external, such as that between Alfio and Turiddu in Verga's *Cavalleria rusticana;* internal, such as that of Henry IV in conflict with himself; or both, either alternating or at once.

At any time a character's objective may coincide as well as collide with that of another character, but in a well-written play, alliances will generally be either tenuous or temporary, until some point of conflict between the two characters is exposed or encountered. Dramatic conflict, divided into individual beats, builds to a climax within a scene, and from scene to scene, to a climax for the play itself.

In order to structure his or her role, an actor should know a character's motivation, whether that character consciously knows his or her motivation or not. Certainly, Truffaldino in *The Servant of Two Masters* knows he is motivated by hunger, but Donna Matilda in *Henry IV* may vary in her degree of awareness as to how much her fear of love motivates her. Sometimes characters on the stage, like people in real life, are driven to realize things about themselves by the intensifying circumstances around them. Similarly, characters may or may not be aware of the strategies and tactics they are employing to achieve their objectives. In Goldoni's plays, Smeraldina often knows she is flirting in order to get something out of Pantalone, but in De Filippo's *Grand Magic,* Calogero may or may not be aware to what extent his fear of rejection motivates his refusal to open the box. Finally, a character may or may not be aware that he or she performs a certain social role. Messer Nicia may be completely ignorant of being the quintessential cuckold, but Henry IV keenly knows that he is participating in a pretense that he does not live in the twentieth century. Questions of self-awareness, awareness of motivations, tactics, and strategies are always appropriate when analyzing a character, but especially so in the case of Italian characters, given the "cultural model" or behavior discussed above.

However, to employ role-play successfully as a strategy to achieve an objective, *"per fare una scena"* on purpose, an Italian must invest in this role-play by connecting with his or her motivation to deploy it. The same holds true for the actor and his or her need to connect with the role assigned. Stanislavski recommends use of "the magic ifs" to help an actor connect with a role. The actor basically asks how he or she would think, feel, react, etc., *if* he or she were in the same situation, motivated by the same objectives, as his or her character. This process of connection is often referred to as "grounding" the character. Emotional memory can also prove helpful at this juncture, if an actor can remember how he or she felt when he or she was in a similar situation. Of course, a character's behavior may diverge drastically from that of the actor, even if the actor imagines himself or herself in the character's situation. At this point, external observation and study of behavior of others, rather than an internal examination of the actor's own, may aid the actor in building the character.

For instance, the greater propensity of Italians to express, to externalize, and to use gesture may be foreign to the actor brought up in an Anglo-American culture. In order "to act Italian," such an actor needs to study Italian interaction and behavior, either directly in Italy, or at one remove, in the residual Italian behavior of Italian Americans, or else as re-created in Italian cinema. In order to gain some mastery of Italian gesture, an actor may take recourse to Pierangela Diadori's book *Senza parole*. However, in order to see such gestures appropriately deployed, an actor unable to observe Italian behavior in the piazza might observe it on film. For example, Lina Wertmüller's *The Seduction of Mimi* (1972) contains an entire scene between Mimi and Fiorella performed solely through gesture, from across a loud and busy street. Films may function well as a source of study of gesture, but since films are primarily visual and only secondarily aural, they may prove highly problematic at helping the actor handle Italian dialogue. In film, the action of the plot may be carried through the verbal, or more often through the relationship of the verbal with the visual, or in some cases exclusively through the visual. Both Pier Paolo Pasolini's *Medea* (1969) and Luchino Visconti's *Death in Venice* (1971), for instance, succeed perfectly well as full-length films almost without any dialogue at all. In contrast, in theater, dialogue most often carries the action of the play, either textually or subtextually.

Failure of actors to connect with, to "ground," or to attain some sort of iconicity with their characters can result in their merely marking a role, indicating a role solely from without rather than playing it from at least partially within. Of course, completely inhabiting the theatrical role, as Diderot noted, can present actors with other problems, such as loss of performative control. After all, theater is not life but represents life. Actors, therefore, may wish to consult the various Stanislavski and Stanislavski-based acting texts listed in the bibliography of this chapter, keeping in mind what modifications might be necessary in building an Italian character. In any case, as actors engage with Italian characters in the text of a play, they also automatically engage with the context of Italian behavior and Italian personal interaction that the play itself represents. Students begin to learn the Italian "invariant cultural model" that affects the formation of an Italian character with their very first Italian class. Since language, culture, and psychology are invariably linked, by merely speaking Italian, a student may already begin to think Italian, and so to act Italian as well.

## Notes

1. Of course, both Italian and Anglo-American cultures are not "invariant" inasmuch as they are continually evolving, neither fixed in time nor uniform throughout. For the purposes of this chapter, however, they are addressed in a generalized or archetypal manner, as "models," in fact.
2. The great nineteenth-century actor Sir Henry Irving (1838–1905) noted the resulting ironic phenomenon of "the experience of the actor often [being] superior to the perceptions of the audience" (quoted in Diderot and Archer, Archer 9).

## Bibliography

Argyle, Michael. *Bodily Communication*. London: Methuen, 1975.

Aristotle. *Poetics*. In Barrett H. Clark, ed. *European Theories of the Drama*. New York: Crown, 1978: 4–22.

Barzini, Luigi. *The Italians*. New York: Atheneum, 1964.

Bentley, Eric, ed. *The Servant of Two Masters and Other Italian Classics*. New York: Applause Books, 2000.

Betti, Ugo. *Crime on Goat Island*. San Francisco: Chandler, 1961.

———. *Frano allo Scalo Nord [Landslide on the North Slope]*. Ed. Alfredo Luzi. Camerino: Università degli Studi di Camerino, 2002.

Chiarelli, Luigi. *La maschera e il volto*. Ed. Michael Vena. Welland, Ontario: Soleil, 2002.

Cole, Toby, ed. *Acting: A Handbook of the Stanislavski Method*. New York: Crown, 1983.

Danesi, Marcel, and Paul Perron. *Analyzing Cultures: An Introduction and Handbook*. Bloomington: University of Indiana Press, 1999.

De Filippo, Eduardo. *Three Plays*. Trans. Carlo Ardito. London: Hamilton, 1976.

De Jorio, Andrea. *Gesture in Naples and Gesture in Classical Antiquity*. Intro. Adam Kendon. Bloomington: Indiana University Press, 2000.

De Marinis, Marco. *The Semiotics of Performance*. Trans. Aine O'Healy. Bloomington: Indiana University Press, 1993.

Derrida, Jacques. *Of Grammatology*. Trans. Gayatri Spivak. Baltimore: Johns Hopkins University Press, 1976.

Diadori, Pierangela. *Senza parole: 100 gesti degli italiani*. Rome: Bonacci, 1990.

Diderot, Denis. *The Paradox of Acting*, and William Archer, *Masks or Faces?* Intro. Lee Strasberg. Trans. Walter Herries Pollock. New York: Hill and Wang, 1963.

Di Giammarco, Rodolfo. *Prima del teatro*. Pisa: Teatro di Pisa, 1985.

Elam, Keir. *The Semiotics of Theatre and Drama*. London: Routledge, 2002.

Fabbri, Diego. *Tutto il teatro*. Vols. 1 and 2. Milano: Rusconi, 1984.

Fawcett, Robin P., M. A. K. Halliday, Sydney M. Lamb, and Adam Makkai, eds. *The Semiotics of Culture and Language. Vol. 1: Language as Social Semiotic*. London: Frances Pinter, 1984.

Fo, Dario. *We Won't Pay! We Won't Pay! and Other Plays: The Collected Plays of Dario Fo*. Trans. Ron Jenkins. New York: Theatre Communications Group, 2001.

Goffman, Erving. *Frame Analysis: An Essay on the Organization of Experience*. New York: Harper and Row, 1974.

———. *The Presentation of the Self in Everyday Life*. New York: Doubleday, 1975.

Hoffman, Paul. *That Fine Italian Hand.* New York: Henry Holt, 1990.

Mayer, Carl Augusto. *Vita popolare a Napoli nell'età romantica.* Trans. Lidia Croce of *Neapel und die Neapolitaner oder Briefe aus Neapel in die Heimat.* Oldenburg: 1840, now Bari: Laterza & Figli, 1948.

McGoldrick, Monica, and Marie Rotunno. "Italian Families." In Monica McGoldrick, John Pearce, and Joseph Giordano, eds. *Ethnicity and Family Therapy.* New York: Guilford, 1982: 340–362.

Moore, Sonia. *The Stanislavski System.* New York: Viking, 1965.

Nunziata, Italo. Personal interview. Rome: June 14, 1991.

Pasolini, Pier Paolo. "Manifesto per un teatro nuovo." In Jean Duflot, ed. *Il sogno del centauro.* Rome: Riuniti, 1983.

Peirce, C. S. *Philosophical Writings of Peirce.* Ed. Justus Buchler. New York: Dover, 1955.

Pirandello, Luigi. *Naked Masks.* Intro. Eric Bentley. New York: Penguin Books, 1957.

Stanislavski, Constantin. *Creating a Role.* Trans. Elizabeth Reynolds Hapgood. London: Eyre Methuen, 1981.

———. *Stanislavski's Legacy.* Ed. and trans. Elizabeth Reynolds Hapgood. New York: Routledge, 1999.

Winner, Irene Portis, and Jean Umiker-Sebeok, eds. *Semiotics of Culture.* New York: Mouton, 1979.

# *II* Theater Courses in the Italian Language Curriculum

# CHAPTER 3

# The Theatrical Workshop in the Italian Curriculum

SALVATORE BANCHERI

This chapter presents two different but equally successful models of teaching theater courses combining academic content and theatrical performance within the Italian academic curriculum: the first model at the University of Toronto at Mississauga (UTM) and the second at the Italian Language School (ILS), Middlebury College, Vermont. The theater and performance courses offered at UTM are part of the undergraduate curriculum and are offered for a full academic year (seventy-eight hours of instruction equally divided in twenty-six weeks). The ILS courses, open to both undergraduate and graduate students, are part of a summer intensive and full-immersion program (thirty hours of instruction equally divided in six weeks).

Les Essif has described theater as a teaching mechanism in its most basic terms: it is "a project that bridges the gap between language and literature studies through the added contextualization of the language offered by performance."[1] I believe that the application of theater to the Italian curriculum is an important educational tool. The course becomes student-centered, as opposed to teacher-centered. A play constitutes a chance for students to use language in a real setting and is an opportunity for real linguistic practice. Furthermore, a performed play serves the simple, though essential, function of generating exposure for and interest in the Italian department. The primary goals of a theater-based course are not only to provide students with practice and experience in dynamic language production, but also to teach them Italian literature and theater from a fresh, different perspective.

When, then, should the theater component of a language-learning program be inserted? My general rule is this: after the intermediate level of instruction has been completed, although it should be noted that this is flexible according to students' pronunciation, skill, and acting abilities. Objections to this kind of course include concerns that it might be too specific or literary, not structured enough, and not goal-oriented enough. In my experience, these concerns are unfounded; the goal of the course is the product—a successful performance. As regards the difficulty of the play, I make a conscious effort when selecting a script to keep the actors, setting, and audience in mind. I have found the implementation of a theater component in a language course to be an enjoyable, intensive, and beneficial educational exercise.

In researching the topic, however, I have realized that theorists of pedagogy have disparate concepts of what the ideal uses, settings, classroom layouts, assignments, and learning goals should be. From Essif's basic description (offered above), theories and practices diverge markedly. I have come to realize that my pedagogical ideas regarding the use of drama in a second-language classroom and, most of all, the setting in which my students have performed for almost twenty years are not in line with the ideas expressed by other theorists and practitioners. First, reading about the use of drama in the classroom reveals that references are generally made to conducting role-plays, short dramatic exercises, and dramatic readings rather than to producing full-fledged plays. Furthermore, these activities seldom result in a performance in front of an audience. This attitude is summarized by Alan Maley and Alan Duff, who define dramatic activities as "activities which give the student an opportunity to use his or her own personality in creating the material on which *part* of the language class is to be based." The two authors then explain what they do *not* mean by dramatic activities: "We do not mean putting on plays in front of a passive audience. . . . Nor do we want students to feel that dramatic activities are part of a preparation for some final performance." Similarly, John McRae feels that drama should be only a part of a language course and believes that it is "wise to restrict to short extracts, and, therefore, to limited class time." For McRae, memorization is therefore not important and "whether or not the students memorize a text for acting should be left to individual circumstances." Harriet Semke, in describing the experiential learning of the German Café-Theater, whose goal is a public performance, explains that "the program is made up basically of skits but it is expanded with musical numbers, folk singing, and group singing." For those few critics, like Charlyn

Wessels, who discuss issues related to the performance of a full-scale play, the staging is identified as a six-week "drama project" exclusively within a language instruction course.[2] I do not intend to diminish the value of the experiences discussed in these books or articles, nor do I argue with the excellent approaches and advice that each of the authors discusses. In this chapter I simply clarify the meaning of "theatrical workshop."

For me, using drama in the classroom means preparing students to perform a full-length play in Italian, in front of a demanding audience. Audience members are fully aware that they are witnessing a language experience and therefore are mentally prepared to appreciate the activity. The students are involved in all aspects of the performance: from the preparation of the program to costumes, from lighting to makeup, from setting the stage to clearing and cleaning it. For the students, it is a 360-degree experience: the teacher is running a real theatrical company, in which the actors are the students registered in his or her course. From an academic perspective, the course may seem like any other academic course in which four to five theatrical pieces are studied, but the students will read the plays studied from a performative perspective. Douglas J. Moody describes this approach as "product-oriented," involving the "various processes in the interpretation, rehearsal, and public performance of a text." He believes it to be "a valuable form of educational drama that should not be excluded from the repertoire that foreign-language teachers have to use in their classrooms."[3] The study of language is also a major component of the course, but only indirectly. This linguistic element is inherent in theater itself; for, as Essif writes, theater is "based on a kind of *parole* concept, on a notion of focused, creative, holistic, communal language production."[4] In order to have a better understanding of the uniqueness of the UTM and ILS models, it is important to analyze in detail the setting of these theatrical experiments in Italian as a second language.

## The Setting and the Courses

The University of Toronto Mississauga, the eastern satellite campus of the University of Toronto founded in 1967, could be considered a typical North American liberal arts university with a strong component in language teaching and learning. Italian plays have been performed annually at UTM since the academic year 1986–1987, first as an extracurricular activity and subsequently, since the academic year 1992–1993, as part of the Italian curriculum. In 1992–1993, two full courses that last the entire academic year, or twenty-six weeks, were introduced: The first, "Italian Comic Theater: Text and Performance," studies Italian comic theater from its origins to Carlo Goldoni; the second, "Italian Comedy and Performance," analyzes theatrical production from the nineteenth century to modern times. In 1995, two independent theater courses were added to give those students who had already taken the previous two courses an opportunity to enhance their study of theater; to focus on some aspect, period, or figure connected with the theater; and to obtain at least a minor in the program. In all courses the production of a play for public performance with Maschere Duemondi, the name adopted by our theatrical company, is also a key requirement.[5]

At the ILS of Middlebury College, the performance of Italian plays has been a prominent part of the program since its inception, first as an extracurricular activity and then, since 1996, as part of the curriculum.[6] What distinguishes the Middlebury program from other Italian programs is the aspect of total immersion, with a pledge students take to use Italian exclusively on and off campus. The pledge constitutes the core of the Middlebury experience and is a binding commitment each student makes in writing that must be respected for the duration of the session. Violation of the pledge may result in dismissal from the school. Since 1996, ILS, following the example of UTM, offers the same two courses, with theater and performance and almost identical course descriptions.[7] Christopher Cairns summarizes the benefits of this double immersion in language and theater at Middlebury College: "So what unique teaching benefits are conferred by foreign-language total immersion in the theater? First and foremost, there is no compromise with the use of Italian. This fits in very well with no compromise in the theater. This is to say that a production with students aims to echo—as far as is reasonably practicable—all the conditions of professional theater. Once they have seen this in action, students readily accept the necessary constraints and discipline of this method, and pull resolutely behind it as a team, with the knock-on-benefit that there will similarly be no compromise in the language—however stressful and fraught the experience may become."[8]

## The Students

At UTM, students taking the theater courses are normally in their second or third year at the university and have already taken two full courses (four semesters) of Italian grammar. Occasionally, students with only one course (two semesters) of Italian grammar will register; only a handful of students in their first year and those just graduated from high school enroll. Originally when the performance was an extracurricular activity and right after it was incorporated in the curriculum, the students acting in the performance were almost exclusively of Italian background and had good pronunciation skills. In the past five to six years, the students participating in the performance have come from more varied backgrounds, and whether or not a student has Italian origins does not necessarily correspond to good or bad pronunciation. Furthermore, every year, one or two drama students with little knowledge of Italian take the course, driven by a genuine interest in the history of theater and in the course's performative aspect. For these students, the course may prove a catalyst for further study in the language. As Sarah L. Dodson puts it, "Drama activities frequently increase students' integrative motivation, instilling a desire to learn the language in order to interact with people of the target culture."[9] The number of students taking the course has increased through the years, with a minimum of about ten and a maximum of about forty.

At ILS, the student pool is composed of highly motivated North American university students. The students registered in the theater and performance courses reflect this pool, and the percentage of students of Italian background is smaller than that of UTM. In general, however, there is no difference in the quality of Italian pronunciation. Fewer students (graduate and undergraduate) register in the Middlebury course: five graduate students in 2000; nine graduate and two undergraduate students in 2002; and thirteen graduate, one undergraduate, and one auditor in 2004. The undergraduate students taking the course have already taken at least two semesters of Italian grammar and take a third grammar course concurrently with the theater course. The majority of the participants, however, are graduate students.

## ILS: Graduate versus Undergraduate Students

At this point, an obvious question comes to mind: Do graduate students perform better than undergraduate students? In general, both graduates and undergraduates perform exceptionally well. Both groups of students have delivered excellent performances of important roles, and they have also distinguished themselves in smaller parts despite the shortness of such parts. What counts in a performance is not the actors' academic preparation, but how they interpret the part; the clearness of their pronunciation; the intonation and projection of their voice; and their ability to move with ease and to dominate the stage, to express emotions, to become one with the character interpreted, and to use appropriate and culturally meaningful gestures and movements. In sum, academic preparation and excellence do not necessarily correspond with performative superiority.

Another question is: Does the preparation of undergraduate students differ from the preparation of graduate students? The preparation is exactly the same, as both graduates and undergraduates need to understand their dramatis personae in order to convincingly interpret the characters; they both need to understand their lines and those of the other actors in the same scene with all their miniscule nuances. However, the timing of this preparation is different, as obviously undergraduate students will generally need more time and help to be on a par with graduate students. Graduate students normally have an advantage as far as understanding their lines in all their nuances; this is not, however, the case when it comes to understanding cultural elements within the play, gestures, and facial expressions. In this case, in fact, one must consider the background of each student. For example, it would not be surprising if an undergraduate student of Italian origin, or one who had lived in Italy for a while, had a more profound understanding of some of the cultural elements within a play. Nevertheless, we must always keep in mind the instructional character of the production and the consequent improvement in the actors' language skills (even those actors at the most rudimentary level). In an intermediate-level French theater class, Essif notes that "the French instruction within this performance project succeeded because the students' attention was directed not to French at all but to performance."[10] In short, students should improve as the process moves along. Graduate students theoretically should have an advantage in the process of memorization as they should be more fluent in the language, but this varies from student to student according to their mnemonic ability. The superior language skills of the graduate students could prove to be an asset in case the actors, during a performance, need to recover from typical stage mistakes such as skipped or forgotten lines. Similar situations, however, are regularly considered in the basic preparation that all students receive in the classroom.[11] In theory, in the extreme case when an actor has to improvise some lines, the graduate students should do a better job, not necessarily in recovering from the mistake, but in expressing those lines in correct Italian and in the appropriate register of the play. In my experience, in similar but rare situations, I have not noticed a gap in level between the two groups of students.

## UTM Students versus ILS Students: Motivation

I have found that in general ILS students have a higher degree of motivation than UTM students.[12] Is this gap in motivation level also evident in the theater courses? Is there a difference in the preparation process between ILS and UTM students? Is the level of proficiency reached during the performance different? Does one group perform better than the other? Even though one might accept the fact that ILS students generally are more motivated than UTM students, when it comes to the theater and performance courses, there is no gap between the two groups; their motivation is extremely high and at the same level of intensity. The reasons why students take the course do not affect the outcome; in the end, as the human motivation of the *bella figura* requires, they reach the same level of proficiency and intensity of concentration. We are not talking about students' motivation for taking courses or studying Italian but the motivation for performing well, to the best of their ability, in front of their peers, families, and teachers.[13] The preparation process is exactly the same for both groups, even though it is brought to fruition differently because of the length of each course and the frequency of meetings.

## Hours of Instruction

At UTM, the number of instruction hours is officially four a week, but in reality, the class meets only three hours; the fourth hour is used for occasional extra rehearsals. During the first term (thirteen weeks), one hour a week is devoted to an academic class on theater (students learn about the history of theater and, as in regular literature courses, analyze plays by authors of the periods studied), and two hours per week are used for rehearsals. In the second term (thirteen weeks), during the first seven weeks, all three hours are exclusively dedicated to rehearsals. The following three to four weeks are for performances: the first performance is on the Thursday of the so-called reading-week, and five to seven performances are normally scheduled for the following three to four weekends. After the first performance, there are no more rehearsals or academic classes. When the performances are over, around the middle of March, the course is considered completed. In short, there are about forty-five actual hours of rehearsal for the play. Rehearsals take place in a fairly large room that has been assigned exclusively to the class, meaning that chairs and furniture do not have to be rearranged for every rehearsal. Students are able to rehearse in the theater/auditorium only two to three days before the first performance.

At ILS, the undergraduate course starts three days before the graduate course. Therefore, the teacher has the opportunity to meet with the undergraduate students for three hours before the joint session starts. In view of the fact that the number of undergraduate students registered in the course is very low, these hours are exploratory in nature. The teacher uses this classroom time to better understand the students and their needs as well as their levels of academic and language achievement. During this time students have the opportunity to familiarize themselves with the script so that they will not be handicapped the first day of the joint session when the process of assigning the parts begins. About ten hours are scheduled for academic classes on theater history, plays, and playwrights, and seventeen hours are dedicated to rehearsals. After the only performance, which takes place the Sunday before the end of the session, there are no more rehearsals or academic classes. Before the final performance we have one dress rehearsal and one regular rehearsal in the theater itself. On the day of the performance, we do not rehearse.

For the academic component of the course, the number of hours of instruction at both institutions is similar: thirteen at UTM and ten at ILS. From an academic point of view, both institutions offer the same program: students read the same works, study the same authors, and discuss the same issues. The three-hour difference does not imply that less material is covered. Since fewer students are enrolled in the ILS course, less time is devoted to student presentations. Furthermore, the continuity of meetings for academic classes (once a week at UTM versus two to three times a week at ILS) accounts for a speedier lesson, with less repetition of the elements covered during the previous class. In both settings, the students, like in other literature courses, are required to do the same amount of academic work, that is, essays, oral presentations, etc.

The difference in rehearsal time between the two settings is, however, substantial: UTM students have a little more than two-and-a-half times the rehearsal time available to ILS students (forty-five hours at UTM and seventeen at ILS).[14]

## UTM Students versus ILS Students: A Director's Perspective

The gap in rehearsal time is also more evident if we consider that at ILS, the students differ every year, which can cause a setback from the director's point of view. Every year at ILS the director needs to start from point zero, as the student pool is almost completely different (90 percent different at the undergraduate level and 80 percent at the graduate level). Furthermore, he or she meets the class for the first time only five-and-a-half weeks before the performance.

An important element that helps to fill the gap in rehearsal hours is the ILS setting. At ILS, one gets to know students faster and better because one lives and eats with them and attends the same co-curricular activities. The fact that everyone lives on campus and in a small town that does not offer a lot of distractions (versus the distractions of a big city at UTM) also helps close the gap because students are able to stay more focused. Furthermore, seeing the students in class every day (versus weekly classes at UTM) is advantageous in that it helps give the learning process more continuity. Finally, it is not uncommon to see students rehearse their parts during meals, while waiting for an activity, or while cheering for the soccer or volleyball team. Similarly, it is not unusual to be invited for private scene rehearsals and to be asked for one-on-one rehearsal sessions.

What also helps to eliminate the gap in rehearsal time is the fact that, at ILS, students do not need to worry about the "commercial" aspects of the performance, that is, preparation and ticket sales and sponsorships. Furthermore, their roles in other aspects of the theatrical company, such as programs, lights, sounds, props, set, costumes, music, and videotaping, are minimal because such things are handled by the director in collaboration with either the school staff or the theater crew. Finally, the rehearsal gap can be completely filled by choosing an appropriate play to be performed and by assigning the parts immediately after the second day of classes.

The discrepancy in preparation time, therefore, does not affect the quality of the performance. At the same time, it does not imply that the UTM students over-rehearse, nor that the ILS students over-achieve. In sum, the gap is fully eliminated through a careful mixture of several factors: having the appropriate mental preparation for the course, being flexible, having experience, having the ability to maximize time and to easily adapt to situations, and having a clear understanding of the setting and parameters of the course. When these factors are carefully considered, the UTM and ILS models can both produce exceptional performances.

## Choosing a Script

Choosing a script is, in my opinion, one of the most important tasks in the course. It is important, as Moody notes, "to present a work of dramatic art that not only [heightens] the learning experience for the students enrolled in the course but [connects] the department with the greater community beyond the classroom." I believe that the use of a proper script is what sets my pedagogy apart from many other drama-based second-language programs. The dramatic activities usually proposed by the instructors or textbooks of such programs "involve one-dimensional situations with a prescribed dialogue and conclusion . . . in which dialogue and action are often restricted to the learning objectives of vocabulary and grammatical structures." Choosing a script requires a process that is quite different from the one used to choose plays to be read during a course. First, it requires the reading of dozens of plays. This reading process, however, differs from what we are accustomed to, as the notion of "text" has to be expanded to mean "scenic text."[15] The play needs to be read as a script, keeping in mind specific actors and audiences, the theater, the lighting, and the set. What works in one setting does not necessarily work in another because perhaps the theater has a different layout, because the audience has its own personality and therefore will not react in the same manner if presented with a particular subject, or simply because it is difficult in one theater to implement scene changes. Antonio Alessio summarizes this process well:

> In un dipartimento di drammaturgia ci si accosta a un testo teatrale con un'ottica e finalità totalmente diverse. Se non è escluso che il valore letterario di un testo possa determinarne la scelta, esso viene innanzitutto avvicinato secondo il grado della sua teatralità, di determinate qualità intrinseche che ne permettano la trasposizione del linguaggio verbale a quello dell'immagine, del colore, del suono, in relazione all'effetto del prodotto scenico finale, tanto a livello di regia che di recitazione. Portato nel laboratorio registico un testo subisce una trasformazione alchimistica al punto che alla fine potrebbe apparire totalmente irriconoscibile rispetto al prodotto originale.

> [In a drama department the approach to a dramatic text is completely different in perspective and scope. Even though we cannot exclude a text's literary value when selecting it for performance, one has to approach the text most of all for its theatricality, for its intrinsic quality, which will allow its transposition from verbal language to that of image, color, and sound, in relation to the efficacy of the final stage product in both directing and acting. When brought into the director's laboratory, a text might undergo such an alchemistic change that at the end it will appear completely unrecognizable with respect to the original product.]

Similarly, Claire M. Mather states: "Theater is a genre that has its own conventions, language, and terminology; above all it is a representational genre. . . . The ideal theatrical experience is a dialogue, or dialectic, between the experience of the spectator and that of the reader: the dialogue is the point of view and the point of departure of the director who must study a text in depth while continuing to assess the effect each of the elements of the mise-en-scène will have on the audience."[16]

The first thing that a director needs to pay attention to while choosing a play is not its artistic quality, but the complexity of the scenes and the number of scene changes. Accessibility to the actors and the audience is an important issue. Whenever possible, I choose plays with only one scene or plays with one scene change between acts. I avoid choosing plays in which one would need to change scenes in the middle of an act. Once I am satisfied with this element, I consider the number of characters in the play, which is one of the key elements in choosing a play. I also ignore a play in which there are few female roles, as the majority of students taking the course are women, with only a handful of men. I do not like having female student-actors play the part of males. So when I read a play, I keep a watchful eye on its flexibility to transform male roles into female roles. At times, this can be easily done; at other times, more complex work is required. In all cases, however, I make sure that these changes do not undermine the quality of the play.

Only after I am satisfied with these initial elements do I start reading the play, trying to picture as much as possible how each scene will be performed onstage. Essif notes that "performance requires a conscious, complex adherence to the reading process."[17] This process is as applicable to myself as director as it is to the students as performers. I envisage the performance of the entire play and how each character should be performed. I also visualize the set, situations, and use of props. It is almost like watching an actual performance of the play. This process is very important, as it helps me identify the main traits, both physical and psychological, of a character. It also helps me identify, in the case of returning students, possible candidates for specific roles. Another important element I always consider while reading is the length of the main parts, as I want to make sure that a play does not rely mainly on one character, with others having only a few lines or secondary presences. Because students' performances are part of a course, equal distribution of the main parts is important.

One last perspective: in choosing a script, I always keep in mind the needs and reaction of the audience. Is the play appropriate for the ILS or UTM audience? How will the audience react to certain lines and scenes? Will they laugh? Will they understand the cultural elements, the dialectal nuances, the situational puns, the wordplay, the metaphorical language? Will the subject of the comedy capture their attention? Is the play too sophisticated or difficult to follow for that specific audience? All these questions need to be considered carefully as they form the basis of the success of a performance. If an audience does not appreciate a play or does not laugh at or understand it, then it cannot be successful. For this reason, another important process is to rewrite the script and prepare it for the actors and the audience.

## Rewriting a Script

Rewriting a script is time-consuming and requires a lot of experience, a clear understanding of the (possible) actors and audiences, and knowledge of the theater and stage. Some teachers, such as Essif, include their students in the rewriting process. In a class production of Alfred Jarry's *Ubu Roi,* Essif assigned different acts to different groups of students for revision, and from these "student suggestions" "a preliminary script of '*Ubu Roi* déformé'" was developed.[18] It takes time to rewrite because it requires continuous changes and many drafts, depending on the play performed.

One of the issues that must be confronted is the feasibility and acceptability of choosing a play that is written in an Italian dialect. Should plays in Venetian by Carlo Goldoni, Neapolitan by Eduardo De Filippo, or Sicilian by Luigi Pirandello, just to name a few, be performed in our language courses? If so, should these plays be performed in dialect or in standard Italian? I will answer these questions with other questions: Are *I rusteghi* or *La casa nova* by Goldoni, *Filomena Marturano* by De Filippo, and *Liolà* by Pirandello part of the literature curriculum in Italian studies in North America? The answer is definitely yes. Then, the next question is, Are these plays studied in the dialect and original version or in a standard Italian translation? The answer, unfortunately, is not that straightforward; it requires both fidelity to the source text and a consideration of the actors' language goals and the audience's cultural background.

Performing in a dialect in our theater and performance courses is definitely a *controsenso* (countersense), as one of the main goals of these courses is strictly linguistic: for the students to improve their language skills of standard Italian. This does not necessarily mean that plays written in dialect should not be considered; on the contrary, they should even be encouraged because dialects are part of Italian language and culture. However, these plays should be translated into standard Italian and adapted for student performance. Translation and adaptation will require a profound knowledge of a specific dialect, as well as much time and preparation. Although these plays are often available in translation, even an excellent translation of a play needs to be modified for the stage, as is the case for plays in standard Italian. What I consider a fundamental element in this translation or adaptation process is making sure that the spirit of the play's dialect is kept in both the language and the settings. For this reason, when revising these translated scripts, I often feel the need to recover and reintroduce typical dialect words and expressions. It is always important to keep a balance between standard Italian and the use of dialect without undermining the audience's understanding of the play.

The process of making cuts takes place partly on paper, before and after the play is typed. There are several different reasons for making cuts: (1) to shorten slightly the length of the major parts, (2) to improve the economy of the play, (3) to shorten a single long *battuta* by a single character, and (4) to shorten the overall length of the play. In the third case, for example, we can point to Goldoni's tendency to give the main character a *battuta* that lasts an entire page as a denouement of the commedia (for example, Cecilia's lines in III, 12 in *La casa nova,* or Giacinta's lines in *Le smanie per la villeggiatura* III, 14). Before implementing any cuts, however, we make sure that the cuts do not undermine the flow or the sense of the play.

Often at the same time as making the cuts, the script is revised with the intent of recovering the dialectal flavor that perhaps was lost during translation. This process consists in reinstating some recurring and key dialect words, expressions, and lines in tune with the setting. Of course, one needs to make sure that the audience will clearly understand the reintroduced words and expressions. We achieve this by preparing, when appropriate, a glossary of such terms, which we include in the play's program. During the play, when the expression or word is not very common or easy to understand, we achieve this by having the dialectal word or expression immediately followed by its translation within the dialogue. For example, I may have an actor say the line "Hai la testa di sceccu, di asino," where *asino* is the Italian translation of the Sicilian *sceccu.* Quite often, some of these words or expressions will become a leitmotif for the play that the audience will recognize and expect whenever a similar situation arises (for example, "nun era ancora 'u momento" in *O tuono e marzo* by Vincenzo Scarpetta).

The process of script revision continues even after classes begin and parts are assigned, for the first few rehearsals. This is because during rehearsals, we have an opportunity to see what works and what doesn't, what could be cut and what could be revised. At the same time, we can restore some of the cuts or changes made previously if we think they were made a bit hastily (this happens rarely). This second phase of revisions is dictated by the need to adapt lines to the personality each actor has created for himself or herself, and at times to consider an actor's pronunciation ability.

One of the changes that has proved to be appreciated during performances are those lines modified or added that reflect a specific audience and that normally could be understood only by them. Such changes "personalize" the play for the audience; they are definitely a *captatio benevolentiae*. For example, in the performance of *Non ti pago!* we introduced some sort of praise of ILS; at UTM we have introduced or modified some of the minor characters to speak *italiese;* in the performance of *Liolà* for an audience of Canadian Sicilians we introduced the holy rosary in Sicilian dialect. These modifications are aimed at recapturing the spirit of the play.

Only when the revision process is complete do we ask the actors to start memorizing their parts. At UTM, by the end of October the actors have to undergo the first test of memorization; the second is by the end of November. The test takes place during a rehearsal, like any other rehearsal; the only difference is that during these rehearsals students are given an official grade.

## Assigning Parts

In my opinion, parts must be assigned immediately. On the first day of class, after the usual explanation of the course and its goals, I proceed to informal auditions. First I present in very general terms the play that will be staged: its setting, plot, and characters. I then ask students to talk about themselves and explain how they intend to contribute to the performance: that is, to discuss their acting capacity; whether they are interested in a small part, larger part, or leading role; and to explain any personal talents, such as painting, music, or singing. Even though I do not automatically grant student requests regarding a particular type of role, I get a sense of what they would like to do and their strengths—most of all their sense of confidence in their ability and their eagerness to play a part. Then we start reading some scenes, and I ask students to play specific parts. After two hours, I have enough information to start the process of assigning roles, and I have one or more of the students' names beside each character in the play.

I take extra care in planning the next class because after more informal rehearsal, I slowly have to start assigning roles, without hurting the students' feelings, especially if there are more students than parts. My policy in facing this arduous task is simple: make sure that all students have been allowed the same opportunity to show their ability; be honest and up-front about the reasons why a specific student has been chosen for a part; and make the students understand that all parts are equally important and that there are no "small parts" but only "small actors." Whatever their assigned part, the student must believe his or her role is important and that he or she can be effective in that role. As the psychologist Albert Bandura writes, the "actions of a partner based on faulty self-precepts of efficacy can produce detrimental consequences for all concerned."[19] Of course, trying to grant, whenever possible, the part that a student requests is helpful.

What criteria do I use to assign parts? First, let me point out that students' academic and/or linguistic preparation, even though important, seldom plays a determining role in assigning parts. I instead consider the following skills or features:

1. *Language skills*—clearness of pronunciation, ability to fully understand the lines read (even though this is related to language level), listening skills (comprehension of the implicit and explicit content of what is said)

2. *Acting skills*—ability to understand and to theatrically render the character's personality, psychological complexity, development, and use of space; and ability to immediately address the director's concerns

3. *Paralinguistic features*, or verbal and vocal behavior—tone and projection of voice, intonation, rhythm, speed of delivery, hesitations, interruptions, conversational fillers, expression of emotions such as irony, sarcasm, and humor

4. *Extralinguistic features*, or face-to-face interaction—body language, movements, and gestures[20]

Similarly useful in the evaluation is understanding the level of students' eagerness in wanting a part, their attitude, their reliability (if I already know a student), and their willingness to work as team players. By applying these criteria, at the end of the informal auditions, the distribution of roles becomes a simple process that, in a way, finds its own natural solution. If I still have doubts, they are normally restricted to one or two parts at the most; in this situation, typecasting could be a determining factor. It is necessary to note that at this initial stage, the director's "actorial" expectations for the students are not set so high as to be unreachable; indeed, research has shown that "high-caliber theater productions result from the most disadvantaged or inexperienced actors, provided there is good social cohesion among the practitioners."[21]

Nevertheless, there are two practical and recurrent issues in the distribution of parts. The first concerns the number of male and female students in the course and the number of male and female roles in the play. In our theater courses, as in language courses in general, the number of female students greatly exceeds that of male students. On the other hand, there are many fewer female roles in comedy "of the remote past" than male roles. For this reason, when the situation arises, I ask female students to audition for those male parts that have been previously identified as "exchangeable."

The second issue is related to the length of the main parts. If a part is excessively long, a student may be intimidated by the amount of work the memorization alone will require. This could negatively affect the tight schedule of memorization set by the instructor, who normally would expect all students to memorize their parts by a particular date. It could also slow down the entire production schedule. For this reason, I try to avoid plays that rely heavily on only one role, unless I see the possibility of splitting that role into two or more parts. This was the case in the 2004 performance at ILS of *Non ti pago!* by De Filippo, in which the part of Don Ferdinando Quagliuolo was split into two with the introduction of Donna Maria, Don Ferdinando's mother. By splitting a few roles, I managed to give an acting part to all the students registered in the course.[22]


## Rehearsals

In theatrical terms, we can say that rehearsal is a process of refinement that, in a relatively short time, will bring an actor from reading a part to living that part, from observing a character to becoming that character; it is a process that will convert a theater space into an eighteenth-century *salotto*, a modern kitchen, a piazza. In the language classroom, however, rehearsal is much more; it is a study of language, culture, movements, and interpretation, as well as the development of reading, writing, listening, speaking, and critical and literary skills.[23] Margaret Haggstrom explains how drama helps students become more effective and critical readers of all literary texts: "To perform their scenes successfully students must make decisions on how to interpret their roles, when and how their characters should enter and exit the scene, what gestures characters should use, how to choose the correct tone to express what the character wants to convey, how to choose the proper décor, etc. These are problems which require the students to link critically to the text. In addition to the problem of understanding the text, students must also decide how to best communicate their ideas to an audience. In making these interpretations and communicative choices, students are actively participating in the creative process, which encourages critical thinking."[24] Rehearsals also build a sense of community even outside the classroom. Producing a play is a unique student-centered process in which the figure of the teacher is, at the beginning, at center stage, with corrections on pronunciation, suggestions on interpretation, clarifications of gestures, explanations of cultural elements, etc. Then the instructor slowly moves out of the spotlight, assuming the role of the director and advisor. Finally, he or she disappears, assuming the role of spectator and coordinator of the event.

The process of transforming students into actors and characters in a play is a slow and gradual one, with four main phases: (1) prerehearsal, (2) rehearsal with the script, (3) rehearsal without the script, and (4) final rehearsals. During prerehearsal, the play is read in a roundtable setting. Pronunciation, understanding of the text and the personality of each character, cultural elements, and settings are stressed. During the second phase, student-actors start the memorization process and rehearse with their scripts in a bare rehearsal classroom that gradually becomes a replica of the final stage setting, with the introduction of the necessary furniture and props. During this phase we concentrate mainly on movements, gestures, interactions between characters, entrances, and exits. One or two of these rehearsals will be used to assign the students' grades for memorization. During the middle of the session, students have a midterm test that consists of the play's performance in front of a selected small audience. Actors are graded on memorization and interpretation of their part. This test marks the beginning of the third phase of rehearsals, which is not different from the second phase except that the script is no longer used. This difference will be noticed in the improvement of the students' interpretations and on the director's comments, which no longer focus on basic elements but on more sophisticated details. One problem at this stage, of course, is the fact that many students are reluctant to let go of their script, which has become a sort of security blanket. The issue is so common that I have coined the expression *svezzarsi dal copione* (to wean themselves from the script). The script is a barrier to nonverbal activity, as the student-actor, just by holding and reading the script, is not able to fully express gestures, make facial expressions, or react to or even see the other characters' movements, body language, and facial reactions. The script also becomes an impediment to language learning, as the student tends to read from it and therefore does not produce real communication. Memory is not perfect, and without a script a student has to fill memory flaws and improvise. This is even truer if memorization has to take place in a second language. We could say that the more the memory gaps, the more real the communication. Given the fact that memory flaws can occur in all student-actors, during many times and at different stages of the rehearsal process, practices are never merely monotonous and boring repetition of lines but constitute real learning and communication where language and cultural interactions occur. Furthermore, the language students produce during a memory gap is never the same as that produced during another identical situation. For this reason, in my opinion, Jean-Marc Caré's distinction between dramatization, simulation, and improvisation is very restrictive:

> Nous appellerons dramatisation tout travail consistant à rendre un texte intelligible et intelligent par d'autres ressources que le linguistique: le corps, la voix, l'espace. Ici, nous avons toujours un texte: frontière nette entre dramatisation et simulation. Elle [la dramatisation] permet à l'élève, libéré de la nécessité d'avoir à construire ses phrases, de pratiquer des activités non verbales.
>
> Dès que l'on aborde la simulation, on quitte le texte.
>
> Or, au-delà de cette dernière frontière, c'est l'improvisation. Le canevas dépassé, on est en face du vide. On doit non seulement faire des phrases mais aussi décider tout le reste: je construis mon personnage, je décide de prendre ou d'abandonner la parole et surtout, je suis le seul à décider de ce que je vais dire.

[We call dramatization any task that is geared toward making a text intelligible and intelligent using resources other than linguistic ones [or: other than linguistic]: body, voice, space. Here we always have a text: a solid border between dramatization and simulation. The former allows the student, free from the necessity to create sentences, to practice nonverbal activities.

Once one approaches simulation, one gets away from the text.

Now, beyond those borders there is improvisation. Beyond the script, one confronts nothing. One must not only create sentences but also decide everything else: I create my character, I decide to take or to abandon the words, and most of all I am the only one to decide what I am going to say.][25]

During rehearsals and performances, the imperfection of memory, more obvious in a second than a native language, will give students ample space for simulation and improvisation. Students have to decide what to do when a character skips a line, does not perform a necessary action, skips to another scene, is late in entering, or has difficulties with a prop. In such cases, real interaction occurs. Also, accepting Caré's distinction, for example, would imply that students' improvisations in a classroom do not involve the process of memorization or that commedia dell'arte actors would actually perform without rehearsing and without memorizing their *zibaldone* (repertoire book). Similarly restrictive is Carol Livingstone's definition of play-acting in contrast with role-playing; play-acting "is not role play as the language is pre-determined and learned by heart. This means that the students need not monitor the speech of others with a view of formulating their own contribution to the discussion. No mental process other than memorization is involved. It does not, therefore, resemble [a] real speech situation."[26]

Few rehearsals take place on the stage where the play will be performed. This is, in a way, unfortunate, as the stage seems to transform students and tremendously improve their performance. The reason for this is not necessarily because the play is at an advanced stage of production; in fact, at UTM we use the stage for the first time in December, after thirteen weeks of classes, for a midterm exam. The intensity reached at this point is high and definitely superior to that of the regular rehearsals that follow. One could argue that such intensity is due to the midterm exam, but I don't believe this is the case. Instead, I think the stage itself transforms the students; the same exam in a regular setting—and we have done this in the past—does not give the same results. I suppose that the stage, costumes, music, and props are all elements that foster in students high levels of concentration and motivation.

## Preparing the Set

Building the set, preparing costumes, finding props, and determining music are time-consuming tasks. But all of these elements constitute an important part of the production. They are essential in the learning process because they require a profound and detailed understanding not only of the play being performed, but also of the period in which the play takes place. In order to prepare for these tasks, students need to research and present to the class such things as the music, habits, fashion, painting, and architecture of the time, as well as basic tools used in daily routines such as cooking, cleaning, or painting a house (as was the case for *La casa nova*). This also gives students the opportunity to show their practical talents and skills. In fact, in particular at UTM, the students design and build the set (buying all the necessary materials, painting, working on the details), work on costumes (taking measurements, buying materials, sewing, conducting fitting sessions), find all props and accessories, tape the music, and create, when necessary, a mechanism for fast scene changes. At UTM we normally have a group of students dedicated only to these tasks, but we expect the collaboration of all students registered in the course.[27] The nonacting students normally set the pace and tone of both rehearsals and the performances. Their preparation of the stage—taking care of the most minute details regarding the set and props and, when necessary, the presence of costumes and music—sends a clear message to all the acting students that cannot be ignored: the preparation of the stage for either a rehearsal or a performance requires a lot of time and effort that should be compensated by an excellent rehearsal. Because the message comes from students themselves, it has a powerful effect on their peers. I often rely on peer pressure during my theater course, especially during phase 3 (rehearsal without the script) and phase 4 (final rehearsals). During these phases the role of the instructor becomes slowly less visible until it finally disappears and rehearsals are taken over by the nonacting students. The role of the instructor becomes that of a spectator, who at the end of the rehearsal will

give a short, critical, constructive, and never discouraging report
to the students, concentrating on elements that could be improved
in acting, movements, use of props, tone of voice, etc.

## The Performances

For the duration of the performance period, the role of the instructor is that of a convener, and his or her place is not backstage but
with the audience. During the performances, the spotlight must
be exclusively on the students; therefore, I refrain from giving last-
minute advice or from conducting concentration exercises. During
classes students have been reminded many times that one of the
most important things during a performance is concentration; they
know that a loss of concentration could negatively affect the entire
performance. It is up to each one of them to find the best way to
concentrate in their acting or stage role, to find their private or group
space, and to become the character they are interpreting. Perhaps
a bit of reassurance is necessary before the first performance, but
it all sums up to a brief talk; the applause at the beginning of the
performance will do the rest.

This technique of noninterference is pedagogically sound in that
it gives students the opportunity to get ready for the performance at
their own pace, and it lowers their affective filters, their anxieties.
The lower the affective filter, the better the performance. However,
the fact that there is a noticeable difference in quality between the
first and the last performance is not necessarily because the affective filters are gradually diminishing. In fact, lower affective filters
often correspond with overconfidence and/or a loss in concentration,
two elements that I always address immediately after the first performance. The main reason for this gap in quality is, in my opinion,
due to the fact that with every performance students get to know the
audience better, and they learn how to "play" with them and react
to their reactions. They learn to adapt to that specific audience. The
audience is, ultimately, the final performance booster: the better
their reaction, the better the students' performances. Interaction
with the audience also means real language acquisition.

In our product-oriented approach, the term *interaction* acquires
more complexity and a meaning that goes well beyond the normal
one, as synthesized by Seán Devitt: "Interaction has many mean-

ings even within the field of language learning. It can refer to oral interaction between two or more people, either over the phone, or written interaction over the Internet."[28] During a theatrical performance, there are different levels and types of interaction. There are interactions between the characters of the play; between acting and nonacting students in the play (through signals to prompt a line or to wait for a music/lighting cue or spoken interaction if backstage); with the director (mainly in remembering his or her acting suggestions); with the audience; even with props and the set.

The use of the language is not limited only to the stage. It also is used before and after the performance and during the intermission, as the students not only perform some of the tasks assigned to them (welcome audience members, take care of tickets) but also mingle and speak with audience members, talk about their experiences, or introduce their relatives and friends to their teachers or fellow students. Even though it is contrary to standard theatrical practices, we encourage student-actors to interact with the audience before or after the performance and during the intermission because we know that often the communication will take place in the target language. We do not want our students to miss such an opportunity to produce "real" language.

One of the issues critics have addressed when writing about theater and performance in a language classroom setting regards this issue of "real" communication. Many critics see the memorization of a theatrical text as unprofitable to students because it does not generate communication; it is merely a matter of transferring words from one container to another. And this is not communication (for a summary of this point of view, see Guido Pugliese and Salvatore Bancheri, "Italiano a tre atti"). To dismiss this type of criticism, however, one need only compare the script of a play with the actual words spoken during a performance to realize how much "real" communication and "real" learning is taking place. The amount of new and different language produced can be quantitatively appreciated only by following the performances with a script in hand. We are referring here not only to additions to the script of gestures, facial expressions, and movements but also to changes to the text itself as reflected in student-actors using synonyms, modifying sentence structure, filling the gap when their memory draws a blank, or simply improvising to solve more complex and unforeseen situations.

## Motivation: The Key to Success

The fact that during a performance language communication in the target language is "real" and complete is one of the main reasons for the success of both theatrical experiments at UTM and ILS. Another main factor in this success could be summed up by Abraham Maslow's motivation theory, which states that real learning will happen and will be retained only if students are highly motivated.[29] The theme of motivation is well presented and dissected by Maley and Duff in all its different facets: "Drama activities . . . help to get rid of the difference and boredom that come from being forced to stay passive all the time. . . . There is no place here for stereotyped responses, set-up discussions, pre-planned arguments or 'free conversations' in which everyone speaks and nobody listens, or else nobody speaks and the teacher is left to quench the fire started by his or her own burning questions. In a sense, motivation is not needed when working through drama, because the enjoyment comes from imaginative *personal* involvement, not from the sense of having successfully carried out someone else's instructions."[30] These activities also fill the learner's need for peer-group acceptance, the sense of belonging and security.

In theater courses that include performance, the students are highly motivated because they have to perform in front of an audience and, of course, they care about the *bella figura;* this is true for both student-actors and those who work behind the scenes. Furthermore, students' motivation is increased because similar courses promote cultural understanding, presenting "intriguing possibilities for students to interpret, rehearse, and embody the target language and culture."[31] This holistic perspective appeals to many different learning styles. Finally, theater courses that include performance are successful because they apply a fundamental approach in language teaching: a student-centered approach. Students become active participants in their own learning process: "A performance approach promotes students' confidence by providing a non-threatening, student-centered stage, where they experience the validity of diverse approaches to texts."[32] The success is also dictated by the fact that the learning experience is total and includes the study of not only literature and languages but also gestures, intonation, pauses, movements, and body language. It implies a deep understanding of the play being performed and of all the psychological nuances of each of its characters. In a few words, during the performance the communication is "real" and complete and combines, in Jun Liu's words, "linguistic accuracy, cultural appropriateness, emotional involvement, active, physical participation, and the language class as a community."[33]

The linguistic fluency and competence in the target language of each student-actor and nonactor will also improve enormously because it is commonly accepted that time spent on a task leads to more learning. In this regard, Semke writes that "skills are developed and strengthened through planning, rehearsing and performing." And through memorization and performance of roles, writes Janet Hegman Shier, "students can overcome problems with language interference, accent, intonation, speaking rhythm and thereby master subtleties of communication in [a second language]." Furthermore, by the time the experiment is over, "most students, even those with minor roles, have learned the entire script just from listening to the others practice."[34]

## Conclusion and Curtain Call

Many benefits result from theater and performance courses. The curriculum becomes student-centered, emphasizing the use of Italian language in creative, practical situations while teaching Italian literature in an integrated way. I believe that any objections to the use of theater in the classroom—that is, its lack of structure, its lack of goal, its being too specific or esoteric—have been answered. Moody points out that the performance course becomes "even more democratically organized and energized because of the rehearsal and staging process of the play." And Semke says that through such performance courses, the on-campus visibility of the language program increases, "stimulating enthusiasm and helping to maintain enrollments."[35] I concur with both statements. My classes are definitely more energized and organized, even though I always point out that my rehearsals are run as a "democratic dictatorship." The performance course revolves around the students, and by focusing enrollment on students with an educational background in intermediate Italian, we ensure a spirited, capable cast and a quality performance. The department of Italian at UTM enjoys a stronger visibility on campus thanks to the theater performances. We attract an average of two thousand spectators yearly, and numerous scholarships are created through the proceedings. This visibility also can be measured by the fact that many university and local authorities as well as community leaders are regularly among our spectators. Former students also at times use UTM theatrical performances as a sort of class reunion, to rekindle friendships, to meet familiar faces, to reminisce about past theatrical and nontheatrical experiences, and most of all to relive the language experience. In brief, the participation in a performance course has the power to build a sense of a language community.

## Notes

1. Essif, "Teaching Literary-Dramatic Texts," 26; Haggstrom, "A Performative Approach." Savoia, using Carter and McRae, presents a practical summary on the way literature in general, and a second or foreign language literature in particular, is taught and learned, and how it needs to be revaluated: "As Carter and McRae explain, traditional approaches to the study of literature tend to be 'product- and teacher-centered': the text or object of study is a canonized, 'fixed and stable entity'; the teacher is the 'expert practitioner' who possesses the techniques to be learned by the student in apprenticeship fashion; the histories of literature and literary criticism books are the other authorities upon which students must rely. Such methods of teaching literature not only 'do not bear any systematic relation to the development of linguistics skills in students,' but they seem to run counter to the language-teaching theories and practices previously described." Savoia, "Teaching Italian Language," 510.
2. Maley and Duff, *Drama Techniques in Language Learning,* 6; Maley and Duff, "Drama Techniques in Language Learning," 151; McRae, *Using Drama in the Classroom,* 13, 8; Semke, "German Café-Theater," 137; Wessels, *Drama,* 110–133. Wessels's book presents a valid discussion on the benefits of "drama projects," even though we are often on opposite sides regarding some of the criteria for setting the "project."
3. Moody, "Undergoing a Process," 135.
4. Essif, "Way Off Broadway," 32.
5. The name Maschere Duemondi (Two-World Players) signifies that each student-actor can function in two worlds. For more information on the theatrical activities at UTM, see Pugliese and Bancheri, "Inscenare Goldoni," Pugliese and Bancheri, "Italiano a tre atti," and http://www.utm.utoronto.ca/~w3ita/theatre.html.

6. Since the early 1990s, all activities outside the classroom (from lectures to soccer or volleyball games, from film viewing and *cinefora* to picnics, from classical concerts to informal singing, from technology roundtables to the variety show) are considered co-curricular as they have, in learning a language, equal value and importance as academic classes. Here are some of the performances presented at ILS since 1990 (professor-director in parentheses): 1990: A. Campanile, *Visita di condoglianze* (M. Lettieri); 1991: L. Pirandello, *La giara* (S. Socci); 1995: M. Bontempelli, *Nostra Dea* (M. C. Papini); 1996: D. Fo and F. Rame, *La donna grassa* (C. Cairns); 1997: scenes from different plays (P. Puppa); 1998: E. De Filippo, *L'arte della commedia* (C. Cairns); 1999: A. Campanile, *Visita di condoglianze* (D. Iuele-Colilli); 2000: L. Riccobene, *Io non mi marito per procura* (S. Bancheri); 2001: P. Aretino, *La talanta* (C. Cairns); 2002: D. Fo, *Non tutti i ladri vengono per nuocere* (S. Bancheri); 2003: G. G. Colli, *Dalla piazza al teatro: il mito di Arlecchino* (G. G. Colli); 2004: E. De Filippo, *Non ti pago!* (S. Bancheri).

7. Here is the 2004 description for IT 6560, Theater Workshop: "A study of representative comic plays from the nineteenth and twentieth centuries with a consideration of acting and staging techniques mainly through the production of a specific comedy. All students in this workshop are expected to act in and/or to help in the production of the play that will be performed prior to the end of the session."

8. Cairns, "Practical Theater," 766–767.

9. Dodson, "The Educational Potential," 162.

10. Essif, "Way Off Broadway," 32.

11. When a similar situation presents itself during the rehearsals, students are given advice on what to do. Also, part of the official evaluation is an oral test, geared at preparing students for these kinds of problems. During the thirty-minute test, all students are asked not only to speak about their character (personality, how to interpret the part, how to move onstage for a specific part, how to dress the character, etc.), but also to translate words or expressions in their lines, to give synonyms and antonyms for words they use, or even to repeat their lines using different words or summarizing them in the case of long speeches.

12. Reasons for the higher degree of motivation are seen in the limited number of students that ILS accepts every summer as well as in the full-immersion concept. On the basis of comments of ILS colleagues, one can safely state that ILS students have a higher motivation than in any other Italian program in North America.

13. Semke explains the success of her experiment: "It is an application of the theory that the goal of public performance can be used as a motivating tool in foreign language learning. . . . Participation in this special event increases identification on the part of students with the

target language group." Also, "The value to the students lies in having a concrete, imminent reason for learning German. For once motivation is not grades. . . . The opportunity for interaction with the German-speaking guests is also of immensurable value to the students. It is a definite thrill for them to discover that they can communicate in authentic situations" (137, 139).

14. Normally, the rehearsal time for a professional company before a performance is about three to four weeks, eight hours every day.

15. Moody, "Undergoing a Process," 149; Fels and McGivern, "Intercultural Recognitions," 20; Mather, "Getting Off the Page," 63.

16. Alessio, "La parola nel testo teatrale," 192; Mather, "Getting Off the Page," 58.

17. Essif, "Teaching Literary-Dramatic Texts," 26.

18. Essif, "Way Off Broadway," 35.

19. Bandura, "Self-Efficacy Mechanism," 131.

20. I have adopted here some of the terminology used by Livingstone, *Role Play in Language Learning,* 5, 56, 60–61; Mather, "Getting Off the Page," 60; Hegman Shier, "The Arts and the Foreign-/Second-Language Curriculum."

21. Moody, "Undergoing a Process," 137. For research on this topic, see also Heath, "Inner City Life," and Courtney, "A Lifetime of Drama Teaching and Research," 205–215.

22. Here are other changes made to the script: we (1) split the part of the priest, Don Raffaele Console, giving him a sister (Lucia Console); (2) changed the role of Luigi Frungillo to Luisa Frungillo; and (3) split the part of the Avvocato Lorenzo Strumillo by adding a second lawyer (Carla Spampinato). In De Filippo's original play, the use of only one lawyer by the two disputing characters (Don Ferdinando and Mario Bertolini) suggests that the decision was dictated by the shortage of one actor in the theatrical company. If this is the case, then our decision to use two different lawyers reinstates what could have been De Filippo's original intention.

23. Barrie K. Joy warns us that social roles should be learned in context. In practical terms, in theatrical workshops we need to bring learners to observe the patterns of the culture as well as its language; otherwise, "they will tend to assume that, with a few quirky exceptions, things are done in the target culture as in their own and that it is only the language, not the culture, which is different in form and structure." Joy, "Role Activities," 169.

24. Haggstrom, "A Performative Approach," 17; Stevick, *Memory, Meaning and Method,* refers to this as the learner's need of a sense of "belonging" and security.

25. Caré, "Approche communicative," 161, 162, 165.

26. Livingstone, *Role Play in Language Learning*, 7.
27. The role of these students, however, does not stop with these tasks alone. They must also work on the programs, develop sponsorships, create and sell tickets, relate with the media (Italian but also non-Italian radio, television, and newspapers), assemble and disassemble the stage before and after weekend performances, put signs up for the audience, and even clean the auditorium after each performance. At ILS, the majority of these tasks are left to the theater crew of Middlebury College. The students act only as coordinators, and their role is limited to a few tasks, such as taking measurements, preparing a list of props, choosing the costumes, doing makeup, etc.
28. Devitt, "Interacting with Authentic Texts," 457.
29. Maslow, *Motivation and Personality*. See also, Richard-Amato, ed., *Making It Happen;* Rivers, ed., *Interactive Language Teaching;* Vigotsky, "Interaction between Learning and Development"; and Whiteson, ed., *New Ways of Using Drama*.
30. Maley and Duff, "Drama Techniques in Language Learning," 157–159; Stevick, *Memory, Meaning and Method*.
31. Moody, "Undergoing a Process," 138.
32. Haggstrom, "A Performative Approach," 9; see also Maley and Duff, "Drama Techniques in Language Learning"; Maley and Duff, *Drama Techniques in Language Learning;* Hegman Shier, "Integrating the Arts in the Foreign/Second Language Curriculum"; Wessels, *Drama*, 10; and Stern, "Drama in Second Language Learning."
33. Liu, "Process Drama," 67.
34. Semke, "German Café-Theater," 137; Hegman Shier, "Integrating the Arts in the Foreign/Second Language Curriculum," 308; Semke, "German Café-Theater," 139; see also Wessels, *Drama*, 10, 13.
35. Moody, "Undergoing a Process," 143; Semke, "German Café-Theater," 137.

## Bibliography

Alessio, Antonio. "La parola nel testo teatrale." In *Italian Literature in North America: Pedagogical Strategies*, edited by John Picchione and Laura Pietropaolo. Ottawa: Canadian Society for Italian Studies, 1990.

Bancheri, Salvatore, and Guido Pugliese. "Italian Theater." In *The Luminous Mosaic: Italian Cultural Organizations in Ontario*, edited by Julius Molinaro and Maddalena Kuitunen. Welland, Canada: Edition Soleil, 1993.

Bandura, Albert. "Self-Efficacy Mechanism in Human Agency." *American Psychologist* 37 (February 1982): 122–148.

Cairns, Christopher. "Practical Theater in a 'Total-Immersion' Language

Learning Context." In *L'Italia nella lingua e nel pensiero,* edited by A. Mollica and R. Campa. Rome: Istituto Poligrafico e Zecca dello Stato, 2002.

Caré, Jean-Marc. "Approche communicative. Un second soufflé?" In *Teaching Modern Languages,* edited by Ann Swarbrick. London: Routledge, 1994.

Courtney, Richard. "A Lifetime of Drama Teaching and Research." In *Building Moral Communities through Educational Drama,* edited by Betty Jane Wagner. Westport, CT: Ablex, 1999.

De Filippo, Eduardo. *Le bugie hanno le gambe lunghe.* Vol. 1, *Cantata dei giorni dispari.* Turin: Einaudi, 1967.

———. *Non ti pago!* Vol. 2, *Cantata dei giorni dispari.* Torino: Einaudi, 1967.

Devitt, Seán. "Interacting with Authentic Texts: Multilayered Processes." *Modern Language Journal* 81 (1997): 457–469.

Dodson, Sarah L. "The Educational Potential of Drama for ESL." In *Body and Language: Intercultural Learning through Drama,* edited by Gerd Bräuer. Westport, CT: Ablex, 2002.

Essif, Les. "Way Off Broadway and Way Out of the Classroom: American Students De-, Re-, and Per-forming the French Dramatic Text." *ADFL Bulletin* 27 (Fall 1997): 32–37.

———. "Teaching Literary-Dramatic Texts as Culture-in-Process in the Foreign Language Theater Practicum: The Strategy of Combining Texts." *ADFL Bulletin* 29 (Spring 1998): 24–33.

Fels, Lynn, and Lynne McGivern. "Intercultural Recognitions through Performative Inquiry." In *Body and Language: Intercultural Learning through Drama,* edited by Gerd Bräuer. Westport, CT: Ablex, 2002.

Goldoni, Carlo. *La casa nova.* Versione italiana dal dialetto e presentazione di Renato Simoni. Turin: Società Editrice Torinese, 1943.

Haggstrom, Margaret A. "A Performative Approach to the Study of Theater: Bridging the Gap between Languages and Literature Courses." *French Review* 61 (October 1992), 7–19.

Heath, Shirley Brice. "Inner City Life through Drama: Imagining the Language Classroom." *TESOL Quarterly* 27 (1993): 177–192.

Hegman Shier, Janet. "Integrating the Arts in the Foreign/Second Language Curriculum: Fusing the Affective and the Cognitive." *Foreign Language Annals* 23 (1990): 301–314.

———. "The Arts and the Foreign-/Second-Language Curriculum: An Interdisciplinary Approach to Actively Engage Students in Their Own Learning." In *Body and Language: Intercultural Learning through Drama,* edited by Gerd Bräuer. Westport, CT: Ablex, 2002.

Joy, Barrie K. "Role Activities in the Foreign Language Classroom." In *Teaching Modern Languages,* edited by Ann Swarbrick. London: Routledge, 1994.

Liu, Jun. "Process Drama in Second- and Foreign-Language Classrooms."
In *Body and Language: Intercultural Learning through Drama,* edited by
Gerd Bräuer. Westport, CT: Ablex, 2002.

Livingstone, Carol. *Role Play in Language Learning.* Essex, UK: Longman,
1983.

Maley, Alan, and Alan Duff. *Drama Techniques in Language Learning.* Cambridge: Cambridge University Press, 1982.

———. "Drama Techniques in Language Learning." In *Teaching Modern
Languages,* edited by Ann Swarbrick. London: Routledge, 1994.

Maslow, Abraham H. *Motivation and Personality.* New York: Harper, 1954.

Mather, M. Clare. "Getting Off the Page and Making a Scene: Teaching
Drama in the Classroom." *ADFL Bulletin* 20 (January 1989): 58–63.

McRae, John. *Using Drama in the Classroom.* New York: Pergamon, 1985.

Moody, Douglas J. "Undergoing a Process and Achieving a Product: A Contradiction in Educational Drama?" In *Body and Language: Intercultural
Learning through Drama,* edited by Gerd Bräuer. Westport, CT: Ablex,
2002.

Pugliese, Guido, and Salvatore Bancheri. "Italiano a tre atti: insegnare reci-
tando." *Romance Languages Annual* 4 (1992): 345–347.

———. "Inscenare Goldoni: un esperimento socio-didattico." *Il Veltro* 40
(1996): 443–447.

Richard-Amato, Patricia A., ed. *Making It Happen: Interaction in the Second
Language Classroom.* New York: Longman, 1996.

Rivers, M. Wilga, ed. *Interactive Language Teaching.* Cambridge: Cambridge
University Press, 1987.

Savoia, Francesca. "Teaching Italian Language, Literature, and Culture
through Performance: The Italian Theatrical Workshop." *Italica* 77
(2002): 509–522.

Semke, Harriet D. "German Café-Theater: A Venture in Experiential Learning." *Foreign Language Annals* 13 (1980): 137–139.

Stern, Susan. "Drama in Second Language Learning from a Psycholinguistic Perspective." *Language Learning* 30 (1980): 77–100.

Stevick, Earl. *Memory, Meaning and Method.* Boston: Newbury House, 1976.

Vigotsky, Lev V. "Interaction between Learning and Development." In *Making It Happen: Interaction in the Second Language Classroom,* edited by
Patricia Richard-Amato. London: Longman, 1996.

Wessels, Charlyn. *Drama.* Oxford: Oxford University Press, 1987.

Whiteson, Valerie, ed. *New Ways of Using Drama and Literature in Language
Teaching.* Bloomington, IL: Pantagraph, 1996.

# CHAPTER 4

# Creative Connections: The Theater Practicum and the Integration of Language and Literature Study

FRANCESCA SAVOIA

More and more teachers of second languages have come to recognize and regard theater as a vehicle for generating communication among students and enhancing both their linguistic abilities and their understanding of foreign literature and culture. Many instructors have developed and regularly offer courses involving a variety of performance projects, the most common of them consisting in the staging of a play in a foreign language. Rather than the pursuit of a full-scale production of a play in Italian, the model discussed in this chapter more specifically aims at providing third-year students with a positive, rewarding experience in the study of literature through the use of theater and performance in the classroom. The aim of this course is to forestall students' fear or mistrust of literature by integrating the goals of language learning and literary study as fully and as seamlessly as possible. Although class activities and assignments do eventually give rise to a performance, they are designed above all to overcome students' misapprehensions about literature and to teach strategies that empower them as readers and interpreters of literary texts.[1]

## Integrating Language and Literature Study: Background

A great divide long existed between lower-level and upper-level second or foreign language courses: the former, traditionally designed to teach basic skills, too often lacked in content; the latter, much richer in content, too often disregarded the students' continuing language learning problems. Fortunately, in the past twenty years or so, much has occurred to facilitate the bridging of this gap.[2]

A change of mind and attitude toward the teaching of second or foreign languages had to occur: applied linguists and language teachers alike have fully realized by now that "a second or foreign language can rarely be learned or taught without addressing the culture of the community in which it is used."[3] The goal of second or foreign language instruction at its best is to enhance the students' acquisition of linguistic skills while raising, at the same time, the level of their cultural consciousness and promoting their understanding of and appreciation for the differences existing between their own histories and systems of beliefs and those expressed by the new language they are studying. The most recently established standards for language teaching reveal this broader definition of language learning, one that embraces cultural knowledge and cross-cultural communication.[4] The fact that in most colleges and universities foreign language is no longer classified as a "basic skill" but as a "general education requirement" is further proof of the general acceptance of these "pedagogical and disciplinary developments which emphasize that language is inextricably tied to the cultural context of which it is part."[5]

New approaches and techniques have been developed to help teachers create a more collaborative learning environment in their classrooms, by providing more opportunity for individual participation and interaction.[6] Content-based language textbooks have been published that help instructors devise and properly sequence activities on the basis of meaningful, authentic material.[7] Nowadays, Italian language classes, like other foreign language classes, are mostly communication oriented; and many good textbooks (and other teaching support tools) are available, especially for the first year of Italian instruction, that effectively discourage the mechanical transmission and reception of the language as a system of rules and require instead that teacher and students be involved in "performing," in "doing" things with the language.

More importantly, from my point of view, the worthiness of literature as a fount of cultural and linguistic exploration has been reaffirmed. Undoubtedly, the development of communicative methodologies—strongly opposed to the grammar-translation approaches of the past, which had made the study of literary texts their cornerstone—helped for a time to shift the focus away from literature, in favor of the introduction of more contingent, less formalized, and less sophisticated linguistic material in the classroom. The popularity of practices emphasizing speaking skills also deterred from the use of much written text in language teaching. Literary texts in particular were deemed by many to be far too difficult, certainly for beginning language students. However, there appears to be wide consensus at present on the belief that doing away with the study of literature altogether severely hampers the acquisition of real cultural and critical literacy, and that the exclusion of literature from the early stages of language learning is unnecessary, unwise, and in fact harmful to the effective articulation of language curricula.[8]

"By integrating the arts, specifically literature, into our teaching," writes Valerie Whiteson in her introduction to a volume addressing teachers of English to speakers of other languages, "we give our students excellent opportunities to express themselves in the target culture."[9] Foreign language teachers have come to the same conclusion and know that "allowing the literature of any language its active and cultural function in the classroom is a sound base for the development of the corporate and individual thought process in both written and oral form."[10] Hence, innovative ways have been sought and found to tap literature as a resource for learning language, as an indispensable means, in fact, for initiating students to the complexities of a second language, its culture, and its values.[11] In this respect as well, materials writers of Italian have striven to keep up with developments in the discipline.[12]

Considering that the specific study of literature constitutes the principal subject matter for advanced courses in most programs of second or foreign language instruction, it is not surprising that the reexamination of the role of literature in language teaching and learning has occurred primarily under pressure from literary faculty, concerned by the students' often insufficient lexical and syntactic knowledge of the target language and general lack of preparation in close textual reading, analysis, and interpretation. However, had the changes occurred solely in language pedagogy, the gap between lower- and upper-tier courses, to which I was referring at the beginning of this discussion, would have not only remained but widened. The way literature in general and a second or foreign language literature in particular is taught and learned also needed to be discussed and reevaluated.

As Ronald Carter and John McRae explain, traditional approaches to the study of literature tend to be "product- and teacher-centered": the text or object of the study is a canonized, "fixed and stable entity";

the teacher is the "expert practitioner" who possesses the techniques to be learned by the students in apprenticeship fashion; the histories of literature or literary criticism books are the other authorities upon which the students must rely.[13] Such methods of teaching literature not only "do not bear any systematic relation to the development of linguistic skills in students," but they seem to run counter to the language-teaching theories and practices previously described. These theories and practices are clearly "more concerned with process and with texts which, if pedagogically required, can be extended, re-written, lexically or grammatically altered, or literally 'cut-up' in order to develop appropriate capacities in the students."[14]

Innovative approaches to the teaching of literature appear to have taken advantage of the new attitudes toward literature and literary texts that various modern trends of literary criticism afford: most notably, perhaps, semiotics (which reconciled literature with linguistics) and reader-response and reception theories (which helped to focus attention on the reader as an active consumer, if not a participant in the artistic creative process). Fully realizing the implications that views such as this have for the teaching of literature in language classes, new pedagogical theories call for a complete integration of language and literary study. Consequently, they also mandate that literary faculty take into consideration the findings of research on first and second language acquisition, reading comprehension, and students' cognitive development.[15]

While most literature professors may find such integration of approaches and goals advisable, the demands of their scholarly career often make it difficult for them to keep abreast of developments outside their immediate field of research. Let us consider also that "for an increasing number of scholars the borders of literary studies are permeable, opening into other areas of the humanities and also the social sciences," and that nowadays the need to develop some competence in more disciplines than one's own is great. The professional separation of language and literature study is most counterproductive given the fact that it is precisely "its focus on language—on coming to know through the power of words, their combinations, their arrangement, and their silences—that characterizes literature within cultural studies." However, the separation risks remaining in place, at least as far as pedagogy is concerned. Too many research-oriented institutions, in fact, effectually continue to discourage faculty from devoting too much time to the development of their teaching skills by rewarding mostly scholarly work in the promotion process.[16]

The solution rests, as many have recently pointed out, on fighting institutional barriers and professional divisions and creating forums of communication and collaboration among diverse faculty, among theorists and practitioners, scholars and teachers of linguistics, language, literature, and culture. Insofar as the success of a foreign language program depends on the adoption of a well-informed, common teaching philosophy, on the coherent articulation of the curriculum, and on a set of progressive goals consistent with the various levels of language instruction and learning, it is crucial for all faculty concerned—from the language coordinators and graduate assistants in charge of early language instruction to the professors of literature—to work together and share their experience and expertise.[17]

## The Theatrical Workshop in Its Local Curricular Context

Teaching Italian literature at the University of Pittsburgh, I found myself facing most of the issues I have discussed above, as well as specific problems related to the institution and the region in which I work (problems that colleagues working elsewhere in the country may or may not have experienced). Notwithstanding the fact that Pittsburgh boasts the fourth largest Italian-American population in the United States, the teaching of Italian in local schools is not supported in any effective way by that community, and, consequently, the language is taught in very few high schools.[18] Thanks to the efforts of a couple of generations of Italian faculty, the number of undergraduates interested in studying Italian at Pitt (a high percentage of whom come from the local Italian-American community) has been steadily growing over the past twenty years, but virtually none of them has sufficient knowledge of the language to enroll in intermediate or advanced classes as a freshman. Furthermore, at this university the foreign language requirement can still be satisfied, most regrettably, with just the first two semesters of elementary language. This makes for high enrollments in elementary Italian classes but reduces considerably the chances of enticing more undergraduates to pursue a rigorous, demanding major, entailing thirty-three credits of work beyond the elementary level.

The negative effect of the above factors on the growth of the program has been partially offset by the Italian faculty's initiative: among other things, we redesigned intermediate Italian courses and made them culturally much richer so that students can take them to satisfy one of three international/foreign culture requirements, and we continue to attend to the successful conduct of the summer study in Italy, so as to engender in all the numerous participants the desire to further their knowledge of Italian culture and pursue advanced Italian courses. Nevertheless, frequently enough my colleagues and I have been caught in a vicious circle, where the cancellation of some advanced language class or literature class taught in Italian (for lack of what the administration considers cost-effective enrollments) disrupts the progress of student majors and stifles in turn the growth in their ranks.

For all of these reasons, we regard the collective, careful planning and articulation of the Italian curriculum as crucial to the success, if not the very existence, of our program. We professors of Italian literature have closely monitored the updating of language-teaching methodologies and course structuring in lower-division classes and asked the language program supervisor and the teaching assistants to introduce the students—in a coordinated fashion, beginning in their first and continuing in the second year of Italian—to as elaborate a linguistic environment as each level allows, through the use of literary and nonliterary texts. Of course, asking the language coordinator and language instructors to lay the curricular foundations for our teaching of literature meant committing ourselves in turn to the creation of advanced courses that could attend to both the productive exploration of literature and the accommodation of the students' continuing language-learning needs.

In 1994, in order to ensure that students satisfy at least one element of their writing requirements within their major, the University of Pittsburgh Art and Science's Curriculum Review Committee determined that each program should develop discipline-specific W-courses (courses with a writing component). This modification of the general education requirements prompted the review of the options offered at the third-year level. The two existing advanced language courses were transformed into courses that could serve (jointly) as both a writing practicum and an introduction to Italian literature for our majors. Each of these two courses was reorganized and similarly articulated in multiple modules, each module focusing on a particular kind of literature and/or art medium (short fiction, autobiography, poetry, song, drama, opera, film) and including materials and activities pertaining to that genre. This organization is still working well in supporting the kind of discourse training that students need to talk and write about different texts and contexts in intellectually adequate and progressively more sophisticated fashion. The subsequent step of choosing one or two overarching themes (for example: emigration and identity, women's role in society, the war experience, generational gaps, etc.) to give the materials proposed in each module cross-genre unity and coherence has also proved successful in helping the students gain a good, solid understanding of some relevant cultural issues. By continuing, in the course of a term, to focus on such issues as the selected themes afford, while moving from one set and type of documents to another, the students' perspective widens, and their ability to interpret the various texts and to elaborate and express their opinion on the topics at hand increases.

It was in the spirit and context of such curricular reform that I created the "Italian Theatrical Workshop," a third-year Italian course that, along with the two described above and perhaps more effectively, could serve as a bridge between phases of the Italian curriculum by making the transition to the mainly literary and increasingly more challenging content of the upper-division classes not only possible but smooth, successful, and desirable. The theatrical workshop was designed to satisfy the creative expression requirement and, as of 2004, has also been approved as a W-course.[19] By offering it, along with the other courses introducing Italian literature, on a three-term rotation basis and giving majors the opportunity to choose two of these three courses, we allow them much more flexibility and provide them with a wider variety of materials and approaches to the advanced study of Italian.

## What Difference Does Theater Make?

Long before I began to develop the Italian theatrical workshop, the writings on communicative language teaching and on the theory of language acquisition through interaction had been referring to role-play, improvisation, and drama as essential tools; drama had been prominently featured in and among the writings that dealt with ways of integrating language and literature study; and ample evidence already existed of the successful implementation of a performative approach to the study of language and literature in English, English as a second language, French, Spanish, and German programs in North America and in Europe. In planning and assembling material for the course I relied on all of these different sources. I also drew (and continue to draw) on the work of some writers, stage directors, and teachers (including my own sister, a junior-high school teacher in Genoa, Italy) who, in the past fifteen years in Europe, have focused on the issue of integrating theater in the primary and secondary school curriculum.[20]

Two notices, signed in Italy in 1995 and 1997 by the prime minister, the minister of education, and the minister of culture, recognized theater as an important component in the education of young people. No national mandate was issued, and no national fund was created for the actual systematic introduction of theatrical education in the Italian public school curricula at all levels; nevertheless, ad hoc workshops, paid for by local authorities, have since been created and offered in most regions of Italy to prepare teachers willing to involve themselves and their students in playwriting and production. AGITA, a national Italian association founded in 1994 with the intent of promoting the culture of theater in schools and communities, has been instrumental in organizing yearly national reviews of middle and high school students' theatrical productions. All this has resulted also in the writing and publication of a number of resource books.[21]

The many theoretical considerations and assumptions upon which the creation of this theater practicum was based were made initially by drawing upon my own teaching experience and subsequently explored in the course of my research. My first concerns and preliminary observations happened to coincide with the ones articulated in the opening statements of an essay by Margaret Haggstrom: first, the primary goal of language, conversation, and civilization courses is not and cannot be to prepare students for literary analysis; second, when and if students overcome their mistrust and/or dread of literature, they come mostly unprepared to their first foreign language literature class; and third, even those students who have acquired some analytical skills in English do not seem to be able to transfer them successfully to their foreign language classes. These observations clearly highlight the need for an introductory literature course in which students can receive "the linguistic and critical skills necessary to think, speak, and write intelligently and confidently about literature, and enjoy it as well."[22]

That such a course be "theatrical" in nature makes sense if one considers that in drama the interdependencies of language and literature can appear more immediately clear to the students. Especially if we understand theater in its broader sense, we cannot fail to realize how one of the natural characteristics of any theatrical work is the tight connection (in fact the circularity) of the fundamental skills involved (writing, reading, listening, and speaking) and how the acquisition of these basic skills also coincides with the main goal of any linguistic education.[23] Among literary studies, then, the study of drama can perhaps more easily be made to accommodate the language learner's need to continue acquiring and mastering skills by actively working on them, provided that a broad, interactive, performative approach be adopted. The particular class dynamic that results from producing, studying, and acting theatrical texts, or in any case the dynamic that results from using a performative approach to texts in general, can break down psycholinguistic barriers to advance language acquisition and cultural knowledge.

Far more than assisting with and providing additional cultural context to language learning, a theater practicum is "especially propitious" for the type of "inductive, constructivist, re-creative teaching and learning" that can, I believe, most naturally draw or reconcile students to the study of literature. In a recent article devoted to the teaching of semiotics through performance, Les Essif reminds us that "dramatic writing is specifically designed by the author to generate another (performance) text and is therefore more obviously a dynamic, regenerative construction process." He observes that "in performance, we get to employ and to manipulate a wide array of concrete signifying materials, whose conjunction necessarily exceeds the meaning of the written text." He consequently warns all teachers involved in foreign language theater workshops against being primarily consumed by the linguistic and artistic/cosmetic dimension of a production and failing "to take advantage of the potential of the project to teach students (and ourselves) about the many and complex ways that signifying processes involved in the text's mise-en-scène create meaning between writer and reader, reader and performer, performer and performer, performer and spectator, and so on."[24] In performance, multiple modalities of communication are activated, and students must necessarily engage in a dynamic, multileveled investigation of the text. By speaking the lines of a text, mimicking the actions the text describes or implies, imagining and re-creating the situations it details or suggests, reconstructing the spaces and times of those actions and situations, in other words by interacting with the text through performance, students become more acutely aware of its constructed, conventional nature. In performance, students are forced to move from what is—to borrow Roland Barthes's well-known terms—simply "readable" (the mere denotative dimension of a text) to what is "writable" (the connotative potential of a text) and can be, must be, therefore, re-constructed or re-created.[25] Thus, through drama, students may indeed become interpreters (players) of literature.[26] Finally, besides the expanded notion of text it implies, what makes theater so helpful in teaching foreign language and literature is the "game" quality of it, the safe and extensive modeling it allows students, the structure it provides for them to practice all skills.

## Course Design, Work Plan, and Procedures

In this theater practicum the students, under the instructor's supervision and working both individually and in groups, engage in a variety of different and yet closely related and interdependent activities.[27] The first five weeks of the semester (a total of nine class meetings of one hour and fifteen minutes each) are devoted primarily to:

  (a) a concise, systematic, and practical introduction to the sounds of the Italian language
  (b) oral reading (of a wide variety of texts of different length, mostly but not exclusively literary)
  (c) storytelling (the telling of preexisting or completely original stories, with or without a predetermined subject)
  (d) role-playing and improvisation

Week six through ten (ten class meetings) are devoted primarily to:

  (a) the writing and enactment of original dialogues and scenarios
  (b) the adaptation of preexisting narrative texts to the stage and their performance
  (c) close reading, analysis, and performance of dramatic texts

The remaining five weeks (nine class meetings) are devoted to:

(a) the selection and preparation of the material to be performed during a final recital

(b) the preparation of detailed program notes, and the publicizing of the recital in all of the other Italian classes

The course has been offered in this format five times so far, and its structure has proved flexible enough to accommodate the needs of small and larger groups. I have worked with as many as sixteen and as few as seven undergraduate students, some beginning their third year, others completing their fourth year of study and displaying, therefore, various levels of ease in performing tasks entirely in Italian, the language in which all class activities are conducted.

The first part of the course is not, and cannot be, a full-fledged phonetics course, nor can it be a course on how to develop a voice suited for the stage, as the objective is not that of making actors out of the students. However, since the aim is rather that of making the students into "conscious readers" by, first of all, making them read aloud, a number of very useful exercises can be drawn and adapted from both phonetics books and actors' manuals.[28] Oral reading, practiced by the students in the classroom and in the language lab (where they can make audio and visual recordings of their performances), represents the first genuine and necessary exploration (if not yet comprehension and interpretation) of the text.[29] Some time is, therefore, devoted to understanding certain basic respiratory and vocal mechanisms connected to reading and speaking Italian. A study of the articulation of sounds in the Italian language, the nature of its consonants and its vowel system, accents, division of words in syllables, and, above all, the practice of such articulation occupy the class for a few weeks. Students work on individual phonemes and words, at first, and then sentences and whole speeches, paying attention to correct pronunciation, to color (suggested by feelings possibly involved in longer passages), to the tone and volume of the voice, to the tempo (that is, the greater or lesser speed at which one reads), and the rhythm (punctuation, pauses, etc.).

While practicing pronunciation students are made aware, however briefly, of the various regional inflections existing in Italy and tackle notions of dialect and language and some of the fundamental issues in the history of Italian. Students are also made to reflect on the implications of mispronunciation, from the standpoint of effective communication, and on common stereotyping based on national inflections (the "American," "British," "French," "German," "Russian," and "Spanish" way of saying things in Italian, according to Italians, versus the "Italian" and other inflected pronunciations of English according to Americans). It is important, in my opinion, that students learn about the huge gap that once existed (and the discrepancies that are still lingering) between written and spoken Italian. Many students of Italian at the University of Pittsburgh are of Italian descent and often ask for clarifications on the subject of dialects and what constitutes "standard" Italian. It is usually somewhat reassuring for all students of Italian to discover that while the "standard" Italian they are taught is the linguistic variety accepted by the whole Italian community as having most recognizable and permanent value, the neutral pronunciation it would require does not necessarily come easy to all Italian natives and may sound almost as foreign to an Italian dialect speaker as to an English-American speaker.[30]

With the help and input of the students the teacher compiles a list of all possible intonations (serious, ironic, emphatic, comic, tragic, decisive, hesitating, phlegmatic, angry, etc.), a list of all possible combinations of volume and tone (for example, high volume/ grave tone, medium volume/ironic tone, etc.), and one of all possible combinations of volume, tone, and speed (for example medium volume/neutral tone/high-speed, etc.). With students sitting in a circle, the teacher gives them specific directions on how to read a given sentence and has them follow the directions to the best of their ability; or each student in turn decides on a particular intonation and delivers the sentence accordingly, while the others guess the choice that has been made. These kinds of preliminary exercises are extremely useful in that they lead the class in a practical exploration of the attributes of language in general, and Italian in particular, while making the students verify and discuss fundamental cultural issues. The exercise on volume, tone, and speed, for example, inevitably leads to the "discovery" that what an American speaker would consider a high-volume or an angry, even threatening, tone of voice does not necessarily sound the same to an Italian speaker.[31] These exercises can also be taken a step further by asking students to accompany each verbal utterance with one particular gesture or body movement (the one that comes more naturally) and inviting them to discuss what additional weight or different character can be given to verbal expression through body language. This already means engaging the students in performance, forcing them to recognize the nature of verbal and nonverbal behaviors involved in people's interaction and communication and how such behaviors differ from culture to culture and according to context. If they had not come to this necessary realization before, students fully understand at this point just how much one tends to interpret and reproduce the foreign language one is studying through the physical and cultural filter of his or her native tongue.[32] Simply warning students against translating in a mechanical fashion what they want to say or write in Italian from their own language is not effective. Students need to realize by themselves how misleading this practice can be. The study abroad or full-immersion experience usually does the trick. But in a classroom students can also be put in the position to reach, on their own and in a practical way, the right conclusion: in order to communicate, to make meaning in a second language, one must think and "act" in that language. Making students "perform" means making them step out of themselves, affording them, at a very minimum, the opportunity to reach such conclusions.

In order to go beyond reading single words or individual sentences, various texts are brought into play: tongue-twisters, proverbs, nursery rhymes, and, finally, literary texts. The latter are chosen among those that more conspicuously and consciously "play" with the sounds of the Italian language. Poetic texts are introduced (one stanza or a few verses at a time, if long poems are selected), in which the sound of the words reinforces the meaning. Students are instructed to find rhyming words, alliterations, repetitions, and onomatopoeia and are helped in establishing the nature of the structure of the verses and/or stanza. They are then asked to keep all of the above in mind as they practice reading the verses aloud, trying as much as possible to recall the sensations and identify with the images suggested by the text.[33] A few very short stories that, again, "play" with words or are centered on word equivocation, such as, for example, the short stories by Achille Campanile "Paganini," "La 'o' larga," and "Galileo," are also used in this phase.

Reading literary texts, poetry in particular, at this stage and in the fashion described above, appears just like another useful, more enjoyable exercise to improve one's pronunciation, rhythm, and intonation. It makes students focus, effortlessly, on vocabulary, sentence structure, and use of imagery. Especially for those who resist reading and studying literature because they consider it abstract and impractical, this represents an opportunity to call their attention to the tools of the literary craft and introduce them to the creative and exciting ways in which poets exploit the richness and beauty of the Italian language.

When, finally, longer readings are introduced, students are asked to treat them as "musical scores."[34] It is recommended that they mark on the text all short or long pauses and where it is necessary to take a breath. They are asked to highlight punctuation marks and to write "?" or "!" at the beginning of a question or exclamation (as the Spanish do). They also underline in different colors the lines of the different characters or write their names at the beginning of their respective speeches. They highlight key words preceding a direct discourse (for example: . . . *e Carlo disse in un sussurro:* ". . . . ) or write something that would remind them of the appropriate tone and volume to be used in delivering the lines of direct discourse. They take notes in the margins based on their interpretation of the text.

Students are also asked to practice various kinds of "reading." The following are some examples:

(a) individual reading with or without change of voice (that is, with or without distinguishing between the narrator's voice and the characters' voices)

(b) "role" reading (for example, one student functions as the narrator and a few other students each read the part of one character)

(c) "choral" reading or "solo" reading with chorus (for example, in poems or folktales with a "refrain," a chorus of voices reads the verses or lines of such refrain, and one other voice reads the rest of the text)[35]

(d) reading accompanied by noises, sounds, mimicry, and/or use of props[36]

While exercising orally with words and sounds, the students must also be encouraged to experiment with them in writing, creating original tongue-twisters, rigmaroles, and simple texts in rhymes or composing blank verse in Italian.[37] I have also adopted the practice of having the students borrow lines from a text in prose and compose a poem with them or "scrambling" the lines of a poem and having the students reassemble it.[38] Some students are successful in coming up with puns and effective plays on words, perhaps based on their own experience as foreign speakers of Italian. I have been fortunate to work with groups that always included one or more students who had spent some time studying or vacationing in Italy and could report some funny incidents caused by word equivocation or other misunderstanding. As their teacher and a native speaker of Italian, I think of course that it is important for me to always volunteer first and tell the students about some of my own mishaps with the English language.

A subsequent set of activities involves the students' creation and account of their own stories and the writing and enactment of their own dialogues and scenarios. As a first step toward playwriting and acting, one particular activity has always proved useful: the instructor selects a number of sentences and asks the students not only to choose how to interpret and read them (to choose whether to deliver them as questions, for example, or in the form of statements; whether to put emphasis on one word or another; whether to say them slowly or fast, in a loud or a low voice, etc.), but to explain in writing the reason for their choice, that is, to provide their own "pretext." Each student receives a sheet of paper that has the list of sentences or lines on the left side; students write their "pretext" or "subtext" on the right side. The students are asked to think of different circumstances in which each of the given sentences could be said. They are directed to read each sentence varying the tone, volume, and color of the voice as a way to find the right context. They have to come up with the situation they feel best suits the words, say the phrase showing consideration for the chosen context, and use the appropriate gestures to accompany their line. Finally, they rehearse the sentence in front of their fellow students to see whether their classmates can guess the situation the performers had thought out for it.[39]

For example, on the sheet of paper provided by the instructor, next to a sentence such as *Sta bruciando tutto* (everything is burning, everything is on fire, or everything is going up in flames), one student may write: "I'm cooking dinner and leave the stove for a few seconds. I smell the food burning. I return to the stove and find out that, in fact, everything is burning." Another student, instead, may think of a more dramatic instance and write: "I'm looking out a window and see that a building not far from my house is going up in flames. I turn to somebody next to me and point out to him or her what is happening." The students then try to "perform" their lines according to their imagined scenarios, and the others tell them what they guessed and critique their performance.

The following are other simple and effective activities in storytelling, story writing and rewriting, as well as creating and acting out dialogues and scenarios (to be carried out around midterm):

1. Provide each student with just a title; ask each of them to think out a story for his or her title, write it down, memorize it, and finally tell the story to the rest of the class.

2. Divide the class into three groups; provide one group with just the beginning of a story, one group with just the end of the same story, and another group with just its rough outline; ask the groups to complete the story and then to share and discuss the results.

3. Make the students listen to a series of recorded sounds, in no particular order (for example: an alarm clock ringing, keys jingling and the opening or shutting of a door, a radio or TV being turned on, a liquid being poured in a container, running water, steps, the shuffling of paper, or the rustling of wind through leaves, etc.); direct the students to take quick notes while identifying the sounds and then to place the sounds in a sequence; ask them to imagine and write briefly about a series of events to suit the sounds; and then have them share the stories they have created.[40]

4. Give each student an open scene to complete.[41]

5. Direct students to think about a phone conversation between two people of their choice; ask each of them to put himself or herself in the place of one of the interlocutors they have thought of and act as such a person in front of their classmates, having them listening in on just one end of the conversation; ask the students to guess who the people involved in each case are, what the nature of their relationship is, and what might the words of the "hidden," unheard interlocutors be. Each student may be asked, subsequently, to complete and write down someone else's "phone call."

The dialogues that the students are asked to create can be *a richiesta* or completely *su improvvisazione*. In the case of open scenes, again, the students are asked to think of possible circumstances that would give meaning to the lines of the dialogues, to read each dialogue in silence, and then read it out loud, each time changing the tone and volume of the voice as a way to envision different possible scenarios. Finally, they are instructed to choose a particular situation and ask themselves the following questions: Where does the scene take place? Who are the characters? What is the relationship between the characters? What is their objective? Are there any obstacles to this objective? If so, are the characters able to overcome them? The scene is then rehearsed according to the situation that the student had thought out and practiced with appropriate gestures and suitable tone and volume of voice, etc. For some of the above activities, it is also possible, and in fact useful, to draw material (bits and pieces of dialogue, situations, characters, or even just vocabulary) and/or inspiration from the narrative and dramatic texts that will be read and studied later in the course. For example, the term in which I had proposed to have the students read and stage Luigi Pirandello's *Così è (se vi pare),* I assigned Pirandellian titles in the first activity, used the story of Signor Ponza and Signora Frola in the second, and borrowed lines of dialogue from the play for the fourth activity. This allowed the students to indirectly familiarize themselves with some elements of the plot and language of the play before actually reading it, and to reflect upon and compare the different ways in which their knowledge, individual experiences, backgrounds, and fancies caused them to respond to (in terms of their creative output) and process the "Pirandellian" input I had given them.

Both at this stage of class activities and later, when the students are required to adapt narrative texts for the stage, they are provided with premade charts on which the process of creation of individual scenes, a *canovaccio,* or a whole script, is outlined. Sheets, divided in columns with various headings such as *atti, scene, personaggi, azioni/parlato, didascalie/dialoghi, movimenti di scena, organizzazione dello spazio scenico,* etc., are carefully filled out by the students while drafting their texts.[42]

One particular chart, or *scheda,* is devoted to the study and/or creation of characters. It provides spaces for the description of the characters' physical aspect, their personality, their movements and actions, the type of voice to be ascribed to each, and the reasons for a certain interpretation or another.[43] The students use it not only when creating their own texts and developing characters of their own invention, but also when analyzing existing plays. Works of various periods are sampled to give the students the opportunity, among other things, to begin to appreciate what constituted formal and/or informal speech in Italian at different times, and to recognize how much the way two characters address each other has to do with the familiarity and knowledge they share, with circumstances inherent to the plot, and/or with their rank and function in the play and in the society they represent. For this purpose, it is useful to select scenes from a couple of plays written in different centuries, involving a significant exchange between two or three characters. The instructor submits the text of these scenes for the students' examination, withholding the names of the playwrights and offering no introduction. Divided into small groups, the students read and discuss the scenes and, on the basis of the information they evince from the text (including names of the characters and all stage directions), try to determine the period in history and the most plausible circumstances in which such exchanges might have taken place, the nature of the characters, of their relationship, of their status, etc.

Scenes taken from Carlo Goldoni's *Le smanie per la villeggiatura* (for example, scene 12 in act 1, entailing Vittoria's visit to Giacinta, their exchange of polite compliments and civilities, as well as veiled threats, challenges, and accusations) or *La bottega del caffè* (for example, scene 3 of act 1, in which don Marzio, a gossip and a very demanding customer, is served by Ridolfo, owner of the coffee shop); from Giuseppe Giacosa's *Come le foglie* (for example, scene 4 in act 1, when Tommy and Nennele, brother and sister, discuss the imminent move to which their family is forced by financial ruin); or Pirandello's *La morsa* (the first dialogue between Giulia and her lover Antonio) all work very well in this kind of exercise.[44]

In mastering such activities, students usually acquire some confidence in their ability to make sense (and make good use) of Italian literary texts and develop an altogether healthier attitude toward literature in general. After completing these exercises, they are ready and willing to read closely, interpret, discuss, and even perform complex plays, going back to some that they may have already partially perused and adding other ones to the list. Some of the plays sampled and/or read in their entirety by the students have included: Pirandello's *La morsa* and *Così è (se vi pare)*; Dario Fo's *Non tutti i ladri vengono per nuocere, Il problema dei vecchi,* and *Il figlio in provetta;* and Luigi Lunari's *Tre sull'altalena*. Scenarios of the commedia dell'arte (selected from the ones collected by Flaminio Scala in *Il teatro delle favole rappresentative* of 1611) have also been studied and used one term as starting points for the creation of original sketches involving the traditional stock characters.

## The Final Recital

A sample of the best products of the students' work during the first ten or twelve weeks of the semester becomes the program for a final public recital, which is scheduled for the last day of classes and to which other members of the Italian faculty, students of Italian from all levels, and members of the local Italian-American community are invited. The recital's aim is to give the students a much more concrete sense of their accomplishments than any final test, instructor's evaluation, or grade could provide. It also serves the purpose of putting the students almost entirely in charge, making them take greater, if not full, responsibility for the choices and conduct that determine the success or failure of the show. The class truly works as a whole at this point. Without much intervention on the part of the teacher, students are usually able to deter, or at least to detect, and correct the behavior of those among them who tend to slack off or act irresponsibly toward the team.

Where funds are available and the use of an auditorium as well as the rental of costumes and other properties is a real possibility, a more elaborate, more polished production can of course be staged. So far, my students have had to content themselves with putting on their shows in auditorium-style classrooms, making due with ill-suited classroom furniture (which we would disguise in various fashions); wearing whatever stage costumes the Pitt theater arts department was not using for its productions (or that we could scavenge out of personal wardrobes); drawing elements of a desirable scenery on the long blackboard, which usually runs the length of one of the classroom's walls; and working under other, similar constraints. This particular course has been designed bearing in mind precisely the sort of limitations against which teachers, especially those working in small foreign language departments, may run up against, but it has also been planned so as to spur inventiveness and avoid the diffidence and reluctance with which many a student would regard his or her participation in more ambitious theatrical projects.

The program of the final recital usually includes (1) the students' production of an existing short play (or excerpts of a full-length play), (2) the students' stage adaptation of a narrative piece, and (3) the students' own play.[45] It is important that the latter be something to which every student enrolled in the class may contribute and each student in the audience may relate. One particular class assignment has proved helpful in assisting and inspiring the students in the creation of their original piece. In the course of the workshop, besides improvising and writing dialogues, students are also asked to practice the form of the monologue, which they inevitably encounter in reading drama. A variety of subjects and situations may be suggested to the students when directing them to create their own soliloquies, but familiar ones always work better.

The first time the course was offered, in 1998, the students were asked to write a monologue in which they articulated the thoughts of a person taking a bus ride. The students of the 2000 class were asked, instead, to think of an "exam situation" and write a monologue in which they articulated the thoughts of a character/student taking an Italian exam. Finally, the members of the 2002 class, all of whom had experienced the excitement and perils of traveling abroad, were instructed to think of an "Italian train scene" and write a monologue in which they expressed the thoughts of someone taking a train ride in Italy. In all three classes, when time came to design an original project to include in the program of the final recital, the majority of the students felt more comfortable working with real-life situations, such as the ones that had served as contexts to the monologues created earlier in the course.

Thus, once those monologues had undergone the review process, the students worked in groups at making a comprehensive text out of them, combining, juxtaposing, timing the individual speeches, and finally producing a sort of "verbal score." In fact, in two classes mini-plays were produced in which the students represented common people on a city bus (*Sinfonia d'autobus*) and students in a classroom (*Sotto esame*). All the characters involved in these plays were created as thinking out loud, with two, three, sometimes more characters expressing their thoughts simultaneously, creating the verbal equivalent of symphonic pieces. In the third class's original piece (*Sette personaggi in cerca di una carrozza vuota*), the monologues relating to travel, which the students had earlier produced, were utilized but inserted in a more traditional fabric of communication, as seven characters were invented who boarded the same train, took their seats in the same car, and struck up various bits of conversation until they had to leave (upon learning of a general rail workers' strike).

## Latest Developments

Different procedures were followed in the 2004 workshop. Rather than a traditional existing stage play, one of Dario Fo and Franca Rame's television sketches was extensively rewritten and produced by the students. The participants also applied themselves to the adaptation and, again, extensive rewriting of a novel and created a one-act play out of various parts of it. Like students in preceding workshops, they also worked at creating monologues, but they transformed them into monodramas, which they individually rehearsed/performed in front of the class and then individually videorecorded in the language lab.

Fo and Rame wrote *Il figlio in provetta* in 1988 and performed it for the Italian television audience as a segment of a show they had created that year for RAI 3 (one of the three state-run Italian television networks). Departing from Fo and Rame's work, the piece my students created (titled *Telesalotto*) took the form of one particular episode of a hypothetical talk show. The students adapted and modified the text to include more than the two original characters in order to each have a part and to elaborate—in a fashion consistent with the farcical nature of the original—on the subject of the sketch. In their play a talk-show host, a doctor, two couples, and a small but lively television audience (consisting of three or four students who sat amidst, but unbeknownst to, the actual public audience) come together to debate the topic of the day: artificial insemination or in vitro fertilization. The couples discussed the issue with each other, responded to the questions that the host or the characters/members of the audience asked of them, and reacted to the scientific information that the doctor supplied. The increasingly lively exchange, just like in Fo and Rame's piece, was aimed at revealing many of the prejudices and taboos still present in our society. While claiming to be open-minded and forward-thinking, for example, the characters of the husbands (both northern Italians) were aghast when considering the possibility that the donor and natural father of their children might be an African immigrant or a man of southern Italian origin.

The second part of the recital consisted in the students' adaptation of parts of Ignazio Silone's *Vino e pane*. I briefly introduced the novel to them and asked them to read carefully Chapter 13 and annotate their individual copies of the text in preparation for group and class discussion. The chapter covers several days in the spring of 1936 in the life of the poor peasants of Pietrasecca, a small village in the Abruzzo region, where the protagonist of the novel, a socialist intellectual wanted by the Fascist police, has taken refuge disguised as a priest. Two separate incidents are featured in this chapter that highlight the relationship of the protagonist of the novel, the anti-Fascist in hiding Pietro Spina, and the village school mistress, the ardent Fascist Signorina Petrignani, with the ignorant *cafoni,* while focusing the reader's attention on the direness of their situation. Students were charged with the task of identifying the chapter's two salient events and thinking of ways to merge such events and work out all relevant narrative material theatrically. After a number of ideas were aired in class, each student wrote in full one of two scenes that we had all agreed should capture the essence of that particular chapter and the spirit of the characters concerned. The students' various versions of the two scenes were shared, compared, and discussed in class, in order to find common ground and make a final collective decision on the components of the created play: the setting, that is, the organization and furnishing of the space; the distribution and timing of lines of speech that in the narrative are assigned to unidentified voices or to the collective voice of the peasants; the smooth transition from one scene to the other; and the number, age, appearance, personality traits, movements, gestures, lines, and mode of delivery of the various characters, etc. A group of the students also did research on the more important characters by reading other chapters of the novel and finding extra material for the portrayal of these characters and their interactions. Other students did research on Italian history and the conditions of rural southern Italy at the time and found original documents from the Fascist era whose language could be incorporated in the play as part of the school mistress's empty political rhetoric.

## Conclusions

All of the tasks that the students perform in the theater practicum described in this chapter involve writing, reading, recording, listening to, discussing, negotiating, critiquing, and even miming in Italian. All of the activities of this class, from the very first warm-up exercises to the rehearsals and final recital, are devised to compel all students to participate and to allow everybody to shine.[46] They reflect and try to accommodate the wide range of learning modalities of our students with an equally wide variety of strategies, sequenced so as to help each student improve in every language function and achieve a certain degree of familiarity with and appreciation for the inner workings of the literary text. The course improves the students' ability to interact effectively in the target language as well as to read some of its literary treasures discerningly. Though other strategies exist, and perhaps better ones can yet be found to introduce students of Italian to literary analysis and literary and cultural history while helping them to master the language, this detailed account of the procedures adopted in my workshop was meant to show how fruitful they can be, what cultural immersion they can provide, and what kind of output they can generate at a very crucial stage in our students' learning.

## Notes

1. This chapter is a much revised and expanded version of an article published a few years ago. Changes have been made to reflect the additional knowledge and experience I gained in teaching four more times the course discussed in the essay, as well as in having fruitful dialogue with colleagues who have similarly integrated drama in the Italian curriculum at their institutions. See Savoia, "Teaching Italian Language."
2. Robert J. Di Pietro was among the first to address this subject in *Strategic Interaction,* 109–110.
3. Hinkel, ed., *Culture in Second Language Teaching,* 2.
4. For a description of these standards, see June K. Phillips's introductory remarks in *Foreign Language Standards,* 1–14.
5. University of Pittsburgh Dean of Arts and Sciences' *Report on the Curriculum Review Process* of April 2001, online at http://www.fcas.pitt .edu/deanmemo/curriculum.html (accessed April 2001).
6. Besides the above-mentioned seminal study by Di Pietro, see Rivers, ed., *Interactive Language Teaching* and Richard-Amato, *Making It Happen.*
7. For models and methods of Content-Based Instruction (CBI) at various levels of proficiency as well as examples of Foreign Language across the Curriculum (FLAC) programs, see Stryker and Leaver, eds., *Content-Based Foreign Language Education.* It goes without saying that, by granting increasingly easy access to up-to-date written or visual and audiovisual cultural documents, new technology and the Internet have

greatly aided foreign language teachers in the introduction of authentic material in their classrooms.

8. For a historical overview of the literary text in the language curriculum, see Schultz, "The Gordian Knot," 3–6. See also Sieloff Magnan, "Rediscovering Text."

9. Whiteson, ed., *New Ways*, vii.

10. Mayer, "Variation on the Scenario," 363.

11. See, for example, Gillian Lazar's guide for teachers and trainers, *Literature and Language Teaching*, and Whiteson, ed., *New Ways*. The latter contains many clearly illustrated activities involving prose, poetry, and drama, designed for teachers of English to speakers of other languages but easily adaptable to other second language classrooms.

12. I have been impressed by some of the Italian readers recently compiled for advanced beginning and intermediate students, such as Berri and Giansiracusa, *In giro per la letteratura;* Jacobsen and Bellezza, *Il reale e il possibile;* and Fedi and Fasoli, *Mercurio.* The latter is for more advanced students of Italian and adopts good strategies for developing students' interpretive abilities through a variety of literary and nonliterary texts and comprehension exercises.

13. Carter and McRae, eds., *Language, Literature and the Learner,* xx–xxi. Along with Christopher Brumfit, Ronald Carter also edited one of the first collections of essays to address the need of integrating literature and language study: *Literature and Language Teaching.* Among the most recent contributions to the subject are the essays collected in Scott and Tucker, eds., *SLA and the Literature Classroom.*

14. Carter and McRae, eds., *Language, Literature and the Learner,* xxi. What Carter and McRae suggest is that a good amount of "irreverence" in the treatment of literary texts in the classroom may prove not only useful but pedagogically necessary. This kind of irreverence, in dealing with literature, has made its way also into Italian textbooks. One good early example was Gloria Paganini, *Issimo. Quaderno di scrittura, livello avanzato,* an advanced manual full of creative and stimulating activities in writing, most often involving the free manipulation of literary texts. About the teaching of Italian literature to speakers of English, see the essays featured in Picchione and Pietropaolo, eds., *Italian Literature in North America.*

15. See Haggstrom, "A Performative Approach," and, more recently, Frantzen, "Rethinking Foreign Language Literature."

16. For the quotations in this paragraph, see Sieloff Magnan, "Rediscovering Text," 96–97.

17. See Byrnes and Kord, "Developing Literacy and Literary Competence."

18. This situation has remained constant over the twenty years that I have been working at the University of Pittsburgh, and there is no sure

indication that it will change in the near future despite the fact that, nationwide, the teaching of Italian in secondary schools is presently expanding.

19. Between first and final drafts, the various writing assignments involved in the theatrical workshop do amount to the required twenty to twenty-five pages of written work per student.

20. Among the studies conducted in the 1980s, besides Di Pietro, see Livingstone, *Role Playing in Language Learning;* Via, "The Magic 'If' of Theater"; and Richard-Amato, *Making It Happen,* 172–191. See Smith, *The Theater Arts;* Lazar, *Literature and Language Teaching,* 133–166. Some of the articles I read in preparation for my first theatrical workshop (Fall 1998) are, in chronological order: Maldaner, "Théâtre et l'enseignement du français"; Semke, "German Café-Theater"; Lederer, "The Play's the Thing"; Vetter, "Second Language Learning through Puppetry"; Hoyt, "Many Ways of Knowing"; Ronke, "Theaterspielen als Didaktisches Mittel im Fremdsprachen-unterricht"; Albert, "Drama in the Classroom"; and Essif, "Way Off Broadway."

21. Savoia and Scaramuzzino, eds., *Tutti giù dal palco.* The text of the ministerial notices mentioned above (the 1995 *Protocollo d'intesa relativo alla educazione al teatro* and the 1997 *Protocollo d'intesa per l'educazione alle discipline dello spettacolo*), as well as a wealth of other documents pertaining to various applications of theater and performance to education, can be found on AGITA's Web page: http://www.agitateatro.it.

22. Haggstrom, "A Performative Approach," 7.

23. See the chapter "Common Principles: Parallels between the Theater Arts and Language Learning and Teaching" in Smith, *The Theater Arts.* See also Pavanello, *Giochi teatrali con la lettura,* 13.

24. Essif, "(Re-)Creating the Critique," 119–120.

25. Barthes, *S/Z,* 10.

26. It is worth noting that, while the first meaning of the word *interpreter* is "an individual who explains or expounds," the term refers to someone who translates (for parties conversing) in different tongues and, in the Italian language, also to an actor playing a part (or a musician playing a piece).

27. For details on the course policies and grading system, see note 15 in Savoia, "Teaching Italian Language," 518–519.

28. Such as Gallarini, *Palcoscenico e dintorni,* and Magnani, *Comunicare a teatro.*

29. Roberto Pavanello calls this first exploration of the texts through the physical means of the voice, a rising of the words to life "una sua risurrezione tridimensionale fatta di voci, di suoni, di dialoghi, di cambi di tono e di volume, di pause sapienti." *Giochi teatrali con la lettura,* 21.

30. See Agar and Di Pietro, *The Sounds of English and Italian,* and Svolac-chia and Kauzner, *Suoni, accento e intonazione,* xvii.

31. See Ekman and Friesen, "The Repertoire of Nonverbal Behavior."

32. Gian Giacomo Colli writes, quite compellingly, about utilizing the practices of theater to sensitize and educate students to gestural expressiveness. See his recent article "Il corpo che parla."

33. For our exercises, we have selected the following poems: the initial *terzine* of Dante's *Inferno:* canto XIII; Petrarch's "Pace non trovo e non ho da far guerra"; Tasso's "Ecco mormorar l'onde"; Pascoli's "L'ora di Barga" and "L'assiuolo"; D'Annunzio's "La pioggia nel pineto" and "La sera fiesolana"; Marinetti's "Sì, sì, così l'aurora sul mare"; Palazzeschi's "La fontana"; Ungaretti's "Sono una creatura"; Montale's "Spesso il male di vivere" and "Clivo"; Campana's "Navi amarrate"; Caproni's "Questo odore marino"; and any of Sanguineti's poems in "Alfabeto apocalittico." See also Savoia and Scaramuzzino, *Tutti giù dal palco,* 59–61.

34. See Pavanello, *Giochi teatrali con la lettura,* 34–35.

35. Poems such as the already mentioned "L'ora di Barga" by Pascoli, "La sera fiesolana" by D'Annunzio, or "Una sera come tante" by Giovanni Giudici (from *La vita in versi*) and "Piangi piangi che ti compero una lunga spada" by Edoardo Sanguineti (from *Purgatorio de l'Inferno*) involve exact repetitions of one line, at regular intervals, and/or veritable refrains, which make them suitable for this kind of reading. A very interesting activity, "choral chant," involving collective reading of folktales, fairy tales, and short stories, has been designed by Geraldine Hetherton for English as a foreign language. See Whiteson, *New Ways,* 144–145.

36. Texts that students have been asked to annotate, study, read aloud, and record, practicing these various ways of reading, include various folktales from the collection *Fiabe italiane* edited by Calvino; *novelle* from day VI of Boccaccio's *Decameron* or from Francesco Sacchetti's *Trecentonovelle;* excerpts from early chapters of Manzoni's *I promessi sposi;* Verga's "Cavalleria rusticana"; and short stories from Calvino's *Marcovaldo* and *Apologhi e racconti.*

37. Much in the way it is suggested by Kenneth Berri and Elisabeth Lee Giansiracusa in the preliminary chapter of *In giro per la letteratura.*

38. Similar exercises have been created by Linda Butler ("Using Borrowed Lines") and Geraldine Hetherton ("Poetic Slips"). See Whiteson, *New Ways,* 66–67 and 69–70.

39. On "subtext," see Savoia and Scaramuzzino, *Tutti giù dal palco,* 77–79.

40. This exercise is described by Courally, "Faire parler les bruits."

41. Barker and Harrigan, *Introduction to Performance,* 41–59.

42. Various narrative texts, and other texts in prose, have been adapted and performed with success by the students of the workshop: short stories by Achille Campanile, Federigo Tozzi, Dino Buzzati, Carlo Castellaneta, and Italo Calvino; chapters from Ignazio Silone's novel *Vino e pane;* and even essays by Natalia Ginzburg. Similar types of charts or *schede* can be found in Pavanello, *Giochi teatrali con la scrittura,* 52–53.

43. Ibid., 51.

44. Marni Baker and Khatarine Ishell created an activity for the English as a second language classroom that requires students to read the same short two-person scene various times, assuming a different social status each time (and therefore a different tone, body language, etc.). See Whiteson, *New Ways,* 92–93.

45. For example, a slightly modified version of *Il problema dei vecchi* (a short one-act play, written some sixty years ago, rediscovered by Franca Rame and Dario Fo and performed as part of one of twenty episodes of the short-lived weekly TV show "Buonasera con Franca Rame") and a very much "condensed" version of Pirandello's *Così è (se vi pare)* (in which the sequence of events, as it unfolds in the original play, was changed, among other things, to accommodate one student's playing the role both of Signor Ponza and of Laudisi) were staged successfully by the first and third group of students that I directed in the theatrical workshop. For the students' stage adaptation of a narrative piece, the following anecdote is worth relating. A story I read with the very first group of students who attended the workshop was "La stessa donna" by Federigo Tozzi. It begins when two friends, Felice and Raffaello, see each other again after a three-year hiatus. It is immediately apparent that their friendship has suffered from the separation. In fact, in the course of what is, at times, a very difficult and awkward conversation, the two realize that they both have loved deeply and have been mercilessly abandoned by the same woman. They decide to assemble everything they have ever received from the woman (letters, portraits, small gifts) and burn them. As they execute their plan, however, they understand that their relationship is irreparably damaged. A great deal of discussion followed the reading of this story in our class: many students argued that one or both of the friends knew or suspected the truth. The ending also puzzled some, and the female students in the class felt that the story was very much a "male" story, with a "male" ending. When asked to adapt this narrative for the stage, the students then came up with two different versions of it (different both from the original and from each other), and we decided to stage them both, presenting them to the public back to back.

46. In 2000, when sixteen students, of quite different backgrounds and

at different levels of preparation in Italian, enrolled in the theatrical workshop, poetry reading was included in the program of the final recital as a way to give everybody the opportunity to showcase some of the work he or she had done. Those who could not master any of the performing roles were also put in charge of introducing the various parts of the program to the public (in Italian) and furnishing English translations of some of the poems being recited (for the less Italian-proficient spectator to read, alongside the original text).

## Bibliography

Agar, Frederick B., and Robert J. Di Pietro. *The Sounds of English and Italian*. Chicago: University of Chicago Press, 1965.

Albert, Eleanor. "Drama in the Classroom." *Middle School Journal* 5 (1994): 20–24.

Barker, Sarah, and Peter Harrigan. *Introduction to Performance: Beginning the Creative Process of the Actor*. Dubuque, IA: Kendall/Hunt, 1997.

Barthes, Roland. *S/Z*. Paris: Seuil, 1970.

Berri, Kenneth, and Elisabeth Lee Giansiracusa. *In giro per la letteratura: Scrivere e leggere nei corsi intermedi d'italiano*. Boston: Heinle & Heinle, 1996.

Brumfit, Christopher, and Ronald Carter, eds. *Literature and Language Teaching*. Oxford: Oxford University Press, 1986.

Byrnes, Heidi, and Susanne Kord. "Developing Literacy and Literary Competence: Challenges for Foreign Language Departments." In *SLA and the Literature Classroom: Fostering Dialogues*, 35–62, edited by Virginia M. Scott and Holly Tucker. Boston: Heinle & Heinle, 2001.

Carter, Ronald, and John McRae, eds. *Language, Literature and the Learner: Creative Classroom Practice*. New York: Longman, 1996.

Colli, Gian Giacomo. "Il corpo che parla: la gestualità e l'italiano fra tradizione teatrale e didattica della lingua." *Italica* 4 (2004): 536–550.

Colussi-Arthur, Gabriella, and Frank Nuessel. "Elementary and Intermediate Italian Readers: A North American Perspective." *Italica* 4 (1998): 564–588.

Courally, Sylvie. "Faire parler les bruits." *Français dans le Monde* 260 (1993): iii–iv.

Di Pietro, Robert J. *Strategic Interaction: Learning Languages through Scenarios*. Cambridge: Cambridge University Press, 1987.

Ekman, Paul, and Wallace V. Friesen. "The Repertoire of Nonverbal Behavior: Categories, Origins, Usage, and Coding." *Semiotica* 1 (1969): 49–98.

Essif, Les. "Way Off Broadway and Way Out of the Classroom: American Students De-, Re-, and Per-forming the French Dramatic Text." *ADFL Bulletin* 1 (1995): 32–37.

————. "(Re-)Creating the Critique: In(tro)ducing the Semiotics of Theatre in the Foreign-Language Performance Project." *Theatre Topics* 2 (2002): 119–142.

Fedi, Andrea, and Paolo Fasoli. *Mercurio: An Intermediate to Advanced Reader in Italian Language and Culture.* New Haven, CT: Yale University Press, 2004.

Frantzen, Diana. "Rethinking Foreign Language Literature: Towards an Integration of Literature and Language at All Levels." In *SLA and the Literature Classroom: Fostering Dialogues,* 109–130, edited by Virginia M. Scott and Holly Tucker. Boston: Heinle & Heinle, 2001.

Gallarini, Cesare. *Palcoscenico e dintorni. Manuale di esercizi teatrali.* Milan: Mursia, 1992.

Galvez-Touzet, Teresa. "El professor de idiomas: el teatro, los titeros y los sketches." Thesis, Universitad Nacional de Trujillo (Peru), 1977.

Haggstrom, Margaret A. "A Performative Approach to the Study of Theater: Bridging the Gap between Language and Literature Courses." *French Review* 1 (1992): 7–19.

Hinkel, Eli, ed. *Culture in Second Language Teaching and Learning.* Cambridge: Cambridge University Press, 1999.

Hoyt, Linda. "Many Ways of Knowing: Using Drama, Oral Interaction, and Visual Arts to Enhance Reading Comprehension." *Reading Teacher* 8 (1992): 580–584.

Jacobsen, Mara Mauri, and Anna Maria Bellezza. *Il reale e il possibile.* Fort Worth, TX: Holt, Rinehart and Winston, 1999.

Lazar, Gillian. *Literature and Language Teaching: A Guide for Teachers and Trainers.* Cambridge: Cambridge University Press, 1993.

Lederer, Herbert. "The Play's the Thing: The Use of Theater in Language Learning." *Studies in Language Learning* 2 (1981): 35–41.

Livingstone, Carol. *Role Playing in Language Learning.* Harlow, UK: Longman, 1983.

Magnani, Silvia. *Comunicare a teatro.* Turin: Omega Edizioni, 1991.

Maldaner, Aurea. "Théâtre et l'enseignement du français, langue étrangère." *Français dans le Monde* 155 (1980): 35–37.

Mayer, Virginia. "Variation on the Scenario: Cooperative and Critical Thinking in the Literature-Based Classroom." In *Strategic Interaction and Language Acquisition: Theory, Practice, and Research,* 363–371, edited by James E. Alatis. Washington, DC: Georgetown University Press, 1993.

Paganini, Gloria. *Issimo. Quaderno di scrittura, livello avanzato.* Rome: Bonacci, 1994.

Pavanello, Roberto. *Giochi teatrali con la lettura. Giochi teatrali con la scrittura. Giochi teatrali con l'oralità.* Milan: San Fedele Edizioni, 1995–1996.

Phillips, June K., ed. *Foreign Language Standards: Linking Research, Theory, and Practices.* Lincolnwood, IL: National Textbook Co., 1999.

Picchione, John, and Laura Pietropaolo, eds. *Italian Literature in North America: Pedagogical Strategies.* Biblioteca di Quaderni d'Italianistica. Vol. 9. Ottawa: Canadian Society for Italian Studies, 1990.

Richard-Amato, Patricia. *Making It Happen. Interaction in the Second Language Classroom. From Theory to Practice.* New York: Longman, 1996.

Rivers, Wilga, ed. *Interactive Language Teaching.* Cambridge: Cambridge University Press, 1987.

Ronke, Astrid. "Theaterspielen als Didaktisches Mittel im Fremdsprachenunterricht: Ergebnisse einer Umfrage an Amerikanischen und Kanadischen Universitaten und Colleges." *Unterrichtspraxis* 2 (1993): 211–219.

Savoia, Francesca. "Teaching Italian Language, Literature and Culture through Performance: The Italian Theatrical Workshop." *Italica* 4 (2000): 509–520.

Savoia, Marina, and Giorgio Scaramuzzino. *Tutti giù dal palco. Fare teatro a scuola dalla materna alle medie.* Rev. ed. Florence: Salani, 2005.

Schultz, Jean Marie. "The Gordian Knot: Language, Literature, and Critical Thinking." In *SLA and the Literature Classroom: Fostering Dialogues,* 3–31, edited by Virginia M. Scott and Holly Tucker. Boston: Heinle & Heinle, 2001.

Scott, Virginia, and Holly Tucker, eds. *SLA and the Literature Classroom: Fostering Dialogues.* Boston: Heinle & Heinle, 2001.

Semke, Harriet D. "German Café-Theater: A Venture in Experiential Learning." *Foreign Language Annals* 2 (1980): 137–138.

Sieloff Magnan, Sally. "Rediscovering Text: Multiple Stories for Language Departments." *Profession 2004.* New York: MLA (2004): 95–106.

Smith, Stephen M. *The Theater Arts and the Teaching of Second Languages.* Reading, MA: Addison-Wesley, 1984.

Stryker, Stephen E., and Betty Lou Leaver, eds. *Content-Based Foreign Language Education: Models and Methods.* Washington, DC: Georgetown University Press, 1997.

Svolacchia, Marco, and Ulrike A. Kauzner. *Suoni, accento e intonazione. Corso di ascolto e pronuncia.* Rome: Bonacci, 2000.

Vetter, Ronald M. "Second Language Learning through Puppetry." *Guidelines* 2 (1991): 57–67.

Via, Richard. "The Magic 'If' of Theater: Enhancing Language Learning through Drama." In *Interactive Language Teaching,* 110–123, edited by Wilga Rivers. Cambridge: Cambridge University Press, 1987.

Whiteson, Valerie, ed. *New Ways of Using Drama and Literature in Language Teaching.* New Ways in TESOL Series II. Bloomington, IL: Pantagraph, 1996.

# CHAPTER 5

# Theater Texts and Techniques in the High School Classroom

LAURA COLANGELO AND
COLLEEN RYAN-SCHEUTZ

Full-scale theater productions and theater-based courses constitute a vibrant part of the foreign language programs in many universities. But is this a valid model for the high school level, where school, state, and national assessment criteria drive curricula and where classes are composed of students with a wide range of intellectual and motivational levels? This chapter will explore techniques for using theatrical texts to provide high school students with rich and meaningful encounters with literature. A theatrical text can form a basis for activities that cater to a variety of learning styles, while successfully implementing the national standards established by the American Council on the Teaching of Foreign Languages (ACTFL) (known as the five Cs of foreign language education for *communication, culture, connections, comparisons,* and *communities*). Furthermore, the creative implementation of dramatic literature can serve as an effective framework for the advanced placement (AP) Italian language and culture course.

## Foreign Language Theatrical Productions and Multiple Intelligences Theory

Perhaps the greatest advantage of theatrical texts is that a creative instructor can easily use these authentic pieces of literature to cater to the range of student learning styles present in any classroom. Moreover, by requiring students to converse only in Italian when completing any task related to the script, the teacher can create an "immersion" environment to give students ample opportunity for realistic communication.[1] In this type of learning environment, logically oriented students are drawn to tasks such as organizing schedules, props, and costume elements, whereas visual learners enjoy creating the "living picture" of the set. And while this attention to diversity of learning styles is useful on the college level, it is even more essential in the extremely heterogeneous high school classroom. After all, college students have already begun to specialize in certain fields; the engineer is oriented toward math courses while students of language classes may have a natural affinity for verbal and written communication. The high school classroom, on the other hand, is not specialized and includes students with diverse interests as well as diverse levels of motivation. Thus, it is extremely important for high school teachers to pursue techniques that will make learning enjoyable and effective for all types of students.

The past decades have seen a shift in educational methodology based partially on the ideas of multiple intelligences theory pioneer and Harvard psychologist Howard Gardner. His seven intelligences are now well-known and widely accepted in the educational community, which continually strives to employ highly varied teaching methods in order to correspond to the diversity of learning styles one finds in most classes. A look at the seven categories of intelligence that Gardner defines in his 1983 landmark book *Frames of Mind: The Theory of Multiple Intelligences* reveals that dramatic literature naturally incorporates all of the seven intelligence areas.

Dissatisfied with standard test–based measures of intelligence such as IQ tests and SATs, Gardner and his colleagues drew from cognitive science and neuroscience to fashion a new way of looking at the issue. They examined a variety of populations, including people considered "gifted" in the traditional sense, individuals with brain damage, prodigies, and autistic children. They studied psychological tests, cross-cultural accounts of cognition, and data regarding cognition from the last millennium. In *Frames of Mind*, Gardner proposed seven intelligence categories that encompass far more than the traditional linguistic and mathematical abilities measured by standardized tests and still emphasized in the classroom.

Each proposed category meets rigorous standards in order to be accepted as a legitimate intelligence.[2] Each type of intelligence is controlled by a precise area of the brain. Linguistic intelligence, for example, is controlled by the left temporal and frontal lobes of the brain. Those with injuries to this portion of the brain demonstrate impaired linguistic abilities but can still accomplish other tasks such as understanding musical rhythm, dancing, relating to others, and reflecting on their own lives. Each intelligence has a distinct developmental sequence, starting at a certain age and tending to peak at another stage in life. Some people are prodigies in particular areas: Albert Einstein in mathematics, for example, or Beethoven in music. Each intelligence has roots in the evolution of humans as well as other species. In addition, each has a particular symbol system, from musical notation to computer languages to social cues. The distinctions between the intelligences are also supported by experimental psychological tasks and findings from psychometric tests and assessment measures.

## Gardner's Seven Intelligences

- *Linguistic intelligence.*[3] Gardner includes in his definition of linguistic intelligence a sensitivity to the meaning and order of words and the capacity to follow rules of grammar. Those with linguistic intelligence have little difficulty explaining information to others and are often adept at using rhetoric in a convincing manner, as politicians and lawyers do. They often employ mnemonic techniques such as lists and written notes in order to remember information.

- *Logical-mathematical intelligence.* A talent for understanding abstract concepts and patterns characterizes those with a strong logical-mathematical intelligence. They can skillfully handle long chains of reasoning, using theories to derive valid results. Ordering information or otherwise framing it in such a way as to emphasize patterns is helpful to learners with strengths in this area.

- *Musical intelligence.* Those with musical intelligence are particularly sensitive to basic musical principles such as rhythm, pitch, dissonance, and harmony. They find it easy to understand and create music. Remembering information becomes simpler for a musically inclined student when it can be set into rhythmic patterns or tied to particular songs or chords.

- *Spatial intelligence.* Those with strengths in spatial intelligence can accurately perceive the visual world and re-create certain aspects of what they see even without the original image before them. Because of their attention to the appearance of the physical world and their ability to re-create it in the mind or on paper, spatially oriented people are often artists, architects, and designers. Such people learn best through images and manipulation of actual physical materials.

- *Bodily-kinesthetic intelligence.* The ability to control one's bodily movements and to skillfully handle objects are attributes of those who possess bodily-kinesthetic intelligence. Such people often excel at activities such as taking objects apart and putting them back together, miming or acting, playing sports, inventing, navigating, and dancing.

- *Interpersonal intelligence.* Those with interpersonal intelligence can easily "read" other people, inferring from their facial expressions, gestures, and voices their inner feelings, motivations, or moods. Such people often excel at persuading and managing (politicians, directors, managers) while others use their skills to help people relate to themselves and to the greater community (therapists or teachers, for example).

- *Intrapersonal intelligence.* This intelligence centers on self-knowledge. One who has self-discipline and self-understanding exhibits this intelligence. Intrapersonal learners are aware of their inner moods, sensitive to their own strengths and weaknesses, and observant of their motivations, desires, and intentions. As learners, they often prefer working alone over working in groups, and enjoy activities that allow them to connect the material being studied to their own lives.

Gardner also noted that individuals exhibit proficiency in more than one intelligence area. A mathematically inclined scientist, for example, needs a solid grasp of language in order to express his or her findings to others through a journal article. A dancer clearly possesses both musical and kinesthetic intelligence. Musicians need a sense of mathematical intelligence to navigate between the various numerical relationships that govern rhythmic patterns and chord compositions. Furthermore, every person has the capacity to actively nurture various kinds of intelligence. Thus the strong musical learner can expand upon his or her musical skills but also use these skills as a tool to better understand linguistic or kinesthetic concepts. This idea of using one's natural areas of strength to improve upon areas of weakness is precisely why the use of theater in the foreign language classroom works so well.

## Full-Scale Theatrical Productions

The nuts and bolts of putting on a full-scale show are discussed elsewhere in this book, and such a production at the high school level is undeniably a worthy goal. However, the high school teacher faces a few technical challenges that are not present at the university level. Before trying to produce a full-scale play with a high school–level class, the instructor needs to consider several factors.

*Class size and composition.* A college instructor has the flexibility to limit the size of the class and audition possible participants, but a high school teacher must involve every student enrolled in the course. Since high school classes tend to have upwards of twenty students, the teacher must choose a large-cast play. Even with a design team (costumes, set, sound, publicity) and a stage manager, the teacher needs plays with large casts, which can be difficult to find.[4]

*Time.* A full-scale production of even a short one-act play in a high school Italian classroom requires at least forty hours of pure rehearsal time, which amounts to more than two months, assuming that the class meets every day for one hour. Beyond the rehearsal time itself, a full-scale production works best when the teacher plans additional enrichment activities such as vocabulary games, comprehension quizzes, character analyses, presentations by designers of costumes and set, and historical and cultural information sessions. All told, then, the high school teacher would likely have to commit about half of the school year to the production. This might not be possible, given that Italian classes at the high school level generally follow a traditional sequence (Italian I, II, III, and IV) in which particular grammatical concepts are taught at specific points. If a full-scale production is a major component of the course, it will be difficult to adhere to this sequence. It is impossible, for example, to find a play in which Act 1 features only the present tense, Act 2 debuts direct object pronouns, Act 3 introduces irregular adjectives, and so forth. While perhaps not practical in the regular classroom, however, the theater immersion project could be offered as an extracurricular activity after or before school.

*Resources.* The availability of a theatrical venue as well as funding for costumes, props, sound effects, and lighting equipment may be limited for the high school teacher. These are not, however, insurmountable difficulties. The teacher and class might work together to generate and implement ideas for fund-raisers. Costumes and props may be borrowed from the school's drama department, or students may find needed items at the homes of family members or friends. To make the production as "professional" as possible (thus increasing students' sense of pride and "ownership" for the project), it would be ideal to secure the school's auditorium for the date of the show. Drama students may be willing to assist with the show's sound and lighting needs. An instructor who manages to address challenges like class size and rehearsal time might find the technical aspects of putting on a production less difficult.

*Varied levels of commitment.* The biggest challenge in the high school setting is perhaps the diverse array of commitment levels among the students. At a university or college, the organization of the academic year into semesters or trimesters and the variety of classes offered give students much flexibility in course selection. The full-immersion theatrical course is just one of many options, and the students who select it have done so for a reason: they are interested in the very specific process of putting on a play as a means for learning a foreign language. They tend to be enthusiastic and committed to the success of the endeavor.

In a typical high school setting, however, the situation is much different. Most schools do not have the luxury of offering Italian courses that focus on a single genre. Rather, students usually follow the traditional I, II, III, IV language sequence mentioned above. Thus a high school Italian class is composed of students who have chosen to study Italian, but they have not necessarily chosen to learn it by means of producing a play. The high school teacher who attempts a full-scale production may encounter much resistance, both from students who do not want to put on a play and from those who are uninterested in school entirely.

One might argue that student resistance to activities is sometimes an unavoidable part of the job of teaching. Students often complain about almost any task assigned to them, from taking tests, to writing compositions, to making presentations. What makes students' disinterest in producing a show different from their resistance to these other activities? The answer lies in the essential community component of the experience. A student may not prepare adequately for a test, but his or her poor performance will not affect the rest of the class. Likewise, students who put together a disappointing individual oral presentation might, at worst, bore their peers for a few minutes, but this will not significantly affect their overall learning experience. For a theatrical production, however, the full commitment of *all* participants is imperative to the success of each individual. In other words, a show is only as good as its weakest link. A student who is uninterested and refuses to commit to the project has a large effect on the rest of the class's ability to gain from the experience.

Therefore, on the high school level, before deciding to base a course entirely around one full-scale production of a text, the teacher should assess the makeup of the class and determine whether the majority of students would be enthusiastic about putting on a show. For certain groups of students, it may be more beneficial to base the course on a work of dramatic literature without putting on a full-scale production, varying the types of activities assigned in order to hold the interest of as many students as possible.

## Theatrical Text Work without a Full-Scale Production

If your class size, time, resources, and commitment level allow for the possibility of a full-scale production . . . congratulations! You will be engaging in an exhilarating language teaching experience. Though the chapters of this book tend to focus on the university classroom, you will find them equally useful for a group of committed high school students.

If a full-scale production is not immediately feasible, however, there is no need to worry; works of dramatic literature will nonetheless prove themselves invaluable texts for your classroom. An intense study of one text over the course of half a year, with a variety of text-based activities interspersed between the normal daily lessons, is a highly enriching way to structure a course.

The following activities are organized into four categories: (1) basic read, (2) production-related activities, (3) writing-based assignments, and (4) exploratory character work. The activities are designed to target different learning styles while encouraging creative and in-depth analysis of the piece.

## *Basic Read*

The first step in engaging students in a foreign language theater text is to have them read through the play slowly and carefully. For a language teacher, it is easy to lose sight of how difficult and frustrating this process can be for students. After all, beginning language learners start out their literary pursuits with short passages, articles, and sometimes simplified readers. It is likely that the script will not only be their first exposure to a genuinely long piece of literature, but will also be the first time that they read a piece that doesn't have footnotes and English translations of the more difficult words. It will also likely expose them to the occasional verb tense or part of speech that they have not yet encountered in their introductory textbook. Some techniques for easing students into reading include the following:

- Proceed slowly, asking students to read no more than three to four pages each night.

- Before students read each section, select about five difficult words to preview with vocabulary games. Do not merely give a list of definitions (though you should engage students in compiling a master list for review later on); rather, make sure that the students can work with the words in other contexts *before* they see them in the script. Do not point out the words' locations in the text in advance; let the students make this discovery for themselves as they read through the passage.

- Incorporate comprehension quizzes at intervals that are appropriate for your students. Some classes may respond best knowing that they will be quizzed after each section, while others may be fine with two or three quizzes in total. Use a variety of input and output activities, and focus on characters, plot, and vocabulary. An example of a comprehension quiz is provided at the end of this chapter. You can also vary your testing format and practice different skills by creating oral, as well as written, quizzes.

- Check comprehension regularly by holding question-and-answer sessions. By leading these sessions yourself, you will be able to determine whether students understood key concepts as they were reading the piece on their own. Alternatively, you might ask a student or small group of students to formulate the questions for the day's session, giving each pupil a chance to demonstrate his or her perception of the text. Or you may prefer to require that every member of the class come up with one or two questions each day, from which you can then select a few upon which to base a brief discussion.

## *Production-Related Activities*

Even if the class will not ultimately perform the play before an audience, engaging them in production-related activities such as designing sets and costumes, performing scenes, and selecting songs for a soundtrack will appeal to almost all of Gardner's multiple intelligences. Linguistically strong students will enjoy the close reading of the text that these activities involve, while spatially oriented students will be stimulated by the task of imagining scenery and costumes. Students with strong bodily-kinesthetic intelligence will deepen their understanding of the text by acting out scenes, and interpersonal learners will thrive through interactions with other students. Those with musical inclinations can better understand the characters by linking them to songs. Students who tend to be logical and mathematical in their thinking will enjoy organizing the information in the text into various lists, charts, tables, and semantic maps, while intrapersonal learners will have ample time to reflect on their own experience in relation to that of the characters in the play.[5]

*Scene production.* Though time constraints may prevent you from producing the entire play, putting on individual scenes in class is an excellent way to create a mini language-through-theater experience. You can also start with individual scene productions as a way to "test the waters" to determine students' interest and commitment in the hopes of producing a full-scale show at a later date or as an extracurricular activity.

Pick a scene that is linguistically and culturally useful, one that demonstrates cultural norms and uses accessible vocabulary and modern colloquialisms. Make sure to put as much care, time, and effort into the scenes as you would were the scene part of a full-scale production. Plan the month's lessons to allow for one, two, or even three weeks of intense rehearsal time, and have students memorize their lines and bring in necessary props and costume items.

It is also advisable to inquire in advance about using the school's auditorium for the performance of the scene, and, if possible, invite other language classes and even parents and siblings. Students can write a summary in English for those who do not speak Italian and can explain to the audience how the scene fits into the greater plot of the show. This is an excellent opportunity to encourage cultural connections and spark true enthusiasm for language learning not only in your own classroom, but within the greater community.[6]

*Design activities.* Guiding students through the process of set and costume design is an excellent way to tap into the talents of spatial and logical-mathematical learners. It is also easy to enhance substantive vocabulary acquisition with these projects because students will invariably need to name unfamiliar nouns (dresser, cabinet, wool, polka dots, etc.) and adjectives to describe the general design.

Here is a sample set design activity based on Dario Fo's *Non tutti i ladri vengono per nuocere.* For this play, in which a robber enters the home of an upper-middle-class couple, a teacher might have students make two collages, one to represent the elegant home of the couple and the other to show what they imagine the robber's home would look like. The teacher can then separate the collages of the elegant home from those of the robber's home and display them on a wall. In comparing and contrasting the images with the class, the teacher can introduce vocabulary such as *spazioso, signorile, di lusso, arredato, ampio, squallido, vuoto, in rovina,* etc. Particularly valuable to students with a strong spatial orientation, this exercise allows them to connect words with concrete images of objects. Alternatively, the teacher may choose to require that the students present their ideas to the class as an exercise in oral proficiency.

The following are a few design activities related to set and costumes. These projects also provide a good starting point for a discussion of the similarities and differences of various students' ideas.

Set design projects:

- Floor plans for each scene, showing the stage from above
- Sketch of each scene, from the perspective of the audience
- Collage(s) of the set to give an idea of the style of the furnishings of the space
- Detailed list or chart of all props used by the actors (requires an extremely careful examination of the text)

Costume design projects:

- Sketches or collages to represent each costume used in the production
- Detailed list of *all* costume items needed by the actors (again, this requires careful thought; students must consider everything from undergarments to wedding bands)
- Communicating (in Italian) with classmates to find and piece together some or all of the costumes used in the show

*Music or soundtrack for the show.* An effective way to spark the interest and draw on the talents of students who are musically inclined is to have them compile a soundtrack for the show. You may want to provide them with some musical selections or point out websites where they can locate songs and lyrics. After reading the lyrics while listening to these songs many times over, students should develop a basic understanding of the themes expressed in each. On the basis of their interpretations of the songs, they can then select a song to represent each character (or, alternatively, to represent each scene) and explain their selections to the class. During their presentations, the students should hand out song lyrics to the class and point out particular words and expressions; this is also an effective and enjoyable way to enhance students' vocabulary base.

*Viewing other productions.* If you have access to cinematic versions of past productions of the selected text (either by a professional troupe or by past groups of students), viewing and discussing a particular cast and crew's interpretation of the work allows for comparison and contrast, debate, and reflection, again incorporating the *connections* and *comparisons* categories of the five Cs of language learning (further discussed below in the context of the AP Italian curriculum). Not only do such viewings stimulate visual learners, but discussions of the production allow those with a strong interpersonal intelligence to explore their ideas by analyzing them with others.

## Writing-Based Assignments

Linguistic and intrapersonal learners will respond well to various writing-based activities, a few of which are suggested below. Many can be used in conjunction with acting activities, engaging bodily-kinesthetic and interpersonal learners as well.

*Character analyses.* Incorporating writing, literature, and creativity, a character analysis is a fantastic tool. Students use their imaginations—combined with the evidence the author gives them in the text—to explore the personality of a character of their choice. These analyses will help students develop a better understanding of the characters' emotions, reactions, and inner thoughts. If the class is producing the entire play (or selected scenes), have each student analyze the character that he or she will be portraying.

Ask students to consider the items listed below as a starting point.

They should not feel the need to answer every question or to structure the composition on the basis of the order in which the questions appear. For best results, the analysis should be as free and creative as possible in tone, structure, and content.

1. General Information
   - Physical description
   - Personality
   - Likes/dislikes (favorite—or least favorite—color, song, type of music, food, season of year, subject in school, sports, hobby, TV show, article of clothing you own, or anything else you want to discuss. Why do you like or dislike these things?)
   - What is your job, if you have one? Do you like it? Why or why not?
   - Where do you live now?
   - What are your hopes and dreams?

2. Personal History
   - When were you born?
   - Where did you grow up?
   - What was your childhood like?
   - Who were the people who influenced you the most?
   - If you have a spouse, how did you meet him or her?
   - If you have a job, how did you get into the profession?
   - What have you learned from your experiences?

3. Relationship to the Other Characters
   - How do you feel about the other characters in the play?
   - To which characters do you feel particularly close? Why?
   - Do any of the other characters annoy or frustrate you? Why?

*Adaptations.* If the play you select is set in modern Italy, having students script a North American version can be an effective way to highlight cultural differences and similarities. Alternatively, students can deepen their knowledge of Italian history by taking a text set in the past and rescripting it in modern times. Advanced students might discover the richness of dialect literature by attempting to translate a dialect piece into modern Italian. Each of these variations especially encourages the standards of connections and comparisons.

The fundamental advantage of adaptations is that they encourage circumlocution, arguably one of the most important strategies for communicative competence. After all, the ultimate goal of language learners is to develop strategies to express their thoughts in their own words. However, to avoid oversimplification, students should be required to incorporate some new vocabulary or expressions into their adapted scripts.

*Journals.* A teacher may choose to have students keep a journal as a way of recording either their experience of reading a text or their thoughts on the process of rehearsing it for a performance. In either case, students should be free to write spontaneously and quickly without being overly concerned with form or grammar. Linguistically oriented students in particular gain from this activity because it gives them the opportunity to experiment with writing, while intrapersonal learners will appreciate the opportunity to reflect on their own learning process.

Depending on students' other responsibilities and assignments for the course, journal entries can be as short as a few sentences or as long as a few paragraphs. If the teacher wants to encourage reflection on a particular point, he or she may choose to assign a journal topic based on a thought-provoking question. Otherwise, free entries give students the opportunity to record their thoughts about the text as well as their personal difficulties and triumphs in reading and interpreting it.

For the instructor, journals can also be an insightful and often surprising glimpse into the learning process. Students are often quite candid in revealing which aspects of reading the text are easy or difficult for them. In reading students' journals, the teacher may also discover specific questions about words or passages that the students have not brought up during class.

*Italian tabloids.* Everyone seems to love a scandal, and high school students are certainly no exception. Have students write tabloid articles divulging shocking news about the main characters. Make sure they incorporate vocabulary from the master list that you compiled. Students, especially those who are spatially oriented, enjoy embellishing their tabloid stories with images clipped from magazines or pictures that they have taken themselves.

*Reviews.* A theatrical review is a way for students to practice another style of writing. Have students read several theatrical reviews from Italian newspapers. Using the Italian reviews as a base, you can lead a discussion of the basic stylistic characteristics of a theatrical review, helping students to understand how a review differs from an essay, an analysis, or a plot summary. If you are staging scenes from the play, students can then write their own review of the scenes produced by their classmates. Alternatively, students can write a review of a cinematic version of the play, or even write a review of an imaginary production.

*Author biographies.* Students can research and report on the life of the play's author, the historical period during which he or she wrote, and the prevalent cultural norms or political situation during his or her lifetime. If the play is set during a time period other than the author's "present," the students can research the history behind the play's setting and explain why the author chose that particular setting. Various secondary activities can then be based on their research. For example, a teacher might offer several options that would appeal to different intelligences such as:

- Create and act out an interview with the author.
- Draw a comic strip involving the author discussing the play with someone.
- Write the author's obituary, highlighting major events and achievements.
- Create an annotated passport for the author showing the important places he or she has been and what he or she did in those places.
- Make an illustrated timeline of the main events in the author's life.
- Pretend you are the author and you just put the finishing touches on the piece and are ready to submit it for publication. Write a letter to a friend explaining what the piece is about, why you wrote it, and how you hope your audience will respond.
- Select a few songs that this author might like and explain the reasoning behind your choices.
- Identify cause and effect patterns in the author's life.
- Discuss how you feel you are similar to or different from the author.

*Commercials.* One way to get students to see the link between the content of the piece and the play's intended audience is through commercial writing. First lead a discussion of the intended audience that the author targets through the play, then pose the challenge: if this were a TV production and you were in charge of selecting commercials for the network, what kind of commercials would you choose? Of course, the types of products advertised would have to correspond to the interests of the author's target audience. Students can then sharpen their communication skills by writing a few commercials and performing them, if desired.

## Exploratory Character Work

Written character analyses (mentioned above in the section on writing-based activities) are not the only way to encourage students to think critically about the lives, personalities, and relationships of the characters. Here are just a few ideas on how to creatively engage high school students in extensive character work. You may assign each student a particular character on which to focus during your study of the play, or alternatively, you may prefer to have students study a variety of characters.

*Character interviews.* Newscast-style interviews are an excellent follow-up activity to character analyses but can also be done as a stand-alone activity. Have the students compose a list of interesting questions to ask each character. You may ask them to compose general questions about the personality and life of the character, or have them grill the character on a specific event in the script. You can have two students improvise an interview, with one asking the questions and the other answering them. If a teacher-facilitated activity might be more useful, you can have a student be the newscaster while you play the part of the character answering the questions. Another option is to collect the students' lists of questions and play the part of the interviewer, with students answering questions as the various characters.

*Character and plot exploration through additional scenes.* Students can probe into the author's plot choices by scripting various new scenes. The following can be done in small groups and then shared with the class as a whole:

- *Past:* Are there points in the script where characters discuss past events that are not portrayed during the course of the play? Students can write out the dialogue for these events and perform their interpretations for their classmates.

- *"Deleted scenes"*: Do some key events occur "offstage," out of the sight of the audience and the characters themselves? Have students imagine these scenes, compose a script for them, and act them out for the class.

- *Future:* Have your students consider what might happen between the characters after the last scene of the play. What is going on in their lives one week later? One year later? Fifteen years later? Students might create or write about these scenes.

- *What if?* Why did the author choose to end the play as he or she did? Challenge students to come up with an alternate ending for the play. If you choose to have them perform these scenes for the class, students can follow up the scenes with a discussion. What effect do the various endings create? Which is most logical? Which most closely corresponds with the author's intentions?

- *Characters out of context:* As a way to focus on characters' interpersonal relationships, have students write a scene demonstrating how they would interact in another context. What if they took a trip to Disneyland together? How would they interact in a supermarket? What if one character were in the hospital having surgery; who would come visit and what would they say? How would things go if the characters were stuck together on a small island with no way to escape?

*Character discovery time capsule.* Select one item to represent each character in the play and place the items in a box. Tell the students that the characters left behind a time capsule and have them guess which item belonged to which character and explain their reasoning. Since the object of this activity is to engage the students in interpersonal exchange and even more structured debate, make sure that some of the items in the capsule could be linked to more than one character. This way, students will need to articulate and defend their opinions with regard to the more controversial time capsule items. Alternatively, small groups of students could put together the time capsule, challenging the other groups to make the connections between the items and the characters.

*Talk show.* Many comedies involve misunderstandings, mistaken identities, and trickery and thus lend themselves wonderfully to Jerry Springer–style talk-show episodes. Always a popular option among students, this exercise allows them to explore character relationships while incorporating modern expressions, colloquialisms, and even (classroom-appropriate) insults.

## Incorporating Grammar

It is easy to incorporate any grammatical structure or vocabulary lesson into any of the above activities; simply instruct the students to focus on the grammatical structure that they are currently studying. For example, a student can practice various verb tenses, direct and indirect objects, and the *piacere* structure by talking about likes and dislikes in a journal, character analysis, or newscast interview. The Jerry Springer talk show is an excellent forum for practicing imperatives ("take your things and move out of my house!"), the past tense ("why did you break into my house and steal my cat?"), indirect objects ("she gave the keys to him!"), or really any concept you choose. The "what if" activity is particularly useful for practicing the *periodo ipotetico*. Even an activity as simple as explaining one's costume design choices could be done in the past ("I chose this because . . . "), the present ("this character wears light colors because . . . "), or the future ("the characters will wear heavy jackets because . . . "). Challenge the students to focus on particular structures or challenge them to incorporate as many as possible.

Lastly, teachers can keep referencing the script during normal grammar lessons simply by transforming and contextualizing the exercises the textbook poses. For example, instead of giving a sample sentence, "A Marta piacciono le mele" during a lesson on *piacere*, ask the students a question that involves the characters in the text. "A quale personaggio piacciono moltissimo i soldi ed i vestiti eleganti?" Use examples like this not only in the classroom, but also in grammar tests and quizzes.

## Theater and Advanced Placement Italian

In *Frames of Mind,* Gardner maintains that traditional testing formats such as multiple choice, fill in the blank, short answer, essay, and mathematical problems are best for linguistic and mathematical learners but may not fully demonstrate the true capabilities of other types of learners. Thus Gardner advocates a change in not only how we teach students, but also how we assess their achievement. A bodily-kinesthetic learner, for example, may be best able to demonstrate the depth of his or her understanding of a novel by acting out a scene rather than by writing about the scene. By providing flexible and varied assessment measures, the teacher can attain a more complete understanding of the students' developing skills.[7]

At the same time, flexible and varied assessment measures can be difficult to conduct on a large scale. First, they tend to be course-specific, since they depend on the primary text chosen. Second, because they need to be conducted in a classroom or theater, they are highly classroom-based. Finally, nontraditional assessment measures are more statistically subjective when compared with multiple choice or fill-in type exams. For instance, the majority, if not all, of the questions appearing on the SAT and the various AP exams are discrete point questions. These are essential on standardized achievement and aptitude tests to ensure objectivity, to strengthen reliability, and, practically speaking, to simplify the correction process.

One challenge, then, for the educator is to find ways to foster the different intelligences so that all students can maximize their learning experience and, at the same time, be as well prepared as possible for the more traditional methods of assessment used by most high schools and by the standardized testing system.

If we take the new AP Italian language and culture exam as an example, we see that although the exam does not specifically test multiple intelligences to assess students' knowledge in the field, the incorporation of a variety of activities into the course can certainly strengthen students' understanding of Italian language and culture in a broader sense. Therefore, a multifaceted course cultivating the interests and talents of the musically, logically, and spatial-kinesthetically inclined, for example, should go far in helping to prepare students not only for the AP test, but also for the fourth- or fifth-semester Italian courses into which one hopes they might place upon entering college.

In the course description for the new AP Italian language and culture exam, the College Board states: "The AP Italian Literature and Culture course is designed to be comparable to college/university Italian courses and linguistics or content-based courses. These courses are usually taught in the fourth semester or equivalent."[8] It then lists the following as course goals and objectives:

> students demonstrate comprehension and comprehensibility in spoken and written Italian in a variety of personal contexts, actively negotiating meaning and drawing appropriate inferences; students appropriately use the formal and informal registers of spoken Italian;

students communicate clearly and effectively in a variety of personal contexts; students comprehend and interpret authentic fiction and nonfiction written texts; students have knowledge of vocabulary, idiomatic expressions, and grammatical structures necessary to comprehend and interpret oral and written texts; students write compositions in Italian on general and cultural topics with clarity and accuracy in a variety of contexts, styles, and registers; and students demonstrate introductory knowledge of contemporary life in Italy, the arts and sciences, social customs and traditions, and contributions of Italians and Italian Americans to the world.

In light of the outlined AP course goals, theater-based courses and theater-based activities such as those described above offer numerous possibilities for the development of the cultural knowledge and language skills necessary for the AP exam. For example, students may speak and write in different communicative modes about the historical context of their text(s), the life and times of their author(s), film adaptations of their text(s), the development of their character/role within the text, or their personal experiences with the theater activities and texts (for example, the journal). And during presentations, dialogues, or scene studies, they have the opportunity to "actively negotiate meaning and draw references." To take another example from the AP exam's stated goals, theater texts and activities impel students to broaden their "knowledge of vocabulary, idiomatic expressions, and grammatical structures" in a lively and active way. In particular, the physicality of scene studies and improvisational dialogue games does much to reinforce the meaning and correct use of such vocabulary, expression, and grammatical structures through contextualized use. As mentioned, teachers may organize their introduction or review of key grammatical structures (for example, imperatives, subjunctives, relative clauses, etc.) around the contextualized use of these structures found in the text. Perhaps more than any other thematic organization, theater provides a thorough basis for practicing all of the College Board's stated goals. Moreover, if provided with opportunities, students can develop skills through theatrical texts and techniques over the course of their entire secondary school foreign language experience.

The AP foreign language exam itself, a primary end goal of the AP course experience, is in fact made up of tasks for which students who complete the theater-based activities listed above are amply prepared. To summarize the exam briefly, there are five main sections, each equally weighted during scoring as 20 percent of the exam. These five sections reflect the four main skills and culture: reading comprehension, listening comprehension, writing (including paragraph completions and a composition on a general topic), speaking (including a story narration and a simulated dialogue), and a composition on a clearly delineated cultural topic.[9] With regard to reading, in addition to practicing reading comprehension strategies by breaking down one or more dramatic texts into manageable and "timeable" sequences, the instructor can seek or create additional texts on a wide variety of cultural subjects stemming from the text.[10] In the case of Fo's *Non tutti i ladri vengono per nuocere* mentioned above, one might consider a politically oriented text on the "historical compromise" between the Left and Right in Italy or a general overview of social classes in Italy from the time of Italian unification through the 1970s. Similarly, for listening comprehension, teachers may prerecord scenes from their texts, use segments from film adaptations or previous productions of the text, use musical recordings if the dramatic text happens to be an opera libretto, or find additional related clips or conversations on topics related to the text.

To help students practice for the written section of the AP test, which begins with paragraph completions, teachers may directly employ excerpts from the theatrical texts or any of the reading and listening comprehension texts. To create practice exams, they can delete important verbs (for the verb completion section) or other parts of speech (see the list in the published exam specifications). This same technique is useful for testing vocabulary and expressions, although the instructor may wish to provide a list or "pool" of possible answers for completing the text.[11] The general composition can creatively stem from any aspect of the theatrical text or techniques being employed. A few examples might be an analysis of one particular character, a reflection on the corporeal particularities of speaking English versus Italian, or a persuasive piece on one of the main themes of the text (such as friendship, work, social rules, childhood, etc.).

To prepare for the speaking sections, the instructor might have students work in pairs or small groups to create picture sequences that reflect "alternate endings" of one or more theatrical texts. The teacher can then duplicate the picture sequences and during subsequent lessons have students practice and "perform" (that is, narrate) their stories aloud. A similar type exercise can be devised for simulated conversations.

Finally, students can prepare for the cultural essay by working together to brainstorm the various ways one or more of the chosen theatrical texts address the general topics chosen by the College Board for the cultural essay, such as contemporary life in Italy, the arts and sciences, social customs and traditions, and contributions of Italians and Italian Americans to the world. Teachers and students alike can then devise essay topics that allow them to use the theatrical texts (along with related topics and texts) to support their written answers. Furthermore, all of the practice and discussions stemming from previous sections of the exam should help prepare students for the cultural segment.

In addition to preparing for the content and specific test-taking formats and conditions for the AP Italian language and culture exam, it is essential that the national standards (the five Cs) play a central role in the three- to five-year foreign language curriculum and in the AP course in particular. As previously discussed, it is easy to see how the single theatrical text or activity can be used to emphasize one or more of the standards. A simple scene study (the memorization and performance of a short scene from the text or even an invented version of one read) allows for practice with different variants of the interpersonal mode of communication. And a more open-ended situation (stemming from one in the text you have read) provides even more opportunity for spontaneous use of the language and authentic negotiation among interlocutors. This same activity, when performed, can also help students practice the presentational and interpretative modes of communication, depending on the listening/speaking tasks the instructor assigns.

At the same time, communication is only one of the five Cs. How might the activity of a scene study or performed situation/scenario address additional standards? For one, the very act of performing already connects the study of foreign language with another academic discipline, namely, theater and performing arts. But depending on the instructor's assignments, this in-class mini-drama might focus on different aspects of history, politics (class difference, gender roles, etc.), or linguistics (nonverbal communication). Equally viable might be a selection of scene studies or invented scenarios that lend themselves to cultural comparisons and the likelihood that a weekly class routine of such scene/scenario performances (to which students from other courses, parents, and Italian-speaking community members might occasionally be invited) can create a broader sense of Italian community.

Regardless of the specific angle from which one approaches the integration of theatrical texts with AP course creation and exam preparation, the primary objective should remain that of creating a rich and comprehensive language and culture learning experience. The exam should be considered but one end goal of a (hopefully) four- to five-year foreign language course and curriculum.

Clearly, close work with a theatrical text, be it through a full-scale production or through a variety of text-based activities, can enhance either a regular or an AP course curriculum. A theatrical text provides a multifaceted and fruitful basis for teaching language and culture, one that incorporates the five Cs of language learning, fulfills AP course objectives, and has the potential to engage students with strengths in all of Gardner's seven intelligence areas. Albert Einstein once claimed, "Learning is experience; everything else is just information." In giving students the hands-on experience of immersing themselves in language, literature, and culture, we are giving them far more than pieces of information; we are giving them a context in which to truly learn.

## Notes

1. In this way, students' learning extends far beyond a simple knowledge of literature and culture; communication in Italian becomes urgent and necessary if they are to succeed in any theater-related task assigned to them. Whether doing something as complex as producing an entire show or something as simple as explaining their ideas for costumes, students must find ways to express their thoughts in Italian.
2. See Gardner, *Frames of Mind*, Chapters 1–4 for more details.
3. Gardner discusses the seven categories in depth in Chapters 5–10 of *Frames of Mind*.
4. Additionally, a college instructor running a theater-based course is able to accept students from beginner to advanced levels of proficiency. Advanced students are appropriately challenged with the more difficult roles while beginners are equally challenged at their own level with smaller parts. At the high school level, however, most students progress through Italian I, II, III, and IV; thus, classes are typically composed of students at the exact same point in their study of Italian. Unless the experience were offered as an extracurricular activity open to students

of all levels, the teacher would have to find a large-cast script whose roles were similar in their level of difficulty.

5. See the "Director's Handbook" in this book for further details about production-related activities.

6. By involving other students as audience members, the presentation of a show or portion of a show promotes the five Cs of communication, culture, connections, comparisons, and communities. These are the main goal areas for foreign language learning as described in the ACTFL publication of the National Standards for Foreign Language Learning.

7. Several of the activities listed above can serve as formal assessment tools for the course. For further discussion see Ryan-Scheutz, "Proficiency and Performance," Chapter 11 of this book.

8. See the 2008–2010 version at http://www.collegeboard.com/prod_downloads/ap/students/italian/ap-cd-italian-0708.pdf (accessed March 2008). This site is updated regularly and subject to change.

9. See published AP Italian language and culture exam questions at http://www.apcentral.collegeboard.com and Boyle, *Ace the AP Advanced Placement Italian Exam,* a recent publication containing numerous practice sections for the exam.

10. While it is never advisable to teach to the test or, in an AP course, to focus solely on practice sections of the exam, it is highly recommended that students practice working under the real time constraints of the exam.

11. Although no one segment on the AP exam explicitly examines vocabulary and expressions, a broad knowledge across a range of content topics and social contexts is important to all sections of the exam.


## Bibliography

Boyle, Bruna Petrarca. *Ace the AP Advanced Placement Italian Exam.* New York: Edizioni Farinelli, 2006.

Fo, Dario. *Non tutti i ladri vengono per nuocere.* In *Le commedie di Dario Fo.* 4th ed. Turin: Einaudi, 1977.

Gardner, Howard. *Frames of Mind: The Theory of Multiple Intelligences.* New York: Basic Books, 1983.

Ryan-Scheutz, Colleen, and Laura Colangelo. "Full-Scale Theater Production and Second Language Learning." *Foreign Language Annals,* 37.3 (Fall 2004): 374–389.

## Sample Quiz: *Non tutti i ladri vengono per nuocere,* pp. 91–96

1. Perché la moglie del ladro gli ha telefonato al suo posto di lavoro?

2. Quale aggettivo è il più preciso per descrivere il tono (tone) che usa la moglie quando dice, "Oh no, figurati . . . Come puoi pensare che io pretenda una cosa simile . . . Tu con un pensiero gentile . . . Tu che pensi a farmi un regalino . . . quando mai!"

    a. amoroso        b. arrabbiato        c. sarcastico

    d. gentile        e. stanco        f. triste

3. La moglie dice, "Non alzare la voce, ti prego" per due ragioni. Quali sono?

4. Scegli la parola giusta per ogni frase. Alla sinistra di ogni frase, indica quale personaggio la dice.

    crepare        apposta        municipio        proprietari

    pendolo        pensiero        basterebbe        già che ci sei

    a. "Mi hai detto tu stesso che i _______________ sono in campagna."

    b. "Scusami, non l'ho fatto _______________, non immaginavo che fossi tu."

    c. "Che bel suono . . . deve essere un ___________ antico. Peserà molto?"

    d. "E perché _________________ non mi dici addirittura di portarti a casa un frigorifero?!"

    e. "Mi _______________ una cosettina qualsiasi . . . è il _____________ che conta."

f. "Mi piacerebbe tanto vedere come è fatta una vera casa signorile . . . e poi farei ________________ d'invidia tutte le mie amiche!"

g. "Sono tua moglie dopo tutto . . . e mi hai sposato anche in chiesa, mica in ________________ come una concubina qualsiasi!"

5. Quando entrano l'uomo e la donna, dove si nasconde il ladro?

6. Che cosa vuole fare l'uomo?

7. Quando l'uomo menziona il marito della donna, lei dice, "Ecco, hai rovinato tutto! Perché hai voluto ricordarmi che ho un marito? E adesso come potrò? Adesso che mi hai fatto rinascere il rimorso, il senso di colpa . . ." A questo punto, l'uomo offre un suggerimento, una cosa che possono fare per calmare e distrarre la donna. Che cos'è?

8. Quando suona il telefono, dove stanno andando l'uomo e la donna?

# III  Genres, Themes, and Techniques of Italian Theater

# CHAPTER 6

# Epic Theater, Comic Mode: Understanding Italian Society through the Works of Dario Fo and Franca Rame

WALTER VALERI

It has become common practice to use the texts of Dario Fo and Franca Rame in Italian language courses in North American universities. Since the late 1970s, Fo and Rame have been the Italian authors whose works are most widely translated and performed in the world, and their texts are excellent instruments for introducing students to Italian popular culture and language. As of 2008, Fo has written eighty theatrical works; his theater lessons are available on video; he has directed nineteen works by other authors (from Molière to John Gay to Rossini); he has written essays and journalistic works, completed paintings, and taught art history courses. He is both a champion of actorial autonomy and a living testimony of political engagement, a kinsman of the playwrights and prolific authors whose works are models for and permanent beacons in Western (not simply Italian) theatrical and literary culture. Franca Rame, Fo's wife and leading actress, has had a primary role in the administration of the Fo-Rame Company and has considerably contributed to the creation, revision, and production of many of the theatrical works that the artistic couple has produced in more than forty-five years.

It is important to remember that contemporary spoken Italian is marked by a particularly complex, living social dynamic. Ancient tradition, a variety of dialects, thirteenth-century literary language, and new, standardized television Italian clash in a permanent dialectic. This phenomenon is a decidedly recent one if, indeed, it was only in 1936, as Corrado Veneziano recalls, that

Italy was in the midst of a complex process of Italianization. The regions had not yet assumed their own, autonomous institutional solidarity; dialectal thrusts were perceived as divergent and distracting; and the valorization of a particular type of "nationality" tended to censor certain sounds, meanings, forms. With little concern for extranational linguistic dialectics (and on the contrary with serious problems of radical isolationism), the Italian language—at the grammatical and syntactic level, but also lexical and phonetic—was devoid of the sense of problematicity and reciprocity that has always characterized human exchange and negotiation. It was encaged in a pre-packaged structure and architecture. In the space of a few decades, the stimuli that always underlie man's activities put aside such abstractions and, in the 1960s and especially the 1970s, there appeared a new generation of intellectual and cultural forces. These, more modernly, attempted to confront an indomitable opposition that exists between "standard" and "minor" languages, languages both erudite and popular that reproduce the unique individuality— creative and reformulative—of linguistic exchange.[1]

One of Dario Fo's first farces, *Non tutti i ladri vengono per nuocere* (1958), is part of an anthology published at the beginning of the 1980s in the United States titled *Teatro, Prosa, Poesia*. Today, this short volume still serves as a practical guide and tool for Italian instructors who view theater as a means for improving students' knowledge of the Italian language. The introductory page of the "Theater" section of this manual suggests: "The theater is said to be a re-creation of life, presented in an imaginative and interpretive form, so as to excite our interest and our participation as well as delight us. The American poet Robert Frost defines literature in general as a 'performance in words.' When we become intellectually and emotionally engaged in a literary work, we experience a kinship with the author to the point of thinking that he has managed to express 'our very feelings,' or has given us at least an entirely different perspective on our concepts."[2] This introduction aptly underlines the expressive mechanisms at work in each of our lives and in the life of theatrical and literary language, mechanisms that actively influence learning and the transference of knowledge. We can say in general that the elements that characterize language learning using theater are based in "imagination," "interpretation," "participation," and active and passive "expression" of the designated text. These fundamental moments of language teaching involve the acquisition, interiorization, exposition, and reinterpretation of the text; its communicative function is equipped and reinforced with grammatical exercises and appropriate thematic and lexical studies. It is also fundamental to reiterate that during the process of learning a text, students must re-create and clarify, with the help of the instructor, the theatrical significance of each scene. Each sentence and each word must be understood in order to give it meaning. That is to say, students must be aware of and take responsibility for their final objective—that of clearly communicating as much of the information contained in the theatrical text as possible to others (their public or other students participating in rehearsals) via voice and action. Here lies the difference between using a passage of prose and using a dramatic text for instruction: in the performance of the dramatic text, multiple languages come together and are optimized. It is clearly the responsibility of the student to effectively transfer the dramatic text from the page to the spectator's imagination via dramatic action. That which remains unique, in many ways not generalizable, is the specific nature of each language and culture. In the case of Italian, the specific context is the history of Italy and of the Italian language: a cultural and political event unique in the history of Western European nations, for reasons that Robert Dombroski aptly summarizes: "What sets the last fifty years apart from the earlier century is an increase in the intensity and consistency of literary activity [in Italy] at a level that could be called at once 'high' and 'popular.' The essential reason for this is that, with the defeat of Fascism and the liberalization of Italian social and political institutions, Italy has become a nation, not just in principle, but in fact. Gramsci's ideal of a 'national-popular' literature, a reality in England and France since the early nineteenth century, has to a large measure now been realized in Italy."[3]

Dario Fo and Franca Rame are without a doubt among the Italian writers and intellectuals who have most participated in the creation of this unique cultural landscape. Both have contributed a vast, consistent theatrical production and have been constantly present on national and international stages for more than fifty years. Their comedies are full of words and syntactic structures that are part of the spoken language: jargon, anecdotes taken from daily life, and historical and cultural references that derive from a direct and attentive observation of society. All of these are part of a comic style of which the actor-author Fo is the undisputed master.

Using the works of Fo and Rame in Italian courses implies re-constructing the meanings and contents of single sentences via comparative linguistic activities that are not excessively difficult (as long as one is aware of the problem). Besides stimulating the student-actors' attention, works by Fo and Rame above all encourage complementary research initiatives. For instance, when students first read and analyze one of their texts, they will have the opportunity to add careful notes to define and explain jargon, identify references to the history of contemporary Italy, and research allusions to popular and scholarly dramatic literature. As in the Western tradition that sees in Aristophanes the great Plantagenet, the satirical theater of Fo and Rame cements itself from the beginning in a comic style written in the presence of a succession of tragic events in society. It is not a comedy of entertainment, but rather it is engaged in un-masking and confronting the ideology of the dominant political and economic powers.

The central figure, the cornerstone of Fo's creation (even from a linguistic point of view), remains the actor: "My growth as an actor has kept pace with my growth as a writer. I learned to write and to think for the theater as I grew as an actor."[4] The reluctance of some critics and academics to speak of Fo as author of theatrical texts, notwithstanding his being awarded the Nobel Prize for literature in 1997, derives from his continual and punctilious return to the actor as mediator of the "oral tradition," not the literary one. "I learned dialect from storytellers," Fo said. "From them I learned a more archaic dialect, that of the old places that absolutely did not hesitate to Italianize dialect, as happens now. They evidently knew idiomatic forms of the language, the structures of language. I learned the structure of dialect, which is different from speaking in dialect. This structure and this language are found in my theatrical works."

Fo's exemplarity as an actor-author lies in his prodigious capac-ity to forge a written, noncanonical language through which he introduces the immediacy and physicality of the expressive body in dynamic sequences of sentences. His is an "eccentric" linguistic the-atrical code, composed of a text interwoven and remixed (tirelessly written and rewritten in collaboration with his audiences) with an explosion of oral creativity, taken from the dialects of the Po Valley, that Fo defines as *grammelot*. Students must become aware that his theater develops in the presence of both structure and improvisa-tion; otherwise, it remains abstract and incomprehensible. "I am not simply a man of letters who writes," Fo has said. "Theater is made of orality, sound, music, timing, rhythms, action, and naturally, writing. We might say that there exist two techniques. There are those who study words exactly, and then recite them mechanically, risking to completely forget their significance. The other way is suggested by a famous quote by Shakespeare, who says: 'you must always act as if it were the first time, and you must re-find the words'—as if the actor does not know, conclusively, the progression of a sentence, and has to reconstruct it as he speaks it."

From the time of the writing of *Dito nell'occhio* (1953) and *Sani da legare* (1954), Fo's writing for the stage, read transparently, teems with extratextual presences. His is truly an "inhabited" language, as Mikhail Bakhtin would say, complemented by a taste for scenic machinations, constructed with the meticulous precision of the perfectly calibrated linguistic and dramaturgical mechanisms of George Feydeau. But the grammelot mentioned above remains the true, mysterious linguistic invention that Fo refers to as a "term of French origin, coined by the comedians of the Arte [commedia dell'arte] and macaronicized by the Venetians, who said 'gramelotto.'" It is a word without intrinsic meaning, a puzzle for teachers of Italian, who often prefer to ignore this linguistic epiphenomenon in order to avoid its complications; it is a pastiche of sounds that manages to evoke the sense of speech. Grammelot means, for Fo, "an onomatopoeic game of speech, articulated arbitrarily, but that can nevertheless transmit, with the help of gestures, rhythms, and particular sounds, an entire, complete discourse."

The term appeared previously in writing by Leon Chacerel, a critic and historian of the theater, an actor in his youth, and a collaborator for some time with Jacques Copeau. Chacerel's work demonstrates how the word *grommelot* was born around 1918 of an act of creativity, an invention, a spontaneous, actorial linguistic game. Marie-Hélène Dasté, Copeau's daughter and also a part of the theatrical school Vieux Colombier, maintained (in a recording of June 16, 1993) that "actors, like children, sometimes invent words. This happened with grommelot. In the beginning the term *grummelot* was used, derived from *gremeau,* and was used to designate a game of linguistic improvisation that imitated expressions, rhythms, and sounds typical of certain situations." According to Dasté, then, the original variation would be *grommelot,* with *grammelot* being the result of a more recent Italian translation, close to that proposed by

Fo, who suggests that it dates to the time of the commedia dell'arte. There exists a homophone, although shorter by a syllable, *grelot*, that means harness-bell or sleigh bell. By extension, it is present in the slang expression *avoir le grelots*, which means "scared stiff," or to become upset and to change the degree of comprehension of the words expressed (to the point of mumbling). This is a state typical of those who find themselves fearful or facing strong emotion. Such an expression (identifying a "situation") was commonly used by the characters and masks of the commedia dell'arte in Paris during the sixteenth century and was, as one says in theatrical jargon, *un tormentone* (a major nuisance). Serious research was conducted on this complex topic for a thesis defended at the Università della Sapienza in Rome, as well as for a precise and illuminating book by Alessandra Pozzo spiritedly titled *Grr. . . Grammelot parlare senza parole*. The fact remains that grammelot is both a textual peculiarity of Fo's theater and a twentieth-century revival of one of the fundamental elements of the *comici dell'arte* (the actors of the commedia dell'arte) in Italy of the sixteenth and seventeenth centuries. As Kostantin Miklasevskij wrote in an old but fundamental essay on the origins and nature of the commedia dell'arte: "Characters all spoke different dialects. That style was particularly favored in that each spectator could find a fellow countryman; the majority of mimed scenes rendered this genre of theater accessible and interesting also abroad."[5]

It is impossible to separate Fo's acting and authorial talents, and when one makes didactic use of his texts, one cannot ignore his striking use of gestures and facial expressions. This bodily language, of French descent (with reference to Marcel Marceau and Etienne Decroux, among others), was transmitted to Fo over the course of his apprenticeship with Jacques Lecoq, master of mime who choreographed the gestures in the performance of *Il dito nell'occhio* staged in collaboration with Franco Parenti and Giustino Durano. The presence of mime remains an important component in Fo, who nonetheless distances mime from "white pantomime," or French aesthetic miming, as Bernard Dort clarified on the occasion of the opening of *Mistero buffo* in the French Theatre du Challot in 1973: "Dario Fo has everything it takes to be a prodigious mime. He knows how to unite, in a gesture of the hand, the arm, or the body, the casual movements to which we never cease to abandon ourselves." Dort then makes clear, "but that which appears is a changeable, transitory figure of man immersed in history and in class struggle."[6] The author-actor Dario Fo is a demiurge, creating around himself all of the elements of the text (pretext) of the performance, constructing his own "permanent mask" as a fulcrum that generates the elements already evident in the writing stage. This radical theory does not try to rebel against written text, in a traditional sense, as happened in Italian theatrical performances in the 1980s that tended to push toward a zero-level of theatrical writing. It is rather a means of emphasizing and valorizing the uniqueness of the individual, whether students (in Italian classes) or actors, re-creating them as bearers of a variety of specific languages that converge in an acting exercise. In this way, the play, and thus the lesson, is saved from the separateness of the roles. The action of the actor and of the student does not simply imitate the only bodies not seen onstage—those of the author and the director-demiurge (the instructor)—but is instead the emanation and presence of the two fundamental roles, brought to life in the performance.

Although Fo is the author of many comedies that have various characters, monologues are the natural precipitate of Fo's production, and he is their foremost master. "The most direct medium, that brings its own force and style from the bowels of popular theater, is the monologue," Fo affirms. From *Poer Nano* (1952) to *Il tempio degli uomini liberi* (2004), and continuing with *Mistero buffo, Tutta casa, letto e chiesa,* and other *Monologhi femminili* written with Franca Rame, the author's talents are clearly involved and interact in this genre, which perfectly demonstrates the extraordinary nature of Fo's art. This incredible "theatrical speaking" is full of hyperbole, sudden deviations in meaning and style, surreal abstraction combined with realistic descriptions, sustained by a rhythm that can only be described as meandering and histrionic. The monologues and sketches of *Mistero buffo* (in the Italian version, edited by Rame) are an extraordinary testing ground for students and a fundamental key to understanding and interpreting Fo and Rame's entire theatrical oeuvre. In his extraordinary capacity to create monologues, Fo oscillates constantly between *canto* (lyric) and *racconto* (narrative) (emblematic in this sense are, for example, *La nascita del giullare, Il matto e la morte, Le nozze di Cana, Il cieco e lo storpio, La fame dello Zanni,* and *Bonifacio VIII*), ultimately reaching a linguistic and theatrical fusion that, notwithstanding its complexity, is immediately enjoyable. These works are capable of capturing the senses of sight and hearing of the students, as well as of the ideal spectator to whom the students address themselves, in a continuous sliding between *grave* and *acute* sounds, making recourse to the diaphragm and shifting the vocal tone of words as they issue from the body, especially during the execution of the grammelot. It is not by chance that in *Manuale minimo dell'attore,* Fo exhorts actors to learn to create their own theater, to weave and to build a text with words, gestures, and situations, but above all to leave aside the false and dangerous idea that theater is nothing more than literature.[7] This exhortation can and must be transferred to the students, inviting them to become aware of the need to personalize the dramatic text when they move from the written page to its oral transposition.

Style, for Fo, is also well defined; it is that of epic theater, where the actor recounts, through the character, a story, a fact, or a real situation. In this way, the author makes frequent reference to examples from the historical past, even if remote: "Identifying with a character is something that has always been abhorred by the ancients," Fo writes. "The Greeks did not act, did not transform themselves, but obviously made clear that there was an actor [in our case, the language student] in the middle, to the point that the principal actor recited all of the parts, unconcerned with imitating the voice of a woman or a man. Rather, through gestures, inflections, vocal dimensions, he suggested the idea of a woman, of a girl, of an old woman, of a man. The concept of great theater was against identification; it is a concept that belongs to all times, that crosses various genres, from Japanese theater to puppet theater. Great actors don't identify with the person; they recount and present him."[8] Drawing on the epos and on popular myths, the theatrical texts of Fo and Rame have an absolute autonomy of dialogue with students and with the public, a historical credibility that has its roots in the system of "man" or "woman." In the moment that one acts or reads one of their monologues, the wall of controlled economy of spectacle (that of bourgeois theater) crumbles. Everything is continually reabsorbed and regenerated—never able to be entirely qualified, and thus mysterious—by the natural element that is the body or voice of the student used as an instrument of representation and performance.

It is clear, in any case, that when one sets about using a text by Fo and Rame in the classroom, one must make students understand what kind of material they are working with. One must not only explain the grammatical and lexical nature of the text, but also consider the following questions: How are its authors considered by their society? Why was it written? And above all, for whom was it written? One cannot overlook the fact that the entire production of Fo and Rame was conceived as an instrument of counterinformation, work of high civic value. It is important to give in-depth, well-developed answers to these three questions, which demand a period of research dedicated to the nature, dynamic, and political and economic history of contemporary Italian society.

In the life of the author, it is essential to trace the line that connects Fo's theater and the text adopted as a linguistic instrument with the origin and traditions of Italian popular epic theater. Such a study is not intended as a digression into the realm of the history of theater and literature, but simply as a way to understand the significance and contents of the text. The originality of the theater of Dario Fo was not derived in the absence of precedents. On the contrary, it is the result of a synthesis between the author's culture and his invention of new linguistic models that are identifiable, to varying degrees, in all of his works. One might also add that fifty years of Italian history can, in large part, be reconstructed and understood through Fo and Rame's texts, in particular thanks to the polemical aspects and political events that are almost never documented in official scholastic texts.

To develop useful linguistic studies using texts by Fo and Rame, students should follow critical, philological, historical, and pedagogical perspectives that at times are challenging; nonetheless, students will find themselves extraordinarily stimulated by the questions and answers they discover in the process of investigating the texts. There is no doubt that popular theater, more than any other literary genre, is able to propose and transmit oral discourse in written form. By the same token, orality is the natural container of the epos tied to the experience of daily life. It is at the same time memory and the permanent elaboration of a people's past, the realization and the extraordinary linguistic synthesis of the culture of the country that expresses it, in the wide sense. In the pedagogical sphere, Fo and Rame's comic theater can truly become the active linguistic experience of a single student inserted in a small community (the class) and stimulated by a fantastic incentive (the performance or final presentation), nourished by themes of common interest.

Students often favor the comic genre. Why is this? In my opinion, beyond a supposed preference of young people for "light" or "not very serious" things, it is because they are naturally attracted to the genre of comedy for its commitment to promoting an alternative point of view, a critical or antagonistic perspective with respect to the official perspective. In performing the satirical monologues or theatrical farces of Fo and Rame, students understand that, while developing their knowledge of the Italian language (including terms and subjects often ignored or repressed if not openly censored), they also are enjoying the pleasure of transgression. Becoming familiar with the comedy contained in satire in a pedagogical context provides an occasion for students to reflect critically on aspects of social life. Moreover, from the point of view of group dynamics, every psychological manual about child development makes evident the important, proxemic role of laughter and its profound function in young people; it is an essential moment of coagulation and socialization within a group of people. The laughter that typically originates from the presence of serious content (sometimes dramatic or even tragic) in a comical situation is one of the important expressive forms in every pedagogical process. Students laugh, if authorized and spurred to a good mood, and at the same time empathetically metabolize the linguistic mechanisms present in educational communication.

In general, as Lucie Olbrechts-Tyteca explains in an essay dedicated to the general theory of the comic, laughter is a conducive instrument for developing a knowledge of reality and of the dynamic of events that compose it, not simply for entertainment, but more because (by way of comedy) one best grasps the meaning of a subject and of the *ideas* of which language is the natural bearer.[9] We know how vital ideas are in the spheres of communication and language, given that "ideas" are generally understood as things to say associated with how to say them. In terms of language, ideas are descriptions (not necessarily and only in prose style) of all the things in life that are seen, heard, touched, and studied; in other words, all of one's own experience. The difference between different languages consists in the different uses that people make of sounds, combining them in such a way that they can apply them to different ideas. Thus, linguistic conventions are based on the association of certain material with its respective system of ideas. The speaker can freely formulate associations between words and ideas in innovative ways. It is part of the common pedagogical experience of every good teacher to recognize in a comic text an excellent means for linking linguistic and didactic objectives. It is important to note the "particular" quality of laughter and of themes often implied and recurrent in the theater of Fo and Rame—a sort of litmus test of relationships between theater and society, between culture and power.

When students are invited to discuss and debate the themes that are associated with the Italian language lesson and that develop during rehearsals and analysis of the text, they are able to reflect (and these reflections pertain to the intimate function of every pedagogical act) on situations, emotions, facts, real contingencies from the written page to the stage, from the school desk to the performance, in what becomes a convincing means of performing criticism. For this reason, comic theater, because of the urgency of the dramatic situation, unites all those aspects of language that the student has previously learned during language courses—verbs, expressions, principles of intonation, accents—connecting them with cultural and historical fragments. The fundamental moment in using theater as an instrument for learning Italian is not to be found in the pleasing performance per se, but rather in the relationship of creativity, analysis, and complicity that the group establishes through laughter and the hypertextual meaning that students develop, conscientiously, during rehearsals. In the theater of Dario Fo and Franca Rame, the two fundamental elements of pedagogy come together admirably: the active presence of the students' ideas and critical thought in an ethical and philosophical as well as a linguistic framework, and the liberating lightness of comic style.

From the first lesson, it is advisable to make students aware that for Fo the text, and thus the play, is the dramatic artifice used to establish a satirical and comic dialogue with the public. Satire has a beneficial effect, according to Fo, given that it is "engaged in an open contrast, tied to rational confutation and public exposition of a different way of conceiving the role and function of culture, and, in perspective, of politics." In making evident the potential of satire, both as a form of logical argumentation and as a persuasive speaking technique, the instructor teaches students how to express critical dissent, channeled rhetorically in a theatrical and cultural rite; it is useful for an analysis of the society's politics and economy. Students should work to perceive the linguistic presence of irony, and through logical analysis, find the various comic elements the satire contains. They will thus learn to produce the dialogic, provocative character of satire in Italian in oral and written form, with appropriate intonations and manipulations of the language. From a linguistic point of view, satire gives access to a vast range of colloquial terminology that enters the living circle of language, providing for the creation of new metaphoric vehicles. Satire uses words in new ways to develop a complete range of potential meanings or to highlight one and the other through the linguistic chessboard of synonyms and antonyms. The theoretical and practical use of satire and of comic discourse, of its argumentative and persuasive ends, is a decisive step in the students' mastery of the Italian language.

The comedies of Fo and Rame are very effective as pedagogical tools to reinforce both communicative competence and cultural knowledge in Italian. They are a formidable means for commenting on historical events through the study of ideas that clash with official ones. They are the ideas (or the ideologies) typical of popular culture, with respect to the Italian public (understood as "a multitude of citizens," as the Zingarelli dictionary defines it); or according to a form of theater that "was born in the traditional life of our people, and particularly in the great annual and seasonal festivals of renewal and propitiation in which the entire society participates, from the most humble people to the aristocrats," as Paolo Toschi writes.[10] It is important to make students understand that the corrosive, polemical elements contained in Fo's satire have a useful, positive social function, not a nihilistic one. Since the time of Aristophanes, Western society has had a psychological need for satire (in that it is fundamental to the psychology of the people).

Video and audiocassettes of Fo and Rame's works are today readily available in Einaudi editions and on the Internet. Critical editions of some of their works, including *Non tutti i ladri vengono per nuocere, Gli imbianchini non hanno ricordi, L'uomo nudo e l'uomo in frack,* and *Morte accidentale di un anarchico,* are also available for students and teachers of Italian who want to use texts that facilitate comprehension. In the classroom, one can make recourse to simple scenes, gags, or sketches from the various farces, or single acts or passages transcribed from television programs. But for the best results, it is highly advisable to introduce students to the study and use of the monologues by Fo and Rame because they are the quintessence of Fo and Rame's theatrical art. Particularly useful are the monologues in *Mistero buffo,* or *Storia della tigre e altre storie, Fabulazzo osceno,* and *Johan Padan a la descoverta de le Americhe* (translated into standard Italian and edited by Franca Rame), or the female monologues in *Tutta casa, letto e chiesa; Coppia aperta, quasi spalancata; L'eroina; Grasso è bello!;* and *Sesso? Grazie, tanto per gradire.* Monologues contain in concentrated form all of the comic and satiric elements that constitute, in an indissoluble network, the intimate linguistic and poetic quality of Fo and Rame's theater. In the narrative monologue one can perceive and experiment with the rhythm, musicality, and simultaneity of meanings typical of spoken Italian that, as in all oral linguistic codes, support and reflect the auditory and tactile perception of reality. The expressive linguistic quality of monologues is stratified and vibrant, able to emotionally involve the student—although unfortunately, this quality tends to be flattened during language acquisition. In the case of *Mistero buffo,* in practical terms, one must choose excerpts that will constitute the dramatic material of the course. I suggest, in chronological order, *La nascita del giullare, Moralità del cieco e dello storpio, Il matto e la morte,* and *Le nozze di Cana,* keeping in mind that single monologues, given the difficulty and actorial engagement they require, can be subdivided and assigned to different students who alternate in portraying the narrating character. It is also important to show (on video) and to comment upon the authors' performances of at least one or two of the chosen excerpts in class; furthermore, one might also use other comedies that give an idea of the popular style and the authors' specific way of acting.

Following are some ideas for instructors as they work with students on a theatrical text:

1. Identify linguistic difficulties and explain idiomatic expressions. Clarify the sense of "obscure" words that will certainly be present, given the texts' oral quality and their use of slang.

2. Explain the historical and sociological cruxes contained in the text, according to the students' need and curiosity. If necessary, collaborate with instructors in other disciplines. Encourage students to use the Internet to find satisfying answers or explanations that they can share with the class, in particular when the text refers to popular culture and history or medieval, Renaissance, or polemical elements of contemporary Italian society.

3. Have students read the original excerpt out loud repeatedly and demonstrate the difference between the written and spoken word, underlining how tone of voice and the speed, rhythm, and situation in which a word is uttered can change its semantic value to the point (in extreme circumstances) of completely changing its meaning.

4. Have students meet in small work groups in order to create a written summary of the text. Then have them present an oral exposition and summary to the class. It is important that this task be completed entirely by the students and not by the instructor, who must, on this occasion, be a passive presence in order to assist students in reaching the didactic objective, the "four abilities" of language: the comprehension and production of spoken language, and the comprehension and production of written language.

5. Encourage conversation and urge students to formulate appropriate questions, comments, and reflections in written and spoken form.

6. Define the Italian text to be memorized and assign parts, taking into account the students' linguistic and acting abilities.

7. Analyze and experiment with scene changes and appropriate gestures for the context suggested by the lines, the stage directions, or the situation contained in the script, in the physical space that will host the final performance. Sometimes it is useful to substitute, in the first phase, some difficult words with a grammelot invented by the students to underline that, in the play, the abilities of the speaker are connected to the mimetic expressive code "natural" to each student. This allows them to affect the meanings and expressive values of the language with their bodies or facial expressions and the volume of their voices.

8. Devise and establish the stage on which the performance happens: the setting and definition of the appointed places, both physical and psychological. Imagine what would happen to the story represented in the text if the setting or the humor of the characters were modified.

9. Have students choose who among them will be the student-actors necessary for the parts, establishing first in written and then in spoken form the physical and psychological characteristics useful for transposing the dramatic text. If necessary, add new characters to develop the situation.

10. Have students choose the stage effects needed: music, natural sounds (wind, rain, the nighttime song of crickets), natural or artificial lights that take into account the day, the hour, and the climactic conditions in which the performance takes place. Decide on appropriate costumes and makeup.

11. Adjust the play for videorecording and for the presence of an audience, or for the students and instructors of other Italian classes, who will review the performance.

12. After the performance, have a debate, in Italian, during which students go back over the salient moments of their experience; or record such reflections during one or more lessons on video, accompanied by oral and written comments.

The dialectic of language learning will thus be entirely realized during the rehearsals, which, in fact, are nothing more than an "Italian class" composed of the exploration of a text, the examination of its contents, and the reformulation and transmission of the ideas within. All this takes place at the level of a game, a game played with a maximum level of engagement and with a lively component of enthusiasm and creative spirit. It is a game that mobilizes all of the students' resources and engages the theatrical supports stimulated by the context explored. The dramatic production involves everything from scenery to lighting, from costumes to music, from ideas transmitted into words (and vice versa) to the representation of those truths and that state of consciousness to which young people, thanks to their innocence and their courage, are fortunately still sensitive.

## Notes

1. Corrado Veneziano, "Laboratorio permanente di perfezionamento della lingua italiana." Unpublished manuscript.
2. Caravacci Reynolds and Brunetti, *Teatro, Prosa, Poesia,* 1.
3. Dombroski, *Italy,* 7.
4. This and following quotations from Dario Fo are from an interview with the author, summer 2004.
5. Miklasevskij, *La commedia dell'arte,* 41.
6. Dort, "Dario Fo," 97.
7. Fo, *Manuale minimo dell'attore,* 283.
8. Fo, *Fabulazzo,* 126.
9. Olbrechts-Tyteca, *Il comico del discorso,* 22.
10. Toschi, *Le origini del teatro italiano,* 7.

## Bibliography

Caravacci Reynolds, Althea, and Argentina Brunetti. *Teatro, Prosa, Poesia.* Saratoga, CA: Anma Libri, 1982.
Dombroski, Robert. *Italy: Fiction, Theatre, Poetry, Film since 1950.* New York: Griffon House, 2000.

Dort, Bernard. "Dario Fo: o l'anti-mimo." In *Dario Fo: il teatro dell'occhio*, edited by Sergio Martin. Florence: La Casa Usher, 1984.

Fo, Dario. *Manuale minimo dell'attore*. Turin: Einaudi Editore, 1987.

———. *Fabulazzo*, edited by Lorenzo Ruggiero and Walter Valeri. Milan: Kaos Edizioni, 1992.

Miklasevskij, Kostantin. *La commedia dell'arte o il teatro dei commedianti italiani nei secoli XVI, XVII e XVIII*. Venice: Marsilio Editori, 1981.

Olbrechts-Tyteca, Lucie. *Il comico del discorso*. Milan: Feltrinelli Editore, 1977.

Pozzo, Alessandra. *Grr . . . Grammelot parlare senza parole. Dai primi balbettii al grammelot di Dario Fo*. Bologna: CLUEB Editore, 1998.

Toschi, Paolo. *Le origini del teatro italiano*. Turin: Editore Boringhieri, 1979.

## Works by Dario Fo and Franca Rame

*Ci ragiono e ci canto*, directed by Dario Fo, video, produzione C.T.F.R. 1976

*Fabulazzo, di Dario Fo*, edited by Lorenzo Ruggiero, Walter Valeri. Milan: Kaos 1992

*Il paese dei mezaràt*, Dario Fo. Milan: Feltrinelli, 2002

*Il Papa e la Strega*, Dario Fo, video, produzione C.T.F.R. 1991

*Isabella tre caravelle e un cacciaballe*, Dario Fo, video, produzione C.T.F.R. 1976

*Le commedie di Dario Fo e Franca Rame*, Vols. I–XIII. Turin: Einaudi, 1996–1998

*Lezioni di teatro*, Dario Fo, libro e video. Turin: Einaudi, 2001

*Lu Santo Jullare Francesco*, Dario Fo, libro e video. Turin: Einaudi, 1999

*Manuale minimo dell'attore*, Dario Fo. Turin: Einaudi, 1987

*Mistero buffo*, Dario Fo, video, produzione C.T.F.R. 1991

*Sesso? Grazie, tanto per gradire*, F. Rame, Jacopo e Dario Fo, video, produzione C.T.F.R. 1998

*Storia della tigre*, Dario Fo, video, produzione C.T.F.R. 1991

*Totò. Manuale dell'attor comico*, Dario Fo. Florence: Vallecchi, 1995

# *Commedia dell'Arte's Techniques: Theater Research and Italian Language Interplay*

GIAN GIACOMO COLLI

## Commedia dell'Arte: Between Myth and Reality

From the point of view of a theater practitioner, learning a foreign language is close to the process of an actor's creating a character, which typically follows a three-step sequence: to assimilate, to rehearse, and to perform the words of a text. The difference for the second language learner is that the text does not preexist in a finished written form, but is the result of a series of choices based on the knowledge of a lexicon and of the rules of grammar making use of it. Nevertheless, in both cases the initial assimilative step is essentially an act of memorization. Western acting technique, at least in the most common and institutionalized forms, still moves around this simple act. Learning a foreign language, despite the diffusion of new educational approaches and sophisticated technological tools, requires some degree of memorization as well.

The following reflections are a direct consequence of my professional career as an actor, director, theater instructor, and, most recently, teacher of Italian. Starting from the simple observation that theater acting and learning a foreign language are rooted in an act of memorization, and my having being involved, between 2000 and 2005, in quite a few university courses of Italian language for English-speaking students, it has been natural to compare the pedagogy necessary to teach such courses with my interest in acting techniques.[1] Even more, the comparison has been unavoidable when the courses were not only about language but also about theater itself. At the Italian Summer School of Middlebury College in 2003, I had the chance to teach a class, "Italian on Stage: The Myth of Commedia dell'Arte," that concluded with the production of the play *Dalla piazza al teatro: il mito di Arlecchino* (*From the Street to the Stage: The Myth of Harlequin*), an educational play on commedia dell'arte that I wrote and directed for the first time in Italy in 1994.[2] In this chapter, however, my attention focuses on an undergraduate course titled simply "Commedia dell'Arte," which did not have at its core the production of a play.

Even if the specifics of the form of theater defined as commedia dell'arte are unfamiliar to students, usually this term rings a lot of bells, though not necessarily the correct ones. A theater expert should at least know that commedia dell'arte refers to an acting technique essentially based on the use of masks and improvisation. These terms have a precise and defined meaning, to the point that commedia dell'arte is known also as *commedia delle maschere* (comedy of masks) or *commedia all'improvviso* (improvised comedy), but they fully belong to contemporary theater culture as well, though variations in their use are often quite remarkable. The starting point of what today are known as theater games, for example, is an improvisation based on a theme or suggestion. Furthermore, the influence of theater workshops such as the Living Theater and that of Jerzy Grotowsky have strongly contributed, in opposition to a passive assimilation of a text, to an idea of corporeal improvisation as a primary source for the creation of a performance.[3] Commedia dell'arte improvisation, on the contrary, invents a text on the basis of a scenario that is known beforehand by all the actors involved in the performance. As John Rudlin defines it, it is "a scenario, literally 'that which is on the scenery,' i.e. pinned up backstage. All it consists of is a plot summary, the bare bones of who does what when."[4] This sort of improvisation is facilitated by the fact that each actor always performs the same role, thus the term *mask* is synonymous with *stock character,* leaving aside the fact of whether the character actually wears a mask (Pantaloon, the Doctor, the Captain, Harlequin, etc.) or not (the Lovers, Columbine, etc.). Again, today there are texts of basic acting in which the term *mask* has a much more extended connotation and indicates "a physicalization used to reveal the character's relationship with itself, or . . . a cover to conceal and hide its true nature and identity from the world."[5] Apart from the confusion generated by different uses of the terms *mask* and *improvisation* in the context of contemporary theater, the investigation of commedia dell'arte from a broader historical and cultural perspective is valuable in unearthing the source of possible further misunderstandings regarding the atypical quality of its dramaturgical aspects.

The fact that commedia dell'arte originated in Italy is amply known. Less known is that the period in question is the second half of the sixteenth century and that Italy, at that time, was substantially an association of sovereign states. Though the Italian of Dante had spread and strengthened its role as a literary language, cultural and linguistic differentiations were still much alive, and "as a pan-Italian form, the commedia dell'arte had, therefore, necessarily to develop in a polyglot manner, using a vocabulary drawn from the northern city states and from the regions of the south."[6] Commedia dell'arte's essential trait, and the main reason for its large success, was consequently its ability to mix dialects and languages, popular and high-class culture, and servants and masters in a highly entertaining form of theater accessible to all kinds of audiences. The success of this eclectic technique in the rest of Europe during the seventeenth century and its influence on the development of certain aspects of European drama, particularly in France, is the proof of its adaptability. As a matter of fact, farces by Molière (1622–1673) were much influenced by commedia dell'arte, and later on we find "masks" in plays by Pierre Carlet de Chamblain de Marivaux (1688–1763), but it would be inaccurate to define Molière's *The Tricks of Scapin* (1671) or Marivaux's *Harlequin Refined by Love* (1720) as commedia dell'arte texts. There is no doubt that commedia dell'arte scenarios could be seen as a sort of prototypical dramatic form for any kind of modern farce, though these farcical elements are strictly related to an acting technique based on the improvisation and the stock-in-trade of the performers and only subsequently can be reduced to a literary genre.[7] Even the full plays written by commedia dell'arte actors should probably be regarded more as the recording of the verbal action performed onstage than as a literary product. This could be the case, for example, for Flaminio Scala's *Il finto marito* (*The False Husband*) (1618), one of the few examples of a full written text that can be compared with its original scenario, published in Scala's collection of scenarios *Il teatro delle favole rappresentative* (1611).[8] In conclusion, the dramaturgical and performance aspects of commedia dell'arte are so interconnected that they tend to disappear into each other. Any attempt to look at a scenario or full text related to or inspired by commedia dell'arte without considering the indispensable contribution of the actor's technique would result in an overestimation of the textual elements.

From this perspective, it is more understandable why the period of decadence and consequent disappearance of commedia dell'arte between the middle of the eighteenth and the beginning of the nineteenth centuries was a direct consequence of a technique that was unable to be renewed and to express new themes. The *commedia all'improvviso* was gradually absorbed by a new form of drama that, to become popular, needed a new acting technique in which the character did not exist but had to be created by the actor before the performance. At least at an academic level, it is known how this last period of commedia dell'arte correlates with the work of Carlo Goldoni (1707–1793), but here again, it is important to avoid the superficial conclusion that he was exclusively a commedia dell'arte author. In 1745, when Goldoni was at the beginning of his career and wrote the scenario *Il servitore di due padroni* (*The Servant of Two Masters*) for the troupe of Antonio Sacchi, one of the greatest Harlequins of the commedia dell'arte tradition, stock characters such as Pantaloon and the Doctor started to assume a more direct reference to society. The production, performed by Sacchi and his troupe in the traditional improvisational style, was a success, but Goldoni was dreaming of a new theater, an expression of the bourgeoisie that emerged with the Enlightenment, and the commedia dell'arte conventions, apart from the inventions of the talented Sacchi, did not allow innovation. As Domenico Pietropaolo concludes, "Goldoni therefore resolved to destroy *commedia* altogether and to embark on a systematic program of reform designed to transform the comic stage, expelling the stock characters, the typical plot situations, the coarse humor, and all vestiges of the genre from the professional theater." Goldoni, in other words, wrote for commedia dell'arte just long enough to realize that this traditional form of theater was an obstacle to the development of a new drama, in which characters reflecting the new times should emerge. The reasons for this change and the difficulties met by the actors who wanted to switch to a new acting technique, in which they could not improvise but had to memorize the lines written by the playwright and to shape full characters, were dramatized by Goldoni in one of the sixteen full-length plays he wrote in 1750 for the troupe of Girolamo Medebach, *Il teatro comico* (*The Comic Theater*). In this text "the expression 'commedia dell'arte' occurs for the first time in history. Goldoni uses the term to distinguish the conventional commedia dell'arte from the character-based comedies, or *commedia di carattere,* by which he intended to replace it."[9] Although for more than twenty years, between 1761 and 1783, Sacchi was able to maintain the public's interest in commedia dell'arte, thanks to the plays written for his troupe by Carlo Gozzi (1720–1806), a fierce rival of Goldoni and his reformist ideas, the collaboration between Goldoni and Medebach quickly established a new model of theater. The *commedia all'improvviso* gradually disappeared, and eventually the masks survived only in the crystallized forms of refined ceramic figurines, in a rich iconography comprising illustrations, paintings, engravings, and frescoes, but also in texts whose unusual feature is, paradoxically, that of having been created by the performance rather than by an author.

Eight years after writing the scenario for Sacchi, Goldoni published *The Servant of Two Masters* "as a fully scripted text, incorporating into it as much of the dialogue and comic business of the original impromptu performance as he had taken down in his notes. In the published version of the play, we therefore have an approximate transcription of the original performance and a good point of access to the creative potential of the performance style."[10] In this sense, Goldoni's text should be regarded more as material originally belonging to the commedia dell'arte tradition and now fixed on the written page. In practical terms, it is the nearest thing to what today would be an audiorecording of the performance by Sacchi and his troupe, and this is another aspect that must be clarified. *The Servant of Two Masters* is quite a popular text; in English there are various translations and adaptations, even for young audiences. Furthermore, the most famous Italian theater production of the twentieth century is *Arlecchino, servitore di due padroni* (*Harlequin, The Servant of Two Masters*) directed by Giorgio Strehler (1921–1997) for the Piccolo Teatro of Milan in 1948 and then restaged several times with performances all over the world. These two facts have created the false myth that commedia dell'arte is a living tradition, when it is not.[11] After its disappearance as a theater technique, commedia dell'arte began to be rediscovered in the second half of the nineteenth century and then effectively recovered, both as an academic subject and as a theater practice, during the course of the 1900s. Piccolo's *The Servant of Two Masters* is probably the contemporary theater production that more than any other has been able to recover the idea of performance belonging to that tradition, but in general Italian theater has simply carried on a sort of sensitivity for gesture, today more observable in cinema than in theater.[12] The physical postures, body rhythms and expressions, and hand mannerisms of commedia dell'arte form a set of gestures that are not easily definable. They have survived fragmentarily in the transmission of knowledge from one interpreter to another, often thanks to the phenomenon of the *famiglia d'arte,* perhaps the only aspect of the commedia dell'arte tradition that in some way has continued to survive after the art form's decay.[13] Nevertheless, because of the international fame of the Piccolo Teatro production, I have met several theater professionals or scholars in North America who asked me whether companies of commedia dell'arte still exist in Italy, as though the tradition had never been interrupted, or even whether commedia dell'arte is still the most common technique of Italian actors, nearly an equivalent of the American "method" popularized by Lee Strasberg at the Actors Studio in the late 1950s.

In planning a university undergraduate course on commedia dell'arte that aims to support the study of Italian language without being just a survey of a cultural phenomenon or a rough introduction to a theater practice, two essential points should be clarified: first, that commedia dell'arte belongs to a period of Italian theater, and Italian theater in Europe, that for various reasons gradually disappeared after the middle of the seventeenth century; and second, that *The Servant of Two Masters* of the Piccolo Teatro can be regarded as one of the best attempts to grasp the technical qualities of the commedia dell'arte tradition, but that the production is not a philological rendering of that tradition. The clarification of these points is necessary in order to detach commedia dell'arte from superficial and erroneous conclusions, and most of all to emphasize the fact that it is a theater form that, in comparison to others, has rich pedagogic implications. Two technical principles make it unique: those strictly related to the acting technique—the physical and vocal expression of the stock characters—that can be experienced in practical workshops inspired by the tradition reinvented by the Piccolo Teatro or by other living practitioners; and those concerning more properly the words performed onstage, what usually is the text but in this case becomes text only in the moment in which it is performed or improvised, as exemplified by the work of Dario Fo (1926– ), who does not consider himself a writer but an actor who writes and rewrites his texts after having tested them with the audience.[14]

The application of these principles implies quite a different approach to that simple act of memorization that is at the origin of my observations. "The Italian comedians learn nothing by heart," wrote the actor Evaristo Gherardi, the Harlequin of the Comédie Italienne in late seventeenth-century Paris. They play, he continues, "more from imagination than from memory."[15] According to this principle, Pietropaolo has observed, "Commedia audiences experience the textual otherness of performance as an entity both immanent and imaginary, an entity that has no existence outside the figurative consciousness of individual spectators, where, at every moment of the performance, it is posited as a script that dissolves immediately into nothingness." Pietropaolo emphasizes that post-Stanislavskian acting theories are not of much help in understanding the peculiarity of commedia dell'arte acting technique. In its various methodological expressions from the twentieth century on, Western acting technique has emphasized the interpreter as a mediator between the written text and the staging of it. For a commedia dell'arte performer, this mediation did not exist for the simple reason that the only textual entity was the one produced by the improvisation onstage. While in the first case the function of memory is predominant, in the second it is imagination that acts as a catalyzing element: "Acting mostly from imagination does not mean creating speech from nothing, having become sufficiently acquainted with the inner life of a character to be able to do so; it means, rather, composing theatrical text, that is to say forming chains of composite units of acted speech from a largely shared repertory of verbal and gestural signs, acquired through long practice and committed to memory."[16] By this explication Pietropaolo opens a pedagogical perspective that, as I will show, is at the root of my commedia dell'arte course.

## A Commedia dell'Arte Course: Structure, Themes, and Objectives

In the fall of 2002, I taught a course called "Commedia dell'Arte" for the Department of Italian Studies at the University of Toronto. As the course was taught in English, there were neither language nor literature prerequisites and it was open to students from other departments and disciplines as well. Nonetheless, almost all the thirty-two students enrolled in the class had attended at least one course of Italian language and a few were majoring in Italian. About a quarter of the class was of Italian background, and their Italian was often influenced by the dialect absorbed from their grandparents, who were first-generation immigrants. Considering that in Toronto there are about a half million people of Italian heritage, this was not a surprise, nor was it a surprise that in such a big multicultural city a few students also had knowledge, sometimes very advanced, of other languages such as French, Spanish, Russian, Chinese, and Portuguese. In the first class, I made it clear to the students that the course was neither a practical theater workshop nor a dramatic literature survey; I introduced Italian words and terms pertinent to commedia dell'arte; I constantly solicited the students to make use of their knowledge of the Italian language and of other subjects relevant to the course such as Italian literature, art history, drama, music, and cultural studies; and whenever possible I made connections with other languages. In this way, by tapping into the polyglot and multicultural background of the class, I was able to parallel the eclecticism that was one of the main characteristics of commedia dell'arte, and, more importantly, I could rely on the linguistic and cultural memory of the students.

Since the initial challenge of the course was to present information that was different from a traditional literature or drama class and, at the same time, was sufficiently stimulating to spark students' interest in an unconventional subject, I decided not to make use of one of the well-known commedia dell'arte surveys such as those by Pierre Louis Duchartre or Allardyce Nicoll. I did not want the students accumulating a bunch of notions without really understanding, and experimenting with, the connections between commedia dell'arte and a variety of cultural, linguistic, and literary issues.[17] That's why the course description was intentionally brief and general: "A study of the conventions of the commedia dell'arte tradition in the context of its performance history from the late Renaissance to the present. Issues examined include acting techniques, improvisation, masks and costumes, iconography, and adaptation to film." I also prepared a set of readings that was more suitable for elaboration rather than just for passive absorption. The required textbooks and readings were:

1. Domenico Pietropaolo, "The Theater." This is the first chapter of Meredith Chilton's *Harlequin Unmasked: The Commedia dell'Arte and Porcelain Sculpture,* a beautiful volume that, together with Cesare Molinari's *La commedia dell'arte,* offers one of the best available iconographic overviews of the subject. Pietropaolo's text is not only an exhaustive and, at the same time, concise introduction to commedia dell'arte from origins to decay, but it is also an enlightening view of how the connection between actors' technique and production of text transformed from improvisation based on a scenario to a fully written play. By reading the first part of this selection at the beginning of the course—the second part, titled "The Commedia dell'Arte in the Age of Enlightenment," was introduced during the sixth week—the students were able to acquire basic historical information, and I could introduce the issues linking improvisation and memorization.

2. Kenneth McKee, "Foreword," *Scenarios of the Commedia dell'Arte: Flaminio Scala's Il teatro delle favole rappresentative.* McKee's introduction to the English translation of the first comprehensive collection of scenarios, published in 1611, is another brief survey that is particularly constructive when describing the influence of commedia dell'arte on European theater.

3. Flaminio Scala, "The Tragic Events." This is a good example of a scenario because its plot, extremely similar to that of *Romeo and Juliet,* is well-known to the students, although Scala's version features a happy ending.[18]

4. Flaminio Scala, "Li tragici successi." Scala's scenario was presented also in the original Italian version so that the students, even with a minimal knowledge of the language, could compare it with the English translation.

5. Stuart Hood, "Introduction," to *Plays: One,* by Dario Fo. Hood's introduction to the first volume of the English translation of Fo's plays offers a concise but informative overview of Fo's theater and traces its roots to the commedia dell'arte techniques.

6. Dario Fo, "The Marriage at Cana." The students had a more direct experience of Fo's technique by watching video clips from his productions, primarily *Mistero buffo* (*Comic Mysteries*), and by reading the English translation of "Le nozze di Cana," one of the texts comprising the "subversive reading of Scriptures" that connects Fo to the traditions of the *giullari* (jesters) and therefore to the origins of commedia dell'arte. It was important for the students to understand how Fo composes his texts through improvisation and how he uses *grammelot,* "a mixture of dialect words

and onomatopoeia, a language that was no language and yet one audiences could latch on to and understand and still do."[19]

7. Dario Fo, "Le nozze di Cana." Like Scala's scenario, the text by Fo was also presented in the original version, which is in dialect but with the standard Italian version presented beside it. This parallelism was particularly interesting for those students of Italian background whose Italian was influenced by the dialect absorbed from their first-generation immigrant grandparents.

8. Dario Fo, excerpts from *The Tricks of the Trade* (pp. 7–12 and 56–59). *The Tricks of the Trade* is the English translation, though with some variations here and there, of the *Manuale minimo dell'attore*, the text in which Fo summarizes, in theoretical and historical terms, his approach to theater. These excerpts most clearly deal with commedia dell'arte.

9. Carlo Goldoni, *Il servitore di due padroni*. The only other mandatory text for the course was Goldoni's play in its original Italian version, easily downloadable from the Internet or in one of the various English translations available.

As we will see, apart from presenting commedia dell'arte as a cultural phenomenon, the function of the readings was to give the students the primary source for later practical exercises and to provide stimuli for further research.

The thirteen weeks of class, two one-hour classes per week, were organized to a great extent in a way that I would describe as "hands-on." In other words, after the first two weeks, which were dedicated to historical background and to the discussion of some general theater-related terms, specific topics were immediately contextualized through the presentation of iconographic, audiovisual, and written material. The variety of information opened a series of perspectives with which the students, in relation to their study interests, could immediately connect and interact, resulting in final essays that featured a markedly interdisciplinary flavor. Moreover, the multiplicity of approaches positively influenced the language skills of the students, for example, by expanding their vocabulary.

The course proceeded according to the following calendar:

Week 1—Presentation of the course and introduction to commedia dell'arte's historical time frame. After the students were introduced to the hands-on approach of the course, an entire class was dedicated to giving them an introduction of commedia dell'arte as a specific historical expression of Italian and then European theater, from 1545, the first notarization of a professional theater company in Padua, to 1780, when not a single Italian actor was left in the cast of the Théâtre des Italiens in Paris. To reflect the general nature of the first reading, commedia dell'arte was framed in the broader context of European history that goes from the Middle Ages to contemporary culture.

Week 2—Discussion of some theater-related key terms: Renaissance drama, dramatic conventions, presentational/representational theater, character, characterization, stock character, text, improvisation, etc. Since the course was offered by the Department of Italian Studies, it was assumed that the students would not necessarily be familiar with the technicality of specific drama terms that, nevertheless, were indispensable to differentiate commedia dell'arte from other, probably more well-known, forms of theater. Therefore, apart from highlighting, in the context of Renaissance drama, the development of two very different types of comedy—*commedia erudita* and commedia dell'arte—it was important to clarify the meaning of some dramatic conventions. In particular, the distinction was made between *presentationalism,* or drama as a frankly theatrical and fictional presentation, and *representationalism,* which is the theater that attempts to create an illusion of the play as real life. The term *text,* though of common usage, was also discussed in its possible specifications—*written text* and *performance text,* for example—and in relation to other terms, such as *improvisation, character,* and *stock character.*[20]

Week 3—Iconography and commedia dell'arte: slide show of stages, theaters, costumes, masks, gestures, performers, etc. The presentation of iconographic material had a double objective: one, clearly, was to offer a visual idea of commedia dell'arte performative practices such as masks in their characteristic physical positions; the other, less predictable objective, was to show to what extent the same practices were the subject for various forms of visual arts that are now one of the main documentary sources for commedia dell'arte studies.[21]

Week 4—(1) Commedia dell'arte between the Middle Ages and Baroque: movie clips from *The Seventh Seal* by Ingmar Bergman and *Molière* by Ariane Mnouchkine; (2) improvisation and grammelot: the language(s) of commedia dell'arte in video clips from Dario Fo's *Mistero buffo:* "Le nozze di Cana" and "La fame dello zanni" ("The Starving Zanni").[22] The clip from *The Seventh Seal* shows a troupe of three strolling actors performing on their wagon, used as a stage in the square of a small country village in the plague-ridden Sweden of the fourteenth century, whereas the scene from *Molière*, a sumptuous film biography of the actor-playwright, is set in the crowded market square of a French town where shows of various kinds are being performed. Bergman's scene conveys the sense of what could be a form of popular entertainment in prehumanistic Europe and, quite interestingly, is immediately followed by an intense portrayal of medieval religiosity, a procession of flagellants, that condenses a vision of the world in which theatricality, as visual category, belongs mainly to the omnipresent fear of God. This second scene works well as a transition to Mnouchkine's. The action, in which Molière is no more than a child, is supposed to take place around 1630, after his mother's death. We see the young Jean-Baptiste Poquelin, Molière's real name, and other spectators while they are watching a sort of commedia dell'arte *lazzo* where it is possible to recognize two masked characters: an old one, a kind of Pantaloon, and another one who is definitely Death. The visual transition from the fear of God to Death as a mask implies a chronological jump of about three centuries, but was of great help in introducing the students to a couple of episodes from Fo's *Mistero buffo*. With his reinterpretation of the gospel, Fo's text rediscovers the medieval jester as a prototypical factor establishing commedia dell'arte's unique technical qualities, most of all improvisation as a tool through which to modify the text while it is performed, while the elaborate physicality and the mix of dialect and grammelot of "La fame dello zanni" is a first form of the servant mask.[23]

Week 5—(1) Commedia dell'arte as improvised theater: analysis of Flaminio Scala's scenario "The Tragic Events"; (2) staging a scenario: video clips from *The World of Harlequin, Then and Now* by Gian Giacomo Colli. Scala's scenario was analyzed with the students in both its textual and performative aspects: the number and the kind of characters in relation to the structure of a commedia dell'arte company, the implicit stage directions, the function of the *lazzi*, and so on. Whenever possible, the Italian scenario was compared with the English translation. Since it was practically impossible to give the students an idea of how a scenario actually works, the best solution was to show them a few scenes from a scenario "Le tre lettere" ("The Three Letters") that, though not entirely, is part of an educational play on commedia dell'arte that was staged for the first time in Italy in 1994 and then also in Canada, in an English version, in 2001. Before inserting these scenes in the educational play, the scenario that I originally wrote for a company of eight actors, five men and three women, became the source for a written text based mostly on *repertori, centoni,* and *zibaldoni* usually written by the actors themselves, of which we still have documentation. The most famous example of these repertoires created by the actors, what Pietropaolo has described as the commedia dell'arte "largely shared repertory of verbal . . . signs," is probably Francesco Andreini's *Bravure del Capitano Spavento* of 1607.[24] The video clips presented to the students, therefore, showed actors who had memorized lines belonging to a fully written text. Nevertheless, since each scene was introduced by the reading of its corresponding plot, the students were at least able to have an indication of how the scenario was the source of a textual entity that, in theory, had to be produced by the improvisation onstage. This week concluded the first part of the course. The students had a few days to review the readings and material discussed so far and to prepare for the first test.

Week 6—First test and introduction to Goldoni's *riforma* (reform) of commedia dell'arte and to Gozzi's reaction: commedia dell'arte as scripted drama. During the first class of the week, the students had fifty minutes to write their first test, composed of twenty multiple-choice and short-answer questions.[25] The second part of the course was based on the latter part of the first reading and on *The Servant of Two Masters*. Having familiarized themselves with the structure of a scenario and with the features of commedia dell'arte's improvisation, the students were able to understand the technical implications of the reform carried on by Goldoni and of the consequent reaction by Gozzi. As I have explained above, in *The Servant of Two Masters* there are traces of the textual entity originally produced by the improvisation of Sacchi and his troupe, and it was therefore crucial that the students knew the text well and were able to identify in it not only the most macroscopic commedia dell'arte elements such as the masks, but also the underlying structure of the original scenario. Excerpts from Gozzi's texts, such as *Re Cervo* (*The King Stag*) (1762) and *Turandot* (1762), were also presented and compared with Goldoni's text.[26]

Week 7—Video of Giorgio Strehler's production of *Il servitore di due padroni*. After a thorough reading of the play, the students were able to watch the video of one of Strehler's productions of *The*

*Servant of Two Masters* with a much clearer sense of the plot and a better understanding of the comic routines. Since the *lazzi,* as the comic routines are more commonly known, were not indicated in the text, the students could have a concrete idea of them only by watching the video.[27]

Week 8—Commedia dell'arte and the other performing arts. The students were stimulated to explore signs of commedia dell'arte in other forms of theater and, more generally, in other performing arts. References were made, for example, to the connections between commedia dell'arte and the origins of classic ballet, and to the similarities between masks and clowns, but what most interested the students were the parallels between masks and film characters, such as the Tramp created by Charlie Chaplin. To provide further examples, video clips of Italian actors were introduced. Totò in *Totò Peppino e . . la malafemmina* (*Totò, Peppino and the Hussy*) (1956) and Roberto Benigni in *La vita è bella* (*Life Is Beautiful*) (1997) not only show off their commedia-like physicality, but also their ability to improvise with the language.[28]

Week 9—Commedia dell'arte as theater training: gestures, physical positions, mask technique, etc. Though the course was not intended as a practical introduction to commedia dell'arte technique, a few basic pointers regarding the use of the body and the mask were presented. Even if minimal, the direct experience helped the students have a wider perspective in their work for two main components of the course: the practical exercise and the final essay.

Weeks 10, 11, and 12—Presentation of the practical exercises. Six classes were devoted to the presentation of the practical exercises, so that each presentation, in which the students could work individually, in pairs, or even in larger groups, could use at least fifteen to twenty minutes. The word "practical" should not deceive, since the intention was not to stage a scene or an entire scenario, but to work with textual material, and therefore with language, in a way as similar as possible to that of the commedia dell'arte actors. From a pedagogical point of view, this was the most innovative part of the course. In nearly every exercise the students had the chance to improve their critical and linguistic skills by elaborating on the primary sources—Scala's, Goldoni's, Fo's—discussed in the course. These are a few examples of the exercises in which the students had to make use of standard Italian, even if their language competence was elementary:

(a) Rewriting scenes or monologues of *Il servitore di due padroni*. The main intent of this exercise was to have the students use contemporary spoken Italian. Two students, for example, rewrote scene II:6 in the form of an e-mail exchange. An interesting variation of this exercise was to have students of Italian background use some form of Italian dialect instead.

(b) Rewriting one act of *Il servitore di due padroni* in scenario form. In this exercise the students had to switch from Goldoni's dialogues to a plain narrative form.

(c) Writing the lines for the first five scenes of Scala's "Li tragici successi." This exercise was basically the reverse of the previous one, though more complex.

(d) Rewriting "Le nozze di Cana" in dialogue form. Since Fo's text is conceived as a monologue, the students had to figure out a sort of one-act play with various characters. When even an elementary competence in Italian was lacking, the students had three alternatives: to use just texts in English, to work together with students who had some competence in Italian, or to work in English and in another language of their knowledge.

(e) Translating in English scenes or monologues of *Il servitore di due padroni*.

(f) Comparing the text of Goldoni's *Il servitore di due padroni* with one or more of its English translations or adaptations.

(g) Rewriting in English grammelot Truffaldino's monologue in I:6 of *Il servitore di due padroni*. This last exercise was also carried out by a student of Russian background with no knowledge of Italian, who on the basis of an English translation rewrote Truffaldino's monologue in Russian grammelot.

Apart from these textual exercises, a few students who were majoring in drama asked to work on more performance-oriented exercises. Some practical examples of the connections between dance and the movements of the commedia dell'arte's masks were quite interesting. Two students staged a scene in English from *The Servant of Two Masters*, but the difference from the other exercises was rather evident: the students concentrated all their efforts on the memorization of the words, while in the other exercises the competence of Italian and/or English forced the students—I am now paraphrasing Pietropaolo—to compose units of speech from their repertory of verbal, and gestural if necessary, signs acquired through practice and committed to memory. Obviously, in the case of students with just elementary Italian, the final result lacked perfection, and often they had to use the dictionary. Nevertheless, the practical exercise gave them a chance to "play" with the language, since the main intent of the exercises was to produce textual material that was entertainingly communicative and not simply grammatically correct.

Week 13—Final review and second test. The penultimate class was reserved for a final review before the second and final test. Structurally similar to the first test, this test concentrated on twenty multiple-choice questions regarding *Il servitore di due padroni* and Goldoni's reform of commedia dell'arte.[29]

The final essay, of at least two thousand words, was due by the last class of the twelfth week of the course. During the third week of class, the students received a list of suggested topics and a bibliography on commedia dell'arte divided in seven main areas: bibliographical sources, general histories and surveys, texts and scenarios, iconography, actresses and actors, acting techniques, and influence on theater/dance/opera/film. Though a few students focused on themes that were too generic—"The Influence of Commedia dell'Arte," for example—in the end, there was a positive tendency for students to explore interdisciplinary territories. The most interesting essays, in this sense, were "Gestures of Greeting in Commedia dell'Arte," "The Influence of Daily Life in Commedia dell'Arte," "An Evolution of Commedia dell'Arte from the Marketplace to Prime-Time Television," and "The Three Stooges: Moe, Larry, Curly Form a Commedia dell'Arte Troupe." Other more theater-oriented essays were nonetheless interesting for their attention to linguistic aspects: "A Comparison of Commedia dell'Arte and Punch and Judy Puppet Theater," for example, and "*Romeo and Juliet* and *Romeo e Giulietta* Revised: 'Re-cycling.'"

The evaluation of the course reflected the emphasis on the hands-on approach. Since one of the main purposes of the course was to stimulate students to explore new approaches to both Italian texts and language, the total grade for the course was calculated by balancing the informative aspects with the creative ones. Consequently, the two tests counted for a total of 40 percent, equally divided, while the 15 percent of the practical exercise and the 30 percent of the final essay counted for another 45 percent. Another 15 percent was calculated for participation: 5 percent for effective class participation and 10 percent for regular attendance.

## A Student-Centered Approach

This chapter began with the observation that learning a foreign language is close to the process of an actor's creating a character, which typically follows a three-step sequence: to assimilate, to rehearse, and to perform the words of a text. In second language acquisition, "to assimilate" corresponds to the study of grammar, syntactic structures, and vocabulary; "to rehearse" relates to the application of what has been learned in the first step to a series of written and/or oral exercises; "to perform" corresponds to the use, in real or almost real situations, of what has been learned and rehearsed in the first two steps. It has also been observed that in both acting technique and second language acquisition the initial assimilative step is essentially an act of memorization. However, the analysis of commedia dell'arte's techniques demonstrates that not all acting systems necessarily follow this three-step process. By directly developing the final or performative moment, as the commedia dell'arte actors did by improvisation, the habitual memorization of a text may be transformed in a more effective process of elaboration and creation.

In the course on the commedia dell'arte, the students were able to apply a few essential aspects of this approach to the practical exercises. Goldoni's and Fo's texts were not passively absorbed as unchangeable entities, surviving only in the way they had been written and/or published, but were utilized as the source of a new textuality that was entertaining and, most of all, produced and contextualized by the students themselves. Through the exercises, from simple sentences to brief dialogues and more complex narrative structures, the students could more easily break barriers and communicate with a language perceived more as an instrument than as a corpus of grammatical rules; this was true also for the students who did not have any competence in Italian and could use only English. In practical terms, the act of memorization of fixed lines was substituted by an act of imagination in which the lines were elaborated on the basis of (1) the knowledge, at any level, the students already had of Italian; (2) the connections the students could establish between the content of the lines and any kind of personal experience, such as in the case of the above-mentioned rewriting of scene II:6 of *Il servitore di due padroni* in the form of an e-mail exchange; and (3) the sharing, between the students working on the same text and then with the other students involved in the course, of both points one and two.

Notice that these three points reflect in some way the three-step sequence by which learning a foreign language mirrors the process of theater acting. The difference is that in this new sequence the focus is more on the students literally producing text(s) than on the text itself. In pure terms of language learning, the process seems limited by the fact that the students do not improve their basic skills, but they definitely improve their language competence. This, obviously, also depends on the approach carried out by the instructor leading the course. In my case, the time dedicated to the grammar and syntax of the texts the students used was limited because of the two one-hour classes a week. However, a commedia dell'arte course like the one discussed here should not be seen as an alternative to more traditional language courses, but rather as a productive integration of them and other courses of the Italian studies curriculum that often rely more on the benefit of a parallel use of technology.

The students highly appreciated the course. In the end, they felt less frightened by the foreignness of Italian and, if we consider the multicultural structure of the class, of other non-English languages as well. Moreover, the opportunity to watch in video the eighteenth-century Italian of Goldoni and the mix of dialect and grammelot of Fo was crucial in reinforcing the idea that the language of theater is always a form of communication in which the body can be as effective as the use of words. The students experienced most vividly how theater can be a living, ever-changing art form with the exercise of writing lines for the first five scenes of "Li tragici successi." To complete this exercise, I encouraged the students to recycle and assemble a wide variety of texts, provided they had some elements of Italian and could work in the context of the scenario: the words of a love song, for example, excerpts from Italian literary texts, or even the adaptation/translation of a Shakespearean passage. Ideally, this kind of work should be the theme of a subsequent half-year course aimed at producing a complete text, eventually staged by the students themselves.

The lack of perfection in the production of Italian language, mainly due to the limited (or lack of) linguistic competence of several students, added an element of unpredictability to the course that in the end emerged as highly experimental, full of potential, and fun. One of the most positive comments came from a student who realized how much she could do with what she already knew in terms of language and, more in general, of theater and culture. As a matter of fact, the most difficult task was to convince the students that theater, as well as Italian or other foreign languages, is not just an intricate communicative structure, but a tool through which we can explore both our culture and others.

## Notes

1. I refer to courses of basic and intermediate Italian I have been teaching at the following Canadian institutions: University of Toronto, University of Toronto at Mississauga, University of Guelph, and Trent University. My interest in acting techniques is a direct corollary of my 1985 thesis, at the University "La Sapienza" of Rome, on the acting approach of the Italian director Orazio Costa (1911–1999). Based on the thesis, I wrote the book *Una pedagogia dell'attore: l'insegnamento di Orazio Costa*.
2. In 1994, I wrote and directed *Dalla commedia dell'arte a Goldoni, il teatro come professione* for the Italian theater company Teatro di Sardegna (Cagliari). The text, originally written for seven performers, was staged again in 1998 by Il Trucco e l'Anima (Brescia) with the title *Dalla maschera al personaggio, il teatro in Italia dalla commedia dell'arte a Goldoni* in a version for only five interpreters. In Italy the play has been presented more than one hundred times, for both student and adult audiences. An English translation of the latter version had its première November 10, 2001, at the George Ignatieff Theatre of Toronto with the title *The World of Harlequin, Then and Now*. The production was sponsored by the Gardiner Museum of Ceramic Art as part of the exhibition "Harlequin Unmasked: Comedy Transformed" and staged by my theater company Heartfeltricks. The original Italian version was staged at the University of Toronto at Mississauga by Professor Salvatore Bancheri in 2003 with about forty students in the course Italian Comic Theatre, and I staged the Italian version in the summer of 2003 with eleven students at the Italian Language School of Middlebury College in Vermont. A video version of the 2001 Toronto production is available on DVD by contacting heartfeltricks@ mac.com.
3. See "Improvisation" in Pavis, *Dictionary of the Theatre,* 181–182.
4. Rudlin, *Commedia dell'Arte: An Actor's Handbook,* 51. Rudlin notes also that *scenario* "came into use late in the development of the [commedia dell'arte] form; earlier names were *canovaccio, centone, soggetto,* even *commedia*" (53).
5. Epstein and Harrop, *Basic Acting,* 165.
6. Rudlin, *Commedia dell'Arte: An Actor's Handbook,* 7.

7. In their text *Acting with Style*, 126–136, for example, Harrop and Epstein seem to pursue this kind of notion by linking commedia dell'arte to other farcical forms of theater.

8. Scala, *Il teatro delle favole rappresentative*. Together with plays written by other commedia dell'arte actors, the text of Scala's *Il finto marito* has been published in Falavolti, ed., *Commedie dei comici dell'arte*, 215–365.

9. Pietropaolo, "The Theater," 21, 22.

10. Ibid., 27.

11. Apart from the classic translation by Eric Bentley in *The Servant of Two Masters and Other Italian Classics* (1958; reprint, New York: Applause Theatre Books, 1986), among the most recent adaptations are Lee Hall's *A Servant to Two Masters* (London: Methuen, 1999), produced by the Royal Shakespeare Company, Constance Congdon's *The Servant of Two Masters* (New York: Broadway Play Publishing, 2000), and Dorothy Louise's *The Servant of Two Masters* (Chicago: Ivan R. Dee, 2003). For Fulvio Fo, who in 1948 was part of the Piccolo Teatro's team, the production was not even the outcome of a preconceived directorial idea. He reports that Strehler was undecided whether or not to stage the text until the actors pulled together subjects from the repertoires, clown gags, and other tricks of their trade. Fulvio Fo is quoted by his more well-known brother, Dario, in *Manuale minimo dell'attore*, 39. Paolo Bosisio clarified that in the first version of the production Strehler's "overwhelming interest seems to be the desire to recover the specific characteristics of a unique theatrical model—the *commedia dell'arte*—and not in any sense to evaluate Goldoni critically. . . . The show appears, then, as an 'original' creation on the part of the director and the troupe, who are only making use of the playwright's text and his dialogues within the limits of the typical practice of the *commedia dell'arte*." Bosisio, "A Clapping of Hands," 8.

12. With regard to this "sensitivity for gesture" in Italian theater, see my article "Il corpo che parla," 537–539.

13. Note that *famiglia d'arte* means literally *artistic family*, and in practical terms indicates a family in which all members are actors or, in any case, are involved in the theater profession. The Andreini family—Isabella (1562–1604), Francesco (ca. 1548–1624), and their son Giovan Battista (ca. 1579–1654)—is one of the best examples of the commedia dell'arte tradition. Another good example, in modern Italian theater, is the De Filippo family, the brothers Eduardo (1900–1984) and Peppino (1903–1980) and their sister Titina (1898–1965).

14. For an overview of the commedia dell'arte practices in the twentieth century, see the third part of Rudlin, *Commedia dell'Arte: An Actor's Handbook*, 161–248. Though not superior to the experience of a practi-

cal workshop, another Rudlin text, written in collaboration with Olly Crick, *Commedia dell'Arte: A Handbook for Troupes*, offers a few useful ideas on how to stage a commedia dell'arte scenario. Fo's technique, in relation to the teaching of Italian, is discussed by Valeri in "Il teatro epico di Dario Fo e Franca Rame."

15. In the whole quote Gherardi praises Italian acting: "The Italian comedians learn nothing by heart; they need but to glance at the subject of a play a moment or two before going upon the stage. It is this very ability to play at a moment's notice which makes a good Italian actor so difficult to replace. Anyone can learn a part and recite it onstage, but something else is required for Italian comedy. For a good Italian actor is a man of infinite resources and resourcefulness, a man who plays more from imagination than from memory; he matches his words and actions so perfectly with those of his colleagues on the stage that he enters instantly into whatever acting and movements are required of him in such a manner as to give the impression that all that they do has been prearranged." Quoted in Duchartre, *The Italian Comedy*, 30–32.

16. Pietropaolo, "Scenario and Performance in the Commedia dell'Arte," 244, 245.

17. As witnessed by Heck's annotated bibliography *Commedia dell'Arte*, worldwide research on commedia dell'arte has progressively increased in the past thirty years. In the context of this growing interest, Duchartre (1929) and Nicoll (1963) still represent two of the best surveys published in English.

18. *The Tragic Events* is not the only scenario whose plot is similar to that of Shakespeare's plays. Giorgio Melchiori notes that Italian commedia dell'arte resonates in Shakespearean theater, even though it is unclear how Shakespeare could have known the text or other scenarios. See Melchiori, *Shakespeare*, 615. He highlights, for example, the similarities between *The Tempest* and the scenario *"Li Tre Satiri"* discussed by Ferdinando Neri in *Scenari delle maschere in Arcadia*. Apart from Scala's, the only other collection of scenarios translated in English is Cotticelli, Heck, and Heck, eds., *Casamarciano*. For a list of the most important collections of scenarios, see Molinari, *La commedia dell'arte*, 42–47.

19. Hood, "Introduction," x, ix. A few years after the course discussed in this chapter, Ron Jenkins published a new translation of *Mistero buffo*, together with a comprehensive introduction: "A Scandal of Epic Proportions," ix–xxxii.

20. For discussion of these terms, the best reference is still Pavis, *Dictionary of the Theatre*.

21. Apart from *Harlequin Unmasked* and Molinari, and for a more detailed approach to the visual records of commedia dell'arte, see the

section "X–The Iconography of the CdA," in Heck, *Commedia dell'Arte*,
293–326.

22. Fo, *The Tricks of the Trade*, 56. For a detailed historical and technical
analysis of grammelot, see Pozzo, *Grr . . . Grammelot*.

23. "Zanni [sometimes translated in English as *zany*] is both singular and
plural, the Venetian diminutive of Giovanni. It can be both a generic
name, referring to all zanni or the name of an actual Mask when the
character is not defined further as being Arlecchino, Brighella, Pe-
drolino, etc. In the sixteenth century it was also shortened to *Zan* as a
prefix to further identification: Zan Paolo, Zan Ganasso, etc." Rudlin,
*Commedia dell'Arte: An Actor's Handbook*, 67. Commedia dell'arte *zanni*
were usually servants and were largely responsible for carrying out the
*lazzi,* the repertoire of verbal and physical gags and buffoonery they
had at their disposal. For a description and a list of *lazzi,* in English,
see Gordon, *Lazzi*.

24. Pietropaolo, "Scenario and Performance," 244–245; Andreini's text
is published nearly integrally in Marotti and Romei, *La commedia
dell'arte e la società barocca*, 209–302. This volume offers an extended
and well-documented anthology of this kind of texts or repertoires,
originally written by commedia dell'arte professionals.

25. An example of a multiple-choice question is: Which one of the following
sentences best describes the modifier *dell'arte* in the term *commedia
dell'arte*? A—a mannered style of acting characterized by nonrealistic
movements; B—an acting technique developed by skilled performers
who wanted to professionalize their craft; C—a spontaneous form of
theater in which all the acting is improvised. An example of a short-
answer question is: Every commedia dell'arte performer had a repertoire of physical and/or verbal gags called *lazzi*. With reference to Fo's
text, to Scala's scenario, or to the videos shown in class, could you give
some examples of them?

26. See Gozzi, *Fiabe teatrali*, and Gozzi, *Five Tales for the Theater*.

27. I showed the students the video of the sixth or "Farewell Edition"
of *Arlecchino, servitore di due padroni*. After the 1948 initial edition,
Strehler staged two new versions of the production, in 1952 and 1956.
In 1963, after the premature death in 1961 of Marcello Moretti, the
actor who had created and performed Harlequin since 1948, Strehler
staged a partially modified summer edition on an open-air stage to
introduce Ferruccio Soleri, the actor who took Moretti's place in the
main role. There was then an official fourth edition in 1973, followed
by a fifth one in 1977, presented on the main stage of the Théâtre de
l'Odéon in Paris. The sixth or so-called Farewell Edition was presented
in 1987, followed by a substantially new one, the seventh, in 1990. In
1997, the same year of his death, Strehler produced an eighth version

by creating a new ending. Ferruccio Soleri has restaged the edition that toured the United States in 2005. See also Douël Dell'Agnola, *Gli spettacoli goldoniani di Giorgio Strehler.*

28. In *Totò, Peppino e . . . la malafemmina,* dir. Camillo Mastrocinque, I refer to the scene in which Totò and Peppino De Filippo arrive in Milan and ask a local police officer for information. In *La vita è bella,* dir. Roberto Benigni, I refer to the scene in which Guido, the character performed by Benigni, pretends to translate from German to Italian the speech of a Nazi guard in the concentration camp.

29. An example of a multiple-choice question on this second test is: In approaching Goldoni's "reform," what was the most difficult task for actors who were used to the technique of commedia dell'arte? A—to memorize fixed lines; B—to perform in Italian and no more in the languages of the stock characters; C—both A and B.

## Bibliography

Benigni, Roberto, dir. *La vita è bella.* Melampo Cindematografica, 1997.

Bergman, Ingmar, dir. *The Seventh Seal.* Svensk Filmindustri, 1957.

Bosisio, Paolo. "A Clapping of Hands as Large as the World." Introduction to the program of the 2005 United States Tour of *Arlecchino, servitore di due padroni.* Milan: Piccolo Teatro di Milano–Teatro d'Europa, 2005.

Chilton, Meredith, ed. *Harlequin Unmasked: The Commedia dell'Arte and Porcelain Sculpture.* Toronto: George R. Gardiner Museum of Ceramic Art, 2001.

Colli, Gian Giacomo. *Una pedagogia dell'attore: l'insegnamento di Orazio Costa.* 2nd ed. Rome: Bulzoni, 1996.

———. "Il corpo che parla: la gestualità e l'italiano fra tradizione teatrale e didattica della lingua." *Italica* 81.4 (2004): 536–550.

Cotticelli, Francesco, Anne Goodrich Heck, and Thomas F. Heck, eds. and trans. *The Commedia dell'Arte in Naples: A Bilingual Edition of the 176 Casamarciano Scenarios.* Lanham, MD: Scarecrow Press, 2001.

Douël Dell'Agnola, Catherine. *Gli spettacoli goldoniani di Giorgio Strehler (1947–1991).* Rome: Bulzoni, 1992.

Duchartre, Pierre Louis. *The Italian Comedy.* Translated by Randolph T. Weaver. Reprint. New York: Dover, 1966.

Epstein, Sabin R., and John D. Harrop. *Basic Acting: The Modular Acting Process.* Boston: Allyn and Bacon, 1996.

Falavolti, Laura, ed. *Commedie dei comici dell'arte.* Torino: UTET, 1982.

Fo, Dario. *Manuale minimo dell'attore.* Turin: Einaudi, 1987.

———. *The Tricks of the Trade.* Translated by Joe Farrell. Edited by Stuart Hood. New York: Routledge, 1991.

————. *Plays: One*. Translated by Ed Emery. London: Methuen, 1992.

————. *Mistero buffo*. 2nd ed. Turin: Einaudi, 1997.

————. *Mistero buffo*. Translated by Ron Jenkins. New York: TCG, 2006.

Fo, Dario, and Franca Rame. *Il meglio di Mistero buffo*. Videocassette. PolyGram, 1995.

————. *Mistero buffo*. Two videocassettes. Einaudi, 1999.

Goldoni, Carlo. *The Servant of Two Masters*. In *The Servant of Two Masters and Other Italian Classics*, translated by Eric Bentley. Reprint. New York: Applause Theatre Books, 1986.

————. *A Servant to Two Masters*. Translated by Gwenda Pandolfi. Adapted by Lee Hall. London: Methuen, 1999.

————. *The Servant of Two Masters*. Translated by Christina Sibul. Adapted by Constance Congdon. New York: Broadway Play Publishing, 2000.

————. *The Servant of Two Masters*. Translated and adapted by Dorothy Louise. Chicago: Ivan R. Dee, 2003.

Gordon, Mel. *Lazzi: Comic Routines of the Commedia dell'Arte*. New York: Johns Hopkins University Press, 1983.

Gozzi, Carlo. *Fiabe teatrali*. Edited by Paolo Bosisio. Rome: Bulzoni, 1984.

————. *Five Tales for the Theater*. Translated and edited by Albert Bermel and Ted Emery. Chicago: University of Chicago Press, 1989.

Harrop, John, and Sabin R. Epstein. *Acting with Style*. Boston: Allyn and Bacon, 2000.

Heck, Thomas F. *Commedia dell'Arte: A Guide to the Primary and Secondary Literature*. 2nd ed. Lincoln, NE: iUniverse, 2000.

Hood, Stuart. "Introduction." In *Plays: One*, by Dario Fo. Translated by Ed Emery. London: Methuen, 1992.

Jenkins, Ron. "A Scandal of Epic Proportions: *Mistero buffo*." In *Mistero buffo*, by Dario Fo. Translated by Ron Jenkins. New York: TCG, 2006.

Marotti, Ferruccio, and Giovanna Romei. *La commedia dell'arte e la società barocca: la professione del teatro*. Rome: Bulzoni, 1991.

Mastrocinque, Camillo, dir. *Totò, Peppino e . . . la malafemmina*. D.D.L., 1956.

McKee, Kenneth. "Foreword." In *Scenarios of the Commedia dell'Arte: Flaminio Scala's Il teatro delle favole rappresentative*. Translated by Henry F. Salerno. New York: New York University Press, 1967.

Melchiori, Giorgio. *Shakespeare*. 4th ed. Bari: Laterza, 2000.

Mnouchkine, Ariane, dir. *Molière*. Films du Soleil et de la Nuit/Films 13/Antenne 2/RAI-TV, 1978.

Molinari, Cesare. *La commedia dell'arte*. Milan: Mondadori, 1985.

Neri, Ferdinando. *Scenari delle maschere in Arcadia*. Reprint. Turin: Bottega d'Erasmo, 1961.

Nicoll, Allardyce. *The World of Harlequin*. Cambridge: Cambridge University Press, 1963.

Pavis, Patrice. *Dictionary of the Theatre: Terms, Concepts, and Analysis.* Trans. Christine Shantz. Toronto: University of Toronto Press, 1998.

Pietropaolo, Domenico. "Scenario and Performance in the Commedia dell'Arte." In *The Performance Text.* Edited by Domenico Pietropaolo. New York: LEGAS, 1999.

———. "The Theater." In *Harlequin Unmasked: The Commedia dell'Arte and Porcelain Sculpture.* Edited by Meredith Chilton. Toronto: George R. Gardiner Museum of Ceramic Art, 2001.

Pozzo, Alessandra. *Grr . . . Grammelot: parlare senza parole. Dai primi balbettii al grammelot di Dario Fo.* Bologna: CLUEB, 1998.

Rudlin, John. *Commedia dell'Arte: An Actor's Handbook.* London: Routledge, 1994.

Rudlin, John, and Olly Crick. *Commedia dell'Arte: A Handbook for Troupes.* London: Routledge, 2001.

Scala, Flaminio. *Scenarios of the Commedia dell'Arte: Flaminio Scala's Il Teatro delle favole rappresentative.* Translated by Henry F. Salerno. New York: New York University Press, 1967.

———. *Il teatro delle favole rappresentative.* Edited by Ferruccio Marotti. Milan: Il Polifilo, 1976.

Valeri, Walter. "Il teatro epico di Dario Fo e Franca Rame nelle classi di italiano in Nord America." *Italica* 81.4 (2004): 504–520.

# CHAPTER 8

# Opera as Theme, Opera as Theater: A Content-Based Approach to the Teaching of Italian Language and Culture

DANIELA NOÈ-LE SASSIER
AND FRANCES BOYD

## Introduction

These are exciting times of renewed interest in modern language education in North America. The pitch of the debate about content and method has risen. While the communicative approach, with its focus on proficiency, has made its influence felt at most colleges and universities and in most textbooks over the past twenty-five to thirty years, critics point out a number of shortcomings: it is still inadequately realized in the teaching of grammar (Aski 2003), and even when fully realized, the approach is inadequate to the teaching of literacy and often results in insubstantial content (Patrikis 2003). At the same time, the foreign language community has put forth another kind of proposition in the form of national standards, suggesting that agreement on goals can add clarity and coherence to the discussion. Nevertheless, through the years, there has been widespread consensus on the importance of modern languages in the liberal arts curriculum, an argument with nineteenth-century roots yet with pressing contemporary relevance (Lalande 1998). Educators continue to agree that language study disciplines the mind, develops sensibilities, is useful, and therefore should be part of what an educated person in our culture learns and values. Professionals in the field are again challenged to find new ways to teach modern languages.

One way to rethink, reorganize, and refresh Italian language curricula, particularly in the early years of college study, is to consider a thematic approach, a form of content-based instruction. What is radical about such an approach is its insistence on content as the organizing principle. Rather than starting from the structure of the language, the thematic approach starts from the conviction that modern languages can be taught in a way that focuses on meaning and combines subject-matter content with language skills (Snow 2001; Brinton, Snow, and Wesche 1989; Swain 1988; Crandall 1987; Mohan 1986). Moreover, theme-based instruction is compatible with the notion that curriculum materials for language study can also be designed to demand some of the analytical thinking commonly expected in any core subject at the college level.

The thematic approach to language teaching and learning, or theme-based instruction, is one version of content-based instruction (Snow and Brinton 1997). It strives to balance subject-matter content with language study, exploring ideas, not just superficial topics, but stopping short of a full-blown content course. The artistry is in the balance. First and foremost, a thematic approach offers an organizing principle, not a method or technique. A thematic syllabus or curriculum comprises a series of units organized around themes that could be "powerful ideas" (Lipson, Valencia, and Peters 1993), social issues, or current events. Texts should be authentic (that is, originally produced for native speakers) or simulated authentic, interesting to students, varied in genre and medium, accessible in language and culture, and potentially valuable for language study. Activities can be developed around language in the texts, as well as language external to the texts but useful for discussing them. Through a range of tasks and exercises that require both receptive and productive use of language, it is possible to give students practice in the four language skills, vocabulary, grammar, culture, and the various communicative competencies, as demanded by the educational setting. Notably, thematic units can easily incorporate multiple texts (readings, listenings, visuals) for integrated skill development and can readily overlap content for constructive redundancy.

As an organizing principle, the thematic approach is flexible, allowing the materials writer to select themes and texts, design and sequence activities, and assess and give feedback to students at different times and for different purposes. Moreover, the approach can accommodate specialized skills such as literacy (Kern 2003) or critical thinking (Benesch 1999), which could also be key objectives in building a thematic syllabus for college-level language courses. Theme-based instruction promotes proficiency and is compatible with communicative methods but elevates content above all other considerations. A thematic approach starts with meaning and sticks with it throughout, as a context to link the various skills, a way to motivate and sustain motivation, and a means to enhance memory and learning.

This chapter explores opera as both theme and genre (theater) for language learning. In the first part, "Opera as Theme," we discuss the elements of an approach to teaching opera thematically (text, activities, assessment) and the special relevance of this approach to teaching culture, sustaining motivation, and connecting to core disciplines through critical thinking. In the second part, "Opera as Theater," we focus on the particular power of the theatrical aspects of opera to encourage language learning. This genre lends itself to playing with identity, collaborating with others, and improvising with language.

## Opera as Theme

In its totality and in its theatricality, opera may easily appear to be wildly unsuited to the early years of college language study. It is, in the end, all about the music and the luscious suitability of the Italian language for singing. If we confine ourselves to the central canon of romantic works written in Italian and by Italians, the repertoire includes operas by Gaetano Donizetti, Ruggero Leoncavallo, Pietro Mascagni, Gioacchino Rossini, Giacomo Puccini, and Giuseppe Verdi (see Appendix A). The text for many of these works is poetry of questionable quality and, with the exception of a few phrases, certainly not a linguistic model for anyone purporting to communicate in modern Italian. Worse yet, opera is elite, highbrow, mannered, formal, artificial, not commonly performed well, and dependent on huge infusions of funds from moneyed patrons. As a group, opera buffs are among the most reactionary of audiences, preferring to hear *Tosca* for the twenty-fifth time to risking the price of a ticket to a lesser-known or unknown work. And yet, even the most haphazardly educated American college student knows that opera is identified with Italian culture and is a central export of Italy to world culture. For this reason alone, it ought to attract our attention as language educators.

Opera can indeed be a strikingly appropriate, effective, and thoroughly enjoyable part of the Italian foreign language curriculum when approached thematically. We envision opera as one theme in a comprehensive Italian language curriculum whose goal is to develop communicative and intercultural competence at a high-beginning to high-intermediate level, or beyond. While some language educators have proposed reading librettos, our idea is to use the opera narrative as a "stimulus to fresh thought" (Maley and Duff 1982). In this sense, study of an opera is viewed not as literary analysis, nor as preparation for public performance, but rather as content for creative exploration. Therefore, opera librettos and scores are not used as texts per se; instead, a recorded performance of an opera on video is used as context and pretext for language learning.

It also must be noted that opera study for language learning is not a new idea. A handful of enthusiasts have written about teaching opera to, for example, high school students learning Italian (Brady 1980; Bruno 1989), college students learning French (Hekmatpanah 1993), and adult students learning English as a second language (Beliavsky 2001). Doubtless, there are many more unsung instructors who have introduced opera in the language classroom to share their passion and awaken students' interest. A number of first- and second-year textbooks for Italian, too, include readings, conversations, or language exercises referring to music, with scattered references to opera. A content-based approach to teaching Italian is not entirely new, either (Bragger and Rice 1999; Dupuy 2000).

When made accessible through thematic units, opera and the world of opera can become generative themes for the first years of Italian language study, offering contexts for teaching culture, sustaining motivation, and connecting to core subjects through both academic content and critical thinking. At the same time, as opera is a kind of theater, theatrical activities within such theme-based opera units lend themselves to playing with identity, collaborating with others, and improvising with language, all of which foster the deep engagement so crucial to successful language learning.

Though units might be arranged to emphasize different sets of skills, the component parts remain essentially the same (Stoller and Grabe 1997). Here, each element will be illustrated with reference to a specific unit on *Tosca*. In this example, the principal learning objectives are development of speaking, vocabulary, and cultural awareness. We selected *Tosca,* one of Puccini's masterpieces, because it is performed more often than any other opera in the repertoire and is characterized by just the mix of intrigue, pageantry, and emotion that is apt to engage students.

## Text

In composing a thematic unit around an opera, materials writers can select texts in various genres and media. To integrate language skills, unit writers will want to select authentic texts or write simulated-authentic reading and listening passages of varied lengths and levels of difficulty.

In this case, the main text is a performance of *Tosca* on an English-subtitled DVD, from which the students learn the story. Other authentic texts include the lyrics of an aria, "Recondita armonia," and two contrasting performances of it on CD, several well-known phrases from the libretto, a few quotations from music or culture critics, and an interview from Italian radio (see Appendix B). These are supplemented by simulated (instructor-written) texts, including an academic lecture, model lecture notes, and program notes. Cast photos are also used. Additional short readings are instructor-written summaries in simple Italian of information from various sources or, in lieu of these, student-selected material from the Internet.

It is important to note that the text of the libretto itself does not provide the main text for the learners. Like many operagoers, students learn to appreciate the opera through familiarization with its plot, not necessarily through reading the libretto word for word, which in their case would present special difficulties and uncertain rewards. With the exception of a few arias, the main texts are visuals, lecture notes, program notes with summaries, interviews, quotations from critics, and newspaper articles. The scarceness of language from the libretto in the units allows the plot to be utilized more as a sort of commedia dell'arte–type *canovaccio* to be explored and supplemented by the students as they spontaneously role-play and/or perform specific skits.

## Activities

It is in the classroom activities that professors can appreciate the delicate balance between content and language that characterizes theme-based instruction. In activities orchestrated by the instructor, learners interact with the texts in ways that guide them to construct an understanding of the narrative and its opera-world context at the same time as they develop language skills. Also, as they work through a thematic unit, "students tend to feel they are on a journey of discovery with the teacher" (Numrich 2001). The journey refers to a state of mind, not a fixed itinerary. Thus, the activities presented here are in a sequence, but the sequence, activities, and "stops" along the way are simply suggestions. Materials writers and instructors will find ways to plan theme-based units to suit their individual educational settings (Noè and Boyd 1997).

1. *Introduction.* The *Tosca* unit begins with a quiz on stereotypes about singers and audiences, which is later followed up by an informed reconsideration. Misinformation, especially if it is widespread, can be a provocative starting point for the teaching of culture (Abrams 2002). Students also match character sketches to people in a cast photo, identifying the archetypal soprano heroine (Tosca), tenor hero (Cavaradossi), baritone villain (Scarpia), and some of the minor characters. Students could also make some interesting cross-cultural observations about this topic by comparing data on opera audiences (age, education, socioeconomic status) and on funding models in Italy and the United States. To complete this introduction, the teacher gives an illustrated academic lecture summarizing background information on the opera's cast of characters, its architectural setting in Rome, and its immediate and enduring popular success. Students take notes to enhance their comprehension, then compare and flesh out their notes, and finally use them to fill in an outline (model notes) of the lecture.

Through these sorts of explicit culture-based activities related to opera, students begin to feel a heightened cultural awareness. To deepen their level of awareness by developing the skills, values, and attitudes that comprise intercultural competence (Bennett 1998; Hinkel 1999), similar critical dialogues, both planned and unplanned, must occur frequently in class and play a part in assessment. The multiple realities within opera and the opera subculture can be useful starting places.

2. *Story.* The purpose of the next (and much longer) set of activities is to help students become familiar with the story as well as the language to describe and discuss it. These tasks get them involved in reading, rereading, telling, and retelling the opera story until it becomes part of their repertoire.

After watching Act I of a subtitled DVD of *Tosca,* students fill in "program notes" with useful vocabulary, then predict Act II, watch it, and do another fill-in exercise. In these notes that simulate the plot summaries commonly available at the theater, the text retells in words the story that students have seen on tape. Other activities focus on characters. To interpret the attitude and intention of characters, students analyze the villainy of the chief of the secret police, Scarpia. Using a graphic organizer, they work together to identify examples of his egregious abuse of political and personal power in each act. After watching a replay of part of the negotiation between Scarpia and Tosca (Act II), students analyze their competing intentions and then act them out in a theater exercise: face-to-face dialogues, first taking one role then the other, then switching partners to negotiate with increasing fluency and confidence. In a number of activities over the course of several classes, including filling in program notes and theme charts, creating dialogues, and participating in small-group discussions, students become increasingly familiar with the plot, characters, and setting of the opera.

3. *Grammar and vocabulary.* In this set of activities, learners use the context of the opera to practice useful grammatical forms and vocabulary. Multiple exposures to these forms in context gradually build and extend their knowledge.

Verb tenses and forms are practiced and reviewed in many controlled and semicontrolled exercises such as imaginative conversations and cued questions and answers. For instance, to practice the formal imperative, they imagine a conversation between a veteran Tosca and a novice who is eager not to incur the wrath of the stagehands:

> Non chieda troppe cose! Sia gentile con tutti! Non perda la pazienza! E guardi bene prima di gettarsi da Castel Sant Angelo!

Or, to practice the subjunctive, students use cues to ask and answer questions about a character's feelings and motivation:

| | |
|---|---|
| *Student A:*<br>(*Tosca/coraggiosa*) | Pensi che Tosca sia coraggiosa? |
| *Student B:* | Sì, penso che Tosca sia coraggiosa perché non fa quello che chiede Scarpia . . . |
| *Student A:*<br>(*Tosca/scenata di gelosia*) | Perché Tosca fa una scenata di gelosia a Mario in chiesa? |

| *Student B:* | Perché crede che Mario l'abbia tradita |
| *(tradire)* | con la donna del ritratto. |

While useful vocabulary appears in the grammatical exercises, it becomes the explicit focus of another set of activities in which students explore meaning, usage, and form. These exercises include narrative discourse frames in which students either fill in the appropriate word ("Quando Scarpia fa vedere il ventaglio a Tosca, questa si ingelosisce") or the appropriate word form ("Scarpia ha fatto di tutto per fare ingelosire Tosca"). Later, the same expressions are recycled in personal contexts ("Sii sincero/a: ti piace fare ingelosire le persone qualche volta? Quando e perché?"). In addition, students become familiar with a handful of famous expressions from the opera that have either entered the vernacular or are standard Italian—for example, "L'ora è fuggita!" and "Quanto? . . . Il prezzo!"—by matching expressions to situations in which they might be used and perhaps using them in dialogues. To provide yet another exposure, students have fun with the language by writing "vocabulary paragraphs" in which they cram as many words and word forms as possible into a short (perhaps humorous) piece related to the opera: a diva's diary, a violinist's view from the orchestra pit, or a fan letter to a singer.

The narrative and the opera world offer a constellation of possibilities for focused practice on grammar and vocabulary.

4. *Music.* Here, the purpose is to analyze in depth one signature piece of music from the opera in order to see how music and lyrics work together in an aria or duet to reveal character. Further, the purpose is to compare performances and express personal preferences.

From *Tosca*, we have chosen "Recondita armonia," with "Vissi d'arte" and "E lucevan le stelle" as close seconds. To begin, students use their knowledge of Italian to fill in a cloze, then listen to the CD to check their work. With carefully constructed exercises, students discover how the lyrics lend themselves to singing, how an emotional high point is punctuated by the music, and how different artists, in this case Luciano Pavarotti and Plácido Domingo, interpret a piece of music. In one class, the students were fascinated when a knowledgeable student explained the considerable differences in training and approach between the two tenors, ending with this trenchant summary: "Domingo è più passionale, Pavarotti ha più tecnica."

With or without technical knowledge of music, students can gain insight into opera and language by close analysis of one aria or duet. Such activities as cloze, comparison of performances, and expression of personal opinions work well for this purpose.

5. *The story interpreted.* At this point, it is helpful to review the story and reflect on its meaning. Using role-play and analysis, students interpret the opera and consider its meaning and appeal. To do this requires familiarity with the story and language they have studied thus far.

In the *Tosca* unit, language learners work through two sustained speaking activities: a panel and an academic discussion. In the panel—an extended role-play in the form of a news conference—students ask provocative questions of the "characters," who use their knowledge and imagination to answer. Students work with the same content and language from the DVD, program notes, and grammar and vocabulary exercises but they now retell the story from the point of view of a particular character and elaborate on it. This activity is followed up with a short writing assignment (in character) and group feedback on language. A videotape of the panel with error-correction worksheets works well in class or lab. This also affords a rare opportunity for learners to observe themselves speaking Italian and to do some useful self-reflection and self-evaluation (in writing). In the academic discussion, students analyze the opera with selected critical concepts or theories. The instructor kicks off the discussion by introducing a pithy quote from the work of a critic of music or culture, for example:

> Quattro opere di Puccini finiscono con il suicidio di quattro donne: Floria Tosca in *Tosca* (1900), Cio-Cio-San in *Madama Butterfly* (1904), Angelica in *Suor Angelica* (1918), Liu in *Turandot* (1924). . . . [E ha aggiunto che] queste donne, attraverso il suicidio, difendono le loro convinzioni e asseriscono la loro integrità fisica, morale e spirituale. (Thierfelder 1992, trans. D. Noè)

Students paraphrase the quotation, stretching their vocabulary, and then continue by discussing how this notion applies or does not apply to Tosca: is she a heroine who commits suicide "in defense of her convictions and of her physical, moral, and spiritual integrity," or is she a victim? The interpretation section ends with a reevaluation of the stereotypes brought up in the introductory opera quiz.

In such activities as the role-play panel, academic discussion, and reevaluation, students are guided to use the story and language they have learned to dig more deeply into interpretation and use their Italian to express meaningful ideas and feelings.

6. *The story in its cultural context.* At this point in the journey, students are ready to broaden their understanding of the opera and its cultural context by inquiring further in one or more ways: by reporting on a particular aspect (cultural, historical, literary, theatrical); by interacting with a guest speaker; by doing research via the Internet; and/or by experiencing a live performance. These activities provide new vantage points from which students can view the opera and new ways for them to apply their Italian language skills. For reports on *Tosca,* language learners can find their own materials in English or Italian on the Internet, or teachers can distribute prepared summaries, controlling the language level (recycling vocabulary and grammatical structures) and quality of information. It works best if three or four students prepare and then report the new information to small groups. During the reporting phase, the other students listen, ask clarifying questions, and take notes on ideas and examples for their final essays. With a two- or three-minute limit, reporters have time to rotate, improving their delivery with practice. Instructors circulate to give the speakers written feedback on fluency, accuracy, and pronunciation.

To find a guest speaker, teachers can turn to Italian speakers either on campus or in the larger community. An interactive presentation by an opera buff has the potential to bring some excitement and perspective on the opera world to the academic setting.

Still, a night at the opera has no equal in its emotional effect. To arrange the event may take a good deal of trouble, but a good performance in the theater is the ultimate culminating event for a thematic unit on opera. It is even more meaningful if followed up in class by activities that encourage learners to react, compare, and express their preferences. At a performance of *Tosca* at the Metropolitan Opera, for example, students were struck by the differences in Scarpia: "Il personaggio di Scarpia ieri sera a teatro era meno cattivo di quello del video, e questo lo ha reso più ambiguo. Forse Tosca avrebbe potuto amarlo." As Pope John Paul II had recently died, students were also eager to compare the political influence of the Catholic Church in the opera as well as in the modern world: "È incredibile che il papa avesse tanto potere politico e non solo spirituale!"

In fieldwork activities such as giving reports, talking with guest speakers, or attending performances, students can reach a new level of sophistication in their understanding of the work and in their practical use of Italian.

7. *Conclusion.* As the journey through the thematic unit comes to an end, it is appropriate to reflect on and evaluate the experience. The well-composed thematic unit prepares students to synthesize information and express an opinion in a longer piece of academic writing. As the redundant and overlapping layers of the unit begin to work on students' awareness of both content and language, many will feel a sense of mastery.

In the *Tosca* unit, instructors prepare with a prewriting discussion on the enduring success of this opera. Does it all boil down to a good story with good music, or can other reasons explain its popularity? When revised essays are ready, teachers choose two or three for classmates to appreciate and analyze. Although some students focus on the historical context as an explanation for the opera's continuing appeal, others highlight its thematic content, for example: "I sentimenti rappresentati nella *Tosca* sono universali: l'amore, il coraggio, la passione politica e l'arte. Per questo è così famosa, perché le persone possono identificarsi con le emozioni dell'opera." By the end of an opera-based thematic unit, learners can draw on a wealth of content and language for a well-developed discussion and academic essay. They also have the knowledge and experience to formulate a critical response to stereotypes about opera and to articulate a personal opinion of an opera.

## *Assessment*

Assessment should harmonize with the thematic approach: balance content and language, integrate skills, and be authentic and ongoing (Turner 1992). To assess and give feedback on productive skills, teachers can use rubrics—grids with ranked performance criteria—to make assessment clearer to students and simpler for themselves. For speaking and writing, a four- or five-point scale with specific criteria indicating the expectations at each level of performance can be created or adapted. To score and give detailed feedback on speaking tasks, the instructors may find it useful to record students' spoken language so that they can listen again later, in tranquility, and write down feedback on positive aspects as well as errors. Similar rubrics, with leveled descriptors in such categories as accuracy, evidence, and stereotypes, have also been proposed for assessing cultural proficiency (Storme and Derakhshani 2002). Independent evaluation of cultural awareness is important, writers are quick to point out, because intercultural competence often develops independently of communicative competence.

In the *Tosca* unit, the objectives include development of skill in speaking, vocabulary, and cultural awareness, with writing and critical thinking as supports. Many of the recommended activities—improvised dialogues, panel discussion, content reports, vocabulary paragraphs, short written pieces, and the final essay—can be assessed as students move through the unit, using rubrics of one's own design. In fact, frequent and balanced feedback on speaking, writing, and culture contributes to proficiency, as it raises learner awareness, expands the learner's repertoire, and increases confidence. As the thematic context repeats and recycles, the positive effect of assessment becomes an additional, overlapping layer for learning. Moreover, ongoing assessment helps instructors, as it gives them information that can help them make learning objectives, classroom activities, and assessment criteria more congruent.

For formal in-class exams, the instructor can create other tasks that fit with a thematic, integrated-skills approach and with the skill focus of their particular unit, for example:

- Read a plot summary of an act or scene, and then rewrite it from the point of view of one of the main characters. Use present (or past) tenses.

- Read a newspaper article (instructor-written) describing key events (say, Cavaradossi's execution, Tosca's jump from the parapet). Rewrite the first paragraph, correcting factual inaccuracies and omissions. Edit the second paragraph for errors in verb tense and form.

- Listen to a dialogue between two audience members (instructor-written) expressing different opinions about a performance of a scene you are familiar with. In writing or speaking, summarize the issue, and then say whose opinion you agree with and why.

- Listen to a dialogue between two students (instructor-written) discussing stereotypes about opera and the world of opera. In writing or speaking, summarize the points and respond to them with examples from the opera you have studied.

- Work in a small group. Pick a question out of a hat about a character's attitude and intention in a particular scene. In a one-minute oral presentation, answer the question. Continue as each student chooses and responds to a different question.

- Work with another student. Choose a problem or situation from a list. Plan and perform a two-minute dialogue between the characters or audience members, as appropriate. Include selected vocabulary and idioms from a list.

At the end of a ten- or twelve-hour thematic unit on opera, students tend to feel that they have covered a lot of ground, that they have learned some opera through Italian and some Italian through opera. Many comments to this effect appear on end-of-course evaluation forms. In the *Tosca* example, we have suggested texts, themes, activities, and assessments that focus primarily on speaking, vocabulary, and culture, with writing and critical thinking as supports; however, an opera context could certainly be exploited differently, as a pretext to highlight other skills in keeping with the focus of the course.

## Teaching Culture

With all the possible subject matter for a theme-based Italian language curriculum, Italian grand opera might be considered an unusual or specialized choice, something for opera buffs, theater lovers, or musicians. In our experience, however, unusual content or an unusual angle on familiar content is, in fact, a positive quality. It makes for "dynamic" language study: students learn something as they learn language. Opera might also be considered too upper class as subject matter, something for the elite and privileged. Again, this prestige value can also have the opposite effect: it can increase opera's appeal for some learners. What might not be readily apparent is the special power of opera to develop sensibilities through its emotional resonance, eliciting empathetic and reflective responses in students (Blasco, Moreto, and Levites 2005). Beyond these qualities, however, the opera repertoire and its world have a great deal more to offer the language learner, in particular. This body of work presents a rich vein for Italian language educators to mine for teaching culture, sustaining motivation, and connecting to core disciplines through academic content and critical thinking.

Yet the issue is how to make this cultural content accessible and meaningful for students. Often, in language classes, if culture is taught explicitly, it may be reduced to the four Fs: food, fairs, folklore, and facts (Kramsch 1991). In other cases, however, it is simply left implicit and not taught at all, as if it were either too obvious or, just the opposite, too elusive. In a real sense, language educators, both native and nonnative speakers, are in a unique position to act as cultural guides and coaches, helping students probe the web of values and beliefs that make up culture. A thematic approach encourages broad thinking about content, including cultural content. With theme-based instruction, instructors can create a critical dialogue between the source and target cultures (Cortazzi and Jin 1999). Thus, in a unit on opera, the question is how to bring twenty-first-century U.S. students into a critical relationship with this rarified nineteenth-century Italian cultural product. Theme-based instruction, with its insistence on content and language, can open the door wide to culture.

Instructors can begin by thinking broadly about cultural aspects of the theme. Using a practical teaching model (Fantini 1997)—culture as products, practices, and perspectives—we can imagine a theme-based unit on opera leading to many stimulating topics: the presence of opera in daily life and language in Italy; the appropriation of opera in popular culture; the contemporary opera world of singers, audiences, conductors, theaters; the social status of opera in Italy and the United States; the subculture of opera; the economics of opera in Italy and the United States; opera as an export; the education and career development of opera singers. Then, once ideas are on the table, teachers can choose narrowly, writing activities on specific topics in order to stimulate critical and comparative dialogue about a few selected aspects of culture.

When composing or teaching a thematic unit, it is helpful to keep in mind an overarching theme, which could be expressed in the form of a question. The materials of the unit can be arranged to suggest many possible answers.

In the *Tosca* unit, for example, the question is: what explains the enduring appeal of *Tosca*? Certainly, the story itself provides some answers. The opera deals with profound human experiences: evil, love, freedom, and sacrifice. The romantic love of the singer Tosca for the painter Cavaradossi is undermined by the evil police chief Scarpia, who tries to manipulate her for his own pleasure. With their political freedom threatened by Scarpia, Cavaradossi and his friend Angelotti fight for the cause but end up sacrificing their lives.

Soon after, Tosca loses her life as a victim or as a martyr for love and art, depending upon the interpretation. This dramatic action is punctuated by inspiring arias and duets in which the characters distill their thoughts and feelings on these transcendent themes. Another answer to the question of the opera's popularity may be found in the fact that the story alludes to the role of art and artists in society: Tosca and Cavaradossi challenge the authorities and, as a result, are forced to act clandestinely. Still other answers crop up in materials related to the opera and to opera production. The work connects to many academic areas of interest to students, such as literary or historical sources, feminist or queer theory, or challenges in set design and staging. Moreover, *Tosca* and other operas lend themselves to a host of cultural topics, including, for instance, stereotypes and preconceptions of opera, the economics of opera, and the growing audience for opera.

In all of these angles, students can find possible answers to the question of the work's appeal, so they can play with ideas throughout the unit and eventually develop an informed opinion.

## Sustaining Motivation

Through a sublime marriage of story, drama, and music, opera motivates students and sustains their motivation through potentially banal exercises on grammar, vocabulary, pronunciation, and so on. The context allows for integration of listening, speaking, reading, and writing skills, as well as integration of content with skill development, so that every activity is more meaningful and memorable (Gianelli 1991). Opera themes—compassion, death, honor, intrigue, love and lust, sacrifice, social class, switched identities—have wide appeal and can be recycled in many variations for language practice. And, it must be said, music makes all the difference. It simply transforms the mood, lowers anxiety and stress, and rewards people with sheer pleasure. Moreover, a theme-based approach motivates instructors, too. It does not require expertise on the part of teachers, some of whom may never have been interested in opera before. In fact, the multifaceted grandeur of opera tends to keep teachers interested, as they make the journey of discovery along with the students.

It is difficult to overstate the importance of attitude and motivation. Some studies suggest that content-based approaches have an advantage over grammar-driven models in this regard. Not only do students learn as much language as they learn in traditional classes, but there is also evidence that they come away with significant gains in motivation, positive attitudes, confidence, and interest (Lafayette and Buscaglia 1985). As we have seen in the *Tosca* unit, activities in theme-based language study can connect to students' interests, awaken new interests, and even link students to opera buffs and opera performances in the surrounding community. As one student remarked: "Adesso tutte le volte che vedrò un'opera penserò al periodo politico e sociale in cui è ambientata." In our experience, opera units can motivate students to continue their Italian studies, consider travel, become educated audience members, or even pursue an Italian connection in their professional lives. Thus, those who may have been simply instrumentally motivated to fulfill a language requirement may perhaps discover a deeper integrative motivation or perhaps rediscover a deeply personal reason for pursuing language study.

## *Connecting to Core Disciplines through Critical Thinking*

Finally, apart from teaching culture and motivating learners, a theme-based approach to opera can help connect the early years of Italian language study to the later years, as well as to the academic subjects and analytical thinking that are at the heart of a liberal arts education. If we continue to agree that students ought to be able to begin study of a language in college, we can be responsible for offering them enriched content-based courses that draw on the same critical thinking skills they routinely use in all of their academic courses. In this sense, theme-based instruction has the potential to blur the dysfunctional division between language and literature courses (Bragger and Rice 1999; Dupuy 2000). In the *Tosca* unit, we see that a thematic opera unit can include content from humanities, social science, and interdisciplinary programs—literature, the arts, history, economics, anthropology, sociology, gender, culture, and media studies—allowing materials writers to match and/or expand the interests of students.

Connecting language learning to academic content is one thing, but connecting it to academic thinking is quite another. Materials writers can help heal the language/literature breach in this even more fundamental way by designing opera-based language activities that depend on analytical thinking. What is important to notice in the *Tosca* example is that the language activities in every section of the unit are crafted to require critical thinking (Brookfield 1987). Introductory activities ask students to share experiences, make observations, and identify assumptions about opera, which they later reconsider. Comprehension activities begin with literal comprehension, but go beyond it to encompass inferential thinking: interpretation of attitude, behavior, and intention. Such interpretation is called for in many of the grammar and vocabulary exercises as well. The unit includes activities requiring classification of data as a prelude to comparison, contrast, and reflection. Other activities require synthesizing of information from more than one source, drawing conclusions, and evaluating information. Taken together, such carefully constructed contextualized exercises, questions, and tasks promote deep processing in the target language. What we are suggesting is that, even with limited language, students can and must engage their analytical minds as part of foreign language study. And, if higher-order cognitive processes are continually stimulated as students speak and write in Italian, they will see their language grow in complexity, fluency, and precision.

The possibilities for language learning with opera are innumerable, but they do not flow inevitably from the raw material. Materials writers and instructors must unearth the potential in works like *Tosca* and make such materials accessible by identifying objectives, selecting texts, designing language-learning activities, crafting assessment tasks, and carefully composing thematic units out of all of these elements (Noè and Boyd 2003).


## Opera as Theater

Like theater, opera is a dramatic art. The essence of drama, according to Ezra Pound, is "persons moving about on a stage using words," and the art of the playwright is to provide the actors with words that develop character and plot (Barnet, Berman, and Burto 1981). In contrast, it would not be meaningful to make a small modification and say that the essence of opera is persons moving about (or, more often, staying put) on a stage singing. Unlike theater, the emotional intensity of grand opera arises from the music in combination with drama, words, dance, costume, and scenery. Moreover, a libretto is not comparable to a literary text: it is likely to be a story from literature, myth, or history retold in poetic form and is a relatively minor part of the experience. Few operagoers know the name of any librettists. In fact, so secondary are the lyrics to many listeners' enjoyment that only with the advent of supertitles and subtitles have most audience members been able to follow the text in any detail.

Despite these important differences, opera is a form of theater, and it is precisely the theatrical aspects of opera that make it an especially appropriate and effective context for language learning. Drama deals with emotion, movement, interaction, with things unfolding before us in time. As drama, opera lends itself to role-play, collaboration, and improvisation. Together, these features provide powerful metaphors and experiences for language learners.

## Playing with Identity

Many operas involve complex, intense, and layered forms of role-play, where social and gender identities are changed or exchanged, disguised or unmasked (Fanselow 1992). Even in *Tosca*, there is an example: the fugitive Angelotti changes into his sister's clothing to escape Scarpia's henchmen (Act I). Students can be encouraged to step into the context of the opera and, using their personalities and imaginations, reenact or create variations on it. As we have illustrated with *Tosca*, they can participate in argumentative dialogues or write letters (or diary entries) in the role of a character. Also, they can take part in a panel discussion, which calls for sustained involvement in the role and, depending on classmates' questions, creative invention of unstated events and feelings. They can role-play through the creation of "missing scenes," prequels, sequels, or even an entire mini-opera based on stereotypical characters, expressions, events, and settings (Whiteson 1996; Noè and Boyd 2003). Not confining students to the language of the libretto makes them freer to explore, create, and express.

For language learners, such role-play is a metaphor for the psychological experience of finding a voice in another language and culture. This immersion is particularly important for those studying in a foreign language environment. Surrounded by their native tongue and natal culture, they have so little exposure to the language that any sustained experience takes on greater significance. In long and short role-play activities, students can act as if they were Italian, can play at being Italian, taking a small step in a safe environment toward an expanded sense of self. Role-play also relates to students' lived lives, to what might be a very real time of experimentation with and search for social, gender, ethnic, and/or racial identity. Although seeking and finding an identity in the second language cannot be accomplished quickly, when complex and culturally challenging activities such as role-play based on rich texts become regular features of the curriculum, language students can begin to construct their "own place" in another culture or a "third place" as a nonnative speaker in another culture (Kramsch 1993).

## Collaborating with Others

Opera and theater production require ensemble work, with close collaboration of the director, the performers, and many people behind the scenes. A collaborative process is also central to dramatic activities for the classroom and even to language learning itself. The work of some learning theorists, such as Vygotsky (1978), emphasizes the social and interactive nature of learning and the principal role of language in the learning process. The value of collaborative learning is further supported by research on learning styles and strategies, which points out that most academic settings are geared for auditory learners while, in fact, significant percentages of the population favor visual or kinesthetic styles. Thus, the movement implied in the more or less kinesthetic role-play activities, even if it means simply getting students out from behind tables and chairs or switching table chairs around, enhances learning for many students (Reid 1995).

On a practical level, by reconfiguring learner-teacher roles, collaborative activities multiply the amount and variety of interaction possible in a classroom setting. In such ensemble tasks as in-character dialogues and panel discussions, time for student speaking and listening is maximized, while teachers are free to observe, listen, and correct errors. Also, in pair and group work, students practice pragmatic competence, both in a broader range of functions such as those involved in planning (proposing, expressing preferences, agreeing, disagreeing) and in a broader range of sociolinguistic registers (an experienced diva to a novice; the chief of police to a prisoner). Finally, student-to-student interaction creates comfort that encourages the shy and less fluent to participate.

Thus, the essentially collaborative nature of classroom activities associated with theater can be seen as extending the range and depth of language learning opportunities for the greatest number of students.

## Improvising with Language

In addition to role-play and collaboration, improvisation is fundamental to acting and, in some sense, to language learning itself: it is analogous to strategic competence. Improvisation requires awareness of the five physical senses and of the communication act, as well as an attitude of engagement and play. The learner uses the linguistic, paralinguistic, and extralinguistic tools at hand, as imperfect as they may be, in order to get the message across. As language educators, it is one of our goals to get students to speak in unrehearsed, unscripted language. Thus, in class, we need to give students opportunities to improvise in Italian, to use their limited language to express meaningful thoughts and feelings.

To create a safe space for improvisation—to set the stage—the role of the instructor is crucial. Above all, the instructor creates a space for experimentation. By believing that something creative and worthwhile can happen, by taking the risk and devoting the time, the instructor allows students a chance to rise to the occasion. Then, by playing the role of audience and judge, the teacher confirms the worth and can improve the quality of students' efforts. Thus, by setting the psychological stage, the teacher gives license for students to play with words, pronunciation, even body language, all of which develop strategic competence.

In addition, the instructor sets the physical stage by encouraging learners to make minimal but significant and "playful" changes in the physical environment, such as adjusting seating or lighting or using a simple prop. As the "good language learner" takes risks, makes errors, and uses circumlocution, the teacher must actively encourage such behavior (Rubin and Thompson 1994). In collaborative role-play activities, instructors are freed to coach individuals and pairs to take risks, to experiment as speakers of Italian. Most students need to be coaxed to use new vocabulary and express emotion in the target language. Some students need help in making the physical changes that result in more comprehensible pronunciation; others need coaching in appropriate use of gestures. Thus, by occasionally turning the classroom into a studio for improvisation, instructors can support the affective processes that aid language acquisition.

For many students, opera in the language class is their first serious exposure to the art form. The novelty and hyperbole of the content can inspire instructors to model an exploratory and playful attitude. Also, it bears remembering that the opera repertoire and opera subculture need not be approached in an overly serious mode. The action is often utterly improbable, as when the gruesomely tortured Cavaradossi lifts his head off the floor to sing a heartrending love duet with Tosca. Seeing the humor in opera is not disrespectful. In fact, it is a great pastime of operagoers, as evidenced by a flourishing grapevine of anecdotes, legends, and operatic scandals. The story about the high-handed and condescending Tosca who jumped to her death and then bounced back on a strategically placed trampoline is just one well-known example.

In sum, as a theatrical genre, opera can be repurposed in thematic units to allow students to participate in collaborative play with identity and language, processes that are instrumental to acquiring a foreign language.

## Conclusion

Theme-based instruction can motivate students, prepare them well for upper-level courses, and provide a foundation in the intercultural communicative competence that is so sorely needed in our era. It can more obviously connect modern languages to the larger undergraduate curriculum by spotlighting robust ideas and sophisticated thinking. Furthermore, by fully engaging foreign language instructors in intellectual content and processes, a thematic approach has the potential to energize teachers as learners in their own right and as critical analysts of their students' learning.

A thematic approach to opera is not widely understood or practiced. Neither has the flexibility of theme-based instruction been explored, particularly as a way to engage learners in sustained critical thinking in the target language. Perhaps this is because, for many departments and programs, thematically organized courses imply dramatic changes. For one thing, those responsible for curriculum materials may have to write more materials, select different textbooks, and perhaps even do away with the all-purpose tomes that seem ubiquitous in first- and second-year courses. Also, instructors may need additional or different preparation to be able to work with theme-based instruction comfortably and effectively. In many cases, assessment practices will need substantial revision in order to be compatible with new classroom practices.

Organizing around themes offers a new kind of answer to the debate about content and method in language teaching: a dynamic balance. Perhaps if languages were approached more like core subjects, more members of the academic community and the society at large would see them as such. For language learners, a thematic approach means becoming more of an independent learner, cultural explorer, and critical thinker in Italian. For language educators, it means becoming more of a composer, coach, and fellow traveler. Since opera, with its theatrical riches, has the power to stimulate fresh thought, we all have our work cut out for us.

## Bibliography

Abrams, Zsuzsanna. "Surfing to Cross-Cultural Awareness: Using Internet-Mediated Projects to Explore Cultural Stereotypes." *Foreign Language Annals* 35.2 (2002): 141–160.

Aski, Janice. "Foreign Language Textbook Activities: Keeping Pace with Second Language Acquisition Research." *Foreign Language Annals* 36.1 (2003): 57–65.

Barnet, Sylvan, Morton Berman, and William Burto. *Types of Drama.* 3d ed. Boston: Little, Brown, 1981.

Beliavsky, Ninah. "English through Opera." *Journal of the Imagination in Language Learning and Teaching* 6 (2001): 72–76.

Benesch, Sarah. "Thinking Critically, Thinking Dialogically." *TESOL Quarterly* 33.3 (1999): 573–580.

Bennett, Milton. *Basic Concepts of Intercultural Communication: Selected Readings.* Yarmouth, ME: Intercultural Press, 1998.

Blasco, Pablo González, Graziela Moreto, and Marcelo Levites. "Teaching Humanities through Opera: Leading Medical Students to Reflective Attitudes." *Literature and the Arts in Medical Education* 37.1 (2005): 19–21.

Brady, Arthur. "Opera as a Motivating Device." *Foreign Language Annals* 13.6 (1980): 59–64.

Bragger, Jeanette, and Donald Rice. "The Message Is the Medium: A New Paradigm for Content-Oriented Instruction." *Foreign Language Annals* 32.3 (1999): 373–391.

Brinton, Donna, Marguerite Snow, and Marjorie Wesche. *Content-Based Second Language Instruction.* Boston: Heinle & Heinle, 1989.

Brookfield, Stephen. *Developing Critical Thinkers.* San Francisco: Jossey-Bass, 1987.

Bruno, Salvatore. "Opera in the Italian Language Classroom." *Italica* 66.1 (1989): 20–28.

Cortazzi, Martin, and Li-xian Jin. "Cultural Mirrors: Materials and Methods in the EFL Classroom." In *Culture in Second Language Teaching and Learning,* edited by E. Hinkel. Cambridge: Cambridge University Press, 1999.

Crandall, Jo Ann, ed. *ESL through Content-Area Instruction.* Englewood Cliffs, NJ: Prentice Hall Regents, 1987.

Dupuy, Beatrice. "Content-Based Instruction: Can It Help Ease the Transition from the Beginning to Advanced Foreign Language Classes?" *Foreign Language Annals* 33.2 (2000): 205–223.

Fanselow, John. "Opera and Role Playing." *Practical English Teaching* 12.4 (1992): 15–16.

Fantini, Alvino, ed. *New Ways in Teaching Culture.* Alexandria, VA: TESOL, 1997.

Gianelli, Marge. "Thematic Units: Creating an Environment for Learning." In *The Content-Based Classroom,* edited by Marguerite Snow and Donna Brinton. White Plains, NY: Longman, 1991.

Hekmatpanah, Lyra. "Opera and Art in the French Foreign Language Classroom." *Mid-Atlantic Journal of Foreign Language Pedagogy* 1 (Spring 1993): 136–141.

Hinkel, Eli, ed. *Culture in Second Language Teaching and Learning.* Cambridge: Cambridge University Press, 1999.

Kern, Richard. "Literacy as a New Organizing Principle for Foreign Language Education." In *Reading between the Lines: Perspectives on Foreign Language Literacy,* edited by Peter Patrikis. New Haven, CT: Yale University Press, 2003.

Kramsch, Claire. "Culture in Language Learning: A View from the States." In *Foreign Language Research in Cross-Cultural Perspective,* edited by Kees de Bot, Ralph Ginsberg, and Claire Kramsch. Amsterdam: John Benjamins, 1991.

———. *Context and Culture in Language Teaching.* Oxford: Oxford University Press, 1993.

Lafayette, Robert, and Michael Buscaglia. "Students Learn Language via a Civilization Course: A Comparison of Second Language Classroom Environments." *Studies in Second Language Acquisition* 7.3 (1985): 323–336.

Lalande, John. "Modern Languages in the American College Curriculum: The Coming of Age." *Foreign Language Annals* 31.1 (1998): 81–90.

Lipson, Marjorie, Sheila Valencia, and Charles Peters. "Integration and Thematic Teaching: Integration to Improve Teaching and Learning." *Language Arts* 70.4 (1993): 252–263.

Maley, Alan, and Alan Duff. *Drama Techniques in Language Learning: A Resource Book of Communication Activities for Language Teachers.* Cambridge: Cambridge University Press, 1982.

Mohan, Bernard. *Language and Content.* Reading, MA: Addison-Wesley, 1986.

Noè, Daniela, and Frances Boyd. "Learning Italian through Opera." *Consortium News* [Yale University] (Autumn 1997): 7–10.

———. *L'italiano con l'opera: Lingua, cultura e conversazione.* New Haven, CT: Yale University Press, 2003.

Numrich, Carol. "Theme-Based Instruction: Fieldwork in a Small Connecticut Town." In *Understanding the Courses We Teach: Local Perspectives on English Language Teaching,* edited by John Murphy and Patricia Byrd. Ann Arbor: University of Michigan Press, 2001.

Patrikis, Peter, ed. *Reading between the Lines: Perspectives on Foreign Language Literacy.* New Haven, CT: Yale University Press, 2003.

Reid, Joy, ed. *Learning Styles in the ESL/EFL Classroom.* Boston: Heinle & Heinle, 1995.

Rubin, Joan, and Irene Thompson. *How to Be a More Successful Language Learner.* 2nd ed. Boston: Heinle & Heinle, 1994.

Snow, Marguerite. "Content-Based and Immersion Models for Second and Foreign Language Teaching." In *Teaching English as a Second or Foreign Language,* 3rd ed., edited by Marianne Celce-Murcia. Boston: Heinle & Heinle, 2001.

Snow, Marguerite, and Donna Brinton, eds. *The Content-Based Classroom: Perspectives on Integrating Language and Content.* White Plains, NY: Longman, 1997.

Stoller, Fedricka, and William Grabe. "A Six-T's Approach to Content-Based Instruction." In *The Content-Based Classroom,* edited by Marguerite Snow and Donna Brinton. White Plains, NY: Longman, 1997.

Storme, Julie, and Mana Derakhshani. "Defining, Teaching, and Evaluating Cultural Proficiency in the Foreign Language Classroom." *Foreign Language Annals* 35.6 (2002): 657–668.

Swain, Merrill. "Manipulating and Complementing Content Teaching to Maximize Second Language Learning." *TESL Canada Journal* 6.1 (1988): 68–83.

Thierfelder, William. "Five Puccini Women." *Italian Journal* 5.6 (1992): 29–32.

Turner, Jean. "Creating Content-Based Language Tests: Guidelines for Teachers." In *The Content-Based Classroom,* edited by Marguerite Snow and Donna Brinton. White Plains, NY: Longman, 1992.

Vygotsky, Lev. *Mind and Society: The Development of Higher Mental Processes.* Cambridge, MA: Harvard University Press, 1978.

Whiteson, Valerie, ed. *New Ways of Using Drama in Literature and Language Teaching.* Washington, DC: TESOL, 1996.

## Appendix A: Selected Operas for Italian Language Study

Gaetano Donizetti
   *L'elisir d'amore*
   *Lucia di Lammermoor*
Ruggero Leoncavallo
   *Pagliacci*
Pietro Mascagni
   *Cavalleria rusticana*
Giacomo Puccini
   *La bohème*
   *Madama Butterfly*
   *Tosca*
Gioacchino Antonio Rossini
   *Il barbiere di Siviglia*
   *La Cenerentola*
Giuseppe Verdi
   *Un ballo in maschera*
   *Otello*
   *Rigoletto*
   *La traviata*


## Appendix B: Selected Texts for *Tosca*

DVD/VHS: The Metropolitan Opera (Sinopoli, Zeffirelli, Domingo, Behrens)
DVD: Deutsche Gramophone (Kabaivanska, Domingo, Milnes, Luccardi,
   Mariotti, Bartoletti)
VHS: Filmed on location in Rome (Domingo, Malfitano, Metha)
VHS: Rome Opera (Pavarotti, Vixel, Kabaivanska, Oren)
CD: Deutsche Gramophone (Freni, Domingo, Ramey, Sinpoli)
CD: EMI Classics (Maria Callas, Di Stefano, Gobbi, DeSabata)
CD: Decca, Opera Gala Series (Freni, Pavarotti)
RAI: http://www.rai.it

# *IV* Methods and Assessment in Italian Theater Workshops

# CHAPTER 9

# *Full-Scale Play Production:*
# *Filling the "Empty Space" between*
# *Language and Literature with*
# *Fo and Pirandello*

NICOLETTA MARINI-MAIO

Instructors of foreign and second languages (L2) who use full-scale play production as a central component of their teaching are a small community with much in common.[1] They share intellectual curiosity for innovative methods, a rich and varied approach to the use of literary texts in the L2 classroom, genuine enthusiasm for theater, and, most of all, the belief that theater can be a transformative experience both personally and pedagogically.[2] In addition, many of them combine the profile of L2 and literature teachers with that of theater aficionados; in most cases they have acted, attended diction courses, or devoted themselves to the study of theater as a literary genre.

Despite their previous experience and passion, the members of this small community generally are reluctant to give an authoritative voice to their innovative pedagogical practices. When asked about their experience in teaching theater performance in the L2 classroom, they typically begin with a disclaimer ("I'm not a theater person, but an L2 teacher!") and then add a justification ("Yet, I have some theatrical experience").[3] Because of the scarcity of theater-specific theoretical contributions in the field of L2 acquisition, they have had to develop their own teaching methods more from hands-on experience in the classroom and on the stage than from an articulated system of thought. Nevertheless, the linguistic, cultural, and emotional growth their students have shown in their productions have convinced them that the combination of communicative practices, disciplinary competencies, theatrical skills, and socio-psychological processes carried out in their theater performance courses may become a new integrated approach to L2 learning and teaching.[4] With their performative approach they claim the right of occupying an "empty space" in L2 education.

Such an empty space, on the one hand, is of a curricular nature. This empty space is the gap, highlighted by several L2 teachers and scholars, between lower- and upper-level courses in the L2 curriculum. Les Essif, Margaret Haggstrom, and Francesca Savoia, among many, emphasize the difficulties that students encounter in the passage from language to literature and culture courses, and indicate theatrical workshops and play production as the most effective tools for bridging the gap between lower and upper divisions.[5] In this delicate transition, they maintain, the act of bringing fixed theatrical texts to life facilitates progress in the acquisition of the L2, promotes student-centered teaching methods, and, overall, furthers a more active, effective, and less stressful approach to the study of complex literary texts and cultural topics.

On the other hand, the image of the empty space suggests an analogy with a different kind of emptiness, one that belongs entirely to the world of theater. This metaphor recalls Brook's paradox of the "bare stage": "I can take any empty space and call it a bare stage. A man walks across this empty space whilst someone else is watching him, and this is all that is needed for an act of theatre to be engaged."[6] When applied to L2 instruction, the process of theater performance, namely, reading, adaptation, rehearsal, and mise-en-scène of a play, corresponds to the gradual metamorphosis from the "bare" class—if a class may be defined as "bare"—into the vibrant dynamics of a play production team.

This chapter hinges on the twofold notion of the empty space on the stage and in the curriculum. First, it shows how theater performance may be an effective and versatile tool for L2 teaching and learning during that curricular segment in which students face, often for the first time, complex cultural and literary content. In other words, it argues for the adoption of theater performance courses at an advanced level, when students are compelled to acquire sophisticated literacy skills while still needing to develop and enhance their ability to communicate in the L2. Second, it maintains that theater performance is also an area of cultural learning and psychological growth per se because it offers students the opportunity to be fully active subjects of the learning process. Following a constructionist approach, I claim that by enriching the learning experience with theater-specific features, theater performance provides an invaluable contribution to the field of L2 education: it lowers the communicative and affective barriers in the L2 classroom, promotes students' creativity, allows for more profound interpretations of the texts' literary and cultural content, and empowers students with the ability to adapt, re-create, and perform such content for real audiences.

## A Holistic Model for Teaching Theater Performance in the L2 Classroom

Since "theater performance" may refer to different approaches, it is helpful to first clarify some terms before proceeding with the three case studies presented in this chapter. On the one end of the spectrum, the performative approach may include the *theatrical workshop*, a widespread practice in performance studies. The workshop's methodology centers on the use of theatrical techniques and the free expression of psycho-physical energy. Improvisation is an essential part of this practice and has an intrinsic value as a creative and liberating moment. For its effect on the psychological and corporeal dynamics of individuals and groups, the theatrical workshop is used as professional training for theater practitioners, an extracurricular activity in schools and universities, a means for promoting self-expression and socialization in cultural associations, and even a tool for rehabilitation in psychological treatments. The theatrical workshop does not necessarily lead to the public presentation of a play. On the other end of the spectrum, we find the *full-scale play production*. This is a team project focusing primarily on the analysis, adaptation, and mise-en-scène of a dramatic text and converging on a public performance of a full-fledged play. It includes the discussion of production issues concerning props, costumes, lights, sounds, publicity, and all the material details necessary to stage a play.

In the belief that the performance component may sustain and advance disciplinary competencies, emotional and cognitive skills, and L2 communicative abilities, I argue that the ideal method to fill the empty space of language learning should harmonize the theatrical workshop with the full-scale play production. The focus on improvisation and performance skills in the theater workshop helps to lower the students' affective filter, liberating their expressive potential, increasing their spontaneous communication and fluency in the L2, and reinforcing their motivation to proceed further in the study of the L2.[7] In addition, the intense work of analysis and adaptation of a preexistent text required by the staging of a full-scale play refines students' analytical and critical skills, introducing them to the historical, literary, and cultural complexity of advanced studies in the L2.

What follows is a holistic model. It is content-based and equally product- and process-oriented because it exposes L2 learners to literary, historical, and cultural content while aiming both to meet learning objectives and to stage a final performance. The model is composed of three modules, in which academic content, performance activities, and language practice are equally means and goals of the learning process. The first module focuses on academic content (content-based module), the second one on improvisation and theatrical techniques (theatrical workshop), and the third one on the final performance (performative module). Each module consists of an ensemble of learning experiences with specific requirements, methods, forms of assessment, and short- and long-term objectives. And each module encompasses a specific curricular segment, in accordance with the overall goals of the course.[8]

The chronological division of the three modules may be flexible, but the best results have been achieved following this pattern: *the content-based module* is conceived as a preparatory phase of about six to eight weeks, in which students acquire familiarity with the cultural, historical, and literary background of the play, depending on the curricular and course objectives. During this phase, they also read and analyze the play. The *theatrical workshop* introduces students to the many facets of theater as a performative art and emphasizes improvisational activities. It starts at the very beginning of the semester and ends when the most intense section of the performative module begins, usually in the last month of class. The theatrical workshop overlaps with the other two modules, with the goal of facilitating the transition from academic content to the more interactive and creative phase of the production. The *performative module* is centered on the adaptation and production of the play. It unfolds as a team project, in which learners have a high degree of autonomy. It usually constitutes the sole activity of the class during the last four weeks of the course.

The organization and temporal segmentation of this model are outlined in Table 1, which includes the suggested requirements of the course.

**Table 1. Organization and temporal segmentation of the holistic model**

| | Introductory section | | | | | | | | | Spring Break | Adaptation and production | | | | |
|---|---|---|---|---|---|---|---|---|---|---|---|---|---|---|---|
| | W1 | W2 | W3 | W4 | W5 | W6 | W7 | W8 | W9 | | W10 | W11 | W12 | W13 | W14 |
| | CM, 2 H | CM, 2 H | CM, 2 H | CM, 2 H | CM, 2 H | CM, 2 H | CM, 2 H | TW, 3 H | TW, 1 H | | TW, 1 H | PM, 3 H | PM, 3 H | PM, 3 H | PM, 4 H |
| | TW, 1 H | TW, 1 H | TW, 1 H | TW, 1 H | TW, 1 H | TW, 1 H | TW, 1 H | | PM, 2 H | | PM, 2 H | | | | |
| | | Quiz | | Quiz | Presen-tations | Presen-tations | Oral exam | Presen-tations | Midterm paper | | 3 extra H | 3–4 extra H | 5–6 extra H | Tech week 7–8 extra H | Final Pro-duction |

*Note:* W indicates week; CM, content-based module; TW, theatrical workshop; PM, performative module; H, hour(s).

This chapter illustrates this holistic model through the description of three teaching and learning experiences, two of which culminated in the production of Dario Fo's *Mamma! I Sanculotti! (Mom! The Sansculottes!)* and one in the public performance of Luigi Pirandello's *Sei personaggi in cerca d'autore (Six Characters in Search of an Author).*[9] These three examples demonstrate how theatrical performance may draw upon various sources and pursue different learning goals while at the same time eliciting a critical and collaborative approach to the learning of Italian language, literature, and culture. They highlight, too, the development of a teacher, who, thanks to the experience of theatrical workshop and play production, has become progressively more willing and confident in increasing her students' autonomy and creative participation in the exciting experience of filling the empty space.

## The Cultural, Linguistic, and Performative Encounter with Fo's *Mamma! I Sanculotti!*

Since the 1950s, Dario Fo, actor, director, and political activist, in collaboration with his artistic partner and wife, Franca Rame, has created numerous politically charged plays, among which are the internationally renowned *"giullarata" Mistero buffo* (1969) and the farce *Morte accidentale di un anarchico* (1970).[10] In 1997 Fo was awarded the Nobel Prize in literature for the novelty of his work, which unites political engagement and the artistic tradition of classic and Italian theater in the figure of a modern *giullare* challenging the arrogance of power. Fo's and Rame's theater is well-known in North American universities, and their plays are often used in theater performance courses.[11]

The two teaching and learning experiments I now describe were both based on Fo's *Mamma! I Sanculotti!,* written in 1993–1994 amidst the corruption scandals that led to the fall of the First Italian Republic or Italy's First Republic.[12] *Mamma!* is an outlandish farce that situates the emergence of the newly elected Prime Minister Silvio Berlusconi, a center-rightwing entrepreneur, the richest man in Italy, and founder of the political party *Forza Italia,* in the framework of postwar Italian history and culture. The main character, Felice Chiappa, is a public prosecutor whose name hilariously translates as "Happy Butt Cheek" in English. He is reminiscent of Judge Antonio

Di Pietro, one of the principal players in the so-called *Mani pulite* inquiry of 1992–1993 that led to the discovery of *Tangentopoli,* a corrupt political network involving many Italian government and business leaders. *Mamma!* includes a variety of information spanning from biting references to popular culture up to the most obscure events of postwar Italian history, such as the Piazza Fontana massacre in 1969 and its aftermath, and culminates in an imaginary coup leading to the arrest of several center-rightwing politicians, who repent for their mischievous actions alongside the pope. The play demonstrates Fo's ability to incorporate wit, intelligence, humor, and current events into his work in order to criticize the Italian government and instigate in his audiences political awareness and willingness to engage in political action.

*Mamma!* is a versatile and powerful text and provides L2 learners with a great quantity of cultural, linguistic, and theatrical stimuli. As is apparent, American students will need a considerable amount of information concerning Italian history and culture in order to analyze, adapt, and perform this text. Staging *Mamma!,* then, becomes an intense learning experience, which may lead L2 learners through an insightful exploration of the Italian cultural context. This theatrical piece also presents students with a vivid expressive mode loaded with a variety of linguistic registers, exceptionally rich vocabulary, and quick-witted humor. Finally, like all of Fo's and Rame's theater, which is profoundly rooted in the Italian dramatic tradition from the medieval mystery plays to the commedia dell'arte, *Mamma!* exposes students to a vibrant component of Italian literature and provides them with a basic knowledge of theater as a performative art. All in all, as Joseph Farrell and Antonio Scuderi argue, Fo's theater is a means for the "decolonization of the mind, of the will, and of the imagination."[13]

The expressive richness of *Mamma!*—and of Fo's entire theatrical production—makes the comprehension of all the nuances and linguistic registers challenging for L2 students. This language is typically anti-intellectual, strongly idiomatic, and often metaphorical. In addition, jargon is repeatedly used to refer to Italian history and politics, including a full range of culturally embedded expressions. Research has shown that reading coherent material extensively improves learners' reading skills and vocabulary and leads to greater content-area learning. However, because of the complexity of the terminology students need to access the historical themes, problems of comprehension may arise, particularly from a cross-cultural perspective.[14] As Anthony Bernier points out, sometimes students spend more time "trying to decode vocabulary than discussing themes, theses, or their own thoughts about the content material itself."[15] Moreover, in the effort to clarify the historical and political concepts texts convey, the instructors, too, frequently use complex vocabulary and refer to cultural imagery that may confuse L2 learners rather than foster their comprehension of the readings.

With regard to history, in particular, Bernier indicates three categories that challenge students' linguistic skills and, subsequently, their ability to decode the information to which they are exposed: content terms, language terms, and language-masking content terms. According to Bernier's taxonomy, *content terms*, which regularly recur in the instructor's lectures, in textbooks, and in the assigned readings, define specific historical notions, ideas, and characters. This first category includes historians' jargon, archaic language, foreign language words, obscure acronyms, and technical terminology borrowed from other disciplines. In many cases, such terms are not common knowledge for students even in the L1. Examples of content terms in *Mamma!* are *strategia delle bombe, monocolore, pentapartito, Sismi, coalizione di destra, stato d'assedio, guerriglia, corpi speciali deviati, strage, lotta armata, strategia della tensione, golpe, colpo di Stato, sindacato, esproprio proletario, brigatista, democristiani, 'ndrangheta, patria, movimento degli operai, campagna elettorale,* and *forza politica.*

*Language terms* are not content-specific and incorporate words that usually do not pertain to history but are persistently used in lectures and academic readings to elucidate historical discourse. Among examples of this second category, Bernier mentions metaphors, colloquial usages, class-based constructions, and cultural idioms: terms and formations that may be fully understood only by individuals already familiar with the L2 culture. In Fo's play, students encountered *esercito, pattuglie, sbattere in prima pagina, sbattere in galera, suscitare polemiche, ordine di arresto, attentato, ordigno, dinamitardo, linciaggio dei mass-media, finimondo, la falciatrice di Sapri, custodia cautelare, reparto indagini, inchiesta, inquisito, mandante, infiltrato, indagine, scorta armata, armi da fuoco, in attesa di giudizio, mandato di cattura, soccombere, presidiare, censura, manifestazione, presa di coscienza, sciopero, imprenditore, onorevole, questore, prefetto, magistrato, senatore a vita,* and *Pontefice.*

Finally, in the category of *language-masking content terms* Bernier includes both language and content vocabulary. These terms have multiple references and may be relevant for historical concepts and ideas while bearing literal and colloquial meanings. Examples from *Mamma!* include, but are not limited to, *strage impunita, appoggio, conoscenze, pezzo grosso, bidone, mazzetta, calare le braghe, saltare in aria, sotto tiro, morire sul colpo, essere in onda,* and *fare domanda.* In *Mamma!* Fo adopts an ample spectrum of all the linguistic typologies Bernier identifies. In addition, these terms appeared extensively in the introductory readings of the theater performance course, and the instructor most likely used some technical or culturally embedded terminology in her lectures. The linguistic density of the play reverberates through this list of terms, giving a clear idea of its complexity. The theatrical medium, however, has the remarkable effect of endowing this fairly intricate language with a concrete communicative context and extralinguistic evidence, facilitating the students' interpretive task. In other words, theater, and Fo's unique style in particular, brings to life an entire system of references that otherwise might remain abstract or incomprehensible information for L2 learners.

A central feature of Fo's theater, inspired by a Brechtian approach and grounded in a Gramscian perspective to literature, combines naturalistic acting with epic storytelling. That is, while the naturalistic acting shows the dramatic action and revives the intensity of the psychological work of the actor onstage, the Brechtian-like epic register interrupts the action with storytelling, comments, direct interaction with the audience, and subtitles, producing a coming to awareness of the spectator in the light of what he or she sees.[16] The purpose of theater for the epic actor is not to reproduce reality, but to present ideas and invite the audience to make judgments about them. In this sense, a process of "estrangement," or alienation, from the story and from the characters portrayed keeps the audience ever-aware that it is watching a play, while activating critical thought about the action.

A remarkable example of "estrangement" is the shifting to the epic mode that occurs at the end of *Mamma!* All of a sudden, Judge Chiappa and his first bodyguard disappear as fictional characters and turn into "Dario" and "Franca," harshly arguing onstage about the finale of the play. While Dario defends the comic ending—the anticonservative coup and the politicians' and the pope's repentance

—Franca presses for a more aggressive finale. Dario eventually changes the ending of the play, denouncing the alleged plan of Berlusconi and his allies to take control of the country and pursue dirty economic and political interests. This finale aims at wakening the audience to political consciousness. The epic mode serves to make this objective explicit and to transform the public into a proactive political subject. This technique recurs throughout the play. The beginning of *Mamma!*, for instance, oscillates between the naturalistic and the epic modes, and in several internal segments the main characters leave their fictional identities, becoming the actors "Dario" and "Franca" who perform comic monologues on political and social topics, discuss current events with the audience, or debate the structure of the play itself.

Fo's metatheatrical technique exerts a fundamental role in theater performance. In the 2001 play production class, students interiorized Fo's idea of theater as a tool to promote critical thinking and political criticism. The course unexpectedly coincided with the controversial election of George W. Bush as the president of the United States in January 2001 and with the equally divisive election of Silvio Berlusconi as the prime minister of the Italian government in April of the same year. Stimulated by Fo's provocative arguments, the students observed the essential traits of U.S. and Italian politics with a cross-cultural focus and gradually became more interested in exploring the historical and political contexts of postwar Italy. Furthermore, they soon realized that their audience, mostly composed of L1 speakers, would not be able to comprehend some of the subtle references to Italian politics included in *Mamma!* Therefore, in their adaptation they replaced such references with references to American society, through which the public could make inferences on the Italian context as well as critically reflect on American culture itself. For example, they turned the names of Giulio Andreotti, one of the most controversial politicians of the First Republic, and Gianni Agnelli, the legendary FIAT owner, into those of their U.S. counterparts par excellence, namely, George W. Bush and Bill Gates. In addition, they provided an analogy by associating Silvio Berlusconi, who in Fo's play enters the scene later, to the Bush-Gates duo:

> *Franca:*   Lasciami dire! [Al pubblico] Allora, abbiamo fatto ironia, parlato delle elezioni, dell'arresto di Berlusconi . . . Dietro il Papa arriva lui, Berlusconi . . . A questo punto manca un

> fax che annuncia che Bill Gates ha regalato la Microsoft a Mac e che Bush si è suicidato ingoiando tutte le ricette mediche degli anziani senza assicurazione!

*Franca:* Let me talk! [To the audience] So, we've created ironic situations, talked about the election and Berlusconi's arrest ... After the pope comes Berlusconi ... All we need is a fax announcing that Bill Gates donated Microsoft to Macintosh and that Bush killed himself by swallowing all the prescriptions of the elderly people without insurance!

## Staging *Mamma!* A Comparative Look at Two Different Experiences

The cultural and linguistic richness of *Mamma!* and its performative potential facilitate different approaches to the play, as shown by two very different experiences. Both courses had as a prerequisite the fulfillment of a two-year language program and were designed to perfect students' communicative skills while providing them with the competencies necessary to access literary and cultural content. Class meetings studied Fo's play in lectures, discussions, and demonstrations as well as provided lab time for extended workshops on acting, directing, design, and production issues. In both cases, students were required to read contextual information; analyze, translate, and subtitle the play; participate in the process of adaptation and mise-en-scène; memorize the assigned parts; and stage the production. The final productions took place at the end of the semester in front of a mixed audience of about a hundred people that included students, faculty, and members of the community. However, due to significant differences in students' backgrounds, their linguistic proficiency, and curricular needs, the main focus of the two courses was decisively different.

The 2001 course was established as an alternative to an advanced conversation course and constituted a transition toward subsequent literature courses, while the 2005 course replaced a survey on Italian twentieth-century literature and was the only option offered for fifth-semester students. Furthermore, the 2001 students were particularly heterogeneous in terms of their motivation, background, and communication skills in Italian and did not have significant theatrical experience. Most of them were unfamiliar with literary analysis (even in English) as well as contemporary Italian culture and history. On the other hand, students in the later course were a more homogeneous group from a liberal arts college, had stronger backgrounds in foreign languages and literary studies, and usually had some theatrical experience—if they were not in fact theater majors. Consequently, the first course focused on the cultural aspects of the play, particularly the history and politics of contemporary Italy, while the second course included a mini-survey of Italian twentieth-century literary texts and centered on the notion of humor as a philosophical, literary, and theatrical category.[17]

Both courses followed the three modules described above, that is, the content-based portion, the theatrical workshop, and the performative section. In the content-based module of the civilization bridge course, students analyzed the economic, social, and political developments that brought Italy from the reconstruction and the industrial boom of the 1960s through the crisis of the 1970s, the Craxi era of the 1980s, the collapse of the First Italian Republic in 1992 to 1993, and Berlusconi's abrupt appearance in the field of politics in 1994.[18] In the content-based segment of the literature survey course, students focused on literary readings, including excerpts from Pirandello's "L'umorismo," *Il Fu Mattia Pascal,* and *Così è (se vi pare);* from Italo Svevo's *La coscienza di Zeno,* Achille Campanile's *Il ciambellone,* and Natalia Ginzburg's *Fragola e panna;* and some short stories in Stefano Benni's *L'ultima lacrima.*[19] In this phase, both courses greatly emphasized reading comprehension and vocabulary. Students worked on prereading and vocabulary activities, such as trivia quizzes, flash cards, text puzzles and jigsaws, and discussion questions. The instructor provided introductory information in brief lectures, with the support of multimedia resources, facilitating the exploration of the cultural content and encouraging cross-cultural reflection. Students read most of the material individually and wrote brief reaction paragraphs in preparation for class discussions.

The content-based module incorporated information on Dario Fo's biography and theater, and the reading of *Mamma!*[20] The analysis of the play was based on a questionnaire, which led students through the "given circumstances," as defined by Konstantin Stanislavski: the dialogues, the action, the setting, the time, the characters and their relationships, and the language.[21] In fact, the reading of the play and the parallel understanding and practice of its performance qualities in the theatrical workshop provided a hands-on perspective on the intricate historical and cultural background of postwar Italy, which, otherwise, would have been difficult for students to interpret.

The intersections among language learning, academic content, and performance were the most significant features in these courses. In both cases, the theatrical workshop acted as a parallel segment to the content-based module. It trained students in diaphragmatic breathing, pronunciation (for example, tongue twisters, reading aloud), intonation (for example, rapid and low reading, same texts performed with different tones), and pragmatics (for example, mirror exercises, individual and group physical expression) and allowed plenty of time for improvisational activities and the exploration of different acting techniques.[22] In addition, some brief readings introduced students to the origins of theater, the codifications of this genre, and its ritual function in society.[23]

Even when reading was required, for the most part the workshop was conducted through performance. Students rearranged and acted out in a theatrical fashion excerpts from Fo's *Manuale minimo dell'attore,* Eduardo De Filippo's *Lezioni di teatro,* and Emanuele Luzzati's *Facciamo insieme teatro.*[24] In their performances, they had to demonstrate, for instance, how to establish a relationship with the audience by breaking the "fourth wall," how to use their bodies in order to have the audience actually "see" actions and objects, how to capture the audience's attention, how to construct a prologue in order to create a meaningful context before the actual performance, how to refer to current events in order to stimulate the audience's self-reflection, how to "exit" from and "reenter" a character in order to avoid the process of identification of the "make believe" of naturalistic theater, how to include unexpected events in the performance, and how to interact in dialogues and perform monologues without losing contact with the audience.[25]

Students prepared for these mini-performances by practicing improvisational drama during specific segments of class time and analyzing some parts of Fo's documentaries and pedagogical video recordings, which were used extensively as tutorials for individual and group activities.[26] Besides being useful instructional materials, these videos also had the interesting effect of familiarizing students with the live figures of Fo and Rame, who amplified with their performances the emotional effect and communicative potency of their texts. In the advanced stages of the performative section of the course, when students were discussing production issues or rehearsing parts of their adaptation of *Mamma!*, the recourse to Fo's authority was not unusual, and such statements as "Dario farebbe così" (Dario would do it this way) or "A Dario questo non piacerebbe!" (Dario would not like this!) were frequently heard among students. This happened, in particular, when technical issues arose during the staging of the play.

The performative module incorporated several small tasks, namely, the auditions and role assignments; the adaptation, translation, and subtitling of the play; the rehearsals; and the mise-en-scène, which eventually converged on the larger task of the final production. This process required many extra hours (see Table 1), during which the instructor and the teaching assistant were not constantly present. A variety of activities, moreover, took place at the same time, and the teacher could not simultaneously be in control of all the groups. In order to optimize their time and performance, therefore, students gradually increased their autonomy and during the last three weeks they worked almost independently in managing the acting, scene design, production issues (lights, audio, props and costumes, playbills, and publicity), translation, and subtitling.

Not only the composite nature of these tasks, but also the necessity for students to make common decisions about them entailed a great deal of meaning and language negotiation, which led to consistent "scaffolding."[27] In other words, as stated by sociocultural theory, learners showed the tendency to co-construct the activities they engaged in, and their relationships with the tasks were more conducive to learning than the inherent features of the tasks themselves.[28] All in all, the intense social interaction that occurred in this phase involved students in a close-knit, collective participation in the undertaking of the play production and led to the gradual transformation of the class into what Robert Di Pietro defines as "a speech community where students cooperate with each other in the work of learning."[29]

In this modular, holistic approach to theater performance, assessment may take place in different forms, with more emphasis on contextual and language competence during the first module, on language and task performance during the theatrical workshop, and on collaborative projects during the performative module. In the content-based sections, the instructor administered two quizzes with multiple-choice and open questions to test the knowledge of the historical background, in the case of the 2001 course, and literary background, in the case of the 2005 course. An oral exam tested students' ability to present and discuss the topics explored, using specific terminology. In addition, in the civilization course learners wrote a midterm paper of six to eight pages in which they explored some specific aspects of the play concerning the characters, the relationship of the play with the historical and political contexts, or Fo's theatrical techniques. In the literature course, besides the midterm paper, students were also required to write two three- to four-page mini-papers on specific literary topics. The evaluation of the oral presentations assessed the two central elements of the theatrical workshop, that is, learners' performance competence and language fluency. In the last module, students' performance was assessed in the small tasks described above, according to heterogeneous indicators such as commitment, teamwork, creativity, and linguistic skills. Both individuals and teams were evaluated on their preparation and the final performance. To this end, the instructor administered a survey in which students anonymously assessed their classmates' contribution to the whole group.

All in all, both courses achieved very positive results. Not only did students undertake advanced cultural, historical, and literary readings with sincere interest, but they also brought this content to life through the experience of the theater performance. They appropriated Fo's play with intellectual curiosity and intelligence, infusing American humor in their adaptations, following Fo's precepts on epic theater and on breaking through the "fourth wall." Their language skills in Italian advanced dramatically, and both their productions of *Mamma!* were enthusiastically received by the local community, the faculty, and fellow students. Obviously, if compared with professional theatrical productions, the public performances were small undertakings, but they were invaluable results for those students who, at the end of their first semester of advanced studies in Italian, had elected the empty space of theater as their own vibrant area of self-expression. And all in Italian, of course.

## The Literary and Pedagogical Challenge of Pirandello's
*Sei personaggi in cerca d'autore*

Compared with Fo's amusing and politically engaged play, Luigi Pirandello's *Sei personaggi in cerca d'autore* (*Six Characters in Search of an Author*), or the *commedia da fare* (play to be done), with its multiple points of view and metatheatrical questions, its intricate structure and conflicts of meaning, and its complex cultural and literary background, is a particularly challenging work for nonnative speakers to analyze and comprehend.[30] However, the philosophical complexity and linguistic and stylistic difficulties of this polyphonic drama may, paradoxically, have a primary role in determining the high quality of the course and the final play production. As shown by the 2003 theater performance course held at the University of Pennsylvania, when academic content merged with social interaction, replicating the learning conditions of a full-immersion environment in which language is used as a means to pursue a collective goal and students are the active subjects of the learning activity, the cultural and literary implications of the text may reverberate positively on learners, determining a significant change in their aptitude toward complex academic content and dramatically advancing their language and disciplinary skills. In other words, like the experiences of performing the Fo plays, the 2003 reading, adaptation, and performance of Pirandello's *Sei personaggi*, too, showed the transformative power of theater and its effectiveness in filling the empty space.

With *Sei personaggi*, Pirandello brings to maturity his long experimental phase initiated with the disintegration of the essential elements of bourgeois theater. In this play, the Sicilian playwright endows the characters with artistic autonomy, submits the authorial process of creation to radical critique, stages the philosophical correlation between art and life, and shows the inconsistency of language as a tool of communication and reciprocal comprehension. Moreover, the mise-en-scène of the play reveals the artifices of the theatrical machinery, demystifying the traditional function of the stage as a barrier between performers and public.

The plot of *Sei personaggi* is well-known. Six characters—the *Padre*, the *Madre*, the *Figlio*, the *Figliastra*, the *Giovinetto*, and the *Bambina*—cannot live their fictional story because the author did not finish writing it. In allegorical terms, the lack of the authorial logos has deprived the characters of their drama as well as of any ideological or aesthetic value. Their subjective and artistic egos are fragmented and incomplete; they can acquire an identity only by reconstructing themselves and enacting their story in the illusively immutable world of theater.[31] This is the reason why they materialize in an actual theater, where a group of performers is rehearsing

Pirandello's play *Il gioco delle parti* (*The Rules of the Game*) directed by an ambitious *capocomico* (director). After some hesitation, the director invites the six characters to act out their *dramma doloroso* (painful drama) and encourages his company of players to imitate them and practice for a future performance. Actions, monologues, dialogues, byplays, and metatheatrical considerations arise on the stage, which turns into a *stanza della tortura* (torture room) where each character's unsettling truth gradually takes shape.[32] The characters' subjective and relative points of view show irremediable conflicts while they recollect the *dramma doloroso*, which pivots both on classic themes (adultery, incest, repentance, vengeance, and death) and modern themes (family, love triangle, and generational conflicts) of the tragic universe. Private dramas and harsh recriminations eventually lead to a melodramatic finale—the *Bambina* dies and the *Giovinetto* commits suicide—which provides the characters with their aesthetic and existential completion.

A multifaceted drama takes place in front of the audience, featuring the *dramma doloroso*, namely, the narrative antecedent reduced to improvised fragments, which are partly narrated, commented on, or enacted on the stage; the drama of the six characters as such, whose fictional nature condemns them to an unsolvable tragedy of identity, only partially relieved by the aesthetic form they can acquire in theater; and the interpretation of the director and the company of players, faithful to the mimetic conventions of nineteenth-century acting. They live the theatrical dimension as a transitory, contingent moment of their existence and cannot comprehend the six characters' irreversible tragedy. Their performances, therefore, ironically result in improvised commedia dell'arte pieces, stemming from the involuntary *canovaccio* (outline) sketched out by the six characters.[33] The final element played out during the performance is the conflicting relationship among the characters, the plot, and the authorship, introduced in the preface by the author-narrator and resurfacing on the stage. Intersecting with the others, each layer creates additional dramatic subtexts and establishes an oblique form of communication with the audience, which is called on to witness the "actual" occurrence of an ongoing drama.

In the 1925 edition of the play, Pirandello includes clear elements of disintegration of the so-called fourth wall, the virtual barrier that conventionally separates the performance from the public.[34] For instance, in this version he differentiates more clearly the two groups present on the stage: the company of actors wear bright clothes, talk cheerfully, sing, and dance, while the six characters wear not only dark clothes—like in the 1921 edition—but also masks and enter the stage from the side of the public.

Remarkably, the *demone dell'esperimento* (demon of the experiment) that delineates the characters in *Sei personaggi* captivated the students of this course, instilling in them the desire to rework the text and create their own original adaptation. They constantly revised the script, discussing the roles of the characters and their relationships with each other, the company of players, the director, and the public. They were particularly intrigued by the authorial issue emerging in *Sei personaggi* and wanted to explore it themselves, integrating Pirandello's text with passages from Edoardo Sanguineti's *Sei personaggi.com;* excerpts from American popular music and film, such as Madonna's *Like a Virgin,* sung by the stepdaughter, and Michael Jackson's *Thriller,* executed by the company of players; and original parts that they created.[35]

The rewriting of the text brought significant changes to the development of the characters and to the drama itself. This process stimulated long discussions on the role of the director, the relationship between author and text, and the question of intertextuality as well as some controversial aspects of contemporary culture. In the students' adaptation, for example, expanding from Sanguineti's interpretation, they transformed the stepdaughter into a provocative Lolita, who morbidly alludes to the sexual abuse she experienced as a child:

| | |
|---|---|
| *La figliastra:* | Eh, come no . . . Ero piccina piccina, sa? con le treccine sulle spalle e le mutandine più lunghe della gonna—piccina così—Veniva a scuola, a prendere me, all'uscita, a guardarmi. Veniva a vedermi come crescevo. Mi aspettava lí, dove c'è il cancello, lí, nel casino delle auto, e quando pioveva, con l'ombrello nero. Non diceva niente: mi faceva un segno, con la mano, un ciao, dietro un albero, mi salutava . . . mi veniva dietro, faceva come . . . delle smorfie, rideva, sorrideva . . . ma no, ghignava, ecco. Avevo quel giacchino Miss Sixty, finta pelle, non so, pelle vera, forse, avevo la mini, una volta, forse, due, mi ha pure come toccata, ma appena, mi ha preso per le trecce . . . |

| *The Stepdaughter:* | Uh, sure . . . I was little, so little! With my hair in pigtails and my panties hanging out below my skirt. Little like this—He would come to school at dismissal to watch me. He wanted to see how I was growing up. He would wait for me there, by the gate, among the mess of the cars, and when it was raining, he had with him a black umbrella. He never said anything, he would wave at me, from behind a tree, making like . . . faces . . . laughing, smiling . . . no, he sneered, yes, he did. I had that Miss Sixty jacket, fake leather, I don't know, real leather maybe. I had a mini skirt. And he touched me once, maybe twice, but only a little bit . . . he took me by the braids . . . |

Seeking to express the legitimacy of his sexual drives, the stepfather attempts a justification:

| *Il padre:*<br>(rivolgendosi al Regista) | Il dramma scoppia, signore, al loro ritorno, quando io, purtroppo . . . lei capisce . . . sono un vecchio, cioè un uomo maturo, un anziano, uno da terza età, da università per anziani: entro gratis nei musei . . . ho lo sconto al cinema . . . mi chiedono la carta d'identità . . . sono vecchio . . . ma non abbastanza . . . sa, l'erotismo senile . . . ha letto le statistiche, signore? Ci stanno, le ragazze, ci stanno e noi . . . l'erotismo senile . . . si ha voglia, si capisce! Si ha voglia! C'è la voglia, ecco! Non potevo farne a meno, però mi vergognavo, a cercarle io, le ragazze, signore, le donne . . . le ragazze . . . però, ci stanno, ecco, ci stanno. È così per tutti! Manca solo il coraggio di dirle, certe cose! |
| *Il padre:*<br>(speaking to the Director) | Our drama broke out, sir, upon our return; when I, unfortunately . . . you must understand . . . I am an old man, that is to say a mature man, a senior, one in the third phase of life, of the university for senior citizens: I enter for free in the |

> museums, I get a discount at the mov-
> ies, they ask me for my i.d. card . . . I
> am old . . . but not old enough . . . you
> know, that senile eroticism . . . have you
> read the statistics, sir? They are easy,
> girls, they are easy and we . . . that
> senile eroticism . . . we get horny, you
> understand! We get horny, of course,
> you know! I couldn't do without them,
> but I was ashamed to look for them,
> for girls, sir, women . . . girls . . . yet,
> they are easy, sure, easy . . . And it's the
> same for everyone! But no one has the
> guts/courage to say these things! every-
> one lacks the courage to say so, these
> certain things!

Their gradual metamorphosis into authors allowed students to become the active and central subjects of the learning process and progressively led them to use the L2 as an interactive tool for working collaboratively toward the common goal of the final per-formance. From a learning objective, the L2 turned into a natural means of communication despite the inevitable differences in lan-guage proficiency and background within the group. Thanks to their involvement in the various activities of the theatrical workshop, in which they invested a considerable part of their spare time, the stu-dents evolved from the "bare" class—as Brook might put it—into a unique micro-society. In the fluid space of the theatrical workshop, students modeled their roles and behaviors on the basis of the lin-guistic norms mediated through Italian language and culture.

It is exactly in this in-between space, a sort of *elsewhere* detached from the outside world (the empty space of theater), that the potential of Pirandello's text had full expression, generating an unexpected excess of interpretations. In fact, students experienced in first person the uncertainty of the condition of the six characters, for whom the stage becomes "la sede dei loro vizi, dei loro peccati segreti, delle loro piaghe che solo a teatro possono essere scoperte, contemplate, giudicate" (the place of their vices, their secret sins, their wounds, which can be exhibited, contemplated, and judged only in theater).[36] In their adaptation of *Sei personaggi*, theater performance students staged a sort of *mise en abîme* of *Sei personaggi* the very play, in which they did not pretend to be but really were characters in search of an identity, a role, and, most of all, words that could express their communicative imperfection. In other words, empathizing with the six characters' condition of incompleteness, lack of communication, and search for identity, students translated their own insecure and unstable status as L2 learners into the Pirandellian *stanza dell'essere* (room of being).[37] On the other hand, the metatheatrical experimentalism that originated from their exploration of the text allowed the critical interpretation of the text and led to the creation of a new *commedia da fare.*

Like the other two courses treating Fo's plays, the 2003 theater performance course, too, had a three-module structure. The primary objective of the content-based section was to provide learners with a general understanding of Pirandello's work and lead them through the reading and analysis of *Sei personaggi.* In this module, extracts from "L'umorismo," *Il fu Mattia Pascal, Uno, nessuno e centomila,* and *Così è (se vi pare)* were read. Prereading, guided reading, and postreading activities facilitated students' approach to the philosophical and linguistic density of the text. In particular, the prereading activities aimed to activate the mental processes that Claire Kramsch categorizes as "predicting topic development" and "schema building," which allow learners to construct information about the content of the text and develop contextual references, particularly concerning the rhetorical (ironical, metaphorical, hypothetical) and linguistic (description, comparison, hypothesis) functions of the text.[38] These activities promoted the use of specific linguistic functions: describe; hypothesize; express opinions, wishes, agreement, and disagreement; compare different ideas. Obviously, these functions required the use of the forms most commonly reviewed in advanced courses, such as the subjunctive mood, the modal use of verbal tenses, and conditional sentences. For the analysis of *Sei personaggi,* students used a questionnaire to help them gain a greater understanding of the environment of the play. At the end of the content-based module, they took an oral exam that tested their comprehension of and critical reflection on the main themes of Pirandello's work. They were also required to write an analytical midterm paper on specific literary topics.

The theatrical workshop constituted an essential component of the 2003 course, perhaps its most original part. Parallel and complementary to the other two, this module had the same objectives and structure as the other courses. Interestingly, Fo's pedagogical readings and taped demonstrations were used as tools to clarify the theatrical style of *Sei personaggi,* to provide specific terminology, and to experiment with the effects of epic versus naturalistic theater on the performance. In addition, Fo's techniques shed light on the contrast, both ontological and aesthetic, between the six characters and the company of players, who take turns acting out the drama and commenting on the others' performances. In other words, Fo's theater was instrumental for introducing learners not only to theatrical techniques, but also to Pirandello's aesthetics of "theater within the theater" and metatheatrical discourse.

The students' commitment and enthusiasm in facing the difficult task of the production of *Sei personaggi* demonstrated one more time the positive pedagogical effect that the combination of the theatrical workshop with academic content and full-scale production may have on students' motivation and learning. Since the play included many long and difficult monologues, the main parts were split and assigned to different performers. Those who executed secondary roles had substantial functions as members of the crew as well. As a result, all contributed to the production in a substantial way, and the opportunities for linguistic interaction intensified. The public performance took place in front of an audience of about 150 people, within the framework of a Pirandello two-day event organized by the university. Besides the students' production of *Sei personaggi,* the Pirandello celebration included a lecture held by the president of the Pirandello Society of America and the screening of the 1976 cinematic adaptation of *Sei personaggi* by Stacy Keach. This context particularly gratified the students, making them feel part of a greater community composed of literary scholars and theater enthusiasts. In the end, the 2003 theater performance course provided learners with a multifaceted, highly fruitful learning experience that impelled most of the students to continue their study of Italian.

Overall, the three teaching experiences described in this chapter led students through the gradual metamorphosis from the "bare" class into a vibrant community of a theatrical team. The reading, adaptation, and staging of Fo's politically engaged satire and Pirandello's metatheatrical drama profoundly influenced students' communication skills in Italian, literary and cultural competencies, and psychological attitude toward Italian. The performative approach to theater offered students the opportunity to develop as active subjects of the learning process, lowered the communicative and affective barriers, promoted their creativity, led them through a deep interpretation of literary and cultural contents, encouraged their looking at the texts with a cross-cultural focus, and gave them the opportunity to adapt, rewrite, and perform such content for real audiences.

Essif suggests that theater may influence L2 pedagogy.[39] I could not agree more. The performative approach to theater may claim a primary position in that delicate stage of the Italian curriculum in which students initiate the exploration of sophisticated literary texts while still needing to enhance their communicative competencies and develop literacy skills. In the field of Italian pedagogy it may indeed provide an invaluable contribution by filling an empty space, a space of cultural transformation, linguistic, and psychological growth.


## Notes

1. In this chapter, the abbreviation L2 will be used for both foreign and second language. L1 refers to the native language.
2. See Essif, *The French Play*, and Whiteson, *New Ways of Using Drama;* and Marini-Maio, "I *Sei Personaggi* siamo noi."
3. Essif, *The French Play*, 4–5, and Chapters 6 and 7 in this book by Walter Valeri and Gian Giacomo Colli, who can both claim professional profiles as theater practitioners.
4. In my experience, students' reactions to theater performance courses has always been enthusiastic. After the 2001 production of Dario Fo's *Mamma! I Sanculotti!,* for instance, a business major at the Wharton School of Economics wrote: "I thank you for the most interesting, creative and possibly challenging class I have taken at Penn. I thoroughly enjoyed it and am sure that the class can only go on to even bigger and brighter things in the future." Mark O'Rorke, personal correspondence, 30 April 2001. O'Rorke and two other 2001 students in this course requested authorization to attend the course again in 2002. Several 2002 students repeated the course in 2003 and one of them even in 2004 as an extracurricular activity for no credit. Thanks to their experience in the original course, three of these students declared Italian as their major. Obviously, each year the theater course was based on a different play.
5. Essif, *The French Play*, 7–9; Haggstrom, "A Performative Approach"; and Chapter 4 in this book.
6. Brook, *The Empty Space*, 9.

7. For the definition of *affective filter,* see Krashen, *Principles and Practice,* 30–32 and 73–76.

8. For a full description of modular pedagogy, see Baldacci, *La didattica per moduli.*

9. See Fo, *Mamma! I Sanculotti!,* and Pirandello, "Sei personaggi in cerca d'autore." A more detailed discussion of the teaching and learning experience developed through the performance of Pirandello's *Sei personaggi* has been published in Marini-Maio, "I *Sei Personaggi* siamo noi."

10. As Scuderi highlights, in his theatrical productions Fo has used numerous genres but mainly two modes of performance: the one-man play, which Fo named *giullarata,* and the satirical farce. Fo derived the term *giullarata* from the Italian word *giullare* (approximately translated in English as *jester*), which in the Middle Ages indicated roving performers of this popular tradition. The *giullarata* is a unique mode of performance that combines popular and oral traditions, storytelling, and acting and relies on Fo's extraordinary talents as a comedian. Fo's satirical farces, instead, are performed with other actors, although Fo's role on the stage is prominent. Satirical farces are translated and performed all over the world by independent theatrical groups. For more detailed information about Fo's modes of performance, see Scuderi, "Unmasking the Holy Jester Dario Fo."

11. For a thorough discussion of Fo's and Rame's theater in North American universities, see Chapter 6 of this book.

12. I have taught two courses based on Fo's *Mamma! I Sanculotti!*: "Italian Play Production" (Spring 2001, University of Pennsylvania) and "Riso amaro" (Fall 2005, Middlebury College).

13. Farrell and Scuderi, eds., *Dario Fo,* 9.

14. Among the many contributions in the field, see, for instance, Warwick, "Acquiring Literacy in a Second Language," and Krashen, *The Power of Reading.*

15. Bernier, "The Challenge of Language and History Terminology," 96. Although Bernier's article concerns the difficulties of L2 students in L1 history instruction, his argument can be easily transferred to L2 content-based instruction.

16. According to the theory of naturalistic acting developed by Stanislavski, actors must strive for absolute psychological identification with the characters. See Stanislavski, *An Actor Prepares.* For a discussion of the Stanislavskian method, see also Chapter 2 in this book. For the notion of epic acting, see Brecht's theory of "estrangement" in Brecht, "Short Description of a New Technique of Acting."

17. For the use of humor as the thematic center of the theater practicum in the L2, see Ryan-Scheutz and Colangelo, "Campanile's Comedic

Theater." Walter Valeri, too, emphasizes the pedagogical effect of Fo's humor on L2 learners in Chapter 6 of this book.

18. The readings consisted of excerpts from Abruzzese, *Elogio del tempo nuovo;* Berlusconi, *L'Italia che ho in mente;* Dalla Chiesa, *La politica della doppiezza;* Di Natale, *Appunti di storia della prima repubblica;* Duggan, *A Concise History of Italy;* McCarthy, *The Crisis of the Italian State;* and Mack Smith, *L'Italia del XX secolo.*

19. See Benni, "Papà va in TV," 9–17, and "Il DDT, o il drogato da telefonino," 119–124; Campanile, *Il ciambellone,* 53–71; Ginzburg, "Fragola e panna," 1261–1284; Pirandello, "L'umorismo," 15–160; Pirandello, *Il Fu Mattia Pascal;* Pirandello, "Così è (se vi pare)"; Svevo, *La coscienza di Zeno.*

20. For information on Fo's biography, political activism, and theatrical productions, students read excerpts from Valentini, *La storia di Dario Fo,* and Behan, *Dario Fo.*

21. The complete Italian version of the questionnaire, adapted and translated into Italian from Ingham, *From Page to Stage,* is in Marini-Maio, "I *Sei Personaggi* siamo noi," 470–471. For a concise definition of *given circumstances,* see Moore, *The Stanislavski System,* 26–27.

22. See Spolin, Sills, and Sills, eds., *Improvisation for the Theater,* and Tosto, *Manuale del laboratorio teatrale.*

23. Brief excerpts from Alfieri, Campo, and Lozio, *Teatro,* provided basic information on theater as a cultural production and performance genre.

24. See Fo and Rame, *Manuale minimo dell'attore;* De Filippo and Quarenghi, *Lezioni di teatro all'università di Roma La Sapienza;* and Luzzati, *Facciamo insieme teatro.*

25. For ideas and discussion about these theatrical techniques, see Fo and Rame, *Manuale minimo dell'attore.*

26. See Piscopo and Luciano, *A Nobel for Two,* and Miti and Fo, *Dario Fo.*

27. In sociocultural theory, *scaffolding* refers to the interactive, social, and affective support that one learner gives to another. See Donato, "Collective Scaffolding."

28. For a full illustration of sociocultural theory, see Vygotsky, *Mind in Society.*

29. Di Pietro, *Strategic Interaction,* 139.

30. See Pirandello, "Sei personaggi in cerca d'autore," 622.

31. For the notion of allegory in Pirandello's work, see Luperini's essays *L'allegoria del moderno,* and "L'atto della significazione allegorica."

32. See Macchia, *Pirandello o la stanza della tortura.*

33. See Ragusa, "Sei personaggi in cerca d'autore," 153.

34. The 1925 revision appears in the Italian edition of Pirandello's plays. In the United States, the 1921 version, included in the English edition

*Naked Masks*, trans. E. Storer (New York: Penguin Books, 1957), has been the only one known for many years.

35. See Sanguineti, *Sei personaggi.com.*
36. Macchia, *Pirandello o la stanza della tortura*, 12.
37. Ibid., 15.
38. Kramsch, "Literary Texts in the Classroom," 360.
39. Essif, "Way Off Broadway and Way Out of the Classroom."


## Bibliography

Abruzzese, Alberto. *Elogio del tempo nuovo: Perché Berlusconi ha vinto.* Genoa: Costa & Nolan, 1994.

Alfieri, R., V. Campo, and G. Lozio. *Teatro.* Naples: Morano, 1996.

Baldacci, Massimo. *La didattica per moduli.* Rome-Bari: Laterza, 2003.

Behan, Tom. *Dario Fo: Revolutionary Theatre.* Sterling, Va.: Pluto Press, 2000.

Benni, Stefano. "Papà va in TV." *L'ultima lacrima.* Milan: Feltrinelli, 1994.

———. "Il DDT, o il drogato da telefonino." *Bar sport duemila.* Milan: Feltrinelli, 1997.

Berlusconi, Silvio. *L'Italia che ho in mente: I discorsi "a braccio" di Silvio Berlusconi.* Milan: Mondadori, 2000.

Bernier, Anthony. "The Challenge of Language and History Terminology from the Student Optic." In *The Content-Based Classroom: Perspectives on Integrating Language and Content,* edited by Margaret Ann and Donna Brinton Snow. White Plains, N.Y.: Longman, 1997.

Bräuer, Gerd, ed. *Body and Language: Intercultural Learning through Drama.* Westport, Conn.: Ablex, 2002.

Brecht, Bertolt. "Short Description of a New Technique of Acting which Produces an Alienation Effect." In *Brecht on Theatre: The Development of an Aesthetic,* translated and edited by John Willet, 136–147. New York: Hill and Wang, 1964.

Brook, Peter. *The Empty Space: A Book about the Theatre: Deadly, Holy, Rough, Immediate.* New York: Atheneum, 1968.

Byrnes, Heidi. "The Role of Task and Task-Based Assessment in a Content-Oriented Collegiate Foreign Language Curriculum." *Language Testing* 19.4 (2002): 419–437.

Campanile, Achille. *Il ciambellone: L'inventore del cavallo e altre quindici commedie.* Milan: BUR, 2002.

Dalla Chiesa, Nando. *La politica della doppiezza: Da Andreotti a Berlusconi.* Turin: Einaudi, 1996.

De Filippo, Eduardo, and Paola Quarenghi. *Lezioni di teatro all'Università di Roma La Sapienza.* Turin: Einaudi, 1986.

Di Natale, Francesco. *Appunti di storia della prima repubblica.* Perugia: Guerra, 2000.

Di Pietro, Robert. *Strategic Interaction: Learning Languages through Scenarios.* Cambridge: Cambridge University Press, 1987.

Donato, Richard. "Collective Scaffolding in Second Language Learning." In *Vygotskian Approaches to Second Language Research,* edited by James P. Lantolf and Gabriela Appel, 33–56. Norwood, N.J.: Ablex, 1994.

Duggan, Christopher. *A Concise History of Italy.* Cambridge: Cambridge University Press, 1994.

Essif, Les. "Way Off Broadway and Way Out of the Classroom: American Students De-, Re-, and Per-forming the French Dramatic Text." *ADFL Bulletin* 1 (1995): 32–37.

———. *The French Play: Exploring Theatre "Re-creatively" with Foreign Language Students.* Calgary: University of Calgary, 2006.

Farrell, Joseph, and Antonio Scuderi. *Dario Fo: Stage, Text, and Tradition.* Carbondale: Southern Illinois University Press, 2000.

Fo, Dario. *Mamma! I Sanculotti!* Turin: Einaudi, 1994.

Fo, Dario, and Franca Rame. *Manuale minimo dell'attore.* Rev. ed. Turin: Einaudi, 1997.

Ginzburg, Natalia. "Fragola e panna." *Teatro.* Turin: Einaudi, 1966.

Haggstrom, Margaret A. "A Performative Approach to the Study of Theater: Bridging the Gap between Language and Literature Courses." *French Review* 66.1 (1992): 7–19.

Ingham, Rosemary. *From Page to Stage: How Theatre Designers Make Connections between Scripts and Images.* Portsmouth, N.H.: Heinemann, 1998.

Kramsch, Claire. "Literary Texts in the Classroom: A Discourse." *Modern Language Journal* 69 (1985): 356–366.

Krashen, Stephen D. *Principles and Practice in Second Language Acquisition.* Oxford: Pergamon Press, 1982.

———. *The Power of Reading: Insights from the Research.* 2nd ed. Westport, Conn.: Libraries Unlimited, 2004.

Luperini, Romano. *L'allegoria del moderno: Saggi sull'allegorismo come forma artistica del moderno e come metodo di conoscenza.* Rome: Editori Riuniti, 1990.

———. "L'atto della significazione allegorica in 'Sei personaggi' e in 'Enrico IV.'" In *Pirandello,* 113–124. Rome-Bari: Laterza, 1999.

Luzzati, Emanuele. *Facciamo insieme teatro.* Rome-Bari: Laterza, 2001.

Macchia, Giovanni. *Pirandello o la stanza della tortura.* Milan: Mondadori, 1981.

Mack Smith, Denis. *L'Italia del XX secolo: Politica e costume con sintesi storiche.* Milan: Rizzoli, 1977.

Marini-Maio, Nicoletta. "I *Sei Personaggi* siamo noi: Pirandello, o la metamorfosi degli studenti nel laboratorio teatrale in italiano." *Italica* 81.4 (2004): 459–482.

McCarthy, Patrick. *The Crisis of the Italian State: From the Origins of the Cold War to the Fall of Berlusconi.* New York: St. Martin's, 1995.

Miti, Ruggero, dir., and Dario Fo. *Dario Fo, lezioni di teatro.* Videorecording. Turin: Einaudi, 2001.

Moore, Sonia. *The Stanislavski System: The Professional Training of an Actor.* New York: Penguin Books, 1984.

Pirandello, Luigi. "L'umorismo." In *Saggi, poesie, scritti varii,* edited by Lo Vecchi-Musti. 2nd ed. Milan: Mondadori, 1965.

———. "Così è (se vi pare)." In *Maschere nude,* edited by Alessandro D'Amico, vol. I, 417–509. Milan: Mondadori, 1993.

———. "Sei personaggi in cerca d'autore." In *Maschere nude,* edited by Alessandro D'Amico, vol. II, 619–758. Milan: Mondadori, 1993.

———. *Il fu Mattia Pascal.* Milan: Mondadori, 2000.

Piscopo, Filippo, and Lorena Luciano. *A Nobel for Two. A Documentary on Dario Fo and Franca Rame.* Videorecording. New York: Cinema Guild, 1998.

Ragusa, Olga. "Sei personaggi in cerca d'autore." In *Luigi Pirandello: An Approach to His Theatre.* Edinburgh: Edinburgh University Press, 1980.

Ryan-Scheutz, Colleen, and Laura Colangelo. "Campanile's Comedic Theater: A Humorous Link between Language and Literature in the Italian Studies Curriculum." *Italica* 81.4 (2004): 483–503.

Sanguineti, Edoardo. *Sei personaggi.com.* Genoa: Il Melangolo, 1998.

Scuderi, Antonio. "Unmasking the Holy Jester Dario Fo." *Theatre Journal* 55 (2003): 275–290.

Spolin, Viola, Paul Sills, and William Sills, eds. *Improvisation for the Theater: A Handbook of Teaching and Directing.* Evanston, Ill.: Northwestern University Press, 1999.

Stanislavski, Konstantin. *An Actor Prepares.* Translated by Elizabeth Reynolds Hapgood. New York: Routledge, 2003.

Svevo, Italo. *La coscienza di Zeno.* Florence: Giunti, 1994.

Tosto, Tonino. *Manuale del laboratorio teatrale.* Rome: EDUP, 2003.

Valentini, Chiara. *La storia di Dario Fo.* 2nd ed. Milan: Feltrinelli, 1997.

Vygotsky, Lev Semenovich. *Mind in Society: The Development of Higher Psychological Processes.* Cambridge, Mass.: Harvard University Press, 1978.

———. *Thought and Language.* Cambridge, Mass.: MIT Press, 1986.

Warwick, Elley. "Acquiring Literacy in a Second Language: The Effect of Book-Based Programs." *Language Learning* 41 (3): 375–411.

Whiteson, Valerie. *New Ways of Using Drama and Literature in Language Teaching.* Bloomington, Ill.: Pantagraph, 1996.

# CHAPTER 10

# *Community, Culture, and Body Language: Staging the Female Voice in the Italian Drama Workshop*

ANTONELLA DEL FATTORE-OLSON

## Theater: A Direction for a Quest

In the past decade, one of the principal goals of departments of foreign languages has been to offer and design new courses that incorporate the many and different interests of students and encourage them to consider a double major in the target language and another branch of learning. Living as we do in an age of globalization, although its meaning is still rather unclear, as Alessandro Baricco wisely points out in his *piccolo libro* (small book), *Next,* it is vital that the cultural identity and historical background of countries all over the world be preserved and taught through a broader spectrum of subjects. Theater is one of the disciplines worth considering for this purpose as it mirrors the history of humankind—its society, language, and feelings. Thus, it can very well represent a direction for the quest of unifying two different interests, Italian and theater.

In the Italian Drama Workshop class, both teachers and students can overcome the boundaries of a regular classroom environment by exploring, as individuals within a community, the social, linguistic, and cultural aspects of the historical period a play presents. Moreover, the play production class, as an advanced course, represents a natural follow-up to the previous years' endeavors. It offers, in fact, the opportunity for students to finally bring together grammar, lexicon, and cultural background in a "whole" by unifying two teaching areas —the performative, linguistic, and literary and the historical and sociocultural—and by reshaping the intentions of first- and second-year courses in a more comprehensive way. It's realistic to think that in the play production class the objective of rendering the students fluent in the target language can be finally attained because, as Nicoletta Marini-Maio points out, bringing together literary and cultural components with linguistic interaction creates a situation of full immersion.[1] In such a course, students don't have to get close to the fictional characters presented in first- and second-year textbooks through dialogues and situations to imagine the meaning of the circumstances of the lives of those fictional characters; instead, students are asked *to be* the characters, to move, breathe, speak, and interact as the characters.[2] The degree of identification with the character is such that students engage in a process of appropriating each line of the play, including its grammatical structures and lexicon. Furthermore, students are forced to think and behave as the characters in the specific historical and cultural period in which the author has placed them; thus the knowledge of history and culture becomes a relevant part in the learning process.

## Dacia Maraini: An Inspiring Voice

The choice of the author whose play constitutes the main component of the Italian Drama Workshop is, like theater itself, a reflection of the goals that the instructor/director wants to reach in the class. If a deeper knowledge of the history and development of the female presence onstage is one of these goals, then undoubtedly Dacia Maraini's theatrical works provide endless sources for a cumulative analysis of the Italian language (including the dialects), culture, and history of periods that range from the Middle Ages to modern times. Her voice is familiar in Italy and abroad, owing to her constant participation in the intellectual, political, academic, and cultural aspects of contemporary society and to the fact that her works have been translated and read in more than twenty countries. Her writing tends to focus on the family and how familiar relationships in Western civilization shape female identity, subjectivity, and their cultural construction—themes with which anyone of any age can identify. As a feminist, Maraini revises the notion of the family in order to allow women to redefine their subjectivity, and she uses literature, poetry, theater, and cinema to empower women by bringing their voices from the private to the public sphere. In this way she enables the reconsideration of women's condition (both historically and in the present), and possibly a revision of their roles in society. For Dacia Maraini, writing is a pleasure, as she states in *Dizionaretto quotidiano,* and the same is true for her readers. Reading her works is indeed a pleasure. Her fluid, harmonious style and her eloquence render the subjects she chooses easy to read, even if they often depict cruel realities. In this chapter, some of her works will serve as guides for describing and explaining the effect that the play production class can have on students of Italian.

## Bringing Together Performative and Linguistic Components with Literary, Historical, and Sociocultural Ones

One strategy for bringing together the different components in the Italian Drama Workshop in order to make students fluent in Italian and more conscious of the historical, social, and cultural backgrounds of the chosen play is, in the first part of the semester, to alternate the reading of the text, with emphasis on language structures and pragmatic aspects, with a literary, historical, and sociocultural analysis.[3] Even though students are eager to step into the theatrical component from the first day of class, they must be advised that the initial approaches during this first phase are to (1) read the chosen play, focusing on grammatical structures, lexicon, and pronunciation, (2) analyze the play in the proper literary and historical contexts along with a study of its author, and (3) discuss the interpretation of the play. In staging any of Maraini's plays, this agenda can be successfully respected. While reading the play, students can research the life and artistic contributions of one of the many female protagonists (for example, Veronica Franco, Isabella di Morra, or Caterina da Siena); read one of Maraini's autobiographical novels, such as *Bagheria* or *La nave per Kobe,* to learn about or deepen their knowledge of the author; and finally, dwell upon the multiple interpretations of the play and its characters.

Although the context in this classroom setting is obviously of a scholastic nature and not of professional acting training, this initial phase is similar to the "planes" suggested by Konstantin Stanislavski: *the external plane* contiguous with *the plane of social situation,* which focus on the plot and historical background of the play, and *the literary plane,* where ideas and style are analyzed.[4] During this first phase, the class, as a community, uses the strategy of rendering logical, thus real, the abstract linguistic and syntactic notions learned so far by memorizing lines in a specific context. In fact, such notions are brought into a real dimension through the play, just as the playwright's vision and ideas are brought to life through the collective endeavor. Furthermore, according to the choice of the play, teachers can present students with a richer linguistic view of the Italian language and its dialects, or at least various forms of regional Italian. Quite often, students claim that the standard Italian they learned in class doesn't always reflect what they heard during their stays in Italy. Pronunciation, intonation, peaks of voice, and regional idiomatic expressions differ from one region to another. Teachers should not shy away from presenting this reality. It would, of course, be unfeasible to teach dialects in an Italian classroom while presenting standard Italian, but students should be aware of the fact that dialects or different kinds of regional Italian do exist and that they have to expect, and accept, such a reality. Among the modern Italian playwrights, Eduardo De Filippo's work immediately comes to mind for his consistent preference for the Neapolitan dialect, but two of Maraini's plays, *Veronica, meretrice e scrittora* and *La lunga vita di Marianna Ucrìa,* also present opportunities for dealing with dialects.

Finally, the play production class offers, along with the challenge of opening new doors to the varied nature of the Italian language, the opportunity for students to face topics that are often controversial and difficult from historical and sociocultural perspectives. After all, the sociocultural context must be the consistent scenery in which the students move throughout their journey in learning a foreign language.

## Creating a Sense of Community

The most important step in making the above-mentioned structure possible is to create among the students a sense of community. The degree of positive results in a performance is proportionate to the level of the collective effort of the participants. It is essential to clarify that the time allowed to the Italian Drama Workshop, an upper-division course, by the legitimate academic credit hours—usually three per week—will be expanded according to the needs of the course. Students know that they will be onstage for a public performance at the end of the semester; therefore, it's not just the final grade and the amount of valuable information they learn that matter, but also and above all the way they perform as actors in the final public performances as well as the style in which the entire show is presented to the audience.

As a community, the play production class has the mission to build its own new space and territory. This is true in any classroom, in any subject. In the enlightening dialogue between bell hooks and Ron Scapp—both strong advocates of progressive, engaged pedagogical practices—while discussing the role of teachers/professors/ critical thinkers in the academy, they stress the importance of establishing a community, an environment in which, as hooks states, "We are all equal . . . to the extent that we are equally committed to create a learning context."[5]

In order to achieve the realization of a community, both teachers and learners must not be afraid to open themselves to others, to let their emotions emerge—in other words, to take risks. In a foreign language classroom, maybe even more than in any other class, teachers ask students to become very vulnerable; not only do students have to express their opinions, but they have to do it as they stumble with different sentence structures and unfamiliar lexicon. Educators can agree, especially in a play production class, that in order for students to feel comfortable in this stressful situation, they have to be vulnerable and be learners as well within the microcosm of the class. The importance of being enthusiastic and interactive in teaching any subject cannot be overemphasized, and teachers should be ready, as Wilga Rivers suggests in her description of the interactive language teaching process, "to step out of the limelight, to cede a full role to the students in developing and carrying through activities, to accept all kinds of opinions, and be tolerant of errors the student makes while attempting to communicate."[6] While directing a play with student-actors, the instructor/director must be, as Michael Bloom says, "creative, inventive, intuitive, and above all passionate"; and he continues, "Passion is what energizes the director's search for the animus or inner life of a play."[7] Establishing a learning community also has to do with respect and trust: respect of everyone's opinions and interpretations and trust in the commitment of each of the participants. Both elements are indispensable in a class whose objective is to make students fluent in Italian by combining subjects of a different nature—foreign language and theatrical production—and by teaching linguistic and cultural components within the framework of a play production course, harmoniously balancing "making theater" and teaching a traditional upper-division Italian course.

As a playwright, Dacia Maraini represents a perfect model for students because of her continuous and unrestrained involvement with all aspects of "making theater." Dealing with any of her plays, students will learn at an early stage how writing a play for Maraini is frequently followed by directing, staging, feeling, and considering all the elements that a theatrical performance implies. Meeting her personally, as many students in the Italian Drama Workshop have had the opportunity to do, can only confirm for them Maraini's deep commitment to theater and inspire them to devote themselves to the project of staging her works. It is quite an experience to observe Maraini participating in dress rehearsals, interacting with students as if they were professional actors and thus encouraging them to give their best as individuals and as participants in a group effort.

Working on Maraini's plays that have just a few characters, such as *Erzbeth Báthory, Da Roma a Milano,* and *Bianca Garofani,* or plays with a multitude of roles, such as *Un treno, una notte; Veronica, meretrice e scrittora;* and *La lunga vita di Marianna Ucrìa,* presents the same necessity of establishing a collective "working force." In fact, if the instructor/director desires a captivating theatrical performance, plays like *Veronica, meretrice e scrittora* and *La lunga vita di Marianna Ucrìa* would certainly be appropriate. They require an attentive study of the costumes of the sixteenth and eighteenth centuries, respectively, of music, and of complex scenography as well as a thoughtful analysis of the text and a collective interpretation. Only strongly committed and dedicated participants can handle such challenging responsibilities. In both plays, Maraini clearly presents her personal and artistic view of two real women—Veronica Franco, the sixteenth-century Venetian courtesan and poetess, and Marianna Ucrìa, an eighteenth-century Sicilian deaf-mute duchess—leaving, however, ample space for the reader's individual interpretation. If these two plays with many roles are to be portrayed onstage, and most likely be interpreted by two different casts, the individual interpretation, even if accurate, will not guarantee a convincing presentation. To present the characters and play in a coherent way, students must undertake intense in-class discussions and listen to one another's views. Only then can the performance reflect a final collective interpretation.

## Culture: Controversial Topics

How theater classes treat culture is a controversial topic that students had to face in the fall of 1999 working on Maraini's two-act play *Veronica, meretrice e scrittora*. It was a special occasion for the students of Italian in general, and the students of the Italian Drama Workshop in particular, because Maraini visited the campus, attending some of the rehearsals of the play she had written in 1991. Her active participation, inspiring enthusiasm, and brilliant input contributed significantly to the success of the production. She spent only a few days at the university, yet she succeeded in sharing with the students her remarkable skills in directing, teaching young people, and helping them understand the text. It was an experience so memorable that it was repeated four years later with the offering of another play by Maraini, *La lunga vita di Marianna Ucrìa*.

In the fall of 1999, the Italian Drama Workshop used the Internet for the first time to release information about the play to be performed at the end of the semester and to share images of relevant moments of the class's work. The following paragraph, posted on the Italian Drama Workshop's website, describes the poetess and courtesan who is the subject of Maraini's play:

> Veronica Franco, poet and courtesan, lived in a world dominated by masculinity and religion. The conventions of sixteenth-century Venice limited women's options in life, and each option carried with it its own set of restrictions. Most women were passed straight from the control of their fathers to that of their husbands, and those who could not afford a dowry often became nuns. Only one role, that of a courtesan, a member of a special class of high-society prostitutes, granted women entrance to libraries, and to artistic and intellectual circles. By choosing this third path in life, Veronica Franco enjoyed freedoms denied to other women. Renowned as much for her wit and intellect as for the other qualities necessary in her profession, Veronica mingled with the upper echelons of Venetian society, and was able to publish her poetry.[8]

The class agreed that such a description reflected Maraini's theatrical depiction of Veronica Franco; it also reflected the way we intended to portray Veronica. However, one of the guest speakers who shared her expertise with the students in the field of Renaissance studies brought up a vision of the poetess that was quite different from Maraini's and that of the students.[9] In fact, Irene Eibenstein-

Alvisi presented us with an interesting argument that constitutes a component of her doctoral dissertation. At the beginning of the semester, during the initial phase when students explored the grammatical, linguistic, and sociocultural components of the play, the historical and contemporary role of women in Italian society and Maraini's contributions to the feminist movement had already elicited a dynamic discussion among the students. Eibenstein-Alvisi added new fuel to the fire of our discussion, making it even more lively. In brief, she argued that, just as Margaret Rosenthal and Sara Maria Adler had appropriated Franco's work as a symbol of positive progression toward self-awareness and self-assurance in their critique of her *Terze Rime,* so had Maraini crafted this character in her play as a heroic role model for women and an iconic symbol of women's issues. Eibenstein-Alvisi maintained that Franco should instead be viewed solely as a poet, and interest in her mainly should be focused on her complex and rich artistic contributions.

Of course, we were all aware that Maraini's Veronica was a fictional character even if based on the poetess's life story; the playwright made imaginative changes, such as having Veronica in a quarantine station during the plague that devastated Venice in 1575. At the end of the play, after having been close to death, Veronica leaves the *lazzaretto* with her new friend Anzola, a young, poor, and simple nun, and together they eagerly face a new reality. I agree with Paola Carù, who sees a similarity between this ending and the ending of Maraini's *La lunga vita di Marianna Ucrìa* (both the novel and the play). There, Marianna and her servant Fila set out on a journey to find a new identity for themselves. Both Maraini's Marianna and her Veronica are dynamic characters who, against all odds, fight to free their spirits from the boundaries to which a patriarchal society confines them. Unlike others of Maraini's female characters who seek refuge from society's rejection in madness (for example, Fede, the protagonist of *Fede o Della perversione matrimoniale,* or Ada and Elvira in *Stravaganza*), Veronica and Marianna succeed in reaching their independence and, especially, their right to communicate and express themselves.

It may be true, as Eibenstein-Alvisi argues, that Maraini's Veronica Franco can be perceived as a heroine and female icon, but only if the readers/spectators decide to apply a particular ideology to the text. One element that greatly impressed the students, and all was done to emphasize it, was the way Veronica is in fact depicted as a "normal" woman with whom both women and men can easily identify. Her fear of dying, her desire to survive and succeed, her pride, her love of love, her questioning of God's will, her honesty, and her need to give to and take from the artistic world are all elements that bring her close to any reader. *Veronica, meretrice e scrittora* was a challenging play to stage because Veronica's character is found simultaneously in two different "spaces" of the stage. In the *lazzaretto*, struggling with the plague, she narrates her life to Anzola, and it seems that they are both kept alive (Veronica physically and Anzola intellectually) by Veronica's words and memories. While she talks, the audience sees a beautiful and healthy Veronica moving in her Venetian home surrounded by lovers, poets, sons, a husband, her servant-friend Gaspara, and, at a certain point, even by a king. In the staging of *La lunga vita di Marianna Ucrìa,* a similar scenario is presented.[10] The soul and reflections of the silent duchess are portrayed by Marianna's narrator, while on the stage the mute Marianna communicates by writing to the people who surround her. As women of the sixteenth and eighteenth centuries, both Marianna and Veronica could have lived their lives in silence, particularly considering that both had experienced an early sexual trauma: Veronica was introduced to her profession by her mother, who was also a courtesan, and Marianna was raped as a child and had to marry the uncle who raped her. These women, however, did not renounce the joy of "speaking," and they fought with the tools that they had at their disposal. If not as heroines or female icons, they are definitely to be considered courageous and strong women whose story must be told and, thanks to Maraini, put on a stage.

In the Italian Drama Workshop of 1999, students as a group decided to see Veronica in the same way as Maraini, and for the same reasons. As Maraini put it: "I liked Veronica Franco because she is sincere, because she is generous, because she writes well, but also because she wanted to be a mother and a woman in love, besides being a courtesan. She took risks and suffered with passion. From this 'human' liking for the *persona* of Franco the inspiration to write the text was born, not from an ideological project. The ideas are parts of the complexity of the character."[11] If the physical presence of the author contributed significantly to interpreting the *persona* and *personaggio* of Veronica Franco, the destiny of the theatrical version of Marianna Ucrìa was entirely determined by the students' choice of having the until-then mute protagonist speak to the audience.[12]

The students were capable of making a collective decision about how to portray the female protagonists, and they did so by functioning as a community. In the same way, they must approach the other components of the course, the ones that belong to the aesthetic, psychological, and physical planes suggested by Stanislavski. Of course, in a classroom it is too ambitious to follow *ad litteram* his sophisticated acting method; however, it is feasible for the instructor/director to keep it in mind while assisting and guiding the students throughout this experience.

## Language and Body Language

In order to avoid an impersonal or, even worse, tedious reading of a play and to create a frame of mind linked to a play, it is useful to ask students to sit in a circle on the stage and read the lines of the characters before they know which character they will perform. They do know though that while reading the lines, both the director and their peers will form an idea for the casting process; therefore, it is to their advantage to "conquer" the role they prefer through a good reading.[13] To offer a convincing reading, students must understand the lines each character is saying as well as grammatical structures and lexicon.

Two one-act plays that are exciting to present in combination, from the perspective of language acquisition and because of their interestingly similar concepts, are *Da Roma a Milano* (1975) by Dacia Maraini and *Cecè* (1913) by Luigi Pirandello. Over sixty years distant from Pirandello's play, Maraini's play confirms the contemporary value of Pirandello's concepts and enlightens the development of the language. From a grammatical point of view, the content of the first play is a superb explanation of the use of past tenses and contains a great deal of descriptive adjectives. Vanna and Geremia travel in a car, living what Maraini called in *Fare teatro* "a gioco pirandelliano."[14] They constantly mix their own identities and the ones of people close to them. Vanna, similarly to Fede in *Fede o Della perversione matrimoniale*, pretends to be two women at the same time, one of whom is dead, and claims she brings the dead one behind her as a corpse. As opposed to Fede's constant anxiety, however, the splitting of Vanna's personality provides a sense of lightness, as she tells Geremia, "Questo essere due, sai, mi rende leggera come una farfalla"—she feels as light as a butterfly. Her often playful state of mind softens the sense of apprehension throughout the play with a hazy, comical atmosphere.

In working on *Cecè,* students began to gain knowledge of a great deal of lexicon from the very first page preceding the play, which lists the characters. In the description of Cesare Vivoli, alias Cecè—whose sound *c'è–c'è* immediately enlightens the eclectic and lively nature of this main character—Pirandello uses expressions, maybe unusual yet not obsolete, such as *avere l'aria stralunata, avere la mente a cento cose a un tempo,* and *al guizzo d'ogni immagine;* for Squatriglia, the wealthy and naive contractor who falls into Cecè's trap, *pezzo d'omone* and *un po' ingoffito;* and continues by describing Nada, *una mondana di lusso,* as a young woman who lives in a precious gallantry but *toccata nel vivo, la perde per cadere o nella sguajataggine o nell'ingenuità.* Other lines from this play show the enrichment of new lexicon (new words and synonyms for students are underlined):

| | |
|---|---|
| *Cecè:* | Ma no! Con te <u>non faccio cerimonie</u>. <u>Sèguito a radermi</u>. <u>L'uscio</u> è aperto; puoi parlare. <u>Anzi</u> se vuoi, entra, entra qua. |
| *Squatriglia:* | No, grazie; <u>fa' pure con comodo</u>; aspetto. |
| *Cecè:* | Cinque minuti. Ho <u>bell'e</u> finito. |

And furthermore:

| | |
|---|---|
| *Nada:* | Il fallimento! La rovina! Il disonore! Tutto <u>a catafascio</u> per le tue <u>nequizie</u>! Un povero padre, a cui <u>hai inzaccherato la canizie veneranda</u>! Una povera madre . . . imbroglione! <u>gaglioffo</u>! Come non ti vergogni? |
| *Cecè: (serio, con freddezza grave)* | Ma tu <u>farnetichi</u>, mia cara! Ti prego di spiegarmi. Io non capisco nulla.[15] |

For any unknown word or idiomatic expression, students are asked to get the gist of it from the context, then to guess the meaning, and finally to come up with a synonym in standard Italian. Translation into English is the last resort. Once everybody understands, students repeat chorally the word or entire idiomatic expression with the correct pronunciation as well as the proper intonation that the context suggests. Thus, the unknown word or expression finds its place in the memory of the learner through repetition and conceptualization within the context of the play, which is becoming the real dimension in which students will be immersed.

The idea of the community can be further clarified here; not only does it refer to the fact that, through antonomasia, theatrical performances are the result of a collective effort, but also that the play itself constitutes the central element in the creation of a microcosm in which the class's community will function and grow. Someone might argue that we will succeed only in establishing an artificial and perhaps restricted dimension—the one of a single play reflecting only a single historical time frame—but this process follows the same kind of limitation imposed by the selection of a textbook or a packet of readings.

Although this play is not one of the most famous or most studied and performed of Pirandello's plays, through Cecè's most significant monologue, students become familiar with many of Pirandello's philosophical concepts. For example, at the beginning, Cecè explains to Squatriglia and the audience that he doesn't know his own identity because he is constantly changing it according to his relationship with different people. He lives his life "sparpagliato in centomila" (scattered in one hundred people), and has a hard time remembering which part of his personality he can safely show to all the many people with whom he constantly interacts. All know him, all have expectations, all love certain characteristics of him, but he knows no one. It is difficult for Cecè to be one for he feels that too many fragments of a human being live inside him, many that perhaps are erasing his own identity. Through the wave of the pleasant comic verve in which *Cecè* is written, students are presented with a not-so-archaic mentality of conducting business pertinent to a certain Italian social class. Cecè does not possess much beyond a charismatic personality and remarkable skills in manipulating the people around him, and, thanks to these characteristics, he is capable of conducting a rich life among "la migliore società" (high society). By means of his connections, Cecè helped Squatriglia with his business by recommending him to an important political figure, and in exchange for this favor, he asks Squatriglia to deceive Nada and persuade her to give him three blank bills, "tre cambiali," that Cecè has given her. Through this particular play, students can master some grammatical structures, which often haunt students even in upper-division courses, and find their rationalization and raison d'être. For instance, subjunctive clauses are more easily understood if presented in an emotional and, in the case of *Cecè*, humorous manner, that is, when a character is using them in a way that resembles the natural flow of a river. In the play, when Squatriglia is following Cecè's request to deceive Nada, he uses "if clauses," verbs in the subjunctive mood, and formal imperatives:

> *Squatriglia:*    Benedetta! Benedetta. Sì .. . Oh <u>creda</u>, signorina, che <u>se lei avesse</u> in pugno veramente un'arma contro di lui, un'arma <u>che potesse</u> colpirlo, colpir solo lui, e distruggerlo, annientarlo, io e il padre, e la madre stessa, <u>le grideremmo</u>: Forte! sù! <u>colpisca</u>! subito! <u>lo distrugga</u>! <u>lo annienti</u>, questo miserabile! questo aborto di natura! questo ributto dell'umanità.—Ma lei non ha nessun'arma contro di lui! Ha lì tre pezzi di carta, che non valgono nulla![16]

Contrary to a lesson in a "regular" Italian classroom, the instructor asks the students to identify and justify the grammatical structures rather than engaging in a lengthy explanation of the rules that students have studied in previous years. Why is Squatriglia using the "if clause"? What are his intentions in repeating so passionately these commands? Why does he not get closer to Nada by begging her in the informal imperative since he obviously accepted his own humiliation? Why is *potesse* in the subjunctive? What effect do his words have on Nada?

Squatriglia's use of grammar is related to his inner motivations. He is an individual who has to reach a goal; specifically in this piece, he has to lie to defeat Nada's resistance and obtain the three blank bills for Cecè. He has to force himself to leave his shyness behind and to repay the favor Cecè has done for him. Thus, the grammatical structures become real components in the communicative process; students no longer view them as abstract concepts unrelated to real-life situations. They are "real" for them because the play is the real dimension in which students live their experience in the play production class.

In lower-division courses, students have been exposed to a learning process that gradually took them from the instruction of individual components in the acquisition of a foreign language—components William Littlewood defines as "part-skills" of communication—to a performance of the "whole task," which should integrate the previous components.[17] Whether we read scholarly works in the field of applied linguistics, pedagogy, or teaching practices, theatrical terminology is constantly used to describe the ideal experience in a foreign language classroom. We are reminded of the importance of the "active roles of the learners," "interaction with other people," "internalization of the language," "motivation," "stimulation," "tasks of repetition," and so on. All this is summarized efficiently in hooks's assertion that "teaching is a performative act" just like learning is a performative act, and both acts should be constantly renewed and reinvented.[18] The important task is to succeed in taking maximal advantage of the material with which we are working from all the different angles: pronunciation, intonation, cultural content, and, last but not least, grammar.

In order to perfect the pragmatic aspects of students' language skills, focusing on pronunciation and intonation, the approach should be based upon a combination of theatrical and pedagogical means: basic theatrical exercises are intermingled with the practice of pronunciation and intonation in order to bring students to a deeper understanding of phonetic rules and a more harmonic rhythm in speaking. First, students practice, as a group and individually, exercises that focus on the pronunciation of Italian vowels and consonants. Short sayings and tongue twisters, such as the popular *tigre contro tigre* or *trentatrè trentini* and other challenging phrases, can be used to correct common errors in English speakers' pronunciation, particularly the ones related to the consonants *t*, *d*, and *tr* and the sound of the vowels *o* and *e*. Students are asked to repeat aloud the expressions that help in such an endeavor. The instructor stands on the opposite side of the auditorium on the left and asks one of the students to stand on the right side: the class has to project toward the instructor specific words, entire proverbs, or creative short sentences in a clear and loud voice. This practice is repeated until students reach the expected phonetic quality. This exercise enables students to stress a crucial element in play production: voice projection. Especially because most of the students are not "real" actors, projecting their voices requires a great deal of effort on their part. John Dolman's statement about elocution explains clearly: "Good elocution is not shouting, not over precise enunciation, not painful exaggerated syllabification, not excessive literalness, not brittle artificiality. Rather it is a subtle, unobtrusive heightening of the natural rhythms and inflection of conversation, in such a way that they [the actors] become clearer than in real life, and project easily to all parts of the theater."[19]

Students need to be as natural as possible but also aware of speaking and moving in a theatrical space. When they enter the stage or move on it, their presence must be felt, regardless of whether they have only one line to deliver or a two-page monologue; they must engage both the ears and the eyes of the spectators. In fact, while practicing this exercise, which we may call *pronuncia in azione* (pronunciation action), students do not stand still on the stage, but rather they move to coordinate their voice projection and movements. (Physical exercises before each rehearsal are a good tool for relaxing body and mind.) Since pronunciation and intonation are such relevant factors in this class, a considerable amount of time must be spent working on the lines individually in and outside the classroom. Students should be encouraged to practice when and where they can by re-creating in different settings the physical position of their characters, thus combining the practice of pronunciation with blocking. In fact, the physical movements and gestures are as important in the final performance as what students say and how they say it.

The student-actors know that some of the spectators attending the final performances will not be fluent in Italian. They are also aware that Italians in general possess a rich repertoire of gestures to express themselves (and some of them have specific meanings); therefore, their bodily actions play a large role in the performance. The commedia dell'arte represents a valuable example in the pantomimic tradition whose roots date back to ancient Greek theater; the students should keep in mind its elements of "simplification, exaggeration, and codified symbolism."[20] Just like the suggestions on wise approaches to elocution, the instructor should constantly stress those about bodily action. On the stage, student-actors must simplify and render clearly their emotions through equivalent movements; at the same time, they need to exaggerate their body language and voice projection during rehearsals in view of the fact that they will have to overcome fear, intimidation, and tension when they are onstage. Since stage fright is a concrete obstacle that can and will interfere with students' performances, the instructor must require of students that both the volume of their voices and intensity of their bodily movements be at least one degree above "normal." One technique for helping students develop confidence is encouraging them to scream and create exaggerated and strange movements during the practice of *pronuncia in azione*. They are merely students facing the challenge of performing before an audience in a foreign language, so any tool to help them feel more comfortable, powerful, and strong onstage is justified. If possible, it is very useful to invite competent experts to rehearsals. For the play *Veronica, meretrice e scrittora,* Claire Marchionne, an actress of the London Stage Theater, gave a skillful contribution by showing the cast the proper postures and gestures of the Renaissance period.

The memorization of lines and accompanying conceptualization of grammatical rules can reinforce students' linguistic accuracy, and the addition of gestures to accompany the lines helps the memorization process, as well as clarifies the meaning of the line. It is true, as Gian Giacomo Colli states, that the gesture is not a "categoria a sè" or a technique, but an expression that reinforces a word and expands its meaning.[21] In the Italian Drama Workshop, however, the instructor should help students choose appropriate gestures because they are working with a language and a cultural product, the play, that are different from their own.

From the start, the student-actors must become aware of the physical relation with their partners onstage as well as the audience. As Stanislavski teaches us, they must create and keep alive an indirect contact with the spectators during the performances but at the same time forget they exist in order to focus on their direct contact with their acting partners. And students have to remember such a concept while trying to project their voices in a comprehensible manner and with the correct intonation. Not an easy task, indeed. However, if at an early stage the instructor presents clearly the inevitable obstacles and problems that the "class community" will face and eventually surmount, students can begin thinking about solutions that will help them individually and collectively. Students will feel a certain degree of pride and gratification because they are performing on a stage and doing it in a foreign language. If, in addition, the play presented includes a partial use of dialect, then the play's production will raise the students' sense of achievement to an even higher level.


## Dealing with Dialects

In order to create an even more profoundly realistic dimension, it is helpful to work on plays that include dialectical expressions and to analyze the reasons why such a practice affects the structure of the plot, reevaluates the role of each character, and further explains the cultural environment in which the play unfolds. Students show a genuine interest in dialects, probably because those of Italian heritage are familiar with their grandparents speaking a language at times different from the standard Italian learned in college classrooms, and those who have visited Italy have noticed the rich variety of Italian spoken by native speakers. Dialects can also elicit discussions of contemporary issues. An example of this is the analysis of the changes that have occurred in language development within Italian society since the 1950s mainly because of the advent of television, which brought to the Italian people a new model of social and linguistic conformism.[22]

Maraini's *Veronica, meretrice e scrittora* and *La lunga vita di Marianna Ucrìa*, together with Eduardo De Filippo's *Filumena Marturano,* offer fine opportunities to stage a female character while investigating the usage of dialect from linguistic and sociocultural points of view. In *Veronica* the Venetian dialect is present in the sonnets written and recited by the nobleman and poet Maffio Venier, who through these sonnets declares his social and poetic positions in disagreement with the ones of his older brother Domenico and Veronica. Veronica's use of Venetian is limited to her interchanges with the only two people with whom she feels deeply connected: Domenico and Anzola. Domenico is one of the two men she has ever truly loved and the one with whom she has been sharing the same poetic ideas for years. The friendship with Anzola reflects Veronica's growth as a woman, and the dialectical exchanges between them reflect their bond, which overcomes social boundaries. Veronica's alternating dialect and standard Italian enables her to subvert the social order and "reappropriate a space of her own."[23] In *La lunga vita di Marianna Ucrìa,* almost entirely, only characters belonging to the lower class use the Sicilian dialect: Innocenza, the cook; Fila, the servant; Peppinedda, the poor daughter of a fisherman; and Calò, a tenant-farmer. For the mute Marianna, writing is the only way of communicating, and none of the dialect-speaking characters can write, so it is relevant that the strongest bond she creates is with Fila. Just like Veronica and Anzola, Marianna and Fila find a harmonic way to share their feelings, positively influence each other, and together embark on a new future. Thus, dialect becomes a linguistic and social symbol of connection. In staging Maraini's two plays, the students chose to leave the dialect unmodified and thereby explore its meaning, analyze its lexicon, and study its phonetics.

De Filippo's *Filumena Marturano* constitutes another great example, although in a different way, of how dialect can be used to enhance the personality of the characters. This powerful play presents a different set of challenges because the entire text is written in Neapolitan dialect; therefore, a translation into Italian is required. For *Filumena Marturano* students memorized the text in Italian but kept the original script as reference. Once students had studied the text during the initial stage of the course, they had the responsibility to contextualize the feelings of the characters and choose the lines in dialect that best translated the emotional elements and enriched them.

Of all of the characters in *Filumena Marturano,* only two always speak standard Italian—Diana, the young new lover of Domenico Soriano, and the attorney Nocella; for the others, dialect is used consistently, and the students portraying them incorporated a few of the original lines in dialect while performing their roles. One student in particular, whose linguistic skills were very advanced, rendered a superb interpretation of Rosalia Solimene, "la confidente di Filumena" as De Filippo defines her. She physically transformed herself into a seventy-five-year-old woman and never forgot her age for a second throughout the entire three acts; even when she was speaking standard Italian, she adopted a southern accent. Her dialogue in the first act with Alfredo, friend of Domenico Soriano, included a monologue that became one of the most relevant moments of comic relief of the play: "A me? E a me nun ce sta niente 'a spiunà . . . 'E fatte mieie so' chiare, titò" ("Me? I do not have anything to be spied . . . My affairs are very clear, my dear").[24] Every word was accompanied by a gesture and a facial expression so real and well planned that the audience was greatly entertained. In such an intense and dramatic play, moments of comic relief are always welcomed.

Rosalia's comic interpretation served us well in defining the drama and the passion of Filumena, almost as if these two women were moving in a chiaroscuro painting. Filumena is undoubtedly one of the most powerful and strongest female characters ever created. The interpreter of Filumena felt the same and gave a remarkable performance both as an actress and as a student of Italian, conveying Filumena's pathos, emotions, and pride in herself as a woman, a mother, and a wife. By means of the sociocultural analysis of the play and through the reading of sections from Maurizio Giammusso's biography of De Filippo, students understood the playwright's intentions to symbolize the three major carrying strengths of Italy in the 1940s through the professions of the three sons (blue-collar worker, merchant, writer) as well as De Filippo's desire to profess the necessity of all human beings' right to equality. In addition, the fact was stressed in class that the play depicts Italy during the hard years after World War II: a country ravaged, once again, by the horror of war, whose people were struggling to find a well-deserved peace and harmony in their lives. Filumena proudly fights to ensure a better life for her children, whom she chose to bring into this world, as well as to assert for them the principle of equality. Furthermore, she worked hard and struggled for twenty-five years, for her choices, and for her presence within the family she had created, to be recognized. She finally succeeds. In the first act, she replies to Domenico—who is questioning her about the fact that not once has he seen her sleep, eat, or cry—by saying that only when one knows the good and cannot have it can one cry, and since she has known only evil thus far, she has been deprived of the joy of crying. In the last scene of the play we see her crying because now, when all her sacrifices and efforts finally have come to fruition, she knows "il bene."

Much time was devoted to the performance of the last exchange between Filumena and Domenico. Once again, as with Maraini's plays, the interpretation of the ending was left to the collective decision of the class. In order to reach a more informative decision, students watched Vittorio De Sica's movie *Matrimonio all'italiana* (1965), with Sophia Loren and Marcello Mastroianni, and talked about the differences between the original play and the cinematographic version. Toward the end of the semester, students also viewed the moving performance of Eduardo and Regina Bianchi in a televised representation of *Filumena Marturano*. For the class, it was important to have the ending of the play convey the victorious and courageous struggle of Filumena through the correct intonation, looks, and postures of *both* the characters Filumena and Domenico. There is, in fact, a certain ambiguity in Eduardo's facial expression, as well as in Mastroianni's, after Filumena's last words, almost as if he were not a true "accomplice" participating in Filumena's happiness, but rather a "tool" she used to achieve her goals. The community of the Italian Drama Workshop wanted to portray onstage that Domenico and Filumena were clearly united and engaged in celebrating the redemption of Filumena's previous sufferings.

Besides the characters of Rosalia and Alfredo, the three sons—

Umberto, Riccardo, and Michele—contribute to creating a brilliant and funny scene while talking in the third act with their "new" father Domenico Soriano after he has agreed finally to marry Filumena. He is trying to find out which one of the three is his biological son, as Filumena chose to keep the name a secret because "'E figlie so' figlie . . . E so' tutte eguale" ("Sons are sons . . . And they are all the same").[25] Just as in Maraini's *Veronica, meretrice e scrittora* and *La lunga vita di Marianna Ucrìa,* in *Filumena Marturano* the use of dialect as a reflection of the creation of a bond among characters is quite clear. The interchanges among Domenico and the three sons, at first in formal standard Italian, progressively turn into dialect to depict the mutation of their inner feelings while they are progressively getting closer to one another. Their use of the language reflect their emotions, and the dialect becomes a way to unite them.

*Filumena Marturano*'s set was easy to prepare because the action takes place only in a few rooms of the Soriano residence; such a factor allowed the cast to focus primarily on the linguistic and sociocultural aspects of the play along with the acting. The students' final performances were extremely touching, and the best satisfaction came from seeing tears in the eyes of some of the native Italian language speakers during the final applause.

The collective decision of the students to incorporate the use of dialect in the performance of these three plays and the final interpretation of the plays did indeed make the Italian Drama Workshop class an Italian microcosm in which students immersed themselves completely. The many components—linguistic, sociocultural, literary, and artistic—of the Italian Drama Workshop class are woven together by a thread that can be broken only with difficulty; and this course constitutes a great opportunity for students to attain a harmonic unity of them all and to let them be creative and active participants in the process of learning the many facets of Italian language and culture, as well as become fluent speakers through performing art skills.

## Notes

1. Marini-Maio, "I *Sei personaggi* siamo noi," 459.
2. I refer here to two textbooks in particular: Pease and Bini, *Italiano in diretta,* in which each grammatical structure is preceded by short dia-

logues, and Olson, Edwards, and Foerster, *In Viaggio, Moving toward Fluency in Italian,* which focuses on and recycles seven major communicative functions and presents situations/dialogues for each of the six friends whose life events are monitored throughout the textbook.

3. My deepest gratitude goes to Robert Olson, who played such an important role in helping me create the structure of this class and skillfully assisted me in the "theatrical" component of the Italian Drama Workshop.

4. Stanislavski discusses the question of interaction between the actor's role, realities in the external plane, and the literary plane in *An Actor Prepares* and *Creating a Role.*

5. hooks, *Teaching to Transgress,* 153.

6. Rivers, "Interaction as the Key."

7. Bloom, *Thinking Like a Director,* 12.

8. See the Italian Drama Workshop's website at http://www.geocities .com/italian_drama_workshop/. I thank Eric Edwards for the website he created for this course, where both my students and I found our space to share relevant information about the play, author, and class. I also thank Eric Edwards, Guy Raffa, and Traci Andrighetti for their suggestions for this chapter as well as Nicoletta Marini-Maio and Colleen Ryan-Scheutz for their admirable strength, commitment, grace, and enthusiasm in making this book possible.

9. Often in this course guest speakers are invited to share with the students their knowledge in various fields. For *Filumena Marturano,* we were pleased to have Michael Bloom, a theater director and professor of drama who explained the basic acting rules in twentieth-century plays; Monica Russo, a lawyer from Naples who helped immensely during rehearsals with her assistance in the correct pronunciation of Neapolitan and above all with her enthusiasm in seeing a much-loved play performed by American students; and Shawna Lucey, an ex-student of Italian and wonderful actress and theater director who volunteered to be my assistant director; for *Veronica, meretrice e scrittora,* besides Claire Marchionne, Heather "Chiara" Butler, who had worked with me as a student and assisted me as a friend in previous plays; and for *La lunga vita di Marianna Ucrìa,* Robert Dawson, professor of French and eighteenth-century scholar.

10. For an extended presentation of staging *La lunga vita di Marianna Ucrìa,* see Del Fattore-Olson, "Dacia Maraini."

11. From a personal conversation with Dacia Maraini (my translation). My warmest gratitude to Dacia Maraini for her participation and constant support.

12. In the fall of 2003, Maraini attended some of the rehearsals of the play and answered many of the students' questions; however, the question about how to represent the ending of the play came up after Maraini left.

13. Casting is based on the students' request of the character they would like to interpret; often, I give my input on what I believe to be the most proper choice. In some cases, we hold auditions.
14. Maraini, *Fare teatro*, 236.
15. Pirandello, "Cecè," 144, 146, 159, 165.
16. Ibid.
17. See Littlewood, *Teaching Oral Communication*, 70–73, 81–89.
18. hooks, *Teaching to Transgress*, 11.
19. Dolman, *Art of Acting*, 107.
20. Ibid., 240.
21. Colli, "Il corpo che parla," 542. I find it useful to show the clip from Lina Wertmüller's movie *Mimì metallurgico ferito nell'onore* (1971), in which Giancarlo Giannini and Mariangela Melato carry on a three-minute silent conversation through gestures.
22. In connection with this linguistic reality, the instructor might explore the two different approaches of Tullio De Mauro and Pier Paolo Pasolini. De Mauro believes that television greatly affected the process of regression of dialects in Italy; however, he views positively the fact that, through television, cultural and linguistic unification has occurred and claims that such unification is the necessary, though not sole, basis for true democracy to occur. On the other hand, Pasolini considered television a controlling tool in the hands of political institutions. He believed that as a means of communication, it was even more dangerous than the means used by fascist rulers. In Pasolini's view, television in the sixties was erasing "healthy" cultural differences among social classes and fostering a homogeneous model of consumerism.
23. Carù, "Vocal marginality," 189.
24. De Filippo, *Filumena Marturano*, 28.
25. Ibid., 67.


## Bibliography

Adler, Sara Maria. "Veronica Franco's Petrarchan *Terze Rime:* Subverting the Master's Plan." *Italica* 65.3 (1988): 213–233.
Baricco, Alessandro. *Next.* Milan: Feltrinelli, 2002.
Bloom, Michael. *Thinking Like a Director: A Practical Handbook.* New York: Faber and Faber, 2001.
Carù, Paola. "Vocal Marginality, Dacia Maraini's Veronica Franco." In *The Pleasure of Writing: Critical Essays on Dacia Maraini,* edited by Rodica Dianescu-Blumenfeld and Ada Testaferri. West Lafayette, IL: Purdue University Press, 2000.
Colli, Gian Giacomo. "Il corpo che parla: la gestualità e l'italiano fra

tradizione teatrale e didattica della lingua." *Italica* 81.4 (2004): 536–550.

De Filippo, Eduardo. *Filumena Marturano.* Turin: Einaudi, 1951.

Del Fattore-Olson, Antonella. "Dacia Maraini e la problematica femminile nel laboratorio teatrale di Italiano." *Italica* 81.4 (2004): 521–535.

De Mauro, Tullio. "Televisione e unificazione linguistica." In *La letteratura e le idee,* edited by Fabio Cioffi et al. Edizioni Scolastiche Bruno Mondatori, 1989.

Dolman, John Jr. *The Art of Acting.* New York: Harper & Brothers, 1949.

Eibenstein-Alvisi, Irene. "The Dialogue Construction of Women in the Italian Renaissance." Ph.D. diss. Cornell University, 2003.

Giammusso, Maurizio. *Vita di Eduardo.* Milan: Arnoldo Mondatori Editore, 1993.

hooks, bell. *Teaching to Transgress: Education as the Practice of Freedom.* New York: Routledge, 1994.

Littlewood, William. *Teaching Oral Communication: A Methodological Framework.* Oxford: Blackwell, 1992.

Maraini, Dacia. *Stravaganza.* Rome: Serarcangeli Editore, 1987.

———. *Dizionaretto quotidiano. Da "amare" a "zonzo": 229 voci raccolte da Gioconda Marinelli.* Milan: Bompiani, 1997.

———. *Fare teatro 1966–2000.* Vol. 1. Milan: Rizzoli, 2000.

———. "Fede o Della perversione matrimoniale." *Fare teatro 1966–2000.* Vol. 1. Milan: Rizzoli, 2000.

———. "La lunga vita di Marianna Ucrìa." *Fare teatro 1966–2000.* Vol. 2. Milan: Rizzoli, 2000.

———. "Veronica, meretrice e scrittora." *Fare teatro 1966–2000.* Vol. 2. Milan: Rizzoli, 2000.

Marini-Maio, Nicoletta. "I *Sei personaggi* siamo noi: Pirandello, o la metamorfosi degli studenti nel laboratorio teatrale in italiano." *Italica* 81.4 (2004); 459–482.

Pasolini, Pier Paolo. *Scritti corsari.* Milan: Garzanti, 1975.

Pease, Antonella, and Daniela Bini. *Italiano in diretta.* 2nd ed. New York: McGraw-Hill, 1993.

Pirandello, Luigi. "Cecè." *La signora Morli, una e due.* Milan: Arnoldo Mondatori Editore, 1951.

Olson, Antonella, Eric Edwards, and Sharon Foerster. *In Viaggio: Moving toward Fluency in Italian.* New York: McGraw-Hill, 2003.

Rivers, Wilga M. "Interaction as the Key to Teaching Language for Communication." In *Interactive Language Teaching,* edited by Wilga M. Rivers. Cambridge: Cambridge University Press, 1987.

Rosenthal, Margaret. *The Honest Courtesan: Veronica Franco, Citizen and Writer in Sixteenth-Century Venice.* Chicago: University of Chicago Press, 1992.

Stanislavski, Konstantin. *An Actor Prepares*. Translated by Elizabeth Reynolds Hapgood. New York: Theatre Arts Books, 1936.
———. *Creating a Role*. Translated by Elizabeth Reynolds Hapgood. New York: Theatre Arts Books, 1961.

## Appendix

### *Plays Directed at the University of Texas at Austin, Department of French and Italian*

*La locandiera*, Carlo Goldoni, Spring 1990
*Ciascuno a suo modo*, Luigi Pirandello, Fall 1991
*Cecè*, Luigi Pirandello; *La verità, Il ballo*, Italo Svevo, Fall 1993
*Questi fantasmi*, Eduardo De Filippo, Fall 1995
*Morte accidentale di un anarchico*, Dario Fo, Fall 1997
*Veronica, meretrice e scrittora*, Dacia Maraini, Fall 1999
*Filumena Marturano*, Eduardo De Filippo, Fall 2001
*La lunga vita di Marianna Ucrìa*, Dacia Maraini, Fall 2003
*Il matto e la morte, La resurrezione di Lazzaro, Una donna sola, L'uomo nudo e l'uomo in frak*, Dario Fo e Franca Rame, Fall 2005
*Notarbartolo, un uomo giusto*, Dacia Maraini, Fall 2007

### *Plays in the Rome Study Program, Rome, Italy, Department of French and Italian*

*Ce n'est qu'un début*, Umberto Marino; *Erzbeth Báthory*, Dacia Maraini, Summer 1996
*Fede*, Dacia Maraini, Summer 1997
*Una casa tra due palme*, Dacia Maraini, Summer 1998
*La nascita del giullare*, Dario Fo; *Bianca Garofani*, Dacia Maraini; *Io, Ulrike, grido*, Franca Rame, Summer 1999
*Da Roma a Milano*, Dacia Maraini; *Il matto e la morte*, Dario Fo, Summer 2000
*Un treno, una notte*, Dacia Maraini, Summer 2001
*La mandragola*, Niccolò Machiavelli, Summer 2002
*Ti ho sposato per allegria*, Natalia Ginzburg, Summer 2003
*Sherlock Barman, il folletto delle brutte figure*, Stefano Benni, Summer 2004
*Astaroth*, Stefano Benni, Summer 2005

# Proficiency and Performance: Assessing Learner Progress in the Italian Theater Workshop

COLLEEN RYAN-SCHEUTZ

The reasons why an instructor might direct a theater production, offer a theater workshop course, or include dramatic texts and techniques in a foreign language curriculum may be many, ranging from a personal passion for theater to a desire for pedagogical variety (creative ways to make students exercise various skills in the target language) to a more formal effort to connect the study of foreign language with other academic disciplines.[1] Likewise, the scope and objectives of combining foreign language and theater vary greatly, depending on the nature and level of the course. While the focus for some may be linguistic accuracy and proficiency, for others it may be pronunciation and fluency, or even cultural content and in-depth literary analysis.

At the same time, the use of theatrical texts and classroom techniques based on educational drama may not be appropriate or appealing to all. To play the devil's advocate for a moment, an unconvinced colleague might ask: "Why theater? It's so much work and the book already offers a variety of other texts and activities—more than we can cover in a year. Why focus on performance? We're in class after all; students don't have to put on a show to learn language and literature." Or, "Who will come to see the performance? Teachers and students are always so busy and I don't want to burden or oblige others." Or, in the case of a non–production-oriented class, "Why insist on dramatic activities in class? I'm not a clown and my students aren't actors or entertainers."

From an alternate perspective, however, the exchanges among curious or convinced colleagues might resemble this: Why theater? It brings language and emotions to life. Why performance? It addresses different learning styles and inspires multiple intelligences such as the audio, the visual, the artistic, and the kinesthetic.[2] Who will see it? Most Italian students and faculty, Italian members of your academic and broader community, friends and family who may not understand Italian but remain mesmerized by students' individual and collective second language talents and artistic and interpretive abilities. Why dramatic activities and techniques? The role-playing mode often (quite magically) helps lower affective boundaries that stifle students' ability to flourish in oral production. It even helps students discover a budding passion for language and culture. It offers variety to any classroom setting and becomes wholly student-centered and creative, even when students are reading or memorizing prewritten texts.[3]

Whether one comes to theatrical texts and techniques with an inherent passion for the genre or with an experimental spirit, it quickly becomes clear that we can teach and students can learn a great deal about language, literature, and culture this way. Yet language professionals have yet to explore in any depth what the most appropriate and effective means of assessment for such activities, units, or courses might be. Indeed, the debate begins with a general question of necessity. As one colleague asked during a presentation I once made on the subject: "Do you really need to conduct assessments? Isn't the fact that your troupe rehearsed and prepared for weeks all in Italian and successfully produced three sold-out performances a sufficient measure of value and efficacy? In my view," she continued, "the course does not require justification; it's clear that students only stand to benefit from this experience."

I wholeheartedly agree with this colleague's statement; but because the Italian Theater Workshop described below is an upper-division course in a rigorous university-level program and the final play production was not an extracurricular activity but a final exercise and exam, it was therefore necessary to identify effective ways of assessing learner progress beyond the overall success and efficacy of the final show. The solution we chose was a hybrid format that included discrete-point testing of vocabulary and grammar as well as spoken and written proficiency exercises that included cultural and literary topics. Affective improvements were measured by means of a qualitative survey, and both individual and collective progress was considered for the final grade. The multifaceted assessment program served well not only to foster the many objectives of the workshop but also to help students perceive the gains they made in several areas.

While it seems obvious that assessments need to reflect the pedagogical goals and learning objectives of a given course or activity, in the Italian Theater Workshop the possible goals and objectives are many. For this reason, it is first necessary to pinpoint and prioritize clear objectives for the individual learner, which may include any or all of the following: language proficiency (productive and receptive skills), literary and cultural analysis, communicative competence (strategies, pronunciation, nonverbal expression), linguistic competence (discrete knowledge of grammatical structures and vocabulary), and self-confidence or visible comfort/ease in the second language.[4] Next, it is necessary to distinguish measures of individual progress from the collective progress or end result, in our case, a performance of the entire class or theater troupe. For the latter, it is helpful not only to generate group statistics on the individual presentations, writing assignments, and exams, but also to build into the course both small- and large-group assessments along the way.

In this chapter, I offer my perspective as a post-secondary foreign language curriculum designer and professor of Italian language, literature, and culture. After outlining some common elements and current debates in foreign language teaching and the assessment of student learning, I will suggest ways to employ such assessments in the context of the Italian Theater Workshop, where multiple linguistic, literary, and affective goals interconnect and overlap, making progress hard to quantify and sometimes (until the end, upon seeing the final product) hard to perceive. To this end, I will use as a primary example the upper-division Italian Theater Workshop course offered each spring at the University of Notre Dame. This fifteen-week course includes assessment procedures for different language skill areas, literary and cultural analysis, and student perceptions about their own language learning. Here, I illustrate how the different learning goals and assessment tools connect with those in other language and literature courses and, thus, contribute to a holistic concept of the foreign language curriculum that emphasizes not only educational drama, but also the integration of language and culture, pedagogical variety, creative and analytical thinking, group dynamics and collaborative work, and even diction and public speaking.

## How to Plan and Prioritize Assessments: Accuracy, Proficiency, Communicative Competence, and Cultural Knowledge

Over the decades, the means and measures of assessment in the foreign language classroom have varied greatly. A review of the well-known multi-edition textbooks geared to the North American market and their accompanying testing materials shows that we are far from the days of giving classroom tests based (solely) on translation, rote repetition, and/or relatively decontextualized discrete-point grammar items. Instead, in contemporary pedagogical materials, we note a widespread commitment to examining competence in a variety of skill areas: vocabulary, listening, reading, grammar, and writing. Most books also incorporate short cultural segments on exams, and some even include (optional) speaking components to be conducted in a lab or with a teacher.

Since the 1980s, researchers and practitioners in second language acquisition and foreign language education have been creating learning materials that call for more interactive, communicative, and student-centered approaches to teaching. Indeed, in the past two decades we have seen a general pedagogical shift away from "traditional" grammar-focused modes of teaching and testing language, mechanically oriented practice, and teacher-centered classroom methodologies toward greater emphasis on communicative competence, strategies for proficiency across different skill areas, and the successful completion of different global functions, which, as Frank Nuessel reminds us, "encompasses the 'receptive skills' (listening and reading), and the 'productive skills' (speaking and writing), as well as 'cultural understanding.'" While the accuracy and proficiency camps are not mutually exclusive, and while grammatical form and accuracy are by no means unimportant for communication-based or proficiency-oriented programs, the focus of classroom goals, writes Alice Omaggio Hadley, "are increasingly articulated in communicative and functional terms . . . encouraging learners to use language in context for real-world purposes." Thus, when we speak about foreign language assessment, we should aim for similarly integrated exams and projects that gauge both what the learner knows about the language *and* what the learner is able to do with this knowledge.[5] As a result, language testing research has recently turned its attention to the development of various approaches to second language performance assessment.[6]

Nevertheless, well into the 1990s, a significant gap in the methods of foreign language teaching and testing remained. As Sally Magnan reports, despite the widespread advocacy of communicative language teaching, classroom teaching was still "largely focused on discrete points of grammar and mastery of isolated components of knowledge and skill." Drawing on Susan Bacon and Michael Finneman's research, she first attributes the lack of discourse-driven or functional language testing to the fact that students and teachers often find discrete-point testing more familiar and straightforward.[7] Second, Magnan maintains that it could be difficult to design and grade other types of tests, and that the profession has not yet developed a widely accepted, practical model of communicative testing. Though many instructors and learners may still prefer traditional modes of testing for the reasons listed above, some fifteen years later we certainly have a much clearer idea of what communicative teaching and testing should entail. Researchers and practitioners have worked hard at the level of textbook production and curriculum development to capture the essence of communicative teaching, and they are beginning to mirror this essence in their assessments.[8]

Indeed, today's foreign language exams often demonstrate a rich set of important criteria such as real-world contextualization of both individual sentences and entire exercises; the input of authentic materials (written for native Italian speakers) from a variety of written and spoken sources; visual stimuli from which learners derive context and information for tasks or activities; and a variety of functions or tasks that require a focus on the meaning and interaction among learners, between learners and teachers, or between learners and texts.[9] These interactive assessments elicit authentic second language use in a spontaneous and relatively unpredictable fashion, as often occurs in the real world.

In her discussion on testing, Magnan also draws an important distinction between assessing the product of learning versus the process of learning. Most language tests, even the more communicative ones, predominantly aim to measure the products or stages in learning. But the processes of acquisition, she asserts, which include learning strategies and styles, communicative strategies, and techniques for conversation and discourse management, offer significant insight into the individual learner's progress and achievements. "Clearly all these processes are highly individual, and thereby seem to defy objective assessment," she writes. "Yet for our testing to reflect what goes on in our [communicative-interactive] class-rooms, we must seek out ways to reward students for their attempts to process language as they direct their own learning." In shifting our conception of assessment to a "dynamic and individual notion of using language for communicative purposes," Magnan echoes Elana Shohamy's call for a broader definition of what constitutes assessment, "to include, in addition to tests, self-evaluation, peer-assessment, and collections of student work in portfolios, diaries, and observations."[10]

Authentic (communicative, performance-based) assessments are generally those that focus on processes and for which there is no one right answer.[11] "Traditional tests," according to Judith Liskin-Gasparro, "are one-time measures that rely on a single correct response to each item; they offer no opportunity for demonstration of thought processes, revision, or interaction with the teacher." She identifies the main tension between authentic assessment and standardized testing to be "the competing demands of test validity and test reliability." According to Liskin-Gasparro, validity is "the faithfulness of a test to the constructs it purports to measure, [and] pulls the test developer in the direction of multifaceted, complex assessments that resemble the problems and situations of the real world. Reliability, which refers to the consistency and precision of test scores, pulls the test developer in the opposite direction, toward assessments that can be evaluated without ambiguity or fear of shifting standards. Well-constructed multiple-choice items that test facts in the absence of their 'messy' contexts result in highly reliable scores but, unfortunately, often at the cost of their resemblance to real-life tasks and problems, i.e., their validity."[12] However, since performance assessments will vary greatly according to the language, level, or types of communication samples elicited, so will the validity and reliability of assessments.

James Brown et al. view the purposes of performance assessment in language programs according to three main sets of goals, which seem reasonable and applicable to almost any language-learning situation. The first purpose of performance assessment is to establish whether or not learners can accomplish specific target tasks that are directly related to course objectives. The second purpose of performance assessment is to evaluate various qualities of learners' language ability, such as accuracy, complexity, fluency, or overall communicative competence. The third purpose is to evaluate the achievements actually occurring within the classrooms and programs from day to day. Overall, the primary objective of language instruction, as these researchers see it, involves both process and product, aiming "to bring about a lasting change in learners' abilities to spontaneously use language." They add, "Fundamental to second language performance assessment is the direct observation and evaluation of learners using the second language to engage in extended acts of communication."[13]

Although we have undoubtedly witnessed a widespread increase in communicative methodologies and the amount of attention given to performance and proficiency, achievement continues to dominate the tone and content of foreign language tests. The truth is that many communication-based practitioners still lack clarity and solid examples of what effective "communicative testing" or performance assessments might be. Micheline Chalhoub-Deville attributes this gap to an underlying difference in the second language construct. Her departure point is Lyle Bachman's cognitive-interactional model. This model views communicative competence ability as an individual-focused cognitive process wherein context is important but not necessarily interconnected with the learner's knowledge and use of language. Instead, Chalhoub-Deville's social-interactional model suggests that the context is essential and the language user/individual ability/context triad is "inextricably meshed." Here, context is critical for communicative competence and thus for test development and test score validation.[14]

If we agree that context is crucial to the interactive notion of communicative competence in a foreign language and if the establishment of context or contexts becomes part of our daily practices, then tests and tasks that examine communicative abilities in a range of designated contexts should prove not only valid and reliable, but also acceptable to the language learner. According to J. B. Carroll, there are four general criteria for good testing: economy, relevance, acceptability, and comparability. James Lee and Bill Van Patten summarize these basic tenets as follows: an *economic* test maximizes the amount of observable information about learners' language in a short amount of time; a *relevant* test refers to "a good match between course goals and the tests we present"; an *acceptable* test implies learners' satisfaction with the test because it inspires confidence in the fact that it is evaluating their progress accurately; and finally, a *comparable* test is one from which we would obtain similar scores across different groups of learners and at different times. But more important, according to Lee and Van Patten, is the fact that "good" tests can have a positive washback effect, meaning that they motivate learners to pay attention and practice and, therefore, have a significant effect on their progress. In sum, "testing cannot be viewed as 'an isolated event'; it must be an integral part of the teaching and learning enterprise."[15] The communicative test or assessment program is thus necessarily hybrid, combining specific features of language—lexical, grammatical, sociolinguistic, and discourse features—and gauging students' progress "as they operate in naturalistic discourse contexts" throughout the different sections of the test. Whether oral or written exams, "it makes sense just in terms of face validity," says Omaggio Hadley, "to give tests that embed the second-language features to be tested in situational formats."[16]

The Italian Theater Workshop (ITW) is an upper-division university-level course that culminates in several public performances of a foreign language play. In this course, the approach to learning goals and assessments is holistic and varied, in that it integrates the study of grammar, vocabulary, and idioms with literary and historical analysis for the purposes of proficiency development and cultural understanding. As its primary framework for assessments, the ITW includes a variety of contextualized activities and assignments that gauge accuracy in forms, proficiency in the four main skills, communicative competence, and cultural knowledge. Typically, assignments and tests combine discrete-point items emphasizing knowledge and achievement with tasks and mini-projects that emphasize the process of learning. Furthermore, the ITW's broad theatrical context and numerous subcontexts (body and actions, clothing and costumes, history and politics, gestures and nonverbal language, gender relations, and cultural norms) enhance not only the validity and economics of situational testing formats but also the acceptability factor for both teachers and students. As a result, the ITW is a rewarding opportunity for collaborative and interdisciplinary learning as well as a far-reaching, highly motivating, and most effective connector between the study of language, literature, and culture in the foreign language curriculum.[17]

## The Italian Theater Workshop: Proficiency and Performance-Based Evaluation Criteria

Each year the Department of Romance Languages and Literatures at the University of Notre Dame offers theater workshop courses in French, Spanish, and Italian. Each course has its own characteristics, format, objectives and, therefore, its own assessment procedures. Whereas the French course is a yearly tribute to Molière, the Spanish one draws upon less canonical works and faces the challenge of balancing native and nonnative Spanish-speaking participants. Some unique features of the ITW course are its immersion-style language pledge, its diversified roles (all aspects of theatrical production beyond acting) for student participants, and its hybrid assessment design, aiming to quantify and qualify student gains in competence, performance, and personal confidence.

The ITW amounts to far more than rehearsing and putting on a play. It involves first and foremost a commitment to language learning, where students come to class, enter a room with Italian music or theatrical games, and agree that they will not utter a word in English (or language other than Italian). The ITW also entails a commitment to literature, since all assignments and activities center on intense work with an Italian author and one or more literary texts under the umbrella context of the theater. Clearly, then, the ITW also requires a commitment to the study of Italian culture, since every aspect of the texts, including their historical setting, character relations, linguistic idioms, and potential for nonverbal language, stimulate a rich variety of cultural discussions. Finally, the ITW calls for a broader concept of language study, one that crosses disciplinary boundaries, thrives on collaboration and communication, and creates a small-scale foreign language community.

Whether one is designing the course or altering and refining it from year to year, it is essential to begin by having a clear idea of its primary and secondary learning goals and where exactly it fits in the language program and curriculum. For example, it is necessary to decide whether the ITW is primarily an Italian language course, focusing on aspects of grammar and syntax, diction and pronunciation, proficiency and fluency in Italian. Or whether it is primarily a literature course that maximizes the potential depth and breadth of textual analysis through the production of a play. Or whether it is mainly an innovative, interdisciplinary course, combining language study with the arts as well as personal talents and creativity (acting, directing, and design). Accordingly, then, the instructor must evaluate the most effective—economic, acceptable, reliable, and comparable—tools for assessing learner progress: discrete-point tests based on factual knowledge; short and long narratives about concepts, history, and literary analysis; performances that evaluate communicative competence as well as literary-interpretative capabilities; or surveys that gauge changes in attitude and affect during the theater production experience. The ITW course at Notre Dame has a hybrid design that focuses on all four aspects of learning and assessment.

## The 2004 Workshop Design

In the spring of 2004, faculty director Laura Colangelo and I chose Dario Fo's *Non tutti i ladri vengono per nuocere* for the course's central text.[18] In preparation, we studied the play for its various actor and nonactor roles; its historical, political, and literary characteristics; and its technical demands in terms of staging and settings. We then advertised the course in all Italian classes midway through the fall term, making it open to all students who would have completed at least two semesters of Italian language study. We held auditions during weeks 13 and 14 of the sixteen-week fall semester so that students could enroll in a timely fashion and begin the course on the first day of the next semester.

Over the years, the ITW has grown in popularity. As a result, it has become increasingly difficult to select only the small number of students necessary for a play, including those who sign on in the role of stage managers, set and costume designers, sound and lighting technicians, and publicity directors. In the case of *Non tutti i ladri*, the show required six actors, two stage managers, two designers, and one publicity agent. Whereas the year before we had sought to accommodate the large number of talented and enthusiastic auditionees by producing two different one-act plays in the same year, the work and time commitment quickly doubled. So we decided to handle 2004's large turnout with an experiment in "double casting": two sets of actors, managers, and designer-technicians, with the publicity agent common to both.

## *Roles and Group Dynamics*

In every walk of life, roles are of great importance for individual development and for the productivity and satisfaction of a group, whether in a family, a set of friends, or a cluster of work colleagues. Zoltán Dörneyi and Tim Murphey maintain that in an academic setting students will become useful members of the team if they are cast in good or appropriate roles. That is, they will perform necessary and complementary functions and, at the same time, be more satisfied with their self-image and contribution to the whole. Roles, claim Dörneyi and Murphey, can be divided into two main types: "naturally emerging" or informal roles, such as a class clown, and "assigned roles" or formal roles, such as the group secretary for a classroom activity.[19] Interestingly, the ITW builds on both types of roles and group dynamics that emerge from group collaborations. The students instinctively bring their bold or shy, witty or serious personality types to the class and assume more or less prominent positions based on these natural character traits that they integrate with the formal class roles—awarded or assigned—as actor, stage manager, designer, agent, or technician. In turn, these roles comprise numerous subroles and related responsibilities that call upon the students' different talents, character traits, and artistic or managerial skills.

What seems most wonderful and efficacious about the ITW is the way it mixes informal and formal roles. Whether in daily improvised warm-up games based on situations, role-plays, or pure corporeal expression, or in spontaneous participation in class discussions, problem-solving, and debates, students instinctively join their informal and assigned roles to create constructive (and oftentimes hilarious) interactions all in the target language. If such roles can be considered the basic building blocks for successful in-class performance, no matter what the task at hand, then they should shed light on the process of language learning and prepare the student for proficiency and in-language performance outside of class. The teacher can encourage students to explore and assume different roles, whether adopting the ones that suit them best or breaking out of their mold or comfort zones to try something different, through the complementary and constructive nature of in-class activities.[20]

## The Participants

Of the eighteen 2004 workshop participants, six were advanced language students (in their third or fourth year of study with a major or minor concentration in the field), and the other twelve had completed two to three semesters of language study in the basic language sequence (whether intensive or regular track) before joining this course. Twelve students were simultaneously enrolled in other Italian classes—six in intermediate-level language classes and six in more advanced Italian literature classes. Four participants had studied abroad for one semester, and all participants, except for two graduating seniors, stated that they would be continuing with Italian in the successive semester, whether on campus or during study abroad.

## The Play

Fo's *Non tutti i ladri vengono per nuocere* satisfied several criteria that the faculty directors have found to be conducive to creating an immersion experience with students at notably different levels of language proficiency and most with little to no theater experience. First, the one-act length makes the play "manageable" in terms of rehearsal times and amount of material to work with (interpret, analyze, practice, memorize, and perfect) and feasible for many students working closely with authentic, unabridged literary pieces for the first time. Second, this play is "modern" in that it is rich with common vocabulary, idiomatic expressions, and language usage. Third, it is a comedy. Comedic plays have the benefit of being more physical and, hence, more visually immediate and conceptually understandable for novice Italian speakers in the audience.[21] Furthermore, comedic plays lend themselves to literary and cultural analyses since, as per the comedic tradition, they also examine and critique societal norms with a focus on class and gender differences.

In brief, the play tells the story of a husband who has brought home another woman to have an extramarital affair, when the wife of a common thief, who had just entered his home, calls to check on her husband for a second time. After the call, the adulterous couple start to panic when suddenly the grandfather clock, in which the thief had been hiding, strikes twelve and the thief is forced to exit with *bozzi* or bumps on his head. As the couple and the thief attempt to sort things out, the homeowner's wife returns home and further cover-ups and misunderstandings ensue. Then, the wife of the thief arrives to save him. Finally, while the five characters seek to cover up or sort things out further, all so that the thief won't go to the police, the wife's lover arrives and sets her in a spin. In the end, the thief is asked to keep everyone's secrets. He agrees, but then quickly escapes with his wife and some goods as the others talk feverishly. The final scene shows a "real" thief entering to find the house "prepared for robbery" while the spouses and lovers attempt to catch the "virtuous" thief. When they reenter the home, the "real" thief feels tricked and threatens to turn himself in. Horrified, the spouses and lovers start explaining all of the evening's mishaps and misunderstandings all over again.

## Class Meetings: Rehearsals

For the first eight weeks of the semester, actors rehearsed and designers met three times a week for sixty to ninety minutes. During the last three weeks of production, the troupe rehearsed five or six times per week, two to three hours at a time, and both actors and designers attended all rehearsals. The time spent together was considered full-immersion workshop time and generally unfolded in the following three-part fashion: warm-up exercises with physical, vocal, and linguistic objectives carefully selected to accomplish specific acting or communicative goals; script-reading for content and analytic discussions; and script-reading for linguistic precision and body movements combined.[22]

## Performances

The 2004 ITW culminated in four public performances, two with each cast and crew. Each group had a matinee and evening performance. Running time was approximately one hour. Students and instructors from all different levels of Italian at Notre Dame attended the show, as did students and faculty from neighboring colleges. Many of the audience members, particularly friends of the cast and crew, had no knowledge of Italian, but the combination of physical humor and a detailed English language synopsis provided in the program made the show comprehensible for those with beginning-level knowledge or no Italian at all.

## *Postproduction Work*

After the final performance, cast and crew stayed on to strike the set and store props and materials. The week after the shows (week 13 of the semester) the ITW members met to discuss the experience, reflect upon their achievements, and take the postproduction test. At this time they also made individual appointments for exit oral proficiency interviews and further arrangements were made (immersion-style still, meaning all in Italian) for returning costumes and set materials, making and distributing video copies of the performances, planning cast parties, and organizing photos for a website.

## Assessing Learner Progress: A Hybrid Model with Comprehensive Curricular Objectives

Given the multifaceted and multipurpose nature of the ITW, it is challenging to find the most appropriate ways to quantify students' progress both as individual learners and as group or language community members with specific roles and responsibilities. Is it generally more appropriate and objective to grade students collectively on the basis of the small- and large-group efforts necessary for the quality and success of a show? Or is it more appropriate and objective to evaluate students on the basis of their individual progress with respect to their own language background and skill levels at the start of the course? Our decision was to do both.

The formal assessment procedures for the ITW include written pretests and posttests, in weeks 1 and 15, respectively. These tests examine (1) knowledge of key vocabulary and expressions from the theatrical text, (2) knowledge of general theater vocabulary and expressions, (3) reading comprehension, and (4) discrete-point grammar questions. The same test was administered both times, though the vocabulary words were presented in a different order on each test to avoid any sequential memory effect. It is important to note that the students did not receive feedback on the pretest so they did not know what they had answered correctly or incorrectly the first time. We simply gave the same exam on the first and last days of the workshop to gauge learner achievement and/or incidental learning in the course of the fifteen-week theater workshop. In addition, we conducted unofficial (single-rated) oral proficiency interviews during weeks 1 and 15 of the semester, while writing was assessed through two formal writing assignments and informal, daily diary entries written in Italian. Finally, we surveyed students' perceptions of their own levels of competence in different skill areas, as well as their cultural knowledge and level of "ease" or "comfort" in the target language.

## Vocabulary and Grammar

The workshop did not include explicit instruction of vocabulary or grammar. The exposure to and practice of certain words and select grammar structures (imperatives, imperfect and pluperfect subjunctives, relative pronouns, object pronouns) came about through the naturalistic discourse necessary to conduct each class (planning, implementation, evaluation, etc.), each rehearsal (preparation, practice, stage notes, and discussion), and all of the other responsibilities (measuring, choosing, sketching, brainstorming, shopping, and budgeting) that took place in between. Workshop participants received the text for *Non tutti i ladri* on the first day of the semester. After an initial read-through with the cast and crew for general comprehension of plot structure and meaning, students received two vocabulary lists to aid their deeper understanding of the text and their ability to function in Italian throughout all class and rehearsal procedures. One list was a significant gloss for the text and the other featured general theater vocabulary and expressions for stage directions. In the absence of explicit instruction, these handouts were a reference and tool for independent study, and our aim was to gauge incidental acquisition of the phrases and terms. Therefore, there was no specific treatment pertaining to vocabulary and grammar, though numerous words and structures were used frequently in the course of class meetings and rehearsals. From pretest to posttest, all students made a minimum gain of ten out of thirty points in vocabulary questions and five out of twenty points in the chosen grammatical structures.

## Second Language Reading

After an initial read-through of the primary text by the whole cast and crew during week 1 for general orientation and comprehension of the text, students read select scenes in depth for homework between meetings and had to reflect upon them in their theater diaries. In class students read the scenes aloud and began to work on blocking and gestures and pronunciation and intonation to get a deeper understanding of the verbal exchanges and the characters' interactions with objects and spaces on the set. Additional reading assignments involved handouts containing announcements, schedules, vocabulary lists, and formal assignments and handouts from peers' biographical, historical, and design presentations to the class. Students also conducted some research-based reading in Italian to complete their literary analyses, character analyses, and presentations. Although pretest and posttest comparisons of second language reading ability (based on similar theatrical texts by Dario Fo) showed an average gain of only two out of ten possible points, the directors noted important gains in certain reading strategies, such as reliance on cognates, and in students' confidence and willingness to make educated guesses about meaning on the basis of context.

## Second Language Writing

Participants were required to keep a daily diary in which they recorded their observations, questions, impressions, emotions, and suggestions after each encounter with the Fo text, whether as homework, during rehearsals, or during meetings. Entries ranged from one paragraph to two pages, depending on the level and personal involvement of the student. Students were encouraged to avoid using dictionaries and grammar books as much as possible. The only fixed requirement was that they add to the journal each day. The journals gave students the chance to explore their ideas on a variety of aspects of production preparation. Actors, for example, explored ways to add depth to their performances by analyzing their characters' reactions to other characters in a given scene. Designers considered choices of colors and styles for costumes and set pieces and how these elements could enhance the comedy of the show. Journals were collected every two weeks and instructors provided feedback on language and content. Generally speaking, students gained confidence and fluency in the course of this fourteen-week writing process. Though in many cases grammatical errors still persisted over the course of the semester, journal entries became voluntarily longer and incorporated new words and idioms, many of which came from the theatrical text.

The second main writing component for the ITW was a more

formal literary analysis in the form of a three-page paper that one might write for an upper-division class. Students had to write about the author, the historical period in which he wrote, and the comic style of the piece. Students were also encouraged to use their personal experiences as an actor, stage manager, or designer in the show in order to analyze the overall message that Fo set out to convey.

The third writing requirement differed slightly among participants. Actors were asked to write detailed character analyses for their parts, including supported interpretations of their relationships with other characters or the setting. These analyses were presented to classmates during a rehearsal, and the final drafts were mounted and displayed around the theater for the performances. The actor writes the analysis in the first person, from the standpoint of the character. The character describes his or her personality, job, relationship with other characters, favorite color, movie, book, hobby, style of clothing, season, time of day, and anything else that the actor chooses to invent. Character analyses also include a detailed description of how certain characters met each other, and how they feel about each other. Actors wrote their analyses about halfway through the production period, and they proved to be a true demonstration of how well the students had come to understand the comic genre, the style of Fo, and the sociocultural reasons why certain things were "funny" within the play.

Stage managers, on the other hand, researched the author's biography, the historical period of the play, and the period in which he wrote.[23] Their reports were distributed to cast and crew before the due date of the literary analyses, giving them a point of reference from which to analyze the piece. The designers had their own unique project: to describe and present their ideas and plans for the set and costumes. They made large poster-board presentations to convey their choices of colors, styles, sounds, songs, and images. They then had to explain these choices and lead a question-and-answer session and general discussion about their presentation. These posters were displayed during the performances as well.[24]

All writing assignments were graded with a similar rubric breaking down points for content (concepts, clarity, organization, originality) and form (accuracy, variation of vocabulary and grammatical structures, and length).

## Speaking and Listening

The skills of speaking and listening were often practiced simultaneously in two different communicative formats: (1) informal interactive exchanges during daily warm-up phases, rehearsing the play, discussing the contents and meaning of the text, or understanding the many additional tasks and responsibilities crucial to the success of the workshop, such as scheduling, measuring for costumes, purchasing props, or preparing the performance program; and (2) formal presentations, whether by faculty directors or by classmates presenting their analyses, design projects, and stage notes.

Pronunciation and diction were the focus of individual and small-group meetings with the faculty directors throughout the second half of the workshop experience. Once actors memorized their lines (ideally, by week 8) they came for intensive hour-long meetings where, one-on-one or in small groups according to scenes, they rehearsed for accent, stresses, and general rules of pronunciation (single versus double consonants, open versus closed vowels, the rolled versus the flipped *r*, etc.), as well as Italian cadence as nuanced through different variations in pitch, volume, and intonation. Speaking and listening were tested through unofficial oral proficiency interviews.

## Oral Proficiency and Communicative Competence

As per the official guidelines for oral proficiency interview (OPI) of the American Council on the Teaching of Foreign Languages, students had individual appointments with an OPI-trained faculty member during which they spoke on a variety of topics (not simply theater or academically oriented items), shifted their context and register through role-play, and demonstrated their ability to carry out global functions such as inviting, debating, convincing, and requesting. Though the interviews were only single-rated and, thus, unofficial, they served an important purpose locally: they showed that during the fifteen-week ITW experience, it was possible for students to improve their oral proficiency by a sublevel (see Table 2). A comparison with pretest scores revealed that nine students maintained their level while the other nine improved by one sublevel.

It is clear that approximately seventy-five hours of second language workshop experience spread out over fifteen weeks, and intensifying greatly at the end, cannot magically enhance oral proficiency for

**Table 2. Unofficial oral proficiency scores in weeks 1 and 15 of the semester**

| Role | Week 1, pretest | Week 15, posttest |
| --- | --- | --- |
| Actor | IM | IM |
| Actor | IM | IM/IH* |
| Actor | IH/AL | AL* |
| Actor | IH | AL* |
| Actor | IM | IM/IH* |
| Actor | IM | IM |
| Actor | IH/AL | AL* |
| Actor | IL | IL |
| Actor | IH | AL* |
| Actor | IH | IH |
| Actor | IH/AL | AL* |
| Actor | IM | IM |
| Stage manager | IM | IH* |
| Designer | IM | IM |
| Designer | IM | IH* |
| Stage manager (NSS) | AL | AM* |
| Designer | IM | IM |
| Designer (NSS) | IM | IM |

*Indicates improvement with respect to pretest.

*Note:* AM indicates advanced midlevel; AL, advanced low level; IH, intermediate high level; IM, intermediate midlevel; IL, intermediate low level; NSS, native Spanish speaker.

all. Admittedly, for some it would be extremely difficult, if not impossible, to improve by a sublevel in this amount of time. However, at the level of pure observation, it was clear that all students sustained performance at the higher sublevel for a significant portion of their posttest, with greater fluency and more strategic competence for smoothing over their limitations. It was also interesting to note that, when compared with the pretests, all students carried out the guided role-play segment of the interview with greater confidence, imagination, enthusiasm, and flair. Once again, their strategies for maintaining the conversation had improved. This improvement is most likely attributable to the rich variety of improvisational-situational warm-up activities conducted throughout the semester at the beginning of each class.[25]

Assessment of students' communicative competence in the oral mode was not limited to preproduction and postproduction OPIs.

Rather, it was monitored and evaluated gradually throughout the workshop experience. For this aspect of the course, the director-instructors used a process- rather than product-oriented approach. The first ten to twenty minutes of each seventy-five-minute class was devoted to linguistic (verbal, emotional, corporeal) activities, scenarios, tasks, etc., in the guise of improvisational warm-up games. The instructors began every class, rehearsal, or meeting with one or two of these planned activities to create spontaneous conversations and interactions between pairs, in small groups, or among the whole cast and crew.[26] At least once a week the director informally took notes on student performance (typically assigning a simple grade such as check, check-plus, or check-minus to each student) during these class segments for criteria such as communicative strategies, pronunciation, use of vocabulary and idioms, ease/fluency/comfort, and grammatical accuracy.

Though the ITW proved beneficial for all categories of Carroll's and, later, Sandra Savignon's models of communicative competence (comprising grammatical, sociolinguistic, discourse, and strategic competence), it affected strategic competence the most. The rich variety of theater games were unmatched in terms of their ability to lower, if not eradicate, affective barriers that inhibit students from employing techniques such as guessing, finding cognates, reformulating, gesticulating, mimicking, and creating circumlocutions in order to successfully complete a task.

## Culture

Content material and discussions of culture (both big *C* and small *c*) were integrated throughout the workshop experience, though never explicitly tested. From the full-immersion environment created from the onset through announcements and auditions and the directors' initial presentation of the course, to numerous discussions about the use of linguistic registers and expressions, the choice of costumes and props, and the exploration of nonverbal self-expression during warm-up games, culture was an integral aspect of the entire workshop experience. In addition, Fo's satiric take on the twentieth-century Italian bourgeoisie and his critiques of the church, state, and middle-class morality provided a basis for teaching and learning about the history of class difference and the basic ideologies of leftwing versus rightwing politics in Italy. Though central to the course, cultural knowledge (facts, dates, figures) and students' ability to interpret character motivations or certain parts of the text were mainly assessed through the "content" portions of their writing assignments, namely, the literary and character analyses and the daily journals.

## Student Perceptions of Their Skills and Comfort in the Target Language

The final assessment tool used in the workshop did not yield a grade or contribute to students' final grade in any fashion. It was a survey of students' perceptions of their own foreign language abilities before and after the play, designed to help us understand the affective and motivational potential of this learning experience. During weeks 1 and 15 students completed a questionnaire in which they had to rate on a scale from one to ten their abilities in some thirty subcategories of the four skills and culture, as well as their awareness of and comfort with each. In brief, the results showed that students generally perceived an increase in their abilities in every category—listening, speaking, reading, writing, grammar, vocabulary, and culture. While these numbers may reflect only subjective impressions, they are extremely valuable for the insight they offer on the students' viewpoints and personal experiences. A course in which students perceive their improvement could also help them gain confidence and confront affective boundaries previously inhibiting or limiting their performance. Moreover, large or small, the gains students consistently perceived in the various subcategories for all skills suggests that the ITW can offer a wonderfully rich and comprehensive learning experience for all.

## Discussion and Future Directions

Individually and collectively, students in the ITW achieved the linguistic, cultural, and literary goals set forth in the course syllabus. Final performances were well attended and widely praised, and several participants went so far as to say that this course was the highlight of their foreign language experience, second only to study abroad. Thus, beyond providing useful information about the ways in which students learn a foreign language and motivating student learning, it seems clear that theater workshops or similar theater-based courses have great potential for vitalizing language programs and achieving multiple learning goals; the ITW allows educators to identify and prioritize learning goals and explore ways of attaining and assessing these goals beyond paper-and-pen exams, one-on-one interviews with the instructor, or even the euphoric finale of a public show. The ITW encourages a multiple and multifaceted model for assessment that evaluates individual and group progress; achievement and performance; the processes involved in learning about language, literature, and culture; the students' individual viewpoints on their learning experiences as well as the final products of the course, including papers, journals, and public performances.

There seem to be many benefits to this holistic and comprehensive approach to Italian language, literature, and culture. For one, thanks to its "language pledge" criterion, the workshop creates an immersion environment unlike others in the university setting. Within this challenging Italian-only environment, teachers have more extensive opportunities in the oral and written modes to discover students' individual strengths and weaknesses and engage them in skill-building practice in a variety of creative and spontaneous ways. As a result of this regular, focused practice within the language community environment, students' "feeling of ease" with different aspects of language and culture quite naturally improves. Even the most reserved students begin to shed their inhibitions and learn outwardly and openly from their mistakes (*sbagliando s'impara!*).

The ITW sets a wide range of learning objectives, including those found in traditional intermediate-level language courses (pronunciation, correct use of imperatives and pronouns, and social registers), in basic acting courses (expanding individual comfort zones, exploring self, talents, emotions, articulation and projection of character, thoughts, and feelings via role-plays and scenarios), and in upper-level literature courses (research, textual analysis, and social criticism). With carefully planned and appropriate assessment tools, these integrated objectives can reveal much about student learning, even providing fruitful comparisons between students with brief versus extensive language learning backgrounds, those contemporaneously enrolled in other language courses (Italian or other), and those in acting versus nonacting roles. For instance, the lack of significant variance between the actors and nonactors in this course underscores the value of the ITW and performance-based methods for those students who are not necessarily "born actors" or comfortable with public performances.

At the same time, the ITW has certain limitations, inherent to the nature of the course, that make it difficult to control certain variables and guarantee the objectivity and scientific soundness of formal results. Among the more prominent variables are (1) different start levels of the students' proficiency, (2) concurrent enrollment in other Italian language or literature courses, and (3) extensive experience and/or study abroad with another Romance language. A further limitation of the evaluation procedures, as conducted, is the lack of any delayed posttest to measure longer-term acquisition of concepts, skills, and oral proficiency.

## Conclusion

The course culminating in a performance of *Non tutti i ladri vengono per nuocere* is but one example of how a foreign language theater workshop might unfold. Such courses allow for great flexibility, permitting instructors to focus on the areas, materials, and elements of foreign language learning—a specific skill, an innovative approach to the study of structures, a certain historical time period or literary author—that they wish to emphasize in their curriculum. With a more homogeneous lower-division group of intermediate-level students, for example, the course could focus on communicative functions necessary for the understanding and interpretation of the theater text such as summarizing a plot; describing, analyzing, or comparing characters; or identifying and discussing the conflicts or problems that arise. The course can also be scaled down to mini-units or single activities integrated with daily or weekly classroom routines, such as preparing an oral exam in small groups at the end of each unit in the form of mini-dramas with a director, designer, and actors. With a more homogeneous upper-division group, composed mainly of senior majors, for example, many of whom have studied abroad, the ITW could take on new, more profound dimensions of literary analysis, incorporate additional primary and secondary texts, and explore semiotics in such a way that "the performance project also could teach the student actors about the complex shifts in meaning production during the artistic and critical passage from text to stage." It would involve practicum participants "in a serious, critical understanding of performance semiotics, i.e., the ways in which the multifarious sign systems of the stage (acting, setting, costumes, props, sound, text, etc.) coalesce and/or compete to convey subtle, complex messages to performers and spectators alike."[27]

Regardless of their level of complexity, the enthusiasm and motivation that fuels these courses are easily visible. This fact alone attests to the courses' intrinsic value, with or without an experimental assessment design or any formal grades. Fostering positive attitudes and helping students overcome the more difficult aspects of language, literature, and cultural studies are important and far-reaching goals that will likely have positive effects on student performance in future courses, both foreign language and other. This approach can also enhance students' more general education and career objectives that call for any number of skills and talents developed in the workshop experience—language proficiency, general approaches to humanities-based materials, analytical thinking, group collaboration, effective communication, and public speaking. Moreover, educational drama, from simple role-play to full-scale theater production, can have a pivotal role in motivating and preparing high school students for formal assessments such as the SAT II subject exams, state exams like the New York State Regents exams, and the new advanced placement exam for Italian Language and Culture, all of which call for competence and proficiency in a one-time and relatively pressure-filled situation—not unlike a theatrical production. Therefore, the theater workshop that requires students to "put it all together" (knowledge and skills) on a regular basis in a variety of assignments and assessments that emphasize both the process and the products of their learning constitutes one of the most singular, comprehensive, and memorable learning experiences a foreign language educator can provide.

## Notes

1. Most current textbooks and course curricula incorporate the national standards as a framework for learning goals. For more information about the "connections" standard in particular, see *Standards for Foreign Language Learning*.
2. See Gardner, *Frames of Mind*.
3. These activities often require other strategies and aspects of communicative competence that make memorized lines in a dialogue or play

much more than a rote learning experience. See, for example, Chapter 3 of this book.

4. The benefits of identifying clear learning goals and appropriate assessments beyond the final show are at least two: from a theoretical perspective, they help identify the ideal place for this course in a given curriculum (level, skills, connecting role between other courses); and clear goals and corresponding assessments allow for better tracking of individual progress as well as the overall progress of the troupe.

5. Nuessel, "Foreign Language Testing Today," 3; Omaggio Hadley, *Teaching Language in Context,* 390. Competence extends well beyond grammatical knowledge to encompass different paralinguistic and pragmatic features of language. And proficiency in the language, as Omaggio Hadley (390–391) makes clear, does not refer to any specific method of teaching or specific set of goals pertaining to the four skills and culture, but rather a learner's ability to function effectively in a second language environment.

6. Brown et al., *An Investigation,* 5. The terminological distinction between *test* and *assessment* made by John Norris et al. is a useful departure point. According to these researchers, a test is an instrument—a procedure or tool for gathering information about learners. Assessment instead describes the use of these tools "for particular inferential purposes relevant to the language education context." They then go on to explain that "the ultimate goal of language assessment is to use tests to better inform the decisions that we make and the actions that we take in language education contexts." Norris et al., "Designing Second Language Performance Assessments," 12.

7. Magnan, "Just Do It," 136; Bacon and Finneman, "A Study of the Attitudes, Motives, and Strategies."

8. See Savignon, *Communicative Competence,* 14.

9. Magnan, "Just Do It," 151–152: "A task-based test activity is defined as one in which students use language in a natural way to accomplish a task they might realistically need to perform in the target culture. They include several types of interaction—between student and input, between student and others, between student and values/conventions of target culture, between student and her developing interlanguage system. Understanding more about the process would mean eliciting information about their strategies along the way." Alan Davies warns against what he calls "heresies" or embracing new and major developments in the field so enthusiastically "that they lead to [an] unbalanced view . . . concerning the construct definition of language, the scope of test impact and the value of new methods of test delivery and analysis." See "Three Heresies," 355.

10. Magnan, "Just Do It," 137.

11. Fulcher, "The 'Communicative' Legacy." The key targets to attack for the new "communicative" language testers were the multiple-choice item as embodied in the Test of English as a Foreign Language (492) as well as the work of Robert Lado, who was concerned with the reliability of such performance-based testing (488). As Fulcher shows, research and debates about the need for performance tests, though speaking generally, date back to the 1920s and 1930s. Even then, the major factor deterring widespread use of such tests was the impracticality of conducting them on a large scale. After the war, however, "testing agencies in the United States were developing the first true communicative performance tests that were to become the models for future test design and development around the world" (486). According to Fulcher, communicative language testing largely developed as "a rejection of the role that reliability and validity had come to play in language testing, mainly in the United States during the 1960s" (486). At the end of his mini-history, however, and despite important concerns raised about reliability and validity in the face of potentially subjective judgment testing formats (oral exams), Fulcher advocates communicative testing when based on tasks. What makes a task communicative and, thus, a valuable assessment tool is "the relationship between the learner and the task, how the learner deals with the task, and what we can learn about the learner as a result of doing the task" (486–487).
12. Liskin-Gasparro, "Assessment," 171, 172.
13. Brown et al., *An Investigation*, 6. Such prioritization of performance ability in the outcomes of second language instruction can also be seen, for example, in the abiding influence of global proficiency models (American Council on the Teaching of Foreign Languages) and the "proficiency movement" in U.S. foreign language education, as well as in recent national policy for foreign language learning.
14. Chalhoub-Deville, "Second Language Interaction," 372, 369, 381.
15. See Carroll, *Testing Communicative Performance;* Lee and Van Patten, *Making Communicative Language Teaching Happen*, 98–99.
16. Omaggio Hadley, *Teaching Language in Context,* 397. Students are more motivated when language-learning materials seem relevant to their communicative needs and interests and resemble authentic language use. Omaggio Hadley cites Shohamy (1982), who found that students had a favorable attitude toward oral interviews for this reason.
17. In 1999, the American Council on the Teaching of Foreign Languages (ACTFL) published its *Standards for Foreign Language Learning in the 21st Century,* applicable to primary, secondary, and postsecondary curricula. The five main categories, widely referred to as the five Cs, are communication, cultures, connections, comparisons, and communi-

ties. Upon reading the description, it is easy to see how the *Standards* necessitate assessment tools that reach beyond measuring accuracy or achievement. They call for context-specific, dynamic, and interactive modes of assessment for which teachers create real-world situations and tasks for language use. As researchers and practitioners adhere more frequently and consistently to the *Standards* as universal objectives for foreign language study, the fundamental context for communication seems clear.

18. See "Test Selection: A Few Criteria" in the "Director's Handbook."
19. Dörneyi and Murphey, *Group Dynamics,* 109–110.
20. Ibid., 110.
21. See Ryan-Scheutz and Colangelo, "Campanile's Comedic Theater."
22. For example, in the beginning stages of the process, the directors selected games to let participants get to know each other, creating a nonthreatening environment in which everyone, regardless of their linguistic level, felt comfortable participating. Games in this stage were less linguistically demanding and more focused on building confidence and trust. When the basic tone of the language community had been set, more grammar- and communication-specific exercises were selected. On a day-to-day basis in response to the difficulties and needs of the group, the director was able to use games that focused on, for example, pronunciation, specific grammar points, or general improvisation of scenes. Finally, after the participants were much more familiar with the script, warm-up games were selected that used lines out of context, explored character relationships, and taught students how to find and convey humor in a variety of situations.
23. Stage managers attended both rehearsals and design meetings. They were responsible for keeping track of line alterations, blocking, pronunciation errors, and general comments during rehearsals. Likewise, at design meetings they kept notes and participated in discussions about costumes, set pieces, and props, offering their comments and suggestions about choices and potential problems.
24. Additionally, designers had to accompany the director to find costumes, props, and supplies. On these trips, the designers and director preserved the immersion environment to the greatest extent possible, continuing to converse only in Italian. Designers were also in charge of writing detailed lists of every prop and costume element and making sure everything was in its proper place at dress rehearsals and performances. The sound and lighting designer wrote sound and lighting cues and ran the sound and light boards for the show.
25. See Kormos, "Simulating Conversations in Oral-Proficiency Assessment." In her study of oral performance, Judith Kormos compared the results of oral interviews and oral role-play exams for intermediate-

level students of English in Hungary. Both tests were analyzed for the number of topics introduced and ratified by the examiner and the candidate, respectively, as well as for the number of interruptions, openings, and closings produced by the examiner and the candidate during the course of the test (163). She found that the conversational interaction is more symmetrical in the guided role-play activity with the candidates introducing and ratifying approximately the same number of topics as the examiners. In addition, the examinees had more opportunities to interrupt and "hold the floor" and demonstrate their ability to open and close conversations. In Kormos's words, "These findings suggest that guided role-play activities used in the study exhibit several characteristics of real-life conversations and therefore can be used for assessing the candidates' conversational competence" (163).

26. See Spolin, *Theater Games for the Classroom.*
27. Essif, "(Re-)Creating the Critique," 119, 120.

## Bibliography

Bachman, Lyle F. *Fundamental Considerations in Language Testing.* Oxford: Oxford University Press, 1990.

Bacon, Susan M., and Michael D. Finneman. "A Study of the Attitudes, Motives, and Strategies of University Foreign Language Students and Their Disposition to Authentic Oral and Written Input." *Modern Language Journal* 74 (1990): 459–473.

Bräuer, Gerd, ed. *Body and Language: Intercultural Learning through Drama.* Westport, CT: Ablex, 2002.

Brown, James Dean, Thom Hudson, John Norris, and William J. Bonk, eds. *An Investigation of Second Language Task-Based Performance Assessments.* Second Language Teaching and Curriculum Center. Manoa: University of Hawai'i, 2002.

Carroll, Brendan J. *Testing Communicative Performance.* London: Pergamon, 1980.

Chalhoub-Deville, Micheline. "Second Language Interaction: Current Perspectives and Future Trends." *Language Testing* 20 (2003): 369–383.

Cohen, Andrew D. *Testing Language Ability in the Classroom.* 2nd ed. Boston: Heinle & Heinle, 1994.

Davies, Alan. "Three Heresies of Language Testing Research." *Language Testing* 20 (2003): 355–368.

Devitt, Sean. "Interacting with Authentic Texts: Multi-Layered Processes." *Modern Language Journal* 81 (1997): 457–469.

DiPietro, Robert. *Strategic Interaction: Learning Languages through Scenarios.* Cambridge: Cambridge University Press, 1987.

Dodson, Sarah. "Language through Theater: Using Drama in the Language Classroom." *Texas Papers in Foreign Language Education* 5 (2000): 129–142.

Dörneyi, Zoltán, and Tim Murphey. *Group Dynamics in the Language Classroom.* Cambridge: Cambridge University Press, 2003.

Essif, Les. "Teaching Literary-Dramatic Texts as Culture-in-Process in the Foreign Language Theatre Practicum: The Strategy of Combining Texts." *ADFL Bulletin* 29 (1998): 24–33.

———. "(Re-)Creating the Critique: In(tro)ducing the Semiotics of Theater in the Foreign-Language Performance Project. *Theater Topics* 12 (2002): 119–142.

Fo, Dario. "Non tutti i ladri vengono per nuocere.." In *Le commedie di Dario Fo.* 4th ed. Turin: Einaudi, 1977.

Fulcher, Glenn. "The 'Communicative' Legacy in Language Testing." *System* 28 (2000): 483–497.

Gardner, Howard. *Frames of Mind: A Theory of Multiple Intelligences.* New York: Basic Books, 1983.

Haggstrom, Margaret. "A Performative Approach to the Study of Theater: Bridging the Gap between Language and Literature Courses." *French Review* 1 (1992): 7–19.

Hudson, Tom, and J. D. Brown, eds. *A Focus on Language Test Development.* Preface. Second Language Teaching and Curriculum Center. Manoa: University of Hawai'i, 2001, ix–x.

Kormos, Judith. "Simulating Conversations in Oral-Proficiency Assessment: A Conversation Analysis of Role-Plays and Non-Scripted Interviews in Language Exams." *Language Testing* 16 (1999): 163–188.

Lee, James, and Bill Van Patten. *Making Communicative Language Teaching Happen.* 2nd ed. New York: McGraw-Hill, 2003.

Liskin-Gasparro, Judith. "Assessment: From Content Standards to Student Performance." In *National Standards: A Catalyst for Reform,* edited by Robert C. Lafayette. The ACTFL Foreign Language Education Series. Lincolnwood, IL: National Textbook Co., 1996.

Little, David, Sean Devitt, and David Singleton. *Learning Foreign Languages from Authentic Texts: Theory and Practice.* Dublin: Authentik, 1988.

———. "The Communicative Approach and Authentic Texts." In *Teaching Modern Languages,* edited by Ann Swarbrick. London: Routledge, 1994.

Magnan, Sally. "Just Do It: Directing TAs toward Task-Based and Process-Oriented Testing." In *Assessing Foreign Language Proficiency of Undergraduates: Issues in Language Program Direction,* edited by Richard V. Teschner. Boston: Heinle & Heinle, 1991.

Maley, Alan, and Alan Duff. *Drama Techniques in Language Learning.* Cambridge: Cambridge University Press, 1982.

———. "Drama Techniques in Language Learning." In *Teaching Modern Languages,* edited by Ann Swarbrick. London: Routledge, 1994.

Mather, Clare. "Getting Off the Page and Making a Scene: Teaching Drama in the Classroom." *ADFL Bulletin* 20 (1989): 58–63.

Norris, John M. "Purposeful Language Assessment: Matching Testing Alternatives with Intended Test Use." *English Teaching Forum* 38 (2000): 18–23.

Norris, John, J. D. Brown, Thom Hudson, and A. Yoshioka. "Designing Second Language Performance Assessments." Second Language Teaching and Curriculum Center, Technical Report no. 18. Honolulu: University of Hawai'i, 1998.

Nuessel, Frank. "Foreign Language Testing Today: Issues in Language Program Direction." In *Assessing Foreign Language Proficiency of Undergraduates: Issues in Language Program Direction,* edited by Richard V. Teschner. Boston: Heinle & Heinle, 1991.

Omaggio Hadley, Alice. *Teaching Language in Context.* 2nd ed. Boston: Heinle & Heinle, 2000.

Ryan-Scheutz, Colleen, and Laura Colangelo. "Campanile's Comedic Theater: A Humorous Link in the Italian Studies Curriculum." *Italica* 81 (2004): 483–503.

Savignon, Sandra. *Communicative Competence: Classroom Theory and Practice.* 2nd ed. New York: McGraw-Hill, 1997.

Savoia, Francesca. "Teaching Italian Language, Literature, and Culture through Performance: The Italian Theatrical Workshop." *Italica* 77 (2002): 509–522.

Schewe, Manfred, and Peter Shaw. *Towards Drama as a Method in the Foreign Language Classroom.* Frankfurt am Main: Peter Lang, 1993.

Shier, Janet. "Integrating the Arts in the Foreign/Second Language Curriculum: Fusing the Affective and the Cognitive." *Foreign Language Annals* 23 (1990): 301–316.

Shohamy, Elana. "Affective Considerations in Language Testing." *Modern Language Journal* 66.1 (1982): 3–17.

Spolin, Viola. *Theater Games for the Classroom: A Teacher's Handbook.* Evanston, IL: Northwestern University Press, 1986.

*Standards for Foreign Language Learning in the 21st Century.* Yonkers, NY: National Standards in Foreign Language Education Project, 1999.

Swender, Elvira, ed. *ACTFL Oral Proficiency Interview Tester Trainer Manual.* Yonkers, NY: American Council for the Teaching of Foreign Languages, 1999.

Teschner, Richard V., ed. *Assessing Foreign Language Proficiency of Undergraduates: Issues in Language Program Direction.* Boston: Heinle & Heinle, 1991.

Whiteson, Valerie, ed. *New Ways of Using Drama and Literature in Language Teaching.* Bloomington, IL: TESOL, 1996.

# *V*  Director's Handbook

## Text Selection: A Few Criteria

The following discussion and list of dramatic texts are by no means intended to be either comprehensive or encyclopedic but rather attempt to provide the aspiring director with a point of departure, a frame of reference, some thoughts for consideration, and some suggestions. Before beginning, keep in mind that, unless you are selling tickets and charging entrance fees to your performance, you will not need to pay for performance rights to the plays.

In choosing a play, the first criterion to keep in mind is the potential cast—the makeup of your course: your enrollment or available actors; their gender, talent level, language ability, personality and physical types; and any special skills they may have. For instance, a former high school gymnast may prove an invaluable asset in the performance of physical *lazzi*. If a director has a group of students who are uncomfortable or self-conscious about their bodies, the more physicalized texts of Carlo Gozzi, Carlo Goldoni, and Dario Fo should be avoided. In aligning a potential play cast with potential play texts, directors must first keep in mind the number and gender of the students at their disposal for the production. The gender composition of Italian drama reflects that of world drama as a whole, with men's roles almost always outnumbering women's roles. In terms of gender, most Goldoni and Gozzi plays, following the composition of most commedia dell'arte troupes, usually have three to four women's roles and six to ten men's roles. Some plays, such as Ugo Betti's *Corruzione al Palazzo di Giustizia* (1944) and Leonardo Sciascia's *I mafiosi* (1976), contain overwhelmingly male cast lists, primarily because of their subject matter. Countering this, Dacia Maraini's more feminist-oriented play texts prioritize women's roles. Franca Rame's *Parti femminili* (1986) addresses this same need of voicing the Italian female, but it does so in a series of monologues. Cross-gender casting can alleviate problems and proves particularly easy when the roles being so cast do not involve romantic or sexual intrigues, when the function of the role itself is gender neutral. Fo's *Quasi per caso una donna: Elisabetta* (1984) calls for the role of Big Mama to be cross-gender cast, as Fo played this ostensibly female role himself. His *I cadaveri si spediscono e le donne si spogliano* (1957) even requires a "Uomo-Donna," so unless you have one readily available, you are bound to do some sort of cross-gender casting in this play.

Some plays, such as many of those by Goldoni and Gozzi, distribute their action somewhat evenly among the various roles, while other plays, such as Dino Buzzati's absurdist critique of medical bureaucracy *Un caso clinico* (1953) and Maraini's critique of absurd patriarchy *I sogni di Clitennestra* (1981), revolve almost entirely around one character, as he or she interacts with others. Smaller roles, if they do not appear onstage at the same time, can be easily doubled and played by a single actor, a change of costume or makeup serving to indicate the different role. In fact, Fo's *Non si paga, non si paga* (1957) explicitly flaunts this device of theatrical convention, as the characters in the play repeatedly comment on the physical similarity of various small characters all intentionally played by the same actor. Perpetually metatheatrical, Fo's original casting for *Gli arcangeli non giocano a flipper* (1959) and *La colpa è sempre del diavolo* (1965) called for actors to play multiple roles, so that the cast lists presented below for these plays may actually be expanded from what is indicated. Dividing a role between more than one actor could prove much more problematic not only for the psychodynamics of the cast but also for the audience. When a role is divided between two actors, it is advisable to have each one alternate performances, having one actor play the entirety of the role for a single performance and then taking turns with the other actor. In addition to doubling roles for plays with large casts, a director might consider doubling plays in order to produce plays with smaller casts. Giovanni Verga, Luigi Pirandello, Fo, and Maraini, among others, have written a number of small-cast one-act plays. By producing one or even two one-act plays, a director-instructor might be able to distribute the responsibility for learning roles more evenly throughout that class or group of available students. Furthermore, while producing multiple one-act plays may upset the unity of a class, the students might actually work better in smaller groups, having less "dead time" as they wait for their time to perform.

In general, unless you are teaching a course or are in a program focusing specifically on Italian verse or on some particular author, such as Torquato Tasso, Gabriele D'Annunzio, or Pier Paolo Pasolini, it is probably best to avoid verse dramas. Such play texts diverge greatly from the underlying psychodynamics of daily speech, frequently containing very long passages and requiring an extra dimension of training and rehearsal. The poetic dialogue itself, quite stilted compared with regular speech, may prove counterproductive to the linguistic goals of your course and production. Similarly, plays in dialect, such as some of the otherwise appealing works of Eduardo De Filippo, for example, *Filumena Marturano* (1946), present additional obstacles to performance and generally should be avoided unless you are teaching a course or are in a program addressing that specific dialect. Learning dialogue in dialect could easily confuse the students' learning process in standard spoken Italian. Furthermore, performance in dialect could easily alienate those members of the audience unfamiliar with that dialect.[1] Some plays, however, both suit linguistic objectives in North American schools and offer a taste of regional culture. Originally intended for continental audiences, Verga's theatrical dialogue retains a Sicilian flavor but remains largely comprehensible and mostly within the idiom of standard Italian. De Filippo's *Il sindaco del Rione Sanità* (1960) employs a similar linguistic strategy, providing a taste of Neapolitan speech within a context of primarily standard Italian dialogue.

Linguistic concerns might prompt initial hesitation in selecting play texts by Niccolò Machiavelli, Gozzi, or Goldoni. Renaissance texts such as Ludovico Ariosto's comic *La Cassaria* (1508), Giovanni Giorgio Trissino's *Sofonisba* (1515), and Giambattista Giraldi Cinthio's *Orbecche* (1541) were written for court academies and remain esoteric and unapproachable, the latter two especially as they are based on archaic models of classical tragedy. Machiavelli's *Clizia* (1525) and especially his *Mandragola* (1519) remain viable, and his language proves accessible, albeit with some extra effort. As for Goldoni and Gozzi, the abbreviations and elisions of eighteenth-century Italian transpose easily into contemporary Italian, and students readily pick up on the various changes in word usage that have occurred in the past two centuries, especially when expressions are used repeatedly, as they frequently are in the dialogue of both of these writers. Some editions of plays such as those of Machiavelli's *Mandragola*, Luigi Chiarelli's *La maschera e il volto* (1916), and Goldoni's *Opere* listed below provide not only footnotes, but also definitions and vocabularies in the margins. Goldoni's plays are numerous and vary greatly in quality. They range in tone and conception from the more farcical *Il servitore di due padroni* (1745), not dissimilar from Gozzi's more fanciful and fantasy-based *Fiabe*, to the more realistic *Trilogia della villeggiatura* (1761) and *La bottega del caffè* (1750), which expose the comic aspects of Venetian social behavior in a more realistic manner. Gozzi's *Fiabe* and *Il servitore di due padroni* require more physical *lazzi* than these other Goldoni works. More broadly comic than his *Villeggiatura* sequence, yet more muted than Gozzi's *Fiabe*, *Il bugiardo* (1750), *La locandiera* (1752), and *Il ventaglio* (1765) remain viably entertaining texts.

While much of Italian theater rests outside the Realist tradition that has dominated much American, English, and northern European theater, certain Italian plays do situate themselves, not only logistically but also temperamentally, more within the realm of the drawing room than that of the piazza. Writing in the wake of Henrik Ibsen and George Bernard Shaw and their international influence, the talky dramas of playwrights Marco Praga and Roberto Bracco, while popular enough in their day, are for the most part justifiably forgotten. Some of Verga's more bourgeois-themed plays, such as *In portineria* (1885) and *Caccia alla volpe* (1902), also fit this mode. Perhaps Giuseppe Giacosa's *Come le foglie* (1900) or Verga's *Dal tuo al mio* (1903) might be a better choice of a play if you are focused on this period for other pedagogical reasons. More contemporary drawing-room dramas include De Filippo's character study *Sabato, domenica, e lunedì* (1959) and Pier Vittorio Tondelli's psychologically savvy *Dinner Party* (1984), both of which are viable options.

Contemplating the disparity between social role-playing and intrapersonal and interpersonal inclinations, Chiarelli's relatively lighthearted *La maschera e il volto* served as a predecessor for the more serious works of Pirandello. Pirandello's works seesaw on the fulcrum of the disparity already scrutinized in Chiarelli's work. Pirandello's plays range in tone from the vivaciousness of *Liolà* to the dark *King Lear*–inspired contemplations of *Enrico IV* (1921). His best works, from a philosophical point of view, risk being his worst, from a dramaturgical point of view. Henry IV in *Enrico IV*, the Father in *Sei personaggi in cerca d'autore* (1921), and Laudisi in *Così è (se vi pare)* (1917) all engage in seemingly interminable set speeches addressing the Cartesian paradox of identity and (self-)consciousness that literally stop the drama.[2] Still, the majority of Pirandello's works contain passages of lively dialogue and colorful characters, many of whom are less self-aware than his primary protagonists. Living more fully within themselves, Verga's peasant characters present other challenges for untrained actors. Unmediated by the bourgeois (self-) consciousness of the Pirandellian hero, Verga's characters readily commit drastic actions of a dramatic magnitude beyond the range of many actors. Plays such as *La lupa* (1896) and *Cavalleria rusticana*

(1884), while certainly not static, constitute daring and potentially difficult choices. The Theater of Moral Trials of Diego Fabbri and Ugo Betti, whose works influenced the French existentialists, furnish characters who live more fully inside themselves than do Pirandello's self-alienated protagonists, yet also within a more accessibly calibrated consciousness than those offered by Verga. Like Fabbri and Betti, De Filippo and Natalia Ginzburg examine the dynamics of role-play within a basically realistic framework. The twentieth-century dialogue of these playwrights, De Filippo's ventures into *Napolitano* aside, generally proves readily comprehensible. Even more than Pirandello, however, Ginzburg has a predilection for long set speeches in her works.

The plays of Dario Fo, often overtly metatheatrical, constitute modernizations of the commedia dell'arte sensibility as applied to the performance of social roles and how such roles affect interpersonal interaction and individual psychology, as well as providing opportunities for comic play. The Marxist-oriented and class-conscious Fo examines and exposes not only the social role-play of his characters, but also the political implications of such roles. Giuseppe Patroni Griffi's *Gli amanti dei miei amanti sono i miei amanti* (1982) examines the giddy role-play involved in the hyperbolically metatheatrical world of opera. For the most part, awareness of role-play in these works generally proves less intellectual and less talky and has greater comic immediacy than that found in the works of Pirandello. These plays may also demand a larger amount of physical *lazzi* than those of Pirandello, making them potentially more lively and energetic in performance as well.

Besides Fo, Maraini probably counts as Italy's most important living playwright. In a manner more focused and radical than Ginzburg before her, she has forged a theater that provokes, engages, and toys with Italian awareness of role-playing specifically as it involves the sociodynamics and psychodynamics of gender. She sometimes juxtaposes soliloquies with dialogue in her effort to contrast internalized intelligence and natural instincts with the externalized demands of social conformity. Her plays confront students with a distinctly feminist consciousness and offer strong roles to women, something to consider, depending on the gender makeup of your course or of available students. The director, however, should be aware that plays such as *I sogni di Clitennestra* and *Un dialogo fra una prostituta e il suo cliente* (1978) deploy foul language as a means of highlighting and challenging patriarchal constructs of language and "appropriate" gender behavior.

In general, Goldoni, Pirandello, Betti, Fabbri, Buzzati, De Filippo, Fo, and Maraini have all written numerous plays that might merit consideration, depending on your interests, potential audience, and available actors. Certainly, the amount of viable Italian dramatic material exceeds what can be addressed here. Below are some cast lists that do not, however, delineate the relative ages of the characters, something else you might want to consider when selecting a play. In the cast lists below, some of the extras listed are simply smaller speaking roles, while others are nonspeaking roles.

## Cast for Selected Plays

| Author | Title | Cast |
| --- | --- | --- |
| Betti, Ugo | *Corruzione al Palazzo di Giustizia* | 8 men, 2 women, extras |
| | *Delitto all'isola delle capre* | 3 women, 2 men |
| | *Frana allo Scalo Nord* | 13 men, 5 women, extras |
| | *La regina e gli insorti* | 4 women, 7 men, extras |
| Buzzati, Dino | *Un caso clinico* | 11 men, 7 women, extras |
| Chiarelli, Luigi | *La maschera e il volto* | 8 men, 5 women |
| De Filippo, Eduardo | *Le bugie con le gambe lunghe* | 8 men, 8 women |
| | *La grande magia* | 11 men, 9 women, extras |
| | *Sabato, domenica e lunedì* | 11 men, 6 women |
| | *Il sindaco del Rione Sanità* | 14 men, 6 women |
| Fabbri, Diego | *La bugiarda* | 4 women, 7 men |
| | *Processo a Gesù* | 17 men, 6 women, extras |
| | *Il seduttore* | 1 man, 3 women, extras |
| Fo, Dario | *Gli arcangeli non giocano a flipper* | 8 men, 4 women |
| | *I cadaveri si spediscono e le donne si spogliano* | 3 men, 4 women, 1 man-woman |
| | *La colpa è sempre del diavolo* | 8 men, 4 women |
| | *Gli imbianchini non hanno ricordi* | 4 men, 4 women |
| | *La marijuana della mamma è la più bella* | 5 men, 2 women |
| | *Morte accidentale di un anarchico* | 4 men, 1 woman, extras |
| | *Non si paga, non si paga* | 6 men (4 of these to be played by one actor), 2 women, extras |
| | *Non tutti i ladri vengono per nuocere* | 4 men, 3 women |
| | *Quasi per caso una donna: Elisabetta* | 3 men, 3 women, extras |
| | *Tutti uniti! Tutti insieme! Ma scusa, quello non è il padrone?* | 13 men, 7 women, extras |

| Author | Title | Cast |
| --- | --- | --- |
| Giacosa, Giuseppe | *Come le foglie* | 8 men, 7 women, extras |
| Ginzburg, Natalia | *Ti ho sposato per allegria* | 1 man, 4 women |
| Goldoni, Carlo | *Le avventure della villeggiatura* | 11 men, 6 women |
| | *La bottega del caffè* | 6 men, 3 women, extras |
| | *Il bugiardo* | 7 men, 3 women, extras |
| | *I due gemelli veneziani* | 11 men, 3 women, extras |
| | *La locandiera* | 3 women, 5 men, extras |
| | *Il ritorno dalla villeggiatura* | 15 men, 6 women |
| | *Il servitore di due padroni* | 5 men, 3 women, extras |
| | *Le smanie per la villeggiatura* | 8 men, 3 women |
| | *Il ventaglio* | 10 men, 4 women |
| Gozzi, Carlo | *Il re cervo* | 7 men, 3 women, extras |
| | *Turandot* | 9 men, 4 women |
| Machiavelli, Niccolò | *Clizia* | 7 men, 3 women |
| | *Mandragola* | 5 men, 3 women |
| Maraini, Dacia | *Bianca Garofani* | 1 man, 3 women |
| | *Don Juan* | 4 men, 6 women, extras |
| | *Donna Lionora Giacubina* | 13 men, 8 women, extras |
| | *Maria Stuarda* | 4 women |
| | *I sogni di Clitennestra* | 4–5 men, 7–8 women |
| | *Stravaganza* | 6 men, 5 women |
| Moravia, Alberto | *La mascherata* | 7 men, 3 women, extras |
| Patroni Griffi, Giuseppe | *Gli amanti dei miei amanti sono i miei amanti* | 5 men, 4 women, extras |
| Pirandello, Luigi | *Ciascuno a suo modo* | 10 men, 4 women, extras |
| | *Come tu mi vuoi* | 7 women, 6 men, extras |
| | *Così è (se vi pare)* | 7 men, 7 women, extras |
| | *Enrico IV* | 9 men, 2 women, extras |
| | *Il giuoco delle parti* | 9 men, 2 women, extras |
| | *Liolà* | 2 men, 9 women, 3 boys, extras |
| | *Lazzaro* | 8 men, 3 women, extras |
| | *Sei personaggi in cerca d'autore* | 12 men, 7 women |
| | *Trovarsi* | 7 men, 6 women, extras |
| | *Vestire gli ignudi* | 4 men, 3 women |
| Sciascia, Leonardo | *I mafiosi* | 9 men, 1 woman |
| Tondelli, Pier Vittorio | *Dinner Party* | 4 men, 4 women |

| Author | Title | Cast |
|---|---|---|
| Verga, Giovanni | *La caccia al lupo* | 2 men, 1 woman |
| | *La caccia alla volpe* | 2 men, 1 woman |
| | *Cavalleria rusticana* | 3 men, 6 women |
| | *Dal tuo al mio* | 14 men, 4 women, extras |
| | *In portineria* | 6 men, 6 women |
| | *La lupa* | 6 men, 5 women |

## —WILLIAM VAN WATSON

## Notes

1. Antonella Del Fattore-Olson and Salvatore Bancheri have a different view on the use of dialect in teaching Italian theater. See Chapters 3 and 10.
2. Other scholars, nevertheless, have used such texts as Pirandello's *Sei personaggi* in theater production courses with great satisfaction and positive feedback from students (see Chapter 9).

## Financial Resources, Publicity, and Community

How can you make your theatrical performances self-funded activities? Here I reflect on my personal experience at the University of Toronto Mississauga (UTM), where six to eight performances attract an average yearly audience of two thousand. In the greater Toronto area, the Italian-Canadian population numbers roughly half a million.

To self-fund a theatrical production, I have found that it is necessary to draw support from as many outside sources as possible. There are a number of options for this, but first, it is of fundamental importance to make sure that the university supports the course and is therefore involved with the production of the play. Any university is an enormous resource, providing technicians, lights, props, and, of course, the theater itself. My approach is simple: since the theater courses I teach are official university courses, I demand from my university the same support other theater courses receive. In this way, I do not have to worry about finding and paying for a theater in which to hold performances. I schedule all my performances in the auditorium or theater as midterm tests or final exams, requesting the necessary support for lighting, videotaping, and anything else that could be justified as part of a final exam. Outside of the university setting, the community and the students themselves can provide ample resources.

Any performance requires an enormous amount of printed material—tickets, programs, and advertisements. Since the performance is part of a theater course, the instructor/director and students are entitled to use the university's resources for printing. Technically, I could even request not to be charged for the cost of printing all programs and tickets. As for the design of the materials, this can be left up to the students, as I have often found it effective to employ the students in all aspects of the production, including the nonperformative aspects. The eight-page program, for which I use a template that I have developed, costs probably less than fifty dollars (150 copies). The filming of the performance is also low-cost, as it is filmed using a university video camera, and the only real cost is that of the videocassette or, more recently, the DVD.

You can easily obtain quality costumes and accessories without spending a fortune on them. First, it is usually possible to get free costumes and accessories through the university's support. Failing this, or if the university's supplies are insufficient for the performance, approach the students' families for assistance. Families are often willing to donate or loan items to a performance if their child is involved. In my experience, I have even had students' relatives create sophisticated eighteenth-century costumes. If you must buy costumes or accessories, thrift stores or the Salvation Army will often suffice; the cost is low and the selection is particularly well suited to theatrical performances. I have found that utilizing the Salvation Army works especially well for modern plays. For props and accessories, old household items stowed away in the back corners of garages or attics are usually effective. However, I must stress that you should exhaust the resources of the university before approaching the students or their families for extra help with the performance.

An excellent way to secure funds, support, and publicity is through sponsorship. The simplest route is through the families of the students involved, who are often more than willing to sponsor the performance, even if they are not Italian. Local associations, clubs, and cultural groups are frequently looking for opportunities to add cultural activities to their profile, so be sure to target them for sponsorships and donations. In our case, we have created a large number of scholarships, and sponsors return to us without being asked. It has become a part of the academic tradition of the school and community. Clubs also provide an excellent partnership because they attract a larger audience for the performance. You do not have to demand a huge sum for sponsorship; anything is acceptable. To ensure that a sponsor, club, or association continues to support future performances, it must feel appreciated; therefore, it is essential to recognize them in the program and perhaps even before or after the performance.

Raffles are another excellent way to secure funds for a performance. Ask individuals or organizations to donate prizes, such as television sets. The money can then be put toward the cost of the performance or toward setting up a scholarship in the donor's name. Even small sponsorships and contributions are acceptable and should never be turned down.

It is always necessary to spread goodwill to the audience and your sponsors to ensure that they come back in subsequent years. In fact, securing a consistent audience must be one of your primary concerns. Always remember to recognize the contribution of the audience, even if they have just come to watch, but especially remember to recognize and show appreciation for the sponsors. Make sure that before and after the performance the stage is reserved for the sponsors and the audience and that you always deal with them personally.

To create publicity for your event, approach local radio and television stations and newspapers. Such media outlets usually have no qualms about participating in or advertising a university theatrical performance, as it is a cultural and academic activity.

At UTM we have managed not only to make our productions self-funded, but also to run them at a profit. We have also succeeded in involving our community in creating endowed scholarships for our students. Most of all, we have earned the respect not only of the community, but of the university administration, which is thrilled that we are not asking, at least directly, for monetary support. In fact, we give our advancement office ample opportunities to meet our community and perhaps discuss more substantial collaborations. The administration recognizes this collaborative support, and for this reason the UTM vice president and principal always attend one of our performances, even though their Italian is limited to only a few words.

—SALVATORE BANCHERI

## The Italian Drama Workshop in Three Acts

The course is divided into three main parts, or acts: presentation and analysis of the play, analysis of the characters, and rehearsal.

*Act I: Presentation and analysis of the chosen play.* The reading constitutes the homework; students focus on lexicon and recognition of grammatical structures. The reading continues in class, with focus on lexicon, recognition of grammatical structures, pronunciation, and intonation. The linguistic and phonetic component alternates with discussion in class of the sociocultural, historical, and literary background that emerges from the content of the chosen play. To deepen the knowledge of the cultural background, students read additional material, such as another work of the author and articles related to the play and its author. Visual aids are presented to make the students familiar with the geographical region in which the play takes place. Immediately after the reading of the entire play, the roles are assigned.

Students who choose small roles are responsible for organizing costumes, lights, scenery, props, and advertising. Music is another important element in theater that deserves serious consideration. It's also wise to select one or two students to act as stage managers.

Memorization of the lines begins in the second part of this initial phase. If films related to the play and to its historical period are available, it is advisable to show them now as they can elicit a useful discussion among students and generate many ideas for the scenery and costumes.

*Act II: Analysis of the characters—their motivations, goals, conflicts, and interactions with one another.* Students write a paper in Italian in which they offer their critical commentary on the play as well as analyze the character they portray. For the paper, they must create a background (from their imagination) that serves to justify their character's behavior. Then, they give an oral presentation in class on their character so that all the student-actors get to know their onstage partners better. Rehearsals in class and blocking of the scenes begin. We continue to talk about the cultural component and, when possible, we invite guest speakers. We put on our website the summaries of the play (possibly in both Italian and English) and all the information we consider useful for our future audience, including students and professors of Italian and members of the Italian community. During the rehearsals, we have some of the scenes filmed, usually the ones that present more difficulties due to an intense interaction among characters.

*Act III: Rehearsal of the play.* We watch the video of the rehearsals in class and give our critique by commenting on what needs to be improved and/or changed. It is very important for students to see themselves on a screen, for the same reason that dancers practice their movements in front of a mirror. Furthermore, the video gives a valid perspective on spatial relations. By this point in the semester, since students have already defined their characters and configured their "personalities," it is safe to watch, if available, a filmed version of the play. The rest of this third act is devoted exclusively to staging the play and giving it the last, finishing touches. The search for the right costumes, props, music, and scenery involves a great deal of effort from the students responsible for this job; although much time is devoted to these tasks outside of class, they seem to get very involved in accomplishing them. The final performances are usually presented in the evenings; their number varies from two to four, according to the number of students enrolled in the class. If the enrollment is elevated and two casts are performing, it is crucial to give at least two final performances to each cast. After three intense months spent together, the bond created by our community will keep us united for a long time.

—ANTONELLA DEL FATTORE-OLSON

## Training the Body, Coaching the Mind: Preliminary Acting Exercises

The following exercises are based on the actor training method developed by Orazio Costa (1911–1999), who is considered one of the forefathers of Italian theater directing, together with Luchino Visconti and Giorgio Strehler. Costa was among the first students at the National Academy of Dramatic Art, founded in Rome in 1936, and started to be interested in theater training just after a significant experience in France as assistant to Jacques Copeau. After World War II, Costa taught acting and directing for more than thirty years at the National Academy and carried out a thorough investigation of the educational practices underlying any form of performing art. Costa's approach is still part of the curriculum of the National Academy as well as of other Italian and European theater and dance schools.

These exercises have been defined as "preliminary" because they do not form part of a specific acting method and therefore a style. They simply warm up the individual's willingness to transform himself or herself, what Costa called the *mimic instinct,* which is at the origin of every form of artistic production: theater, dance, music, painting, sculpture, poetry, or other. When first introducing students to the technique, it is advisable to keep the timing suggested for each section of the routine, for a total of at least forty minutes. Then, when the process has been practiced, understood, and absorbed, all the elements can be sped up and adapted to specific needs. In the end it becomes an effective creative warm-up activity, running no more than twenty minutes and without the instructor having to explain the structure of the exercises.

## Rhythm (four minutes)

On our knees and with our hands resting on our legs, we breathe without closing our eyes. We breathe in with our mouths closed and breathe out with our mouths slightly open. We listen to the breath entering and exiting the body, and we try to get into its rhythm. We continue by transferring the rhythm to one of our hands, right or left does not matter, though probably we start with the one we use to write. We observe our breath represented by the hand that, through a movement of alternating releases and contractions, becomes a metaphor of the breathing body. Gradually we experiment also with the other hand, then with both. We widen the rhythm of our breath to our arms, and finally we stand up to transfer the rhythm to our entire bodies that will move like a big hand in which the five limbs— arms, legs, and head—correspond to the five fingers.

## Tension (four minutes)

On our knees, like before, we position our hands over our hearts. We feel the heartbeat and concentrate on the fact that the circulation of blood in our bodies depends on the tension of the heart's muscular mass alternatively increasing and diminishing. It is important to focus on the tension and not on the rhythm of the heartbeat; then, like in the previous exercise, we transfer the tension to one hand, then to both, and finally to the whole body. The structure of the exercise is similar to the previous one. The result is a free movement shaped by our attention to an essentially internal process that depends on breathing, while in the first case the attention is directly on breathing.

## Volume or Weight *(six minutes)*

We start again on our knees, but in this exercise we must be ready to extend the movement more rapidly to the entire body. We begin directly with one of our hands representing our breathing, clenching and unclenching, but quite soon we transform it into the breathing of a little animal, possibly an animal that we have held in our hands before, such as a kitten, a canary, or a mouse. From the rhythm of our breath, we pass to the tension of the heartbeat of the same animal. We repeat this same process with animals of average size, such as a dog, a goat, or a chimpanzee, and finally with large animals, such as a horse, an elephant, or a lion. During this exercise it is important to stress that rhythms and tensions are not necessarily similar in animals of the same size or analogous weight.

## Temperie *(Temper) or Balance (eight minutes)*

The physical representation of any kind of natural or abstract phenomenon implies a different series of relationships between rhythm, tension, and volume, which Costa summarizes by the Italian word *temperie,* from the Latin verb *temperare,* which means to find a suitable proportion or balance of qualities. This exercise looks for such *temperie* within four natural conditions and their variations: water, smoke, fire, and ground. For each one of the representations we rapidly follow the usual process, starting from expressing the condition with one hand, and when the process has been assimilated, starting directly with the whole body. It is advisable to keep to the sequence of the four conditions as indicated above, then, the variations for each condition can follow different patterns:

> *Water:* steam, fog, cloud, rain, snow, ice
>
> *Smoke of a:* cigarette, fireplace, chimney
>
> *Fire of a:* fireplace, lighter, furnace
>
> *Ground:* mud, sand, stone, rock

During this exercise it is very important to clarify that our aim is not to imitate the phenomena, but by tapping into our experiences, feelings, and inclinations, to look for a representation of them by using our hands and body. The idea, just to give an example, is not to represent a generic idea of "fog" but a "fog" that we have experienced, if not physically, by being there, at least visually in a movie, on television, in a picture, or even by reading about it.

## The Tree (six minutes)

In the tree exercise we stress even more that our goal is not to imitate but to represent our interpretations of these natural phenomena. We do not look for a generic tree but for a tree with which we are familiar, of which we have some real experience. This exercise helps the actors to understand how the *temperie* or balance also involves a sensitive dimension that is further enhanced by situating the tree under different atmospheric conditions. Starting with one hand we gradually represent our tree, whether it be an oak, willow, pine, olive, cherry, walnut, etc., with all our body, and then, without interruptions, we represent its condition on a sunny day with a light breeze, at night with a strong wind, during a thunderstorm, under the snow, during a hot and humid day, and so forth. The point is, to give another example, that the very same tree can be the object of different paintings or poems, with each painter or poet offering his or her personal interpretation of that tree. The tree exercise also becomes extremely useful if we point out that not necessarily our feet are the roots and our arms are the branches: in our representation we are free to use our body in all possible and less obvious ways.

## Organic Dramaturgy (twelve minutes)

This final exercise elaborates on the previous ones and introduces what Costa calls *organic dramaturgy,* which is basically the experience of all those variations and contrasts usually defined in theater as conflicts. As a consequence, the exercise focuses our attention on transformations and our ability to move from one *temperie* or balance to another. To do so, we have to rely on our basic observations and knowledge of natural phenomena and animals in order to put them in complex and articulated relations. In the end, this exercise enlightens the inner structure of what, in a text, are complications and developments, crises, denouements, etc. Since the examples of organic dramaturgy are practically endless, we will suggest just a few of them here. Sometimes we can create the representation in pairs or even as a group, but feel free to propose your own. Eventually, if you are working on a specific text, the best solution is to create one or more exercises of organic dramaturgy strictly connected to it.

Examples:

- A spring bursting from a mountain becomes a waterfall, then a torrent, a stream, and finally a river that flows into a sea.
- A match is lit, burns, extinguishes itself, and leaves a trace of smoke.
- A sea wave smashes against a rock.
- A wet sheet hung out in the open air is dried by the wind.
- A fire of green wood is suddenly extinguished by a pot of water.
- A freshly plowed field under a heavy rain becomes an expanse of mud.
- A pot of water on a stove begins to boil.
- Balls of different materials—billiard, heavy rubber, tennis balls—fall on different kinds of surfaces.
- In couples, we present a fight or a courtship between animals of the same kind.

During any organic dramaturgy exercise, we must be intent on showing everything, which means, for example, not only the "wave," but also the "rock covered by water."


## *Note on Voice*

Costa's approach does not look at voice training as something apart from body movement. From the very first exercises the students should be prepared and encouraged to present the mimic activity together with a vocalization of sounds—murmurs, grumbles, whines, cries, syllables, and, progressively, articulated words. A specific session can be devoted just to the mutable aspects of the voice: pitch, volume, timbre or tone, etc.


—GIAN GIACOMO COLLI

## Monologue/Monodrama Projects

This project requires each student to choose an important figure in Italian history or culture (present or past) and to "impersonate" him or her in a monologue or monodrama.[1] Students create the text of their solo performance after researching the character, life, and work of their chosen person. Guidelines, including the selection of appropriate material to incorporate in the script, the choice of props and other useful tools to enhance the performance, etc., are provided.

The scope of the project can easily vary; the exercise can be used in different courses and contexts and be made to serve diverse purposes. For example:

- Students involved in the full production of a stage play could use this exercise in the study of the various characters of the play, writing and delivering original monologues aimed at capturing the essence of each character (as each student sees him or her).

- Students involved in the study of a particular period of literary history or a particular literary genre could be asked to choose, as characters for their monologues, important representatives of that period or genre of literature. The exercise would afford them an unconventional approach to literature within a traditional literature course.

- Teachers of broad Italian civilization courses could use this exercise to make students confront particularly difficult-to-comprehend or harsh historical, social, or political realities, by inhabiting the lives of people who experienced and wrote about those realities.

In the context of the specific theatrical workshop I discussed in Chapter 4, this project fits in the sequence of activities of the last few weeks and can easily be geared to the background research the students have been conducting in order to write or rewrite and perform the pieces to be included in the final recital.

The following are general guidelines for students (here in a dual-language version):

—Scegli un personaggio importante della storia o della cultura italiana, attuale o del passato, che hai incontrato nei tuoi studi (in qualsiasi campo: letteratura, arti figurative, musica, scienze, politica, ecc.).

—Fai un po' di ricerca sul tuo personaggio, se non hai già sufficienti informazioni sulla sua vita e le sue opere, sui tratti della sua personalità, ecc.

—Decidi quali aspetti della vita, del carattere, dell'opera di questa persona pensi siano fondamentali e ritieni di dover includere nel tuo monologo/monodramma e condividere con il pubblico.

—Puoi, anzi devi usare la tua immaginazione: considerando i dati che possiedi, come immagini che sia stata la vita del tuo personaggio? Quali idee, opinioni, emozioni, eventi, ecc. hanno informato la sua vita e la sua attività? O, in alternativa, quali fra le idee, opinioni, sentimenti, ecc. che informano la tua vita credi che questo personaggio condivida con te e possa trasmettere in scena al pubblico?

—Dunque: devi scegliere una figura o personaggio che possa (1) parlare di se stesso/a per mezzo della tua interpretazione della sua vita e della sua opera, oppure (2) diventare un veicolo per esprimere drammaticamente quello che tu pensi sia importante nella vita.

—Tieni presente che il teatro deve avere sia la funzione di educare che quella di divertire. Non essere troppo semplicistico e superficiale, né troppo didattico e pedante. Per esempio, non fornire un lungo elenco di attributi del tuo personaggio o una lista degli eventi occorsigli. Pensa a presentare il tuo personaggio in maniera suggestiva, lasciando che il pubblico deduca da quello che gli fai dire e fare tutte le questioni su cui tu hai riflettuto e vuoi che gli spettatori, a loro volta, riflettano.



—Choose an important figure from Italian history or culture, present or past, whom you have encountered in your studies (the person's work may be in any field: literature, arts, music, science, politics, etc.).

—Conduct some research on the person if you do not have sufficient information on his or her life and work, the traits of his or her personality, etc.

—Decide what aspects of the life, character, and work of this person are important, need to be included in your monologue/monodrama, and shared with the audience.

—You may, in fact you must, use your imagination. Given the data you have collected, how do you imagine the life of this person to have been? What ideas, opinions, feelings, events, etc. informed his or her life and work? Or, alternatively, what ideas, emotions, attitudes, and opinions do you feel this person shares with you, and—as a stage character—could convey to your audience?

—So, you must choose a figure/character capable of (1) talking about himself or herself through your own interpretation of his or her life and work, or (2) becoming a dramatic vehicle for expressing what you believe is important in life.

—Keep in mind that theater should both educate and entertain. Do not be too simplistic and superficial, nor too didactic and pedantic. For example, avoid making a long list of your character's attributes or of the events that occurred in his or her life. Think of presenting your figure in a suggestive way, letting the audience deduce all the issues upon which you have reflected and that you want them to consider from what you make your character say and do.

The first draft of this assignment is "tested" for efficacy in the classroom; that is, each student, closely following the guidelines provided above (modified according to the focus and needs of the course), chooses a character to interpret and drafts the text of a monologue to perform in front of the class. The draft is then submitted to the instructor, who comments upon it and recommends revisions on the basis of the following points:

- *Accuracy:* Are there any errors in grammar and syntax that obscure meaning?

- *Vocabulary:* Is the vocabulary used adequate to the task? Is the choice of words precise? Should more complex, richer words be used? Is the tone of the speech appropriate to the character and the aspects of his or her life and work that have been selected for the presentation? Or is the choice too limited and the usage bad or inadequate?

- *Background preparation:* How in-depth was the research conducted about the chosen figure and his or her life and work? Was it sufficient to sustain a highly meaningful and/or comprehensive presentation of such a figure?

- *Content and interest:* Is the text of the presentation sufficiently interesting, informative, and substantive? Does it include excellent, good, or just adequate material? Important, useful, or irrelevant details?

- *Organization:* How well or poorly could the text, as conceived and organized, serve the in-class performance? Could the audience follow it? Could the audience understand and react in a positive way? Are there/should there be a clear introduction and a conclusion? Do the lines of the text make for a natural or unnatural pace?

- *Clarity and scope:* Were all aspects of the character's life, work, and personality selected by the student relevant? Did they form a truly interesting, significant portrayal of the figure in question? Is there anything that needs clarification, that leads to misunderstanding, or that distorts the reality of the person and his or her life and work?

— FRANCESCA SAVOIA

## Notes

1. In the fall of 2004, at the Seventh Annual Symposium of Theater in Academe (Washington and Lee University, 28–30 October 2004), Nancy Nanney, chair of the humanities division at West Virginia University at Parkesburg and a professor of drama, made a presentation on the following topic: "Encountering International Cultures through Monodramas." The idea of designing a project modeled after the one Dr. Nanney described in her conference paper came to me at that time, and I am forever indebted to her.

## English Translations and Surtitles for the Public Performance: Rationale and Practicalities

One might wonder whether preparing English translations and surtitles for a play performed in Italian by foreign language students in an academic environment is necessary. At first glance, there seem to be several reasons to avoid this enterprise. The translation of a text is a complex and time-consuming endeavor for both students and the instructor. It imposes a painstaking work of editing and line-by-line comparison between the original and its rendition in English. Although the translation could be rendered as a communicative and/or collaborative assignment, the goal is the production of an English text. The focus on English required by translating and surtitling may seem contradictory and even counterproductive in theater performance–based courses, in which speaking the second language is both a central goal and a decisive tool for language enhancement. And, after all, surtitles in English would allow only an audience of non-Italian speakers to enjoy the performance. However, despite these concerns, translating and surtitling a full play into English may be tremendously fruitful and rewarding. The development of surtitles fosters the comprehension, analysis, and enactment of the play; reinforces learners' linguistic skills; helps develop their cross-cultural competence; boosts their motivation; and, more generally, promotes an interest in and appreciation for Italian theater within and beyond the Italian programs.

The practical motivations for translating and surtitling a play should not be overlooked. Making an Italian language production comprehensible to audiences composed of both speakers and non-speakers of Italian can serve as an effective tool for advertising the Italian program. The reception of the five productions I directed at the University of Pennsylvania and Middlebury College—all surtitled in English for non-Italian speakers—was enthusiastic and the number of spectators (from 100 to 150) always exceeded our expectations. This positive feedback made the Italian program particularly popular within the community, reaching students not previously interested in Italian language and culture. Furthermore, this response increased Italian students' willingness to further their study of Italian, developed their sense of belonging to a group, and encouraged some of them to declare their major or minor in Italian.

The complex process of translating and surtitling a text can also enhance students' language learning and cultural enrichment. First of all, an accurate translation made by students ensures that they understand the play in all its nuances, which leads to their being more effective in performing it. Translating a text could seem an obvious and simple first step for a performance-based course, but may become, in fact, a challenging task for beginning students or for those who are working with more linguistically or culturally complex texts. At the advanced level, the in-depth analysis required by translation enables learners to thoroughly explore and interpret the idiomatic, technical, and literary vocabulary the playwright chose. The attempt to render the richness of the original in English may considerably reinforce learners' linguistic competencies.

Translating stage directions also contributes to the students' understanding of the text. Since the student translators are usually part of the crew, translating the stage directions helps them to better discern all the details of the mise-en-scène and enriches their vocabulary with many technical terms. Stage directions not only serve as indications for scenery, but they also connect the dialogues and explain the characters' behavior and are therefore necessary for producing a coherent translation.

The translation of a theatrical text, which has been written not to be read but to be performed, does not exhaust its function in the linguistic and cognitive areas. The student translators should consider the interactive, that is, semiotic quality of the performance and seek to elicit in the English-speaking audience the same emotional reaction as from a public of native speakers. In order to pursue this objective, they need to make substantial changes to the play because certain cultural references or performance details aimed at an audience of native speakers might prove to be incomprehensible to spectators who understand the Italian language but are not immersed in its culture. Such a work of adaptation provides learners with a broad exposure to the sociocultural dimension of language and may significantly help develop their cross-cultural competence.

An example from Luigi Pirandello's *Sei personaggi* may clarify this process. Wishing to adhere to Pirandello's choice of breaking the "fourth wall" from the opening scene, students began their adaptation of the play with the stagehand and the stage manager discussing in English the preparation of the surtitles. Once the stagehand sets up the screen for surtitles and turns the projector on, the two naturally switch to Italian and the surtitles appear on the screen. Then, two actors enter the scene discussing the issue of double casting until the teacher/director intrudes, telling them to share the same role and take turns acting out their parts. By means of this opening scene the actors inform the audience about important organizational features (surtitling and double casting) and, at the same time, enact Pirandello's metatheatrical poetic, breaking the "fourth wall" and extending the theatrical discourse to the stage and the public. If, instead, the students had followed Pirandello's original version, the opening scene would have featured a dialogue in Italian about scenery and scheduling, which would have worked perfectly well to introduce the audience to the novelty of the metatheatrical design of the play but would not have highlighted the unique features of this particular production.

Overall, translating and surtitling a play are extremely useful tasks, both from a practical perspective and as learning practices. They require, nonetheless, a rigorous organization. The following sections provide suggestions for successfully arranging and coordinating the work of translation, converting the translation to surtitles, and handling the surtitles during the production.

## *Translating the Original: Work Distribution and Coordination*

Although the actual starting time and duration of the work of translation may vary depending on the overall organization of the course, students, the instructor, and assistants (if any) should begin to plan the organization and coordination of the whole enterprise far in advance of the performance of the play. The first step is to decide on the distribution of the translation assignments. There are at least three options, based on the number of students, the complexity of the text, and the length of the main parts:

1. *Each student-actor in charge of his or her part.* In the case of texts that are not particularly long or complex, such as Achille Campanile's plays or Dario Fo's shortest or earliest works, each student may translate a part of the play, which will usually coincide with his or her role. This is the simplest choice in terms of organization but a difficult one with regard to revision and copyediting, phases that require a great deal of coordination. In order to avoid having a huge amount of work bounce back on the instructor, it is recommended that students work in pairs and be responsible for each other's part.

2. *A group of students in charge of the whole translation.* When the texts are more challenging and/or longer, for example, plays by Carlo Goldoni, Pirandello, Dacia Maraini, and some by Fo, the instructor should carefully balance the amount of work assigned to each student. The actors playing the main parts should be exempted from translation assignments, and a group selected from those who play secondary roles should be in charge of the entire translation. However, the instructor should be cautious that the least proficient students, who usually play the smallest roles, are not in charge of the challenging work of translation by themselves. This issue may be overcome by splitting the translators into smaller groups and assigning an assistant or a more advanced student to coordinate each team. This model is normally more difficult to organize but ensures the consistency of the format and a great deal of collaboration among students.

3. *A group of students in charge of the translation with some volunteer collaborators.* Some student-actors performing the main roles may be willing to translate (selections from) their own parts because they feel that translating helps them to fully assimilate and memorize their roles, particularly in the case of long monologues. This solution is not easy to coordinate because in performance-based courses the main actors are likely to overdo it in each aspect of the play, while the others tend to feel their contributions are subsidiary and easily remain on the side. For this reason, the main actors should be free to join the translators but should not be responsible for the same amount of translation as the others. They should translate only brief excerpts of their parts and collaborate in revising the rest.

In any of the three combinations listed above, we suggest that the instructor split the class into small groups and ask those students who are particularly proficient in Italian, more familiar with literary analysis, or knowledgeable in linguistics to coordinate the work of one or two groups, provided that these individuals are not main actors as well. They will collect and revise the translations and pass them on to the assistants and/or instructor, who will then return the pieces to the translators with requests and suggestions for correction. The student coordinators will perform a second revision of the corrected translations and will return this second version to the assistants and/or instructor. If no additional work is needed, the coordinators will collate all the translations and will do the necessary changes to standardize the format.

The instructor should make every effort to make the translators understand the importance of their task. To this end we recommend that during the work of translation, and especially after the first revision, instructor and assistants meet groups and coordinators to briefly discuss relevant topics or translation issues. These meetings may be held during rehearsals, when the translators are usually less busy than the other students. After the meetings each group may continue the discussion separately with their coordinators.

## From Translation to Surtitles

As soon as the translators have finished their work, a small group of three or four students will prepare the surtitles in the form of a PowerPoint presentation to be projected on a screen during the performance. The following outline provides directions to successfully carry out this project.

1. *Get the equipment.* In order to project the surtitles, the following equipment is needed:

   a. A laptop computer, from which to run the PowerPoint presentation. If possible, the same laptop should be used for both the rehearsals and the final performance. Using a different, unknown laptop during the final production is never recommended because unforeseen problems of compatibility often surface at the last minute.

   b. An LCD projector, through which to project the surtitles on a screen. Nowadays many rooms are "smart," that is, they are provided with the most advanced technological equipment, but this is not always the case with the rooms, lounges, and small- or medium-sized theaters that are normally used for student productions. If the production takes place in a smart room, a screen and an LCD projector will already be incorporated into the system and directly connected. If the play is performed in a more traditional room, both the screen (even an old-fashioned model will be perfect) and the LCD projector may be borrowed from media services. In this case, a technician will have to connect all the devices.

2. *Streamline the translation.* The translation of the text will need some additional touches to be ready for surtitles. Students need to eliminate the stage directions, which should not appear in the surtitles. They will also need to condense or simplify sentences that are too long or intricate, which could be hard to read on the screen during the performance.

3. *Create the slide template.* Designing a slide template will allow students to easily enter text, which will be automatically formatted on each slide. In making their decision, students should keep in mind several practical details, such as lighting, distance of the public, presence and movements of the actors, and height and position of cumbersome items on the stage. The following suggestions are particularly useful for creating a slide template:

   a. *Color layout:* Fancy background and extravagant nuances are distracting and should always be avoided in surtitles. Black backgrounds and white characters are the most (if not the only) visible layouts in dark environments.

   b. *Font:* The font should be plain, such as Times New Roman 30-point type, which will be readable even for audience members sitting far away. Again, readability is the most important quality for surtitles; decoration can be counterproductive. Students should understand that the objective of the surtitles is not to excite the spectators with special effects but to allow them to read with the slightest effort possible.

   c. *Amount of text:* The text should fill no more than one-third of each slide, possibly less. This means that each slide should include no more than four or five lines. If there is more text, the actors' bodies or shadows and other items positioned on the stage can cover the words and make reading difficult. Moreover, the public might feel overwhelmed by the reading task and lose contact with the scene. On the other hand, in order for the spectators to have time to read all the surtitles while watching the scene, it is important that the slides do not run too fast and display a fair amount of text on each one. For these reasons, one- or two-line slides should be avoided, except in the case of small pauses, changes of scene, or the arrival of new characters on the stage.

Here is an excerpt from the surtitles created for the scene of Pirandello's *Sei personaggi* discussed above. Note the black and white, plain layout, the absence of stage directions, and the combination of shorter and longer texts.

MIKE: Okay, enough, you're exaggerating! From the beginning of this Italian Play Production course you've been trying to get all the most important parts. But my dear primadonna, that part's mine, is that clear?
NICOLETTA: Okay, guys, we can start rehearsals.

4. *Test the surtitles.* Students should test the readability and pace of the slides during rehearsals. This step will help avoid problems in the final performance. In fact, too fast a pace or overly busy slides can obstruct or delay the audience's ability to read the translation and eventually make them feel tired. A fair speed in changing the slides is also easier to handle for the students who will have to manage it during the actual production.

5. *Project the surtitles.* Since they know the translation and the surtitling system better than their fellow students, the students who have authored the translations and created the surtitles should manage the surtitles during the performance. This task requires a great deal of concentration and readiness to face technical or acting problems. The slides must synchronize with the student-actors' performances and follow not only their pace, but also their unforeseen pauses, oversights, and omissions. Although inadvertently, actors may even skip an entire scene (it happened in one of our productions!), and the surtitles must catch up with their performance. Therefore, in order to maintain a high level of concentration throughout the entire performance, students should take turns running the surtitles.

Overall, if the team of translators, assistants, and the instructor has coordinated the work in an effective fashion, then the result will be extremely rewarding. All the spectators will be able to grasp even the most subtle nuances: the non-Italian speakers, who need the translation in order to understand the play, as well as the Italian speakers, who, in certain cases, will find the translation helpful. After the first five or ten minutes, both Italian and non-Italian speakers will have grown accustomed to reading the surtitles while watching the play. Naturally, some minor discrepancies between the two audiences' reactions to comic situations may signal the presence of the surtitles; for example, the non-Italian speakers will laugh only after they have finished reading the lines, while the Italian speakers will burst into laughter some seconds earlier.

The PowerPoint presentation created for the surtitles may also offer an opportunity to integrate the final performance with pictures and video clips, which are easily embedded in the slides using the many possibilities offered by today's technology. In the team of translators there is usually a computer enthusiast who will help to set up these extra features.

Finally, and most important, the translators will accomplish two crucial results through their work in the class: they will concretely enhance their language skills and perceive their role as central in the final production, even if they have been assigned secondary acting roles. Therefore, though it may seem only an ancillary undertaking, the task of translating and surtitling a play may contribute to accomplishing the central goals of a student-centered pedagogy in teaching a foreign language.

—NICOLETTA MARINI-MAIO

## "It's Showtime!" A Concise Guide to Italian Theater Production for New Directors

### *Getting Started*

#### SECURING A LOCATION AND DATE

The first step in organizing a foreign language theater production is to secure a venue and establish performance dates and times. Since most theatrical spaces have a constant flow of productions throughout the course of a semester, it is relatively rare to find a theater that will allow you to rehearse there from day one. Usually, you rehearse a show in any space available (in a classroom, for example) and move into the theater one week before opening night.

Start your search as early as possible, since various groups tend to book up theatrical spaces surprisingly quickly. Though it is possible to have a last-minute stroke of luck, making initial inquiries early on—even up to a year before the performance—will ensure that you have the most available options. Seek information on all theatrical spaces on your campus, including theaters, auditoriums, classrooms, coffeehouses, and lounges. Ask your students whether they can recall any unusual locations in which they have seen shows performed. Contact student theatrical groups and the school's theater department for suggestions.

Here are some important questions to ask:

- *Is there a cost?* Some theaters might charge you for use of the space for your entire technical week (usually called *tech week*—the week before the production) and performance nights.

- *Are we qualified to use the venue?* Some spaces are available only to academic classes or only to student-run clubs and organizations. If you are running your program for credit, you may have access to more (or possibly fewer) choices in theaters.

- *Will we have full control of the space for the entire week before our performances?* The Notre Dame Italian Theater Company once put on a production in the university's library auditorium, where we had to dismantle the set each night to allow for daytime activities. Our tech week was even punctuated by a few evening lectures that had already been scheduled in the space. Interruptions like these add unnecessary confusion and stress to a week that is already, by its nature, the busiest and most trying week of the whole process.

- *Are our preferred dates available?* You may have to be flexible in choosing dates, but do not schedule a performance too close to midterm or final exams, as you will have a stressed cast and crew and likely a very small audience. Likewise, try to avoid performing just before a holiday or vacation, as students often plan to travel a few days early.

- *Is there a backstage area?* Most theaters will have a backstage area in which actors can wait for their entrances. Props and set pieces are kept here, and any quick costume changes also take place backstage rather than in the dressing rooms. If a space that does not have a backstage area seems promising in other ways, visit it anyway; you may find that there are doors that lead to a hallway that would serve the same purpose. Make sure you have the permission of the building staff for use of spaces such as hallways, closets, or anterooms.

- *Is there a dressing room?* While not absolutely essential, it is very convenient to have dressing rooms that you can lock when they are not in use. Dressing rooms let you leave costumes and makeup neat and organized from one rehearsal or performance to the next. It is far less stressful for actors as well as for the costume designer, and having dressing rooms also reduces the chance that items will get lost.

- *What are the lighting features of the space?* A lecture hall or auditorium will often have fixed lights that are limited to "on," "off," and "slow dim." If this is the case, and you want special lighting effects, you may need to rent lights. If you do find a traditional theater, ask around in language classes to find a student who has experience with theatrical lighting. If no language students are qualified, ask the theater department for a list of students who have completed or are currently enrolled in a lighting design class. Many students are glad for the opportunity to acquire additional experience with designing and running lights for a show. Even if this concession breaks the total-immersion rule, the element of excitement and professionalism that well-orchestrated lighting adds is significant, and in any case, the lighting designer does not need to have significant verbal exchanges with the cast.

- *Is there a sound system?* Many university spaces have microphones and the ability to play CDs or DVDs. Even without a sound system, however, it is easy to bring portable CD players into any space for your audio needs. And in the absence of microphones, actors can learn to project their voices.

FUNDING

You can put together a wonderful production on a limited budget, but more money obviously gives you more flexibility and more possibilities. Look into grants from local and national organizations well in advance. You might also consider asking for donations from student groups, as well as from local shops, restaurants, and bakeries in exchange for a full-, half-, or quarter-page advertisement in your program.

Planning fund-raising events such as cooking classes, bake sales, movie nights, or music concerts—all with an Italian theme—is a fantastic way to target your school's foreign language community while providing a little advance promotion for the show. Similarly, you could design an Italian T-shirt incorporating the school's name; this could be a big seller among students enrolled in language courses. Not only do T-shirt sales make money for the show, they promote the department itself.

TEXT SELECTION

Text selection is one of your most important tasks as director (see also "Text Selection: A Few Criteria," above). Here are some considerations:

- *Language.* Is the language accessible for participants and audience members? Does it contain colorful and up-to-date expressions and vocabulary words that participants will enjoy incorporating into their everyday speech? If the play is written in dialect or in an antiquated version of Italian, you may want to consider whether at the end of the experience participants will feel more confident with using modern Italian, in addition to gaining cultural knowledge and familiarity with a famous text, since students often find the sharpening of their growing language skills to be the most fulfilling aspect of participation. You may be able to find "Italianized" versions of some dialect plays, or you may consider working with students to "translate" dialect into Italian. Similarly, for texts that use an antiquated Italian, you might have students use their creativity to script a modern-day version of the play. A first-time director would be well-advised to avoid the process of rescripting by selecting a modern text in standard Italian.

- *Scope.* Are the scenic requirements within the realm of the possible given your budgetary restrictions? If not, are there ways you can improvise without compromising the integrity of the piece? Think of the theatrical space in which the play will take place; you do not need an absolutely clear picture of exactly how the set and audience will look, but you must be comfortable with the idea of producing the play within the space. Lastly, is the length appropriate for your actors given their limited expertise with the language? Remember that you can always cut some lines.

- *Casting.* How big is the cast? Are the roles relatively balanced, and if not, do you anticipate finding students linguistically strong enough to carry the burdens of a demanding leading role? If you would like to have some actors play more than one part, think about which roles might work well for double casting. Make sure actors will have enough time to change their costumes between appearances onstage.

- *Tone.* Comedies tend to work well in the context of foreign language productions. Not only do the cast and crew members enjoy finding ways to render their performance more comical, but audiences unfamiliar with the language tend to easily grasp slapstick and physical humor.

- *Rights.* Are the rights accessible? Does the cost of the rights fit in your budget?

ENROLLMENT CONSIDERATIONS

Once you have chosen your text, the next potentially challenging task you will face is selecting your cast and design staff. It is unlikely that the number of students interested in the course will correspond exactly to your needs. Too few participants will usually not pose insurmountable difficulties, as students can always play multiple roles or take on both design and acting responsibilities. The opposite situation—having too many students for the available roles—often turns out to be more of a challenge for the director of a foreign language production. You may want to limit enrollment by instituting a "first come first served" policy or by using auditions to thin out the group. If you would like to involve as many students as possible, here are a few suggestions on how to handle larger groups.

*Double Casting.* Taking one show and producing it with two different groups of students can be an effective way of reaching the linguistic and social goals inherent in the foreign language theater workshop experience. It will require extra organization and patience on your part, however. The easiest way for you as the director to accomplish this task is to require that all students attend all rehearsals, rather than rehearsing with Group A separately from Group B. That way you can concentrate on one cast if you choose, or you may decide to switch back and forth, repeating scenes first with one group and then with the other. There are many benefits to this strategy.

1. In comparing their own interpretation of the text with that of the other cast and crew, students come to understand the dynamic between written and performed theater. They see in an immediate way how the same script can be performed in sometimes strik-

ingly different manners depending on the artistic choices of the director, performers, and designers.

2. Actors internalize their lines both actively during their own rehearsals and passively as they watch the rehearsals of the other group. Also, as actors hear their own lines spoken by their counterparts in the other cast, differences in memorization or pronunciation will jump out at them, enabling the actors to correct any errors that had begun to fossilize in their own performance.

3. When an actor is absent, you can facilitate the rehearsal by substituting the corresponding actor from the other group.

4. For extra practice with lines, you can pair up corresponding actors from the two groups. For example, the actor who plays Giuseppe in Group A can practice reading with the Giuseppe from Group B. One student reads from the script, taking the part of any other character in the scene, while the other tries to accurately execute the lines of his own character, Giuseppe. As they alternate reading the other parts and correcting each other, they will not only learn their own lines, but get a better sense of how the lines of the other characters affect their responses.

5. Students form close bonds with the members in their own group but also become a supportive presence for the students in the other cast and crew, particularly during performances.

*Multiple Shows.* In 2003 at the University of Notre Dame, the Italian Theater Company put on two different shows on the same night, *I cadaveri si spediscono e le donne si spogliano* by Dario Fo and *Il ciambellone* by Achille Campanile. Here are some of my thoughts and suggestions based on what we learned from the experience.

- The two one-act plays that we produced were relatively lengthy, which impeded attempts to provide adequate rehearsal time for both groups. It might have been better to have had an "Evening of One-Acts" with a greater number of shorter texts, allowing students to appear in more than one play where feasible.

- Organization is the key to juggling multiple productions. Make sure each show has a separate stage manager, students whom you know to be responsible and willing to take initiative. The stage manager can keep an eye on the progress of costumes and sets, organize supplemental rehearsals when necessary, and facilitate communication between you, the designers, and the cast.

- When you double cast one show (as discussed above), requiring students to attend all rehearsals is useful and logical. But if you are producing two or more shows, it is not necessary (and can be problematic) to request participants' presence at rehearsals for shows in which they are not involved.

- Do, however, require students to read the script for all the shows. Organize periodic "viewing nights" when all participants sit in on a rehearsal for one show (perhaps three to four viewing nights per cast over the course of the rehearsal period). This allows the viewers to understand the text better, contribute their suggestions and comments, and identify areas that are linguistically difficult enough to warrant more attention to physical movement and gesture. In essence, they are a "practice" or "test" audience. There are also benefits for the rehearsing cast; the chance to practice performing in front of others is a good way to decrease stage jitters and also gives actors a better sense of how the timing of their lines and movements will be received by a live audience.

*Large-Cast Shows.* The fear with larger cast shows tends to be that some students' roles will be so small that they will not gain much from the experience. We have found that this is not necessarily the case. When we chose a production with a very large cast at the University of Notre Dame in 2005 (*Il campionato di calcio ovvero fare l'amore non è peccato* by Campanile), even students with smaller roles enjoyed the project and gained much from participating in warm-up exercises and repeatedly viewing the play and coming to understand its subtleties at each rehearsal. Since we insist on a total-immersion environment, they also benefited from communicating in Italian with other cast and crew members.

However, holding everyone's attention is no small feat and involves a large amount of creativity and persistence. Therefore, it is probably best to take on the challenges of a large-cast show only after having started out with a few smaller productions. A few shows' worth of experience will familiarize you with the process and give you the background and confidence you need to better manage a large cast. Here are some suggestions for when you do feel ready to take on a big group of participants.

- Be insistent about attendance and punctuality. Students will be tempted to think that their absence will go unfelt in a large group, but their presence is important for their own progress and for that of the group as a whole. Have your stage managers take attendance and phone students who are not there on time, leaving urgent-sounding messages on their voicemail.

- Make a conscious and consistent effort to involve students with small roles to the greatest extent possible every single day. After you rehearse scenes, ask for their impressions and suggestions. Make all students aware that watching a rehearsal is not a passive activity and that you will be expecting them to contribute frequently to discussions.

- Make sure your stage manager is ready to be heavily involved in working with the design team to stay on task and organized through every step of the process. This can be particularly important for the costume designer because the greater the number of actors and costume changes, the greater the risk of unexpected glitches.

- Make sure that the stage manager and designers are absolutely committed to using the target language in all of their communication, despite how difficult it will be at times. While actors do much of their work in front of your watchful eyes, designers complete many of their tasks together on their own time, and thus the temptation to slip into their native language is much greater.

## Auditioning

It is useful to hold auditions before the beginning of the enrollment period for the upcoming semester's courses so that students can appropriately plan their schedules. Auditions may be used to reduce course enrollment numbers if interest is too high or simply to properly place students in design and acting roles. What does an audition entail and what does a director look for in an auditioning student?

### HANDOUTS AND PAPERWORK

First and foremost, an audition is meant to present your expectations to the student. Provide all the information necessary about the course itself: show dates, rough rehearsal schedule, written requirements (essays, presentations, diaries), and your policy on attendance and punctuality. (See Appendix A for an example.) Be as clear and as thorough as possible. You do not want students to drop out of the course later in the semester because they did not have all of the information necessary to make an informed decision at the outset.

Next, you will need information from students: their preferred role in the production, their schedules, conflicts, contact information, and so forth. (See Appendix B.) They should fill out the information and then return the sheet to you so that you can take notes as you watch them audition.

Lastly, the students need to have some idea of the background of the play and the characters in order to have an effective audition. If you have already chosen a stage manager (it is extremely helpful to choose one before the audition process), he or she can write a brief summary of the play (or of the audition scenes only, if preferred) and the characters. If you have not yet selected your stage manager, you will have to write these yourself.

ORGANIZATION OF AUDITIONS

You may choose to schedule auditions in advance so you can see small groups of students at a time without having to make anyone wait. This can be accomplished by creating a sign-up website or by leaving a list in a central location such as the school's Department of Foreign Languages. Students, however, often prefer "drop-in" auditions, which afford them more flexibility. If you are having drop-in auditions, your stage manager can coordinate the distribution of materials and periodically send groups who have finished the paperwork to the audition room.

RUNNING THE AUDITION

With each group of auditioning students, start out with a brief warm-up exercise to ease any tension. Even though you have distributed a written summary, take a few minutes to explain the play and the specific scene or scenes chosen for the audition. Give ample time for students to read the selection and encourage them to ask questions. Finally, have them perform the scene, using the photocopied excerpt that you distributed.

Remember that your most important task during this stage of the experience is to identify those students who have the potential to be convincing and interesting actors. Look for creativity, willingness to take risks, and the ability to try different approaches to a scene. Of course, the students' linguistic capability is important, particularly for the roles that require the memorization of many lines. However, remember that problems of cadence, pronunciation, and even comprehension should not necessarily keep you from casting a student.

These trouble spots are sometimes more easily addressed than acting-related problems such as a lack of ability to experiment and vary one's interpretation of a role.

Always let each student act the scene or scenes at least twice, and give them specific suggestions in between. This coaching is of fundamental importance because it lets you see how well they respond to instruction, and you will be able to better judge their potential as actors. For instance, if you ask for "angrier" and a student gives the exact same interpretation of the scene as before, you might consider casting that student in a smaller role or using him or her as a designer.

If you feel that a performance was lifeless or awkward because the student did not understand the sense of the scene, explain it again, answer any questions he or she may have, and ask for a second performance. It can be difficult to spot potential when a student's comprehension of the language itself can get in the way of acting ability, but sometimes a simple explanation will yield a marked improvement in the audition.

When the auditions are over, discuss your impressions with your stage manager. If you are undecided over a few roles, you can hold a callback audition, asking students under consideration to return for another reading. Alternatively, you can post a general cast list, without assigning specific roles, and decide later during the first few rehearsals.

## The Rehearsal Process: A General Overview

In general, the rehearsal period for a foreign language production can be broken up into the four stages below. Of course, this format is by no means the only way to structure the rehearsal process, and each director will find his or her own methods for running rehearsals. The suggestions listed here are merely meant to provide a starting point for new directors.

*Stage 1 (the first few rehearsals): First read-through and general comprehension.* As many of the participants will not entirely understand the play by reading it through on their own, this step is crucial. You will need to spend the first few rehearsals simply reading through the text with the entire cast and crew. Cast and crew may remain seated for the read-through, or you may ask that readers stand up and attempt some rudimentary movements and gestures.

This is a good opportunity to allow stage managers, designers, and minor characters to do the bulk of the reading, since for most of the rest of the process, the actors themselves will be reading their own lines. Since students tend to skip stage directions and, in doing so, often miss some of the most important keys to comprehension, assign one person to read all stage directions.

As you read through the script, stop frequently to discuss the play's setting, explore the personalities and motivations of the characters, and check students' comprehension of the plot. Provide ample opportunity for questions. Be careful, however, not to be too detailed. Your goal in the read-through stage of the process is to introduce the key facts of the play so that students have a clear framework for in-depth work with the script in later rehearsals. They will come to understand the subtleties later on, and in fact the most exhilarating aspect of the whole experience is seeing students' flashes of comprehension as they hit on the perfect interpretation of a line, and their pride as, in doing so, they truly make it their own.

*Stage 2 (roughly one-third to one-half the rehearsal process): Addition of blocking (movement) while actors are reading from script.* After spending a few days reading the script one time through, have actors begin to read their parts while adding movements. At the beginning, this is often a very loose, experimental process, particularly since your set designer will still be determining the setup of the acting area. You may choose to go through scenes relatively quickly, to provide a general sense of the flow of the piece. Alternatively, you may elect to proceed slowly, repeating each scene a few times before moving on to the next. In either case, make sure participants begin to focus on using their bodies and facial expressions to convey meaning, communicate emotion, and engage audience members. Encourage students to ask questions if the meaning of certain words or passages is unclear.

One technique that has proved useful in the initial stages of rehearsals is simultaneous blocking work. Before trying simultaneous blocking, make sure that students have blocked at least one scene under your guidance so that they understand how to work through a scene. Divide the cast and crew into small groups, giving each a set amount of time to work on a particular scene in a sequence of consecutive scenes (for example, group A does scene 3; group B, scene 4; and group C, scene 5). Next, one at a time, the groups perform the scenes for the rest of the class, which responds with comments and suggestions. When using this technique, actors should be playing their own parts, but they cannot, of course, be in multiple places at once. When a character appears in more than one scene, you can assign a designer or stage manager to step into the role. Simultaneous blocking is a good way to speed along the initial blocking process while intimately involving as many people as possible.

As soon as you and your set designer have a clear idea of the placement of entranceways, exits, and significant set pieces, your blocking will become more precise and more consistent. Have your stage manager take blocking notes in the margins of his or her script, noting any changes or adjustments made from one rehearsal to the next.

*Stage 3 (one-half to two-thirds of the rehearsal process): Off-book perfection of lines.* Actors are "off book" when they have their lines more or less memorized. It is a major turning point in the rehearsal process, as it will allow actors to truly get into character and act freely with their bodies and hands without the hindrance of holding a script. This will not happen immediately, however; at first, you will see a major step back because all the emotion and energy that the actors had begun to add in past weeks will vanish with the sheer force of concentration needed to memorize their lines. The off-book phase will at first require much patience and lots of prompting of lines on the part of your stage manager, but soon students' focus will shift from the words of the lines themselves to their actual message and their character's relationship with the other characters in the play. They will make great strides as they perfect their blocking and gestures and delve further into the complexities of the piece.

At the beginning of this stage, you will be running only a few scenes at a time. Actors will be deep into emotions and delivery and precise blocking, and thus the beginning of the off-book stage lends itself to spending a significant amount of time with each scene, repeating and repeating it before moving on to the next. At the tail end of the off-book phase, you are working toward putting it all back together into one cohesive play, and thus you will start to have rehearsals that encompass more and more scenes without stopping to repeat them. Eventually you will be able to rehearse the entire first half or the second half, and finally, the whole show.

*Stage 4 (the final week): Tech week.* Tech week refers to the week before the production, when you will move into the theater space where the show will take place. The first day or two will be devoted to setting up and perfecting lighting and sound cues. These cue-to-cue rehearsals, run by the stage manager, are more for the technical staff than for the actors. Essentially, you start with "house lights down," then "lights up," and skip ahead to the next time there is a light or sound cue. The stage manager tells the actors to start a few lines before the cue (*"Ragazzi, cominciate da 'Oddio, siamo persi!'"*), then the operator of the lights or sound practices the cue, and then the stage manager tells the actors to stop and either go back to that same cue or, if everyone is satisfied with the cue's timing, proceed to the next. Perfecting a cue may take a few tries, but it is essential that the operators of the light and sound systems are comfortable with their tasks. A cue-to-cue rehearsal requires a good deal of patience on the part of the actors, and it is best to explain the process ahead of time. Don't forget to start with an upbeat warm-up activity.

One cue-to-cue rehearsal is often sufficient, and the next step is the dress rehearsal. Actors will rehearse with all costumes and props, with set and costume designers taking note of anything that they need to change, fix, or adjust. You will spend the last few rehearsals under show conditions, without any stops at all, running the show from start to finish just as it will be during performances, including the final bow. Do not forget to leave some time after one of the dress rehearsals for photos. Though everyone will be tired, they will later be glad for pictures of the cast and crew's favorite scenes and shots of their costumes and sets.

## *The Rehearsal Schedule*

### OVERVIEW OF SCHEDULING

Before starting on a schedule, make sure you have a complete list of any foreseeable scheduling conflicts that your cast might have. Inevitably, students have to be away for track meets, weddings, job interviews, choir concerts, etc. Though one or two missed rehearsals do not seem significant to the individual actor, you as the director will find yourself extremely frustrated when all of these conflicts add up, and you seem to go for weeks without having all of the actors needed at the rehearsal. In sum, let the students know that it is imperative that they take a careful look at their calendars and identify all potential conflicts at the outset of the process.

Next, sit down with your stage manager, a big calendar, and your actors' conflict sheets and begin planning. Start by working backwards from tech week and set an "off-book" date. How many rehearsals before tech week do you want students to be working without their scripts? Three to four weeks before tech week is a good guide; however, this will depend on the frequency and length of your rehearsals. You should aim to have a total of a little more than a third of the rehearsal process be off book.

While it is certainly possible to take things day by day—determining which scenes to rehearse as you are going along—the inexperienced director may feel more comfortable with a relatively detailed plan of action. A rehearsal schedule that specifies exactly which scenes you will rehearse on which days will also make it easier for the actors and design staff to stay on top of their responsibilities. Creating this type of schedule can be one of the most time- and labor-intensive steps of directing a play, but you may find the organization extremely useful.

FRENCH SCENES

In order to establish a detailed rehearsal calendar, it is useful to first break down the show into what are referred to in the world of theater as *French scenes*. The creation of a French scene is simple: whenever a character enters or exits, this marks the close of one French scene and the beginning of the next. Note that these will not necessarily correspond to the scene breaks delineated by the author.

Why is this helpful? Imagine a scene that starts out with two characters. After a bit of conversation, a third enters. They converse a while, then one of the original two leaves. After a few more minutes of conversation, the third person leaves and a fourth person enters. If you were to look at only the scene itself, you would see:

Scene 1: Characters A, B, C, D

However, if you subdivide the scene into French scenes based on characters' entrances and exits, it looks like this:

Scene 1: Characters A, B

Scene 2: Characters A, B, C

Scene 3: Characters B, C

Scene 4: Characters B, D

Now, imagine you are trying to put together an efficient rehearsal schedule. Actor A cannot make rehearsals on Wednesdays? No problem.

You have an easily referenced list and can simply avoid scheduling French scenes 1 and 2 on Wednesdays. Actor D will be out of town for a week? You know to schedule rehearsal of French scenes 1 through 3 during that week. Without French scenes, all of these would be classified as scene 1, but the French scene breakdown allows you to set the rehearsal schedule any way you choose. You can stray from chronological order, focusing, for example, on the four French scenes scattered throughout the course of the play that involve only characters A, B, and C together.

Make a chart of your French scenes, noting page numbers, actors, and characters. For your own reference, you may want to write down the total rehearsal time necessary for each scene. Also, give each a title so you can easily remember the action that takes place. Here is an example of the beginning of a French scene chart.

| Scena | Pagine | Tempo | Azione | Attori | Personaggi |
|---|---|---|---|---|---|
| 1 | 91–94 | 1.5 ore | Prima telefonata | Stefano, Teresa | ladro/moglie |
| 2 | 94–97 | 45 min | Entrata della coppia | Genna, Giovanni | donna/uomo (ladro nascosto) |
| 3 | 97–100 | 2 ore | Che botta! | Stefano, Teresa, Genna, Giovanni | donna/uomo/ ladro/moglie |

For an example of a more simplified French scene breakdown (the one you might want to distribute to cast and crew), see Appendix C.

TIMING YOUR REHEARSAL SCHEDULE

Some directors calculate an hour of rehearsal time per page of script. Since the amount of space dedicated to stage directions and the general pace of the lines might vary, however, many directors feel that it is more accurate to estimate the performance time of the show and schedule an hour of rehearsal for each minute of performance. To do this, read your script out loud and time yourself, writing down not only the starting and ending times for the whole script, but also times for each individual scene or segment. If you read lines at a normal pace and read stage directions quickly, you will often have a good estimate of how many minutes it will take to perform the play. If you estimate that the play will be thirty minutes long, plan on a minimum of thirty hours of rehearsal. As foreign language plays present additional challenges for actors, you may want to plan for extra time because it is far easier to cancel an unnecessary rehearsal than coordinate the schedules of cast and crew to add a rehearsal at the last minute.

Using your timed reading of the play, you can estimate how much time to spend on each scene. The same rule of thumb applies: if it took you three minutes to read a scene, allow at least three hours of rehearsal. Of course, you will not spend these three hours all at once. Plan your schedule so that you spend some time on the scene near the beginning of the process (the blocking period discussed above, while actors are still on script), more time near the beginning of the off-book period, and still more time closer to the end of the off-book phase. In planning your schedule, remember to leave a few flexible days scattered throughout in which you have no specific plan, but for which you call in all cast members. This way, if particular scenes need extra work, all the appropriate actors will be present. And, again, keep in mind students' individual conflicts, as well as campus events that might interfere, such as large sporting events, parents' weekend, exam weeks, and vacations.

The schedule that you distribute to actors may look like a calendar, or even a sort of list, if you prefer. However you decide to do it, be sure to indicate which scenes will be covered at each rehearsal and, if you want to be extra safe, which actors will be in them as well. The students can refer to their French scenes guide for page numbers. While you are at it, you can also decide when you would like students to hand in any written work that you wish to assign, such as character studies, literary analyses, research regarding the playwright and setting of the show, and diaries.

## Running Rehearsals

At all stages of your rehearsal process (read-through, blocking, off-book, and tech week), you will likely find it both useful and energizing to begin each rehearsal with three things: music, stretching, and a warm-up activity. Putting some modern Italian pop or rock music on in the background while you are leading stretches not only energizes the group, but also familiarizes students with Italian music. If you use the same few songs throughout the process, students will come to identify with them and regard them as "their" songs. You will find that students will eventually start to sing along, especially if you provide copies of the lyrics. If you put together a soundtrack for the show, make sure it includes students' favorite warm-up songs.

Opening with a few minutes of stretching is important because it helps students release the physical and emotional tension that has built up during the day. It marks a separation from everyday life and gets them into "theater mode." Additionally, it exposes them to *voi* form imperatives, body vocabulary, and possibly a few new verbs. After leading stretches yourself for several weeks, try allowing different students to lead them each time, using their own favorite stretches along with the ones you have been teaching. Stretches can also incorporate massages, which often turn into one of the most popular loosening-up activities. You may choose to have students "stretch" their voices as well through vocal activities such as saying tongue twisters, making noise, singing scales, humming, etc.

Finally, do ten to fifteen minutes of short theater games. This is a great way to involve the whole cast and crew, target specific linguistic or theatrical goals, energize the group, and build a sense of community. For a list of a few warm-up activities, see Appendix D.

Once your group is ready, you can begin working with the text. Keep in mind your overall goal for the day because it can be easy to get wrapped up in details. If a scene is being stubbornly problematic, let it rest. Before moving onto the next scene, express to the students what you see as the problem, ask for their input, and tell them all to think over possible solutions. By the next rehearsal you, or possibly the students themselves, might have already found a way to improve the scene. Remember to involve students who are not acting in the scenes as much as possible with follow-up questions and comments.

Be sure to give lots of praise. Laugh out loud, let them know when a scene is fantastic, encourage them when they need it. As a director, it is natural for you to want to constantly improve the performance and therefore to notice all the things that go wrong, but be careful to balance suggestions for improvement with positive feedback.


## Involving Designers and Stage Managers

Give designers and stage managers as many opportunities for practicing communication as possible. Hold weekly design team meetings outside of rehearsal hours. Set the agenda for the meeting yourself but have the stage manager run it, with your assistance. At your first meeting, discuss the responsibilities and expectations of designers and stage managers, distributing, if possible, a list of tasks that they will need to complete. (See Appendix E.)

At this first meeting, you can also discuss the timelines for costume, set, lighting, audio, and publicity designers and establish a firm calendar of deadlines. At subsequent meetings, you will discuss general ideas and impressions, progress, problems, and solutions.

COSTUME DESIGN TIMELINE

Within the first week, after the initial read-through of the play, the costume designer should already have an idea of the types of colors, fabrics, and styles for each character. During this time period, actors should also fill out a form listing their sizes (shirt, dress, pants, shoes, ring, bra, coat, etc.). During the second to the fourth week, depending on the number of characters in the play, the designer should prepare a sketch or watercolor for each costume that each character wears. Alternatively, he or she could assemble a stylized collage, with bits of color cut from magazines and swatches of fabric, if possible. After a presentation of his or her ideas to the troupe and a discussion of the choices, the designer should be ready to start seeking costumes—borrowing, renting, or buying them. College students tend to be able to find almost anything among their friends, and your local Goodwill store or Salvation Army will surely have some treasures.

In order to set the costume design timeline, it is necessary to work backward from the dress rehearsal when the costumes have to be perfect. Schedule a fittings day, during which actors try on each of their costumes, a full week or two before the first dress rehearsal. This fitting will give the designer time to fix problems and find replacement items for anything that does not work well. Schedule the due date for complete detailed costume lists at least two weeks before the fittings date, so that the designer does not miss anything. The costume lists should include everything that the actor must wear, from socks or hose to jewelry and hats.

Again, planning in advance and staying on top of deadlines will not only make things run more smoothly near the end, it will also create opportunities for discussion about costumes throughout the process. Actors tend to become excited when they know what they will be wearing for their production.

SET DESIGN TIMELINE

Determining a timeline for the set is similar to determining one for costumes. Everything must be completed by the cue-to-cue day, so work backward from that date and set specific guidelines. The earlier you can find or build the bigger elements, such as couches and cabinets, the better. Even if you are not able to practice with them because of practical concerns, you will at least know how big they are for blocking purposes, and you can also begin to choose accessories that will go with the items, such as decorative pillows, matching carpets, or picture frames. Any props that the actors actually use, such as plates, trays, guns, canes, swords, etc., should be incorporated into rehearsals as soon as possible. Even a substitute "rehearsal" prop is fine until you locate a real one. The sooner the actors have real items in their hands, the more comfortable they will feel.

On the same day that the costume designer submits costume lists, the set designer should submit a detailed prop list, listing all props and where they are to be placed at the start of the show as well as who brings them out (where appropriate). Here is an example:

4 red dishes—on center table at start of show

Small gray umbrella—stage left prop table, brought out by Giovanni in scene 2

Photo of Carolina—stage right prop table, placed on white nightstand by stagehand #1 at blackout before scene 4

And, again working backward, on the same day that the costume designer presents sketches or collages, the set designer should already have a working ground plan. This means that he or she will have visited the space in which the play will be performed, measured it, and decided how to set up furniture and other major set pieces for each scene. Having an accurate ground plan is extremely important, as it will determine all blocking. The less confusion there is, the better!

LIGHTING AND AUDIO TIMELINE

Unless the lighting designer is familiar with hanging and focusing theatrical lights and running a light board, lighting will likely be rather simplistic. But the same general rules apply: the designer should have an idea of basic lighting cues and a detailed cue sheet before tech week. The sound designer is responsible for any sound effects that occur during the production but can also be given the responsibility of compiling a soundtrack for the show. From the very first day, the student should be listening to all types of different Italian music, reading lyrics, and trying to find some fun and interesting songs that in some way remind him or her of the show. After explaining the songs to the cast and crew, they can then be used during warm-ups each day and will become a group energizer.

PUBLICITY TIMELINE

Depending on how much you want to publicize your show, you may want to have a publicity designer responsible for putting together the program, making and selling the tickets, and advertising for the production. Below is a list of details you might leave in the hands of either the publicity director (if you have one) or the stage manager.

Publicity
    School newspaper (ad or story)
    School magazine (ad or story)
    Advertisement in language classes
    General posters around campus
    Advertisement in local restaurants, bakeries, stores
    National Public Radio
    Local newspaper (ad or story)
Program
    Director's notes/thank you's
    English synopsis of play
    List of participants and their roles
    List of scenes and settings of each
    Bios of each member of cast and crew
    Ads, if you decide to sell them
Tickets
    Available beforehand? If so, where will they be sold?
    Cost
    On the tickets themselves: title of show, date, time
    Different colors for different evenings?

Extras

> Refreshments for "meet and greet" after the show
>
> Flowers/thank-you gifts or notes for the troupe
>
> A videotape of the performances
>
> T-shirts for cast and crew to be finished at least a week before the start of tech week
>
> Soundtrack CDs for troupe, including songs used in show or favorites from warm-ups

—LAURA COLANGELO

## *Appendix A: Sample Course Syllabus*

Welcome to the Italian Theater Workshop, and congratulations on choosing this exciting total-immersion initiative! By its nature, the experience of working on a theatrical show involves constant speaking, listening, reading, and writing—communication, *insomma*. Though it may be challenging at first, if you put your all into what you do, you'll soon realize that your Italian is improving by leaps and bounds.

Be prepared during the following months to forge friendships, overcome obstacles, laugh a ton, and have a lot of fun. Leave your inhibitions at the door; we are all friends here, and will all, without exception, look ridiculous at times and make *abundant* mistakes.

All participants will be required to complete the following:

*Attendance at rehearsals and meetings:* Our time slot is 5–6:15 Tuesday/Thursday, but extra rehearsals and meetings will be essential, particularly as we move closer to our opening night. We will hammer out a schedule together. Since we make every effort to work around all of your conflicts, unexcused absences will not be permitted. A theatrical troupe is a unified team that *cannot function* without the presence of everyone scheduled to be there for any given rehearsal or meeting. If you have questions, problems, or emergencies at any time, please contact Laura immediately.

*Pre- and post-experience testing:* Pretests and posttests include a short written portion and an oral interview with Professor Ryan-Scheutz. Don't feel stress about these tests. They are not designed to "judge" you; rather, they help us assess the utility of the theater project as a whole. They are for research purposes.

*Il diario:* The diary is an indispensable tool for actors and anyone involved in the theater. It helps you to see your progress, capture your first impressions of things, and remember little touches that you added at a rehearsal or design meeting and want to try again next time. Get into the habit of writing in it after every rehearsal or meeting. I suggest you really convince yourself not to go to bed without doing that entry—from the very first day! It's a real pain—and not remotely useful to you—to try to catch up on 4 weeks in one night.

I will collect diaries three times during the semester. You can hand write or type your diary, but you must write in Italian. I expect at the very minimum one entry per rehearsal or meeting, half a page or more. (That will work out to one or two entries a week at the beginning and more toward the end of the semester.) You will probably find that you'll want to write more, and I *strongly* encourage you to do that. Just that small—and easy—step of writing even a little bit each day will work miracles for your Italian!

*L'analisi:* Everyone will write a literary analysis of the play. You will be provided with some information regarding Campanile and the historical literary environment in which he wrote. Believe me, after working on these plays for the bulk of the semester, this assignment will be a breeze!

*Appendix B: Documents to Distribute at Auditions*

Informazioni per le audizioni

Nome: ______________________________________________

Email: ______________________________________________

# telefono: __________________________________________

# telefono al lavoro: _________________________________

# cellulare: _________________________________________

Indirizzo, ND: _______________________________________

Indirizzo, casa: ______________________________________

Contatto di emergenza: (nome, # telefono, chi è): ________

______________________________________________________

Sesso: ______________________________________________

Età: ________________________________________________

Altezza: _____________________________________________

Capelli: _____________________________________________


Mi interesserebbe fare:

Attore    Scenografo    Costumista/truccatore
Pubblicità/Direttore tecnico    Direttore di scena

I agree to accept any role if cast. Y  N

I agree to cut/dye/alter my hair if asked by the director to do so. Y  N

I agree not to cut/dye/alter my hair before discussing it with the
director. Y  N

I will smoke (cigarettes/herbal cigarettes, cigar, or pipe) if the role requires. Y  N

Please describe the outfit you are wearing right now (this is so I can put names to faces later on):

Please indicate all weekly commitments (include class, work, etc.), and list one-time commitments (weddings, concerts, etc.) on the chart below. Grazie!

| Time | Mon | Tues | Wed | Thurs | Fri | Sat | Sun |
| --- | --- | --- | --- | --- | --- | --- | --- |
| 8 A.M. | | | | | | | |
| 9 | | | | | | | |
| 10 | | | | | | | |
| 11 | | | | | | | |
| Noon | | | | | | | |
| 1 P.M. | | | | | | | |
| 2 | | | | | | | |
| 3 | | | | | | | |
| 4 | | | | | | | |
| 5 | | | | | | | |
| 6 | | | | | | | |
| 7 | | | | | | | |
| 8 | | | | | | | |
| 9 | | | | | | | |
| 10 | | | | | | | |
| 11 | | | | | | | |

Other commitments/conflicts (please give date and time):

## Appendix C: Sample French Scene Breakdown

The following table shows the French scenes for *Non tutti i ladri vengono per nuocere.*

| Scena | Pagine | Attori | Personaggi |
|---|---|---|---|
| 1 | 91–94 | Stefano, Teresa | ladro/moglie |
| 2 | 94–97 | Genna, Giovanni | donna/uomo (ladro nascosto) |
| 3 | 97–100 | Stefano, Teresa, Genna, Giovanni | donna/uomo/ladro/moglie |
| 4 | 100–102 | Genna, Giovanni | donna/uomo |
| 5 | 102–107 | Genna, Giovanni, Stefano | donna/uomo/ladro |
| 6 | 107–110 | Genna, Giovanni, Stefano, Kate | donna/uomo/ladro/Anna |
| 7 | 111 | Giovanni, Stefano | uomo/ladro |
| 8 | 112 | Giovanni, Stefano, Teresa | uomo/ladro/moglie |
| 9 | 112–114 | Giovanni, Stefano, Teresa, Kate | uomo/ladro/moglie/Anna |
| 10 | 115 | Kate, Patrizio | Anna/Antonio |
| 11 | 115–118 | Stefano, Teresa, Genna, Giovanni, Kate, Patrizio, SL | Tutti |
| 12 | 118–119 | Genna, Giovanni, Kate, Patrizio, SL | Tutti eccetto ladro e moglie |

## Appendix D: Warm-Up Games

Many of the games suggested below are variants of well-known exercises for theater courses, production rehearsals, or educational drama-based approaches to teaching in general.

### GIOCHI DI RISCALDAMENTO

Prima del "gioco di riscaldamento," si consiglia di distendere il corpo e fare esercizi che riscaldino e rilassino la voce. Gli scioglilingua, per esempio, sono sia utili che divertenti. Poi, per poter proiettare meglio la voce, gli studenti devono imparare a respirare bene e profondamente, usando il diaframma per riempire i polmoni fino in fondo. Il massaggio piace sempre a tutti, ed è anche utile (particolarmente quando si canticchia simultaneamente) per rilassare i muscoli del tronco, facilitando il respiro e la proiezione della voce.

I vari giochi qui descritti sono ordinati secondo un criterio cronologico di esecuzione: quelli iniziali pongono l'enfasi sul movimento, mentre quelli che seguono sono sempre più difficili e richiedono varie capacità linguistiche. Si tratta di giochi che abbiamo trovato particolarmente utili per chi studia una lingua straniera, ma rappresentano soltanto un campione della gran quantità di giochi teatrali esistenti, o che si possono inventare.

### Tiro alla fune immaginario

*Scopo:* Sollevare lo spirito e dare energia al gruppo, creare un senso di unità fra gli studenti, sviluppare la consapevolezza dei movimenti degli altri, rilassare il corpo

*Tempo:* 5 minuti

*Descrizione:* I partecipanti si dividono in due squadre. Ciascuna squadra si dispone in fila. Gli studenti fingono che ci sia una corda e le due squadre tirano questa corda immaginaria alle due estremità. Ogni squadra prova a tirare la corda in modo che l'altra squadra oltrepassi il punto centrale.

### Caduta di fiducia

*Scopo:* Creare un senso di unità e promuovere la fiducia fra i partecipanti, abituare gli studenti a cadere all'indietro senza piegare le ginocchia (molto utile per le farse)

*Tempo:* 7 minuti

*Descrizione:* Gli studenti (preferibilmente di altezza simile) si dividono in coppie. I due studenti si dispongono uno dietro all'altro, così che il secondo possa prendere il primo fra le braccia quando questo cade. Senza guardare il compagno dietro le spalle, lo studente che cadrà chiede all'amico: "sei pronto?" e l'altro risponde "Sì, fai pure!" Questo dialogo è importante per stimolare un rapporto di fiducia tra gli studenti e per evitare che qualcuno si faccia male. Poi, lo studente si lascia cadere all'indietro, e viene preso dal suo compagno. Dopo aver praticato la caduta varie volte, gli studenti dovrebbero essere capaci di cadere quasi fino al pavimento senza piegare le ginocchia.

                                                   

### Il ritmo

*Scopo:* Sviluppare la concentrazione e la consapevolezza degli altri, creare un senso di unità fra gli studenti

*Tempo:* 3 minuti

*Descrizione:* Tutti i presenti si stendono in posizione supina, formando con i loro corpi un cerchio con i piedi rivolti verso l'esterno e le braccia distese verso l'interno. L'iniziatore batte la mano destra, e poi la mano sinistra sul pavimento per cominciare un ritmo. La persona seguente continua il ritmo, battendo prima la mano destra, poi la mano sinistra. Questo battere sul pavimento continua a fare il giro del cerchio. Quando la persona di turno batte con la mano due volte invece di una, si cambia direzione. Chi sbaglia deve lasciare il cerchio. Il ritmo comincerà ad andare sempre più veloce, e sarà sempre più difficile non sbagliare!

### Alzati se . . .

*Scopo:* Dare energia al gruppo; far divertire

*Tempo:* 5 minuti

*Descrizione:* Ogni partecipante, eccetto uno, prende una sedia. Gli studenti mettono le sedie nella forma di un cerchio, e si siedono. Tocca alla persona senza sedia cominciare il gioco con la frase, "alzati se . . . ," seguita da una condizione ("alzati se i tuoi nonni sono italiani"). A quel punto, tutti quelli che hanno i nonni italiani si alzano e corrono a trovare una nuova sedia. Chi rimane senza sedia comincia di nuovo con "alzati se . . ."

### Libere associazioni

*Scopo:* Rilassare i partecipanti; incoraggiare la creatività

*Tempo:* 3–5 minuti

*Descrizione:* Tutti si siedono formando un cerchio. Uno studente inizia il gioco dicendo una parola. La persona seguente deve dire la prima parola che gli viene in mente, associandola alla parola appena sentita. A sua volta, il terzo studente dice la prima parola che gli viene in mente, associandola alla parola pronunciata dalla persona che lo precede. Per esempio, se la prima persona dice "casa" e la seconda persona dice "bianca," la terza persona deve rispondere alla parola "bianca" (per esempio, "sale"): se dicesse "tetto," questa parola sarebbe associata a "casa" e non a "bianca."

### Avverbi e imperativi

*Scopo:* Esercitare l'uso degli avverbi e degli imperativi, creare un senso di unità fra gli studenti

*Tempo:* 10 minuti

*Descrizione:* Uno studente lascia la stanza e sceglie un avverbio senza svelarlo agli altri. Quando rientra, gli altri studenti, a turno, gli danno degli ordini, usando l'imperativo. Il primo studente deve eseguire gli ordini, e tutte le sue azioni devono essere compiute secondo l'avverbio. Se l'avverbio è "tristemente," e qualcuno gli chiede "dammi un abbraccio," per esempio, deve trovare un modo di "dare un abbraccio tristemente."

### Alibi

*Scopo:* Migliorare la capacità di parlare spontaneamente; porre enfasi sulla rilevanza dei dettagli di una scena e delle motivazioni del personaggio rappresentato

*Tempo:* 10 minuti

*Descrizione:* Due studenti escono dalla stanza. Immaginando di aver passato tre ore insieme il giorno prima, devono costruire un racconto dettagliato per spiegare ciò che hanno fatto in quelle ore. I due vengono interrogati separatamente davanti agli altri partecipanti, che costituiscono "la giuria." Se i due racconti non coincidono in tutti i dettagli ("ma di che colore è la sua macchina?"), la giuria giudica le persone colpevoli.

### Finire la favola

*Scopo:* Migliorare la capacità di parlare spontaneamente

*Tempo:* 5–10 minuti

*Descrizione:* I partecipanti si dispongono seduti in cerchio. Uno studente inizia a raccontare una favola, pronunciando solo una frase. La persona seguente continua la storia con un'altra frase. Ogni persona aggiunge una frase, e la favola si sviluppa liberamente secondo la fantasia dei partecipanti.

### Distrazioni

*Scopo:* Far capire le differenze di prestigio fra diverse persone; rendere gli studenti consapevoli di alcuni principi fondamentali della farsa

*Tempo:* 5 minuti

*Descrizione:* Due studenti prescelti devono rappresentare una scena in cui l'uno prova a fare bella figura con l'altro. Si può trattare, per esempio, di un appuntamento fra un uomo e una donna nota per la sua bellezza, o di un operaio che ha invitato il suo capo a cena a casa sua. Gli altri studenti fanno di tutto per creare distrazioni e disastri: spostano le sedie perché le persone cadano per terra, capovolgono le forchette, ecc. I due attori impegnati nella scena non vedono le persone, ma soltanto gli effetti delle loro azioni. Lo studente intento a fare bella figura deve cercare di riparare ogni nuovo disastro velocemente e con efficienza, offrendo una spiegazione su ciò che di strano continua a succedere.

### Il campo minato

*Scopo:* Dare energia al gruppo, creare un senso d'unità fra gli studenti, essere il punto di partenza per una discussione su che cos'è il teatro, abituare gli studenti a scegliere parole specifiche

*Tempo:* Almeno 15 minuti

*Descrizione:* Gli studenti si dividono in due squadre composte, rispettivamente, da un gruppo di soldati e un gruppo di prigionieri. I prigionieri sono soldati alleati che sono stati catturati e accecati dai nemici e, per questo motivo, devono stare ad occhi chiusi per tutta la durata del gioco. I gruppi sono separati da uno spazio di circa quattro o cinque metri: il campo minato. Tutti i partecipanti si tolgono le scarpe e le distribuiscono sul campo minato in ordine sparso: le scarpe rappresentano le mine. Un membro della squadra dei soldati deve aiutare un individuo dell'altro gruppo (che, essendo cieco, deve chiudere gli occhi) ad attraversare il campo minato. La persona che guida può usare soltanto le parole e per questo, ovviamente, le istruzioni devono essere ben specifiche. Si possono aggiungere altri fattori per rendere più difficile il compito: un limite di tempo, per esempio, o vari rumori di disturbo fatti dagli altri studenti (cani che abbaiano, mitragliatrici, nemici che gridano, ecc.).

### Espressioni fuori posto

*Scopo:* Aiutare gli studenti a capire le espressioni e gli idiomi nel testo e ad incorporarli nel proprio vocabolario personale; migliorare la loro capacità di interagire spontaneamente nella lingua insegnata

*Tempo:* 15–25 minuti

*Descrizione:* Ogni partecipante riceve un foglio di carta sul quale è scritta una battuta presa dal testo ("Non avete ancora capito che sono pazzo di voi?"). Poi, senza rivelare la battuta agli altri, gli studenti si dividono in gruppi di due o tre. Il regista inventa una situazione per ciascun gruppo ("Voi siete un prete e una persona che confessa i propri peccati," per esempio). Il compito degli studenti è di creare e rappresentare una scena, cercando di inserire la battuta nel dialogo in modo appropriato. NB: questo gioco è particolarmente utile, e può essere usato molte volte durante le settimane di prove.

**Ascoltami!**

*Scopo:* Sottolineare l'importanza degli obiettivi dei personaggi; dare l'opportunità di esercitare modi di dire e frasi alternative per un medesimo concetto

*Tempo:* Non più di 10 minuti e secondo il numero dei partecipanti

*Descrizione:* Questo gioco richiede non più di sei o sette partecipanti, ma si possono fare tre o quatto versioni del gioco simultaneamente, se la stanza è abbastanza grande. Il regista assegna ad ogni partecipante un obiettivo, cioè, un desiderio o un sogno che motiva la sua vita. La scena comincia con due persone, ciascuna delle quali prova disperatamente a comunicare i propri desideri all'altra persona. Poi, una terza persona entra, e prova a farsi ascoltare. Tutti devono cercare di usare vari modi per esprimere quello che vogliono dire ("Ho fame. Ci sarebbe un ristorante qui vicino? Scusa, sapresti dov'è un supermercato? Hai un panino a portata di mano, per caso?"). Si può fare questo gioco usando i personaggi dello spettacolo per esagerare i loro desideri e le loro motivazioni. Nel particolare caso delle farse e delle commedie, il risultato è spesso molto buffo quando gli attori esagerano i desideri dei personaggi. Questo gioco può essere difficile, perciò sarà bene evitarlo nelle prime settimane di prove.

## *Appendix E: Duties of the Design Team Members*

Doveri del direttore tecnico

- La tua presenza alle riunioni degli scenografi e alle prove
- Il diario
- L'analisi letteraria

- Trovare suoni per gli effetti speciali di cui abbiamo bisogno (un cane che abbaia, un campanello, una porta che si chiude, ecc.)
- Ascoltare tante canzoni italiane, e compilare una colonna sonora (soundtrack) per lo spettacolo. (Canzoni che ti ricordano i personaggi, canzoni che sembrano adatte allo spettacolo in generale, canzoni che usiamo durante lo spettacolo, ecc.)
- Presenza alle prove generali e allo spettacolo
- Una presentazione: una spiegazione delle tue scelte per la musica per la colonna sonora

Doveri del direttore della pubblicità
- La tua presenza alle riunioni degli scenografi e alle prove
- Il diario
- L'analisi letteraria
- Creare: (1) un poster da affiggere per il campus, (2) una pubblicità da distribuire agli studenti di tutti i corsi d'italiano, (3) un poster in inglese da distribuire a vari ristoranti italiani a South Bend (Rocco's, Macri's, Parigi's, Ciao's, Sunny Italy, Francesco's)
- Contattare l'Observer e la Scholastic (giornali dell'università); invitarli a venire a fotografarci!
- Organizzare la serata delle fotografie (gli attori devono essere fotografati in costume)
- Compilare il programma
- Creare le magliette per tutti i partecipanti

Doveri degli attori
- La tua presenza alle prove
- Il diario
- L'analisi letteraria
- L'analisi del tuo personaggio
- Memorizzare le tue battute e i tuoi movimenti!!!

Doveri del direttore di scena
- La tua presenza alle riunioni degli scenografi e alle prove
- Il diario
- L'analisi letteraria

- Una presentazione: ricerca sull'autore
- Prima delle prove: misurare lo spazio del teatro
- Alle riunioni degli scenografi: assistere e prendere appunti

Alle prove:

- compilare le cronache delle prove durante ogni prova
- prendere appunti durante le prove sui movimenti ("blocking"), e sui cambiamenti dei movimenti
- dopo la memorizzazione delle battute, scrivere errori di battuta, di pronuncia e di movimento: leggere tutti gli appunti agli attori alla fine della prova
- fare il suggeritore: cioè, leggere il testo mentre gli attori recitano, e se dimenticano una battuta e dicono "battuta!" (che, in questo caso, vuol dire "aiutami!"), leggere la battuta con voce forte e chiara
- praticare le battute con gli attori, se ne hanno bisogno
- mantenere il libro del suggeritore

Alle prove generali e agli spettacoli:

- assicurare che tutto sia a posto (i materiali di scena, i costumi, ecc.)
- assicurare che tutti gli attori e gli scenografi siano presenti alle prove generali e agli spettacoli
- sederti nel cabina con i tecnici delle luci e del suono per aiutarli
- distribuire i programmi agli spettatori

Documenti che devono essere nel libro del suggeritore

- Una copia del testo con i tuoi appunti (usare una matita, non una penna!) sui movimenti, sulla pronuncia, ecc.
- L'elenco dei partecipanti con numeri di telefono ecc.
- Il programma delle date importanti per i disegnatori
- Le scene francesi
- L'orario delle prove
- La lista dei segnali per luci e suoni

Doveri del costumista e dello scenografo

- La tua presenza alle riunioni degli scenografi e alle prove

- Il diario
- L'analisi letteraria
- Una presentazione: la spiegazione delle tue scelte artistiche

Scenografo:

- La pianta del teatro (floor plan)
- Lista (molto dettagliata!!!) dei materiali di scena necessari

Costumista:

- Un collage o un disegno per ogni personaggio
- Una lista dettagliata di tutti gli elementi dei costumi di ogni personaggio

1. *Autoritratto* (self-portrait) by Dario Fo, 1949. Oil painting. Courtesy of Dario Fo and Franca Rame.

2. Dario Fo's drawing for *Gli amici della battoneria,* 1963. Courtesy of Dario Fo and Franca Rame.

3. Dario Fo's drawing for *Arlecchino,* 1985. Courtesy of Dario Fo and Franca Rame.

4. Dario Fo's drawing for *Gli arcangeli non giocano a flipper,* 1959. Courtesy of Dario Fo and Franca Rame.

5. Dario Fo's drawing for *Elisabetta. Quasi per caso una donna,* 1984. Courtesy of Dario Fo and Franca Rame.

6. *Studio di movimenti.* Drawing by Dario Fo, 1983. Courtesy of Dario Fo and Franca Rame.

7. *Studio di manifesto.* Drawing by Dario Fo, 1979. Courtesy of Dario Fo and Franca Rame.

8. Dario Fo's drawing for *L'italiana in Algeri* (curtain detail), 1994. Courtesy of Dario Fo and Franca Rame, and Amati Ricciardi.

9. Dario Fo's drawing for *L'italiana in Algeri* (curtain detail), 1994. Courtesy of Dario Fo and Franca Rame, and Amati Ricciardi.

10. Dario Fo's drawing for *L'italiana in Algeri* (curtain), 1994. Courtesy of Dario Fo and Franca Rame, and Amati Ricciardi.

11. Dario Fo with mask and lion, 1985. Courtesy of Dario Fo and Franca Rame.

12. Dario Fo in *Mistero buffo,* 1970. Courtesy of Dario Fo and Franca Rame, and Corrado M. Falsini.

13. Dario Fo in *Mistero buffo,* 1970. Courtesy of Dario Fo and Franca Rame, and Corrado M. Falsini.

14. Franca Rame in *Tutta casa, letto e chiesa,* 1970. Courtesy of Dario Fo and Franca Rame.

15. Franca Rame in *Parliamo di donne,* 1991. Courtesy of Dario Fo and Franca Rame, and Giuseppe Briguglio.

16. Franca Rame in *Sesso? Grazie, tanto per gradire,* 1992. Courtesy of Dario Fo and Franca Rame, and Tommaso La Pera.

# Afterword: An Interview with Dario Fo and Franca Rame. Thoughts on Theater, Engagement, and the Comic. Examples for a New Pedagogy

WALTER VALERI, TRANSLATED BY
GIUSEPPE GAZZOLA

**Q:** Is it possible to trace a progression in your work as an actor and author?

**Dario Fo:** Actually, my early artistic training was in painting and architecture; that is, the main components of scene design. My growth as an actor was linked to my activity as a writer. On the other hand, I learned to write and to think for the theater while growing as a performer. When I write a comedy, or a monologue, I'm not particularly interested in depicting the state of mind of various characters. Rather, I'm interested in the scenic fact, the main event, which is the object of the narration developed in the comic stage, and which must always reflect reality. This scenic element determines the development of the comedy and of the plot, and at a later stage it will determine the behavior of the actor. I need this scenic element to create the various characters, their actions onstage. A good theatrical work, paradoxically, should not be pleasing to a reader: it should reveal its pleasures and qualities only on the stage. When I write a play, before deciding the dialogue, I imagine the physical place where the performance will be staged, where the actors will be arranged, and the position of the audience. When I develop a work, I'm rarely uncertain of the entrances and exits; I never decide them afterwards. This is also true for monologues, which normally do not have a specific setting. For me, the idea of sequences is important, as are the dynamic, chromatic, and perspectival characteristics of the actor. I have transposed all my knowledge into theater, not only at the figurative level but also at the directorial one, in my conception of rhythms and tempos. I like synthesis and I often use comics, with their series of successive images, as inspiration. For example, in rewriting and staging Stravinsky's *Histoire du Soldat* at the Teatro alla Scala of Milan in 1978, before thinking about direction, I made around two hundred drawings. I drew on Plexiglas, so that the images could be moved on their transparent background, in order to study the infinite possibilities of composition. We used the drawings to improvise the final versions. In some cases the images were even generated before the words. It was truly a didactic activity, playing on many possibilities—painting, acting, movement—offering many levels of study and work for thirty-three young apprentice actors who had just graduated from the Scuola del Piccolo Teatro and other Italian acting schools. In my history as an actor, author, scene designer, director, and costume designer, everything has been combined.

*Q:*  What has changed since the beginning of your careers, both yours and Franca Rame's, since *Gli arcangeli non giocano a flipper* [*Archangels Don't Play Pinball*], your first play in the traditional form of three acts, dated 1948?

*Dario Fo:*  More than fifty years have passed. Certainly, things change with time, even if some themes, stylistic elements, and values have remained the same. When we performed the so-called traditional theater, with a strong will and desire to experiment always, to intervene in the political and cultural debate with regard to the national standard of the times, we used a variety of theatrical effects: pauses, contrasts of lights, cosmetics, wigs, sound effects, whatever was useful in that context. In short, we used the magic of theater to its full effect. Then, in the seventies, we needed a more agile theatrical structure. Theatrical action no longer unfolded on traditional stages, but in new spaces with specific characteristics: open-air settings, in the street, in city squares, inside factories or in deconsecrated churches, in the Case del Popolo, which no longer exist, but which used to be the cultural centers of the working classes. Then, in the eighties, we went back to using the traditional structure, even if dramaturgically and content-wise the separation was not quite so neat and clean.

*Q:*     How could theater today have an important pedagogical function in schools and universities?

*Dario Fo:*     Good theatrical text is never banal. More than any other art, theater is an expression of thought and the exercise of intelligence, though that does not necessarily translate into a positive intelligence, used for the common good. On this subject, Sartre used to say that a character who freely expresses his human condition represents the most moving manifestation of theater. It is the moment of choice, of free will, which engages all moral values and an entire existence.

*Q:*     What are the most obvious dangers for an educator who makes use of theater?

*Dario Fo:*     In every culture and in every country, one of the greatest dangers in which "educators" and all those professionally involved in the transmission of culture, history, or language are caught, is the censorship of sources, which are the most direct expression of that language and culture. Not always, but often, teachers perform a reductive or sterile adaptation. In the worst case, they use manuals and texts that superficially respond to their needs, rather than to those of their students. This is especially true in the United States, where synthesis and simplification dominate mass culture. Everything must be rapid and digestible in a short period: fast food, *Reader's Digest,* the universe in miniature form, etc. The myth of velocity is a tempting siren who pushes the masses onto the rocks of insufficient consciousness or, if you prefer, of insufficient knowledge of the principles of reality—and thus, of its loss. I remember when I performed *Mistero buffo* [*Comic Mysteries*] in New York. While introducing the play, I used to tease the audience explicitly with the main characteristic of the average American: the ability to synthesize. The audience used to react immediately, with a loud hysterical laugh, since I was touching on a nerve of American culture and daily life which they recognized with a sense of guilt.

*Q:*  An everyday culture, different from the one proposed inside academia.

*Dario Fo:*  These two are only seemingly separated; in reality, they interpenetrate each other. They remind one of the cat and the fox in Pinocchio's tale. The fox is smarter than the cat, more educated, its language is more refined, haughty, and well mannered. The cat, on the other hand, is a sort of *Zanni*, a brainless figure, nothing but stomach and muscles. But both, in the end, want the same thing: to steal the gold coins from Pinocchio, with which he was supposed to reward his old father who had created him by carving a piece of wood for a life of sacrifice.

*Q:*  This is a precise criticism and also a suggestive metaphor. How could it be explained more clearly?

*Dario Fo:*  Unfortunately, in America the only known version of Pinocchio's tale is the one by Walt Disney, which is extremely deficient when compared with Collodi's masterpiece. And not by chance, I must say. What I mean to say is that a professor or a textbook of Italian language and literature, most of the time for marketing or editorial reasons, tends to fabricate or to reproduce a simplified vision of reality as though it were reality itself. One ends up forgetting the original text. And yet we know that original texts are a precious thing, to which students must be directly exposed. They are the only true memory of the past. Original texts, specifically where popular language and culture are concerned, are like the gold coins Pinocchio received from history. We had better not take the coins away from him.

*Q:*  But students demonstrate a great interest for those expressions and phrases which refer to events that actually happened.

*Dario Fo:*      Yes, because they are a direct transposition of the facts themselves. And also because students naturally desire to use their abilities for interpretation and imagination. They want to use their fantasy, to test their intelligence, rather than assimilate or digest somebody else's interpretation. The autonomous exercise of one's intelligence is a source of great pleasure, and not the opposite, as we are often led to believe. Students must have the opportunity to partake in this pleasure during the learning process. Otherwise frustration and resentment will build and they will take things out sadistically on others.

*Q:*            It is possible to provide an example?

*Dario Fo:*      In our country, but also elsewhere in recent years, a discussion about dialect and popular culture has finally taken off. Folklore is no longer considered folkloristic. After years and years of inattention, we now pay attention to this nonliterary language (rather, as opposed to the literary one) which almost always uses dialect for its fundamental structure. When Luigi Pirandello, just to mention an important author, began to write for the theater, he did so in his dialect. The use of dialect as a matrix for theatrical language by the Sicilian playwright is evident and explicitly declared. Moreover, when he translated or adapted novellas written in the literary language for theater, he profoundly modified them by using dialect. Dialect as syntax, dialect as structure, dialect as a rhythmic value which dictates the entire verbal construction of the dialogues. The same thing is true for Eduardo De Filippo, even if, in fact, Eduardo was preoccupied with inventing a language that started from dialects (and not only the Neapolitan dialect, since he also used forms which originated from Sicilian and even Roman dialects). Dialect is an essentially oral and dynamic language, full of immediate references through which the reality it describes is immediately recognizable. In a theatrical situation, this particularity helps enormously to reproduce the process of communication. Theatrical language is synthetic and does not permit descriptive pauses for situations or states of mind, unless they are part of the intended rhythm.

Q:

What is the relationship between your theater and dialect?

*Dario Fo:*

I learned dialect from the storytellers of my region; from them, I learned the most archaic dialect, the one spoken by the elderly and not contaminated with Italian, as happens nowadays. The dialect was their natural language. It was their only universe of expression, their only possible language. Of course, they knew the idiomatic forms, the very structures of the language. Hence, I learned the structure of the dialect, which is different from speaking the dialect. This structure and this reinvented language can be found in my theatrical work.

Q:

With the addition and the invention of *grammelot.*

*Dario Fo:*

I did not invent *grammelot.* I used it in my own manner, as I deemed it necessary. It is a term of French origin, coined by the actors of the commedia dell'arte and imported by the people from the Veneto region, who would call it *gramelotto.* It is an onomatopoeic play on words that belongs to an arbitrarily articulated discourse which can encompass a complete discourse with the help of gestures, rhythms, and particular sonorities. In the United States, for example, there was a great television actor, Sid Caesar, who put it to good use in the mid-sixties. It is a tradition of comic actors, the origin of which is as old as the world. For precise historical and social reasons, this tradition resurfaced in Italy and Europe with the commedia dell'arte and the theatrical profession, as we know it in modern times.

Q:

In your work there are references to the texts of classical authors, both Greek and Latin, to the works of Ruzante, of the commedia dell'arte of the sixteenth century, of Shakespeare, Molière, Feydeau, Brecht.

*Dario Fo:*

And many others, as it were. But I think that I have principally assimilated the lessons of Ruzante, to whom I dedicated an entire performance. He constructed a language for the theater. It is said that he used the Paduan dialect, but I've done some research and discovered that it is not true. In his language there are various dialects. There is a linguistic root for every situation, and every situation dictates the right word in some dialect or another. I do not consider myself a literary figure who writes; my theater is made of orality, sounds, music, tempos, rhythms, actions, all sources related to the manifestation of life, and also, by their nature, to writing. We can say, roughly, that two different approaches exist to the use of theatrical texts. There are those who learn the words by heart, the grammatical structure of the phrases, and then recite them, or have them recited mechanically by actors, and thereby risk forgetting their original significance, the real causes which have generated them. The other approach comes from a famous quotation from Shakespeare, which says more or less, "One should always recite as if for the first time; one should always rediscover the line." As though one did not entirely know the continuation of the line and had to reconstruct it as it was being uttered.

*Q:*   After having received the Nobel Prize for literature, you acknowledged as your mentor and inspiration the north Italian writer and author Ruzante, from the end of the fifteenth century. You spoke to him, as if he were onstage next to you, dedicating to him four verses in dialect: "Beolco Ruzante / bestia animál de palco / càta 'sto tòco del méo medajón / l'è ànca tòo! Salùt!" ["Beolco Ruzante / animal beast of the stage / take this piece of my medallion / it's also yours! Cheers!"] Why?

*Dario Fo:*   Yes, it is true. Ruzante and Molière have been my true mentors. Both actors and authors, somewhat ridiculed and opposed by academics and literary officials of their time. In reality, they were misfits who showed everyday life onstage, the suffering and joy of the common people, and, above all, the violence that they received from the political, economic, and cultural establishment. While the book industry associated with theater was being born in Italy, Ruzante, like Shakespeare, never saw his own work printed. And yet Ruzante is a great author, one of the greatest in Italian—even European—theater. His ability to include comedy and tragedy in the same performance is magisterial. It should be made clear that this is a "Dionysian" laughter. The comedy, often overlapping with tragedy, is used to demolish the ideological structure of the ruling classes, of religion imposed from above, of an economy imposed by the authorities, of a language controlled by the academy, of the customs and the sexual morality that result from expropriation. Clearly the teaching of Ruzante remained an important guide for me, when I composed *Mistero buffo.*

*Q:* When one wants to communicate to students the nature of the culture where they belong in some critical sense, are laughter and the comic quality useful? Are they useful to their understanding of reality?

*Dario Fo:* Yes, definitely. Vincenti, a comedian from the beginning of the twentieth century who harshly satirized the Nazi movement, said something that I believe is interesting with regard to the relationship between the comic spirit, irony, the grotesque, and youth. He cleverly made a distinction between those circumstances in which comedy and laughter were meant to be liberating and those that underscored a sort of sadomasochistic play which generates false, hypocritical laughter. For example, students often laugh out of compliance, to oblige, to be likeable, because they fear the teacher or another authority. The act of laughing, for them, becomes an instrument to be accepted with benevolence. We know very well how, often, the professor or the teacher clumsily tries to be funny without really having a clue; and the student, or the hypocritical child, laughs ostentatiously so that the professor or the teacher may think, "Today I've been really amusing." Rather, they have simply created a situation of conflict, of expectation, acting from their position of power. Naturally, the students act accordingly, showing submission.

*Q:* Children and students learn these behaviors from the world of adults.

*Dario Fo:* It is true. Students and children, especially when they are very young, quickly learn the worst behaviors from adults. They understand that this is the only way to find an equilibrium that allows them to survive and remain of this world. These behaviors are imposed on the child by the family at first, then by teachers at school, then by professors in the academy. Or they are taught in the street, by television programs, by the advertisements created expressly for them. But they clearly understand the existence of a power struggle which they must resolve to their advantage. On the other hand, especially when the child is very young, he or she does not really have any power to oppose the situation. When we speak about a child's laughter, we must always consider the relationship between power and the action derived from it—conscience, knowledge, morbidity, repression. The key to laughter is mainly linked, for children and teenagers, to the repression that adults impose on them. Let me clarify that this repression is not always, a priori, negative.

*Q:*  What differentiates their way of laughing from that of adults?

*Dario Fo:*  We can look at clowns to understand this difference. We must return to the origin of the comic quality in order to understand it and interpret it. Clowns engage with primordial mechanisms. A child inevitably laughs if somebody falls; naturally that laughter is linked to the anxiety to have to walk in an erect position, a precarious equilibrium on which we must rely all our lives. But from a theatrical point of view, the redeeming laughter happens when the person who falls is dressed as an emperor or king. When the character embodying political power trips with a somersault, the child claps enthusiastically, full of redeeming happiness. This is also one of the classic pranks in the French circus over the course of the entire show: the White Clown, as Ringmaster, shouts to August, the humble clown, a little clumsy, with whom the child identifies. August is denigrated by everybody: by the sparkling trapeze artist who walks the tightrope, by the elephant keeper, by the lion tamer, in short everyone maltreats him and makes him carry the buckets, insults him, tells him not to pick his nose, not to raise his voice, not to laugh in this manner, not to waste his time chasing butterflies, not to eat the cake, not to harass the elephant. They build a world of constriction and suffering that, at a certain point, gets overturned. The trapeze artist slips on elephant dung, the Ringmaster trips on his whip, the buckets are suddenly filled with firecrackers, the elephants go wild for a caramel, etc. And when this happens, all the children laugh uncontrollably. It suffices to choreograph the items with a little rhythm, a little theatrical know-how, and voilà.

*Q:* Even classical theater, from Aristophanes to Plautus, from Machiavelli to Goldoni, and all contemporary comic theater, uses these ingredients.

*Dario Fo:* The key to theater is always the same: the fall of the powerful, that collapse, the balance of power overturned in favor of the spectator, of her mindset. This is the fundamental condition for a comedy that impresses children and students.

*Q:* Could we say there are rules to evoke laughter?

*Dario Fo:* No, there aren't any specific rules, but there is a play on opposites. Ideally, before selecting a play, a comedian approaching an audience or a professor at a school should enquire what recent events have affected the community or have had an impact on the students. Or what are the great current concerns that menace the community. At that point, one would have the exact content for a plot in a comic register. We must always remember that the use of irony facilitates the search for a smile, irony that derives from the parody of commonplace dogmas, wherever they might be: from rigid rules, from customs and norms, or, in other words, the sacred essence of royal power, of hierarchies and their modern derivatives. There are a thousand ways to tell the stories of everyday life, those which unfold in individual lives of students or in the street; each one is more intelligent than the official and established narratives. Bad teachers often do not realize their own comic lapses while they are teaching. Instead, if they used such moments to communicate with their students, they would escape the trap of embarrassment and boredom in which they are perennially caught. They would increase their authority and credibility. Even gossip, which normally circulates in a classroom, can be reshaped wisely and saved from its inevitably sordid nature through the instruments of comic theater—which are always handy—and revealed in the light of a smile.

*Q:* Your theatrical texts always have a clear political content and a specific dramaturgical structure. What is the origin of these two aspects, and how have they developed over the years?

*Franca Rame:* Our theater is socially committed. It has always been this way, since the beginning. It is a theater concerned with problems of the people, engaged with daily events of a political or economic nature, or with civil law, injustice, or discrimination based on sex or the manipulation of public opinion. We do not invent anything; the content of our theater consists of elements already present in society, in the culture that surrounds us. We treat facts or events that society needs to discuss, but which have not yet come to light. Our theater, in its comic, satiric, and grotesque incarnation, is the synthesis or the fantastic reinvention of things that already exist. It offers a shift in perspective, a moment of information and collective growth. Not everybody, obviously, feels this necessity; in fact, those who wield political power and hold special privileges seek to intimidate and inhibit the debate. They do not want us to talk and laugh publicly about certain causes and episodes of violence and social corruption, least of all about their responsibilities. They want to appear as saviors even when they do evil.

*Q:* And what about dramaturgy?

*Franca Rame:* With regard to form—the practical manner in which we stage our plays—it's clear that we draw on the richness and style of popular theater. Dario knows everything about theater. I don't know if I could be considered an author. Dario, who is a Nobel Prize winner and one of the most popular playwrights in the world, says so—perhaps I am. But most importantly, I owe my style as an actress and an author to my parents. And I need to clarify: it's not as if my father and my mother ever gave me express directions, or taught me to construct a plot outline, or to block a scene, or to follow the lights according to the stage directions, or anything else of the sort, as we say in technical language. Ours was a family of professional actors, linked to the tradition of the old Italian *commedia*. At home, we talked about theater using everyday language. Behind the scenes, my mother, before sending me onstage, used to ask me if I had done my homework, what Uncle Tommaso, the playwright for our company, had said, or if I had a clean handkerchief, and so on. As soon as our troupe arrived in a city, we began to inquire about the most salient and important events that had recently taken place. We would then select a play to perform from either the classical or popular repertory, making appropriate adaptations based on the results of our earlier inquiries. Often, the protagonists of an injustice or a local crime could be recognized in the plot or the introduction to the performance. I learned the concepts of dramaturgy and direction, the distinction between erudite and popular theater, only after I worked in other companies, and later on with Dario, in fifty years of close collaboration. In fact, even today these words sound strange to me. Obviously, one changes with time and experience, and refines the tools of the trade. One perceives more clearly what the audience wants to see onstage, and how it should be performed. But these suggestions aren't always to be followed mechanically, especially in a comic context. Sometimes one must surprise the audience and contradict its expectations in order to realize the aim of the performance fully. Theater, in its simplicity, is a very complicated matter. Evoking laughter is serious business, we often say.

Q:     *Tutta casa, letto e chiesa* [*Adult Orgasm Escapes from the Zoo*] is the first highly successful text with feminist content written together with Dario Fo, and it is also the most translated and performed among your monologues in the United States. From what facts and imperatives was it generated?

*Franca Rame:* The original version of *Tutta casa, letto e chiesa* was written in 1977, in a single afternoon or a little more. It contains all the ferment and the most important themes of the feminist movement that emerged in the decade from 1968 to 1977. It concerns abortion, pregnancy, motherhood, sexual violence against women, the double economic exploitation of women as both housewives and members of the workforce, the pill, etc. After this first draft, the text was gradually refined and elaborated through an uninterrupted relationship with the audience, almost like a living creature or organism. Other texts, developed over years of political work and social intervention, were added later. These are now collected in three volumes of monologues edited by Einaudi.

*Q:* Could we distinguish two moments within your theatrical output: one personal, and one more clearly linked to the political and social sphere?

*Franca Rame:* It is clear that our theater is not about interiority, nor is it psychological or autobiographical. But, that said, I think it is difficult to separate the two moments: an act of solidarity also implies a transformation of one's own personal experience, an exchange of one's own life with someone else's. It is always like this if one believes in what one does, especially in theater. For example, the monologue *Una madre* [*A Mother*] tormented me for a long time. It was born in 1980, after months—in fact, years—of contact and interaction with mothers of drug addicts and terrorists whom I helped or simply met in the course of my social work in jails and rehab centers. Two different reasons for suffering, two similar human afflictions—that of a mother of a terrorist and of a mother of a drug addict—were combined in a single character: a woman who recounts her story aloud onstage. It is the story of a son who ends up in jail, and who could easily be the son of any mother in the audience. I remember that the first night I performed the text in Turin (or rather, I read it, since I had not yet memorized it), it created a palpable chill in the audience, an almost physically perceptible tension.

*Q:* After these monologues, you and Dario have written

many others about the female condition. How has the audience changed since the first monologues?

*Franca Rame:* The real tragedy is that we are still at the same place—a little ahead or a little behind, but we are still here. Those early monologues are still relevant because the condition of women is more or less the same. I do not say that pessimistically, but that is how things are. What has improved, if there has been a small improvement, affects a small minority. A minority that, sometimes, risks arrogance by judging or considering passé the restatement of female reality as it still is. Reality never proceeds, or almost never does, with the abstract rhythm of the thoughts of a few intellectuals, with the patterns of intellectual consumption.

*Q:* In the course of innumerable international tours you have encountered other actresses who have translated and performed your feminist monologues. What impression do you have of them?

*Franca Rame:* In some cases I have been happily surprised, as in the case of Yvonne Braysland, in a production of the National Theater of London, or in Amsterdam, Buenos Aires, Berlin, Istanbul. In other cases I have been profoundly disappointed: when the actresses have aligned themselves with theatrical stereotypes, or when they have tried to portray what, according to them, is a typical Italian woman, a specimen who, notoriously, does not exist—or exists only in fashion magazines. In short, I have almost always been disappointed when there has been scarcely any engagement or consciousness of the content of the performance. I include great American actresses, those who have won Oscars—such as Estelle Parsons—who at a certain point in their careers decided to stage our monologues without understanding the profound spirit that animates them, or our idea and form of theater and the performative style appropriate to it. But on the whole, between the two extremes, I must say that I have encountered much enthusiasm and, almost always, a sincere desire to contribute to the success of the performance and, above all—what matters most to me—a desire to communicate with the audience.

# *Index*

**R**

Rame, Franca, 10, 13, 47, 134, 140, 171, 173, 177, 181, 182, 186, 244, 323, 384, 393–396

reading (activities): close, 123, 152; dramatic, 84; for librettos, 215; literary, 250; oral, 123, 124; peer, 5; pre-, guided, and post-, 259; process, 92; rapid and low, 251; strategies, 12; techniques, 151

realism: as a formal aesthetic, 72–73; Goldoni's, 37; realistic theater, 44. *See also* acting: naturalistic

*recitar cantando*, 36. *See also* opera

rehearsals (time commitment, planning). *See under* theater production

Renaissance theater, 2, 29–33, 34, 194, 197, 325

resources and funding. *See under* theater production

rhythm: body, 192; of Fo and Rame, 177, 183; of Italian language, 63; musical, 146, 147; of the play, 51; reading, 124, 126; speaking, 107, 280; study of, 6; of theater, 24, 175. *See also* Costa, Orazio; *grammelot;* paralinguistic features

Rinuccini, Ottavio, 35. *See also* melodrama

role-play, 2, 3, 8, 12, 54, 65, 68, 69, 77, 84, 102, 123, 216, 220, 229–231, 292, 301, 308, 309, 312, 314, 317–318, 326–327

roles (parts), assigning, 97–99; student, 184. *See also* theater production

Rossini, Gioacchino, 40, 236. *See also* opera

Rosso di San Secondo, Pier Maria, 42

Ruzante (Angelo Beolco), 32, 388–390

**S**

Sacchi, Antonio, 190–191, 199

*sacre rappresentazioni*, 27–29

Sanguineti, Edoardo, 256

Sannazaro, Jacopo, 30

Sartre, Jean Paul, 70, 385

scaffolding, 15, 252. *See also* community

Scala, Flaminio, 131, 189, 198

*scapigliatura*, 40

scenarios: commedia dell'arte, 131, 188–191, 195–199; creating, 123; performing, 128–129; relationship of, with the five Cs, 164; rewriting in the form of, 201. *See also* adaptation; writing activities

scene production, 152. *See also* theater production: set design

Sciascia, Leonardo, 323–329

script, choosing a, 92–95. *See also* adaptation; text selection

semiotics: cultural (ethnosemiotics), 51, 117, 122, 313–314; performance (theater), 6, 67, 122, 313–314

set design. *See under* theater production

Shakespeare, William, 11, 30, 52, 65, 175, 207, 388–389

show (final performance), 42, 184, 303; large-cast, 148, 356–357; multiple, 24, 276, 300, 355–356; one-act (play), 134, 140, 201, 276, 302, 324, 355; recital, 5, 124, 132–133, 134, 339; small-cast, 324. *See also* theater production

Sicily, 8, 23, 43

Silone, Ignazio, 134, 140

skills: acting, 98; analytical and critical (thinking), 5, 121–122, 180–181, 213, 227; communication (linguistic), 2, 8, 11, 98, 122, 158, 213, 221, 249, 279

sociocultural and linguistic behaviors: Anglo-American, 75;